THOMAS TOMKI
THE LAST ELIZABE

For Gregory and Thomas
with a grandfather's love

Thomas Tomkins:
The Last Elizabethan

Edited by

ANTHONY BODEN
With commentaries on Tomkins's music
by
Denis Stevens
Bernard Rose
Peter James
and
David R.A. Evans

LONDON AND NEW YORK

First published 2005 by Ashgate Publishing

Published 2016 by Routledge
2 Park Square, Milton Park, Abingdon, Oxfordshire OX14 4RN
711 Third Avenue, New York, NY 10017, USA

First issued in paperback 2016

Routledge is an imprint of the Taylor & Francis Group, an informa business

Copyright © The individual contributors, 2005

The individual contributors have asserted their moral right under the Copyright, Designs and Patents Act, 1988, to be identified as the editors of their chapters.

All rights reserved. No part of this book may be reprinted or reproduced or utilised in any form or by any electronic, mechanical, or other means, now known or hereafter invented, including photocopying and recording, or in any information storage or retrieval system, without permission in writing from the publishers.

Notice:
Product or corporate names may be trademarks or registered trademarks, and are used only for identification and explanation without intent to infringe.

British Library Cataloguing-in-Publication Data
Thomas Tomkins: The Last Elizabethan
  1. Tomkins, Thomas, 1572–1656 2. Tomkins, Thomas, 1572–1656 – Family
  3. Composers – England – Bibliography 4. Music – England – 17th century –
  History and criticism 5. Music – England – 16th century – History and criticism
  6. Worcester (England) – History
  I. Boden, Anthony II. Stevens, Denis 1922–2004 III. Bernard Rose 1916–96
  IV. Peter James V. David R.A. Evans
  780.9'2

Library of Congress Cataloging-in-Publication Data
Thomas Tomkins: The Last Elizabethan / edited by Anthony Boden.
     p. cm.
  Includes list of works.
  Includes bibliographical references (p.   ) and index.
  ISBN 0–7546–5118–5 (alk. paper)
  1. Tomkins, Thomas, 1572–1656. 2. Composers – England – Biography. I. Boden,
Anthony.

ML410.T65T56 2005
780'.92–dc22

2004013967

ISBN 13: 978-1-138-24859-5 (pbk)
ISBN 13: 978-0-7546-5118-5 (hbk)

Contents

List of Illustrations	vii
Notes on Contributors	ix
Acknowledgements	xi
Abbreviations	xiii
Introduction	1

Part One   The Lives and Times of Thomas Tomkins and his Family

Anthony Boden

1	Lostwithiel	7
2	St David's	17
3	Menevia Sacra	27
4	Gloucester	41
5	Her Majesty's Chapel	53
6	Worcester	65
7	Awfull Majestie	87
8	The Greatest Maecenas	99
9	Sceptre and Crown	115
10	Sacred and Profane	129
11	A Faithful City	143
12	Distracted Times	161

vi   *Contents*

Part Two   The Music of Thomas Tomkins

Denis Stevens

13	*Musica Deo sacra*	197
14	Songs of 3, 4, 5 and 6 Parts	217
15	Music for Keyboard Instruments	233
16	Consort Music	259

Part Three   Further Commentaries

17	Thomas Tomkins: An Appreciation *Bernard Rose*	273
18	Sacred Music omitted from *Musica Deo sacra* *Peter James*	285
19	Thomas Tomkins: Borrowings, Self-borrowings and Homage *David R.A. Evans*	301

List of Works and their Sources	325
Bibliography	353
Index	359

List of Illustrations

1.1 South-east view of Lostwithiel in the eighteenth century
(*The Courtney Library, The Royal Institution of Cornwall,
Truro*) — 10

2.1 St David's Cathedral. An early nineteenth-century engraving
by I.H. Shepherd, from a drawing by H. Gastineau
(*St David's Cathedral Library, Pembrokeshire*) — 21

4.1 MS page of a Fantasia *a* 3 by Tomkins, in the hand of John
Merro
(*Bodleian Library, University of Oxford: MS Mus. Sch.
D 247, fol. 36r*) — 50

6.1 Internal view of Worcester Cathedral, drawn and engraved by
James Ross for Valentine Green's *A History of Worcester* (1794)
(*Photograph by Mr Christopher Guy, Worcester Cathedral
Archeologist, reproduced by permission of the Chapter of
Worcester Cathedral (UK)*) — 66

6.2 Worcester Cathedral. (*Three Choirs Festival Collection*) — 71

6.3 Map of Worcester, *c.*1610 (*Worcestershire Record Office*) — 72

6.4a Old Pull (Poole) Court House, 1538 to 1798
(*Courtesy Peter and Lucille Elms*) — 75

6.4b Pull Court today
(*Courtesy Douglas Sharp and Martin Roberts, Bredon School*) — 75

6.5 Frontispiece of Thomas Tomkins's own, signed, copy of
Morley's *Plain and Easy Introduction to Practical Music*
(*The President and Fellows of Magdalen College, Oxford*) — 80

6.6 Additions, mostly in the hand of Thomas Tomkins, to his own
copy of Morley's *Plain and Easy Introduction to Practical
Music.* The names added by Tomkins are those of Bevin,
Mudd, Blitheman, Mundy, Bull, Hooper, Morley, Carleton,
Gibbons, Warwick and John Tomkins
(*The President and Fellows of Magdalen College, Oxford*) — 82

viii *List of Illustrations*

7.1 Bishop Henry Parry (1561–1616). A portrait by an unknown artist
(*Courtesy the Bishop of Worcester*) 91

7.2 Henry, Prince of Wales (1594–1612). A portrait drawing by William Hold 96

8.1 William Herbert, 3rd Earl of Pembroke (1580–1630). A portrait by Anthony Van Dyck
(*The Collection of The Earl of Pembroke and the Trustees of Wilton House Trust, Salisbury, UK*) 108

9.1 The ending of the *Offertory*, signed 'Mr Thomas Tomkins:– organist of His Majesty's Chapel, 1637'.
Two short pieces 'for Edward' – Edward Thornborough, archdeacon of Worcester
(*Bodleian Library, Oxford: MS Mus. Sch. D 247, fol. 36r*) 117

10.1 Warrant of Charles I for the appointment of Thomas Tomkins as Composer-in-Ordinary
(*The National Archives, SP 39-23-53*) 130

11.1 Record of Benefactors of Worcester Charities, 1627, fol. 15r.
(*Worcestershire Record Office: City of Worcester Archives*) 144

12.1 Archbishop William Laud (1573–1645). A portrait by an unknown artist, after van Dyck
(*National Portrait Gallery, London*) 162

12.2 Certificate of the Mayor and Aldermen of Worcester, dated 17 June 1650, showing that Thomas Tomkins was 78 years of age in that year (*Worcester City Council*)
(*The National Archives, SP 23-124-273*) 183

12.3 Martin Hussingtree Church, Worcestershire
(*Photograph: Anthony Boden*) 188

15.1 Thomas Tomkins's List of Books
(*Bibliothèque nationale de France, Paris: Réserve MS 1122*) 236

15.2 Thomas Tomkins: 'A Toy made at Poole Court'
(*Bibliothèque nationale de France, Paris: Réserve MS 1122*) 240

15.3 Thomas Tomkins: 'Fortune my foe' (4 July 1654)
(*Bibliothèque nationale de France, Paris: Réserve MS 1122*) 243

15.4 Thomas Tomkins: 'A Short Pavan' (19 July 1654)
(*Bibliothèque nationale de France, Paris: Réserve MS 1122*) 254

Notes on Contributors

Anthony Boden is a writer with particular interests in British music and literature. In 1989, following a career in the medical services of the Royal Air Force, he was appointed Administrator of the Three Choirs Festival in Gloucester, a post he held until his retirement in 1999. He remains a member of the Council of the Three Choirs Festival Association, as well as member of the Gloucester Three Choirs Festival Committee. In 1995, he became the founding Chairman of the Ivor Gurney Society, and, in 2001, Trustee of the Ivor Gurney Trust. His books include: *Stars in a Dark Night: the Letters of Ivor Gurney to the Chapman Family* (Sutton, 1986; rev. 2004); *F.W. Harvey: Soldier, Poet* (Sutton, 1988; rev. 1998); *Three Choirs: A History of the Festival* (Sutton, 1992); and *The Parrys of the Golden Vale* (Thames, 1998).

David Evans is a senior lecturer and Deputy Head at the School of Music, University of Wales, Bangor and is also a member of the editorial board of the bilingual journal *Welsh Music History/Hanes Cerddoriaeth Cymru*. His main research areas are English church music of the sixteenth and early seventeenth centuries and the history of music in Wales, particularly Welsh collections of music manuscripts. At present he is working on an edition of services and anthems from the Chirk Castle manuscripts for the projected series *Musica Cambriae*. He is known in Wales as a choral conductor, specializing in Renaissance and twentieth-century music.

Peter James completed his doctorate on the early English verse anthem and has published numerous music editions, articles and reviews. He was Director of Studies at the Birmingham Conservatoire for nine years before being appointed Vice-Principal of the Royal Academy of Music, London, a post he held for twelve years until his retirement in 1995. During his time in the Midlands he was also a vicar choral at Lichfield Cathedral and chorus master of the CBSO Chorus. As Series Editor of *Cathedral Press* since 1997, he has produced some three dozen editions of sacred music of the sixteenth, seventeenth and eighteenth centuries, including six anthems and services omitted from Tomkins's *Musica Deo sacra*. In recent years he has been a Consultant to the Royal College of Organists and has overseen restoration of an important organ in his native South Wales.

Bernard Rose was a chorister at Salisbury Cathedral, where he began playing the organ, studied at the Royal College of Music, attracting there the attention of Sir Adrian Boult, and was Organ Scholar at St Catharine's College, Cambridge. In 1939 he was appointed Organist and Tutor in Music, later Fellow, at the Queen's College, Oxford, a post that included being conductor of the Eglesfield Music Society, where he engaged some of the finest soloists of the time and commissioned works by composers such as Vaughan Williams and Edmund Rubbra. During the war years, he fought with the 'Desert Rats' at El Alamein and Italy, before being captured in northern France and spending the remainder of the war as a POW in Germany. From 1957 to 1981 he was Fellow, Organist and Informator Choristarum at Magdalen College, developing the choir into one of the finest in the country. Whilst at Magdalen he composed some forty works, mostly sacred, including his well-known *Preces and Responses*. He edited the complete anthems of Thomas Tomkins included in *Musica Deo sacra* (*Early English Church Music*, 6 vols) and Handel's *Susanna* for the complete German edition. His pupils have become composers, conductors, performers, professors, lecturers and teachers. He was President of the Royal College of organists 1974–76, and was made OBE in 1980. He died aged 80 in November 1996.

Denis Stevens was born at High Wycombe, Buckinghamshire, in 1922. He was educated at the Royal Grammar School there, and later at Jesus College, Oxford. His main fields of study were languages and musicology: in the latter subject he was a pupil of Dr Egon Wellesz. In London, he was for a short time a member of the Philharmonia Orchestra, in which he played violin and viola. He worked at the BBC from 1949 to 1954 as a producer, specializing in Third Programme broadcasts of medieval, Renaissance, and Baroque music. In 1955 he was invited to Cornell University, NY, as Visiting Professor of Music, and in the following year acted in a similar capacity at Columbia University, where subsequently he was Professor of Musicology from 1964 to 1974. He was Professor of Music at the Royal Academy of Music in 1960, and was founder conductor of the Ambrosian Singers from 1956 to 1960.

Professor Stevens's published transcriptions of early music range over nearly five centuries, including an edition of Monteverdi's *Vespers* (1961, revised 1993) and *Orfeo* (1967). He conducted at numerous European Festivals, including at Salzburg in 1967, and in that same year introduced the works of Monteverdi to the Promenade Concerts in London. His contributions to musical literature in Britain, France and America were numerous. He was the author of books on Tudor church music and Thomas Tomkins, editions of English madrigals, Tudor organ music, etc., and in 1980 he published a translation of the letters of Monteverdi.

Denis Stevens was made CBE in 1984. He died in April 2004.

Acknowledgements

Since starting out in 2001 to research the life of Thomas Tomkins, the list of those to whom I turned for information, advice and assistance steadily and inevitably increased. First and foremost, I owe a particular debt of gratitude to the late Denis Stevens, without whose wisdom, friendship, unfailing encouragement and guidance this book could not have been written.

In addition to agreeing readily to contribute chapters of their own, David R.A. Evans and Peter James have given me invaluable advice on many aspects of the book as a whole. I am more than grateful to them both for giving so willingly of their time and expertise over many months.

On my travels in search of Tomkins and his family I have been greatly assisted by many whose local knowledge was vital to the direction of my researches. I owe thanks to Jory Bennett for his help in directing my steps in the search for information in Cornwall; to Joanna Mattingley for bringing to my attention a Tomkins family connection with the medieval St George's guild at Lostwithiel, as well as for much other advice on Cornish history; to Marie Humphrey, the Secretary of the Lostwithiel Old Cornwall Society; to Henry Sneyd and Carole Vivian for information about the Trelawney family and Poole Menheniot; and to Angela Broome at the Courtney Library, Royal Institution of Cornwall, for her aid and efficiency in helping me to seek out references to the Tomkins family in sixteenth-century legal documents.

I am grateful to Nona Rees, the Librarian at St David's Cathedral; to Peter Marks for sharing his profound knowledge of Pembrokeshire history with me; to Lowinger Maddison, the Librarian at Gloucester Cathedral and his counterpart at Worcester Cathedral, David Morrison; Judith Dickinson, Secretary to the Bishop of Worcester; Chris Banks, the Curator of Music Manuscripts at the British Library; Peter Ward Jones, the Music Librarian at the Bodleian Library; Christine Ferdinand, the Fellow Librarian at Magdalen College, Oxford, and her assistant, Sally Speirs; Robert Tucker, Music Librarian at the Barbican, London; the staffs of the Bibliothèque Nationale, Paris; the National Archives at Kew; the National Portrait Gallery; the Wilton Estate; the Churchdown Library; and the County Record Offices of Gloucestershire, Herefordshire and Worcestershire, all of whom have shown me the utmost courtesy and cooperation.

I am indebted to Mrs Molly Rose and to Gregory Rose for permission to include an edited text of a lecture on Thomas Tomkins, given by the late

xii *Acknowledgements*

Bernard Rose to the Royal Musical Association in 1956 and published in the Proceedings of the RMA, 82nd Session (1955/56). I am also most grateful to Hugh Cobbe, President of the RMA, for permission to reprint it.

Martin Roberts and Douglas Sharp of Bredon School, and Lucille and Peter Elms kindly shared much fascinating information about Poole Court. William Reynolds generously permitted me to quote passages about John Fido from his Ph.D. thesis, 'A Study of Music and Liturgy, Choirs and Organs in Monastic and Secular Foundations in Wales and the Borderlands 1485–1645', and I am equally indebted to Patricia Hughes for allowing me to extract details about Robert Kettle and Humphrey Withey from her Ph.D. thesis, 'Buildings and the Building Trade in Worcester 1540–1650'.

I owe thanks to Peter Phillips for permission to quote a paragraph from his sleeve notes to the Tallis Scholars' CD recording of Tomkins's *Great Service*, and to both John Irving and Andrew Ashbee, who gave me invaluable advice on the listing of Tomkins's instrumental music. I am also most grateful to the late William A. Grieve-Smith, who was the first to use the title 'Thomas Tomkins, the last Elizabethan', in a review of Tomkins CDs published in the *La Folia* online music review, and to Mike Silverton, editor of *La Folia*, for permission to adopt the title for this present book. And I owe an especial debt of gratitude to Richard Newsholme, not only for permission to quote from his two articles on Tomkins, published in *Leading Notes* (the Journal of the Early Music Association), but also for the wealth of additional advice and information, the fruits of his own meticulous Tomkins research, that he so generously shared with me.

Many others have responded kindly and readily to my requests for help, including Roger Buckley and Christian Wilson, who agreed to read through my typescript with critical eyes and made numerous helpful observations and suggestions; Michael James, who gave editorial advice; and John Aukett and Chris Gorringe, who came to my aid when technical computer problems threatened to thwart my efforts. For valuable suggestions, assistance and advice of many kinds I am also grateful to Jonathan Boden, Lionel Carley, Pamela Coren, Jeremy Dibble, Roderic Dunnett, Gordon Cumming, Tony Kemp, Leslie Ryan, Sylvie Pierce, Brian Schiele, Lesley Scott, Paul Spicer, the Reverend John Tadman and Peter Wallace.

Finally, I would like to thank my dear wife, Anne, for her constant support and for her patience with a husband too often preoccupied during the past three years.

A.B.
2004

Abbreviations

BL	British Library
Cheque Book	Edward F. Rimbault (ed. 1872), *The Old Cheque Book or Book of Remembrance of the Chapel Royal*, repr. New York, 1966
DNB	*Dictionary of National Biography* (1900)
GRO	Gloucestershire Record Office
NLW	National Library of Wales
RCM	Royal College of Music
Stevens	Denis Stevens (1957), *Thomas Tomkins: 1572–1656*, London (rev. New York, 1967)
TCM	*Tudor Church Music* (Oxford University Press, 1928)
TNA	The National Archives
WCL	Worcester Cathedral Library
WHS	Worcester Historical Society
WRO	Worcestershire Record Office

Introduction

Ask any music lover to identify a great British composer whose career was centred on Worcester, giving as an extra clue that he was married to a lady whose name was Alice, and the reply will almost certainly be Sir Edward Elgar. And yet there was another musician who spent sixty years of his life in Worcester, whose wife Alice was dearly loved, and who has a distinctive claim to be remembered as the last great composer of the 'golden age' of British music: Thomas Tomkins (1572–1656).

Tomkins lived through one of the most revolutionary periods in our history. Born in Wales during the reign of a seemingly popular queen, Tomkins's professional life was spent in the service, at both the Chapel Royal and Worcester Cathedral, of three monarchs and the Church of which those monarchs were successively head. For more than sixty of his eighty-four years the security of the English Crown had appeared to be beyond question, only to be cast, literally, into the melting pot to augment the funds of a country wasted by civil war and ruled by a regicide commoner. And yet Tomkins was not only able to survive the suppression of the music of the English Church, the closure of the Chapel Royal, the destruction of the organ at Worcester, the despoliation and shutting up of the cathedral there, and the devastation of much of the city, but also to find strength and inspiration to continue composing secular music of fine quality. Furthermore, it was his distinction to be the pre-eminent member of a family which, as Charles Burney acknowledged, 'produced more able musicians, during the sixteenth and seventeenth centuries, than any other which England can boast',[1] thus inevitably prompting comparison with the family of J.S. Bach.

Ever hopeful that his music would be valued by posterity, Tomkins died too soon to see the Restoration of 1660, but by great good fortune much of his output has survived, including his collection of music for the Anglican rite, *Musica Deo sacra*, published posthumously in 1668. One of the most versatile figures of English Renaissance music, Tomkins's work embraces both sacred and secular vocal music, pieces for keyboard and for viol consort. A superb contrapuntalist, he is perhaps best known today for his sacred vocal music. The anthems *Almighty God, the fountain of all wisdom* and *Above the stars*

---

[1] Charles Burney (1776–89), *A General History of Music*, ed. F. Mercer (London, 1935), II, 290.

come immediately to mind, as does his best-known composition *When David heard that Absalom was slain,* a masterpiece which seems to have been acclaimed in his lifetime. Following a performance of it at the Oxford Music School in 1636, Charles Butler was moved to write of 'the melodious harmony whereof ... whether I should more admire the sweet well-governed voices, (with consonant instruments) of the singers; or the exquisite invention, wit, and art of the composer, it was hard to determine'.[2]

In Part One of this book I have tried to set the lives of Thomas Tomkins and his family into historical context in such a way as to interest the general reader, music lover and musician alike. I have deliberately limited the amount of technical information contained in the biography and have, in the main, modernized sixteenth- and seventeenth-century spelling and punctuation, leaving archaisms only where they add authenticity and flavour to the text.

In an attempt to give an overall picture of Tomkins's achievement as a composer, Parts Two and Three contain chapters on his music, written by four leading Tomkins scholars: Peter James, David R.A. Evans, the late Bernard Rose and Denis Stevens, who died soon after the completion of this book.

In musical examples the original printed/written pitch is retained, as are the note-values in examples of vocal music, except for those in 6/4 and/or 3/2 time, where they are halved. In the instrumental examples the note-values are retained in the majority of cases; in some which were included in Denis Stevens's earlier study,[3] the halved note-values have been retained. In most examples the original mensuration indications are retained; bar-lines are editorial; and modern clefs have been substituted for the original ones. Symbols in brackets are editorial, as are accidentals in small type; small-sized accidentals in brackets are cautionary; and spelling and punctuation have been modernized.

The advent of compact discs has opened up the world of English Renaissance music to a much wider audience than could possibly have been imagined only twenty years ago. As a result, interest in Tomkins's superb secular madrigals and his inventive works for consort and for keyboard, almost entirely neglected in the past, is steadily gaining ground. Recently released recordings have done much to stimulate awareness of this repertoire as well as of Tomkins's more familiar anthems. It is also gratifying to see that transfers to CD of classic performances originally recorded on vinyl discs are becoming available to a new generation of collectors.

Sir Ivor Atkins (1869–1953), late organist and master of the choristers at

---

[2] Charles Butler (1636), *The Principles of Music,* London (repr. New York, 1970, with an introduction by Gilbert Reaney), 5.

[3] Denis Stevens (1957), *Thomas Tomkins 1572–1656,* London (rev. New York, 1967).

Introduction 3

Worcester Cathedral, writing in 1918 about his most illustrious predecessor, expressed the view that 'with the publication of the *Songs* and the still greater *Musica Deo sacra* in score form one may safely prophesy that Thomas Tomkins will stand out as one of the greatest figures in English musical history of the seventeenth century'.[4] More than eighty years on, Tomkins has still not quite achieved the 'household name' status of his great teacher, William Byrd, or of his close friend, Orlando Gibbons. He is undoubtedly worthy of much greater recognition, and those who may be unfamiliar with his music but prepared to explore will find it never less than movingly sincere and, at its best, sublime.

---

[4] Sir Ivor Atkins (1918), *The Early Occupants of the Office of Organist and Master of the Choristers of the Cathedral Church of Christ and the Blessed Virgin Mary, Worcester*, Worcester (WHS).

PART ONE

THE LIVES AND TIMES OF THOMAS TOMKINS AND HIS FAMILY

Anthony Boden

Chapter 1

Lostwithiel

Thomas Tomkins was a son of Wales, born and bred at St David's in Pembrokeshire, the county in which, as he put it, he 'first breathed and beheld the sun'. His father, Thomas Tomkins the elder, a Cornishman, had crossed the Bristol Channel in 1565, leaving Lostwithiel where his forebears, from beginnings as mercers, had built up a business in the luxury cloth trade, risen to become merchants and, within four generations, established themselves as 'gentlemen'. Thomas Tomkins himself signed as correct a short family tree contained in the Visitation of the County of Worcester (1634), and an extended genealogy included in the *Visitation of Hereford and Monmouth* (1683) shows that three of Tomkins's Cornish forefathers were named Ralph;[1] but throughout their long years in once 'famous and glorious' Lostwithiel, the town was in steady and irreversible economic decline.

One of the ancient Stannary (or Coinage) towns, Lostwithiel sits quietly on the banks of the River Fowey, its street plan little changed since medieval times. In the late thirteenth century a range of buildings was erected in the town to serve as the administrative centre of Cornwall, within its bounds a Hall of Exchequer and Exchange known as the Shire Hall, a prison, and the Coinage Hall or Stannary. There were also smaller buildings for the stamping, assaying and weighing of tin. In 1337 these buildings, the remnants of which still stand, gained added lustre when Edward III conferred on his eldest son, Edward of Woodstock, the Black Prince, the title of duke of Cornwall: the complex becoming known thereafter as the Duchy Palace, even though no earl or duke ever stayed there.[2]

On his travels through the length and breadth of Henry VIII's kingdom between 1534 and 1543, the first English antiquary, John Leland, found that many of Lostwithiel's ancient buildings were already in ruin. 'It is evidently known', he wrote, 'that The River Fowey had flowed to Lostwithiel; but the spewing of the sands of the tin works has stopped it now.' Two centuries later the presumed cause of the town's decline was still open to dispute. Daniel Defoe visited and lamented 'an ancient and once flourishing but now decayed town; and as to trade and navigation, quite destitute; which is occasioned by

---

[1] Atkins, *Early Occupants*.

[2] See N.J.G. Pounds (1979), 'The Duchy Palace at Lostwithiel', *Cornwall Archeological Journal*, 136: 203–17.

The Lives and Times of Thomas Tomkins and his Family

the river, formerly navigable by ships as far as Lostwithiel, being filled up with sands, which some say, the tides drive up in stormy weather from the sea; others say it is by sands washed from the lead-mines [*sic*] in the hills; the last of which, by the way, I take to be a mistake, the sand from the hills being not of a quantity sufficient to fill the channel of a navigable river.'[3]

The Tomkins family observed this decline with dismay and, over time, drifted away from Cornwall, the county in which for several generations they had clearly enjoyed influential patronage. In the twentieth year of the reign of Henry VII, on 18 August 1505, Richard Chynowith of the parish of St Cuthbert, a member of a leading Cornish family, signed over a parcel of land to Ralph Tomkins:

> To Ralph Thomkyn of Lostwithiel, mercer, and Matilda his wife, a close and a piece of land in the Burghs of Lostwithiel and Penknight, at Greenway Head, his piece between the land of St Bartholomew on the S and the Close of Henry Nicholls on the N and E, and his Close between Greenway Head on the E and the Wood of St Bartholomew on the W and the Mill there on the N and the Close of John Kyllyo on the S. to hold forever.[4]

Perhaps this was a reward for services rendered, or maybe Matilda was related to Chynowith and this was a wedding gift.

In 1546 a long and purposeless war, waged by Henry VIII against France, came to an end. 'The war had been prodigiously expensive. Henry's last parliament passed an act empowering him to take into his hands all chantries, hospitals, colleges, free chapels, fraternities, guilds and their possessions ... but the exigencies of history are stronger than the will of kings. The machinery was in operation for the dissolution of the chantries and guilds; the commissions were appointed; all that was necessary was the final impulse. This was provided by the financial stringency bequeathed by Henry to his son's government, the members of which, so far from nourishing any scruple on the subject of the chantries, were actively in favour of suppressing them as a further advance in the Reformation.'[5]

> The government began with a new Chantries Act, mainly re-enacting Henry's provisions, but making them more extensive and more complicated: lands given for the endowment of anniversaries, obits, lights before images, were annexed to the Crown, while various bodies – colleges, schools, chapels-at-ease, were exempted. It was all very complicated, and the Act necessitated the appointment of new commissions in every county to make surveys not only of chantry lands and goods ... but of all their plate, jewels, ornaments, bells, vestments.[6]

---

[3] Daniel Defoe (1724), *A Tour through Great Britain*, London.

[4] Kendall Deeds, Part III, K/7/20. The Courtney Library, the Royal Institution of Cornwall.

[5] A.L. Rowse (1969), *Tudor Cornwall*, London, 252.

[6] Ibid., 253.

Lostwithiel   9

The dissolution of chantries and guilds was no small measure. Life was, and always had been, harsh for the humbler classes; death their frequent and unwelcome guest. Disease and war ensured that few made old bones. Powerless to improve their lot on earth, the living, terrified of judgement after death, could only seek ways of relieving the supposed sufferings of souls in purgatory. The wealthy and powerful might bequeath money in their wills towards a chantry, where prayers for the souls of the faithful departed would be offered regularly; the less affluent, obliged to accept second best, might join together in guilds, created with the primary purpose of maintaining chantries on behalf of their members. The St George's guild at Lostwithiel was one of these. But the Reformation brought with it condemnation of the doctrine of purgatory. Salvation, insisted the Protestants, could be assured by faith alone; no amount of good works could compensate for sins committed.

In 1548 the St George's chapel in the parish church at Lostwithiel was defaced by order of the mayor, acting in accordance with the Chantries Act, but the chantry lands of St George's guild appear to have been 'concealed', leading, seven years later, to a dispute in court.[7] The case included the deposition of Thomas Halwell, clerk, aged 54 in 1552, of St Nighten's chapel, who had been the last St George's guild priest for four years and more, i.e. 1543–48. When asked what lands belonged to St George, he replied that 'He knew one Raff [Ralph] Tomkyn to be a tenant of [a] parcel of it in Lostwithiel'.[8]

Among the papers presented in this case is an account book kept by Richard Courtes, the St George's steward, and probably dated October 1536 to September 1537 (although perhaps copied in 1553). The book includes references to the mill, the local festival known as the Lostwithiel Riding and associated requiem mass, and, at the end, a list of 'Offering pence for the de[a]d', which includes 1*d.* each for Thomas Tomkyn and Margaret Tomkyn, and the omission of this Thomas from all tax documents suggests that he was dead by 1522. Making offerings for one's parents' souls was common at this time, and Thomas and Margaret may well have been the first Ralph's father and mother. Two separate rentals are included in the account book, one concerning the rental of St George's lands in Lostwithiel for 1536–37, showing that 'Raffe Tomkyn did holde a tenemente in the high streete & r[enders] per annum xijd' [twelve pence],[9] and on a later folio that 'Raff Tomkyn did holde a house and garden with an orchard in the Som[er]lane & r[enders] per annum iiijs' [4*s.*].[10] The rental accounts for St Bartholomew's

---

[7] The National Archives (TNA), E315/122. I am grateful to Dr Joanna Mattingley for bringing this information to my attention. See also her article (1989), 'The Medieval Parish Guilds of Cornwall', *Journal of the Royal Institution of Cornwall*, NS, 3: 290–329.

[8] TNA, E315/122, fol. 17.

[9] Ibid., fol. 23.

[10] Ibid., fol. 23v.

Fig. 1.1 South-east view of Lostwithiel in the eighteenth century.

lands in the borough of Lostwithiel and Penkneighe at the same date record that 'Raff Tomkyn did beare for a garden in the Crockenstrete per annum xijd' [12*d*.].[11]

The Riding of St George at Lostwithiel took place on the Sunday after St George's day, with a man in armour (and presumably a dragon) being paraded through the town, the only musician mentioned being a piper, possibly a bagpiper. Various payments for the cleaning of the rider's harness or armour are recorded in the steward's accounts of 1538. Several such festivals were celebrated in Cornwall, like the Bodmin Riding, Hobby-horse Day at Padstow, and Furry Day at Helston, only the last two of which still survive. It is probable that Ralph Tomkyn was a member of the guild of St George and perhaps of other pre-Reformation religious guilds too, a proposition supported by his offering pence, given for deceased family members in 1536–37.

In any event, land in Lostwithiel was still in Tomkins hands when, on 14 October 1549, the last known Ralph Tomkins bequeathed property to his two sons, Thomas and John:

> Ralph Tomkyn of Lostwithiel, merchant, to Thomas his son. Messuage and garden in Lostwithiel near the Great Hall, commonly called The Kings Shire Hall, between the lands of John Day, lands of Richard Curtes of Pylle, the highway and stream called The King's Water. Also a garden in the *venella*, called Summer Lane near *Imaginem Crucis*, called Galbert's Cross, between the highway on two sides The King's Moor. Also, Close at Greenway Head in fee of Penketh and borough of Lostwithiel between lands of Henry Nicholls on two sides, the hereditary lands of Morlowe and the highway. To hold to him entail forever, remainder to John Tomkyn, another son.[12]

Although the spelling of the surname varies, as was common until the eighteenth century, it is clear that this document represents the inheritance of Thomas Tomkins the elder, father of the composer, and also that the last Ralph Tomkins had another son, John, who inherited the remainder of his father's estate. Ralph Tomkins seems to have had a brother, Edward, who appears to have bought out the property inherited by Thomas and John, the value of which may be estimated from information given in the lists of taxpayers (the Subsidy Rolls) for 1525 and 1543, and for the Benevolence Tax of 1545. In 1525 Ralph Tomkins was taxed on his goods at a rate that applied to only 4 per cent of the wealthiest taxpayers in Lostwithiel; in 1543 he was included in an even smaller and more affluent group, 3 per cent, whereas his son John was one of 19 per cent of taxpayers of similar worth. In 1545 Ralph was charged a Benevolence Tax of 10*s*. 8*d*. and was one of only ten persons in the borough paying Benevolence. The highest levy was 12*s*. 8*d*.: the lowest,

---

[11] Ibid, fol. 25.

[12] Ibid., K/7, 32. The *venella* was a granite-paved pathway over which tin ingots were dragged to waiting barges.

12   *The Lives and Times of Thomas Tomkins and his Family*

6*s.* 8*d.* The going rate was eight pence in the pound on lands and goods up to £20, and from £20 upwards, one shilling in the pound. From this assessment it seems therefore that Ralph Tomkins's land and goods were valued at £16, a typical sum for a prosperous master tradesman.

The interval between the Chynowith grant of 1505 and that of the last Ralph Tomkins to his sons in 1549 embraced a splintering epoch: the closing years of the life of Henry VII, the whole reign of his pleasure-loving son, Henry VIII, and the first two years of Edward VI's short life. Within those four decades Thomas Wolsey rose to power as cardinal and chancellor, failed to secure a divorce for his king, and as quickly fell. Henry VIII, having severed the bonds between Rome and the English Church and State, was acknowledged nationally as Supreme Head of the Church of England. Archbishop Cranmer drew up forms of prayer in English, which, by the first Edwardian Act of Uniformity of 1549, gained the force of statute and found their way into the Book of Common Prayer. Nothing was to be read in church other than 'the very pure Word of God, the Holy Scriptures, or that which is evidently grounded upon the same, and that in such a language and order as is most easy and plain for the understanding, both of readers and hearers'.[13] The impact of the Reformation upon the development of sacred music in England was to be profound. Catholic music, some of the most ornate, complicated and beautiful in Europe, was denounced for concealing the clarity of the Word of God; as early as 1516 the Dutch theologian Erasmus (1466–1536) had condemned both its performance and the means of training its performers:

> Modern church music is so constructed that the congregation cannot hear one distinct word. The choristers themselves do not understand what they are singing, yet according to priests and monks it constitutes the whole of religion ... money must be raised to buy organs and train boys to squeal, and to learn no other thing that is good for them ... Boys are kept in the English Benedictine Colleges solely and simply to sing morning hymns to the Virgin. If they want music let them sing psalms like rational beings, and not too many of these.[14]

Extreme Protestants such as Thomas Ridley, the bishop of London, and John Hooper, bishop of Gloucester and Worcester, saw no purpose in choral and instrumental music in public worship, and reduced it at every opportunity. Was church music to be sacrificed along with rich and colourful church decoration: the gilded wall painting, stained glass and intricate carving through which artists and craftsmen had striven to recreate in the medieval church the imagined sounds and visions of paradise? Was the celestial dream to give way to earthly black and white?

---

[13] 1559 Prayer Book, Preface.
[14] Percy A. Scholes (1934), *The Puritans and Music in England and New England*, London, 216, citing *Life and Letters of Erasmus* (ed. Froude), ch. 7.

Cranmer, although no musician, went so far as attempting to add 'plainsong' tunes of his own devising to the Litany (or English procession), and expressed his view on the matter of church music in a letter to the king:

> in mine opinion, the song that shall be made thereunto would not be full of notes, but, as near as may be, for every syllable a note; so that it may be sung distinctly and devoutly, as be in Matins and Evensong *Venite*, the hymns *Te Deum, Benedictus, Magnificat, Nunc dimittis*, and all the Psalms and Versicles; and in the mass *Gloria in excelsis, Gloria Patri*, the Creed, the Preface, the *Pater noster* and some of the *Sanctus* and *Agnus*.[15]

But in the years that followed, 'Cranmer's more radical colleagues were to insist more and more that church music of all kinds – both monodic and polyphonic – should be in the simplest note-against-note style'.[16] Then, in 1553, the death of the boy-king Edward VI brought Henry VIII's elder daughter, Mary Tudor, to the throne, driven by a relentless ambition to throw the Reformation into reverse and to restore the Roman Catholic Church to its former power and influence in England. Church musicians were, for a while, released from the restrictions of Protestantism, but the reinstatement of the Latin rite was notoriously and cruelly accompanied by the agonized screams of heretics committed to the flames. Amongst their number was Hooper, burnt at Gloucester in 1555, and Latimer and Ridley at Oxford in that same year. 'Play the man, Master Ridley', cried Bishop Latimer famously, as the flames shot up around him; 'we shall this day light such a candle, by God's grace, in England, as I trust shall never be put out.' On the same spot, a few months later, Archbishop Cranmer, even though 68 years old, met a similar fate.

Mary's death, after a rule of six years, brought her Protestant half-sister Elizabeth I to the throne in November 1558. English-language services were restored in 1559, and in her Injunctions of that year Elizabeth set out her wishes in regard to church music:

> Item, because in divers Collegiate, and also some parish Churches heretofore there have been livings appointed for the maintenance of men and children, to use singing in the church, by means whereof, the laudable science of music has been had in estimation, and perceived in knowledge: the Queen's Majesty, neither meaning in any wise the decay of any thing that might conveniently tend to the use and continuance of the said science, neither to have the same in any part so abused in the church, that thereby the common prayer should be the worse understood of the hearers, willeth and commandeth, that first no alteration be made of such assignments of living, as heretofore have been appointed to the use of singing or music in the Church, but that the same so remain. And that there be a modest distinct song, so used in all parts of the common prayers in the Church, that the same may be as plainly understood, as if it were read without singing, and yet nevertheless, for the comforting of such that delight in music, it

---

15 F.E. Brightman (1915), *The English Rite*, I, London.
16 Peter Le Huray (1967), *Music and the Reformation in England 1549–1660*, London, 7.

14 *The Lives and Times of Thomas Tomkins and his Family*

> may be permitted that in the beginning, or in the end of common prayers, either
> at morning or evening, there may be sung an Hymn, or such like song, to the
> praise of Almighty God, in the best sort of melody and music that may be
> conveniently devised, having respect that the sentence of the Hymn may be
> understood and perceived.[17]

But what *was* 'the best sort of melody and music that may be conveniently devised'? Elizabeth, for the sake of peace, clearly sought a middle way between the radicals and traditionalists. It would of course be impossible for her to please all shades of opinion, but her own love of music and tradition became self-evident in the form of services that she ordered in her own chapels. When she directed that a crucifix and candles should be placed upon the altar of the Chapel Royal for the marriage of one of her ladies-in-waiting, her chaplains and Council took such great exception that the intention was temporarily abandoned. None the less, as the visiting bishop of Arras recorded, 'it was done at Vespers [Evensong] on Saturday, and on Sunday the clergy wore vestments as they do in our services, and so great was the crowd at the palace that disturbance was feared in the city. The fact is that crucifixes and vestments that were burnt a month ago publicly are now set up in the royal chapel, as they soon will be all over the kingdom, unless, God forbid, there is another change next week.'[18]

The fanaticism of Mary Tudor was still a recent memory; 300 Protestants had been burnt in just four years and the old religion made to appear to the English as a foreign creed, unpatriotic and cruel. Little wonder that the crowd was frightened or that a thing no more sinister than the outward show of Elizabeth's chosen style of worship appeared to point once again to Rome. Against this restless background there were to be years of confusion and uncertainty for church musicians, and Ralph Tomkins's younger son, Thomas, growing to maturity, had already determined that he wished to be a church musician.

Born about 1545, Thomas Tomkins the elder, the first known member of his family to abandon the cloth trade, was to become the founding father of a distinguished family of musicians. Given the declining fortunes of Lostwithiel and his own lack of any substantial inheritance, it is not surprising to find that Thomas sought his living elsewhere. By 1564 he had married Margaret Poher (or Pore), and soon afterwards was offered and accepted a post as a vicar choral at St David's Cathedral in Pembrokeshire. (All cathedral choirs included priests, called variously minor canons or vicars choral; laymen, also called vicars choral, singing men or lay clerks; a master of choristers; and choristers or singing boys.) Still in his early twenties, Thomas sold his land in

---

[17] From the Injunctions of 1559.

[18] H. Robinson (ed., 1842), *Original Letters Relative to the English Reformation*, 'Zurich Letters', I, London.

Lostwithiel and, with his young bride, left Cornwall, probably embarking by boat from Padstow to begin a new life in Wales.

A Muster Roll for Cornwall drawn up in 1569 named all men available in the county to help repel any Spanish invasion. Thomas's uncle, Edward, was listed, alongside William Kendall and Thomas Hellyer, as one of the three leading gentlemen in Lostwithiel; he was also credited with being both an archer and harquebusier. Three years later, on 24 March 1571, Edward sold most of the remaining Tomkins lands to Thomas Hellyer's son: 'Sale: Edward Tomkyn of Lostwithiel, gent, to John Mayhow alias Hellyer of Lostwithiel, gent, all those lands in the borough of Lostwithiel and Penknight ... reserving only his own mansion house there now inhabited by John Stowell and himself.'[19]

Thomas Hellyer's granddaughter, Katherine, married William Kendall's son, Walter, and following the death of her father, John, in 1601, Katharine Kendall inherited the former Tomkins property in Lostwithiel. The wealthy Kendalls, who had benefited from the dissolution of Tywardreath Priory, were undoubtedly well acquainted with the Tomkins family. They were singled out by Richard Carew in his 1602 *Survey of Cornwall*, where especial mention is made of William Kendall's hospitality at Lostwithiel as deserving remembrance 'while he lived here and kept house because for store of resort and frankness of entertainment it exceeded all others of his sort'. But by 1602 the Tomkins family was long gone from Lostwithiel. There, in the ancient Church of St Bartholomew, family memorials record the Kendalls' passing; but of Thomas Tomkins's ancestors not one inscription remains.

---

[19] Kendall Deeds, Part III, K/7/37 (see n. 4).

Chapter 2

St David's

Upon the furthest pointe of that unfruitful shore …
there, void of all delite, cold, barren, bleak and dry,
no pleasure might allure, nor steal the wandering eye.

(Michael Drayton, *Poly-Olbion*, Song 5)

The St David's peninsula in Pembrokeshire, a county affectionately known as 'little England beyond Wales', is a place of natural beauty and peace, its cathedral a fine example of medieval architecture in a perfect setting. But to travellers and pilgrims of the distant past, access presented a daunting prospect. Giraldus Cambrensis, who oversaw the construction of St David's Cathedral in the twelfth century, described its surroundings as remote, out of the way, barren, unfruitful and stony, without woodland, rivers or meadows; ever exposed to winds and storms. Even five hundred years later when, in 1793, Sir Richard Colt Hoare of Stourhead journeyed on horseback into Wales he concluded that 'nothing can be more dreary than the country about St David's; not even a hedge can be reared on account of the high winds which prevail here', and by then, the cathedral, as well as all the adjoining buildings, were 'either in an absolute state of ruin, or decay'.[1] Thomas Tomkins the elder had arrived in St David's by July 1565, the month in which his name first appears in a series of entries in the Cathedral Chapter Act Books.[2] As elsewhere in the kingdom, the religious and political life of Pembrokeshire had undergone considerable upheaval in the previous three decades, but in Wales there was the added dimension of English hegemony.

In 1536 Wales had been annexed to England by statute, but there were few educated men to be found in the principality capable of taking up the essential offices of Church or local government:

When King Henry the eighth came … to establish good and wholesome laws among them [the Welsh], and to give them magistrates of their own nation, I mean Sheriffs and Justices of ye Peace in every shire, he then was fain and forced

---

[1] M.W. Thompson (ed., 1983), *The Journeys of Sir Richard Colt Hoare*, Stroud, 45.
[2] See David Evans (1987), 'A Cornish Musician in Wales', *Journal of The Institute of Cornish Studies*, 15: 19–28; and St David's Chapter Act Book 'A', 102, 105, 108 and 112. National Library of Wales (NLW), Aberystwyth.

18   *The Lives and Times of Thomas Tomkins and his Family*

> to admit such to be Justices of Peace as were to be found in the country, for then there was not sufficient number to be found in many shires of Wales that might dispend £20 of lands or were learned, for most gentlemen could neither write nor read for they were clean barred from all manner of learning and good education.[3]

In that same year, 1536, William Barlow, an Englishman and ardent advocate of religious reform, was installed as bishop of St David's. He was appalled at what he found there, and was bitterly outspoken on the condition of religious life in his diocese: 'Habit, superstition and ignorance were the order of the day among the peasantry. They accepted the Church simply because it had formed an essential part of the daily routine of life.'[4] Barlow set about ridding the Church of what he saw as its most glaring abuses, particularly the use of 'idolatrous images'. He also, coincidentally, set out to benefit the dowries of his five daughters by stripping the lead from the roof of the episcopal palace at St David's and selling it for a sum so great that, according to a sixteenth-century account, twelve years' revenue of the bishopric would have been insufficient to cover the cost of repairs. So successful was Barlow's shameless pocket-lining that he was enabled to match his five daughters to five bishops!

Barlow's successor at St David's, Robert Farrar was, on the accession of Mary I to the Crown, condemned as a heretic and burnt at the stake in Carmarthen on 30 March 1555. The next bishop, Henry Morgan, a devoted Roman Catholic, was acceptable to Mary but was ejected by Elizabeth in 1559. Amongst others deprived was Morgan Phillips, precentor at St David's, who, with other exiles, settled at Douai in the Netherlands. Phillips was replaced as precentor by Thomas Young, who, after Henry Morgan had been ejected from his See, remained at St David's as bishop for only a few months before being translated to the archbishopric of York in 1560. Then, at last, came a man to make a real difference: Richard Davies, bishop of St David's from 1561 until his death at the age of 80 in 1581.

Davies, a highly educated man, is still remembered as one of the translators of the Bible into Welsh. William Salesbury had already completed much of the work of translating the New Testament, but legislation passed in 1563 had directed that Welsh translations were to be made of both the Bible and the Book of Common Prayer; moreover, this enormous task was to be completed by 1 March 1567. The Welsh peasantry had accepted the Reformation with indifference: 'If they did not understand the Prayer Book and Bible in the foreign tongue of England, neither had they understood the Latin Mass. As yet religion passed them by. Early in Elizabeth's reign the Welsh peasantry were in a state of intellectual torpor and educational neglect.'[5]

Richard Davies and William Salesbury, assisted by Thomas Huett,

---

[3] H. Owen (ed., 1906), *George Owen, The Description of Pembrokeshire*, London, III, 55–6.
[4] J. Gwynfor Jones (1989), *Wales and the Tudor State*, Cardiff, 81.
[5] G.M. Trevelyan (1949), *Illustrated English Social History*, London, II, 13.

St David's   19

precentor of St David's, set to work on the much-needed translation, working at the bishop's palace at Abergwili, near Carmarthen, the palace at St David's, thanks to Barlow's greed, being already ruinous: 'The Bishop's Palace at Abergwili was a prime centre of cultural activity where professional bards were welcomed and granted hospitality ... The household was open to men of learning and Davies's own contacts with laymen and clergy within and outside Wales testified to his wider cultural and scholastic interests.'[6]

The fame of Richard Davies and his pioneering work at St David's quickly spread. A contemporary of Davies, Sir John Wynn of Gwydir, recorded that 'he governed ... for ye honour of our nation. He also kept an exceeding great post [staff], having in his service younger brothers of most of the best houses in that country to whom ... he gave good maintenance and education.'[7] All seemed to augur well for Thomas Tomkins the elder as he and his bride embarked for Wales.

Tomkins's appointment as a vicar choral at St David's in 1565 coincided with efforts made by the dean and chapter to bring about improvements in the standard of music at the cathedral; indeed, his recruitment, following the appointment in 1563 of a new master of the choristers, Thomas Eliot, and the imposition of greater discipline upon the vicars choral and choristers, may well have been elements in a comprehensive strategy. Eliot had been directed by the precentor to 'teach the choristers their plainsong, prick-song [written music] and discant' and to 'play the organ when time requireth'.[8] Consequently, 'during that year a number of significant changes were made ... including the addition of several new stops to the organ and the purchase of three metrical psalters and three other books of "Geneva Psalms"'.[9]

The introduction of metrical psalms was no straightforward step in a community still smarting from the ejection of a Roman Catholic bishop, Henry Morgan, just six years earlier. Even as late as 1582, Bishop Marmaduke Middleton, on his translation to St David's, continued to rail against 'the idolatrous mass' and all other practices 'after the use of popish superstition'. The Welsh were not easily to be severed from tradition, and Middleton's 'denunciation of Roman Catholic survivals was, at that time, amongst the most scathing in Wales'.[10] It was a giant stride from the Latin mass to sermon, prayers, and psalms sung by church congregations in rhymed, metrical English.

A collection of metrical psalms compiled by Thomas Sternhold, 'groom of

---

[6]   G. Williams (1967), *Welsh Reformation Essays*, Cardiff, 180–86.

[7]   Jones, *Wales and the Tudor State*, 95.

[8]   National Library of Wales (NLW), MSS SD/Ch/B27-28; H.T. Payne, *Collecteanea Menvensia*, I, 8.

[9]   Evans, 'A Cornish Musician in Wales', 19. See also W. Jones and E. Freeman (1856), *History of the Antiquities of St David's*, London, 389.

[10]   Jones, *Wales and the Tudor State*, 114.

the King's Majesty's robes' and gentleman of the Privy Chamber, had appeared as early as 1549. A second edition, published in the December of that same year, contained thirty-seven translations by Sternhold and seven by Hopkins, and this over the next dozen years became the standard English psalter. The introduction of 'Sternhold and Hopkins' with music, first published in Geneva in 1556, was issued at the same time as a form of prayers used by the English congregation in Geneva and approved by John Calvin himself: anathema in England of course during the Marian reaction of 1553 to 1558, but thereafter an essential part of compulsory worship at a time when church attendance was enforced by the State on pain of a fine for absence.

Elizabeth might have wished for all her subjects to accept the middle way of 'one religion' but this could hardly be expected given so diverse a society as that in England, and not everyone answered the Sunday peal willingly. Perhaps Tomkins *père* knew of his fellow Cornishman, John Trevelyan, a Catholic gentleman 'who used to attend church to avoid the fine, endured the reading of the lesson and the singing of the "Geneva jig", which was his name for Sternhold and Hopkins' psalms, but always went out before the sermon, calling aloud to the parson in the pulpit "when thou hast said what thou hast to say, come and dine with me". He used to frighten the Protestant old ladies of his acquaintance by telling them "they should expect worse days than they suffered in Queen Mary's time, and that faggotts should be dear!" He was a merry old gentleman of whom many stories were told.'[11]

The arrival of Tomkins the elder in 1565 probably coincided with the first introduction of metrical psalms and the relatively new style of psalm singing to the St David's choir. 'Thomas Eliot may not have found teaching the new repertoire to the singers an easy task. Discipline among the vicars choral and choristers had for many years been a problem, and by 1565 it had become so bad that the cathedral authorities decided to bring matters to a head. The first serious complaint was made by Mr Morgans, the cathedral schoolmaster, against William Huett – probably a relative of the precentor, Thomas Huett.'[12] On 27 April 1565, William was accused of:

> Diverse faults worthy to be reformed as the said Mr Morgans doth allege and is always ready to prove: to which Complaint the said William Huett would not make answer nor obey such order as Mr Chancellor debate and the rest of the chapter would order but ostinantly [*sic*] and unreverantly [*sic*] contrary to his oath against all good order of the statute of this Cathedral, disobediently and unreasonably used himself that all honest ears might be sorry and ashamed to hear, whereupon Mr President commanded the said William Huett out of the

---

[11] Trevelyan Papers, *Camden Soc.*, Pt. II [1863, pp. 113–18] and Pt. III [1872, p. xxii]. *See also* Trevelyan, *Illustrated English Social History*, 40.

[12] Evans, 'A Cornish Musician in Wales', 19.

Fig. 2.1   St David's Cathedral. An early nineteenth-century engraving by I.H. Shepherd, from a drawing by H. Gastineau.

choir ... And also to obey and reverence his said schoolmaster according to the order and decree made of late for good order of vicar chorals [*sic*].[13]

The chapter were obliged to deal firmly with several more cases of serious misbehaviour and incompetence in the months that followed, after which, for a while, the musicians of the cathedral caused relatively little trouble. Meanwhile, Thomas and Margaret Tomkins settled in at St David's and were in time blessed with children. Within two years of her arrival at St David's, Margaret Tomkins gave birth to a son, Thomas, followed by a daughter, Bridget, around 1570. But then, in 1571, the seemingly calm progress of their married life together was shattered. Thomas Tomkins the elder found himself among several of the vicars choral who by various misdemeanours had incurred the censure of the chapter; and in his case the charge was a particularly personal and painful one concerning an extramarital affair. On 14 July 1571 he was:

> Admonished by Mr Chantor [the precentor] etc ... to procure and get home his wedded wife as is supposed betwixt this present day and one fortnight after Lammas Day next, and for his sinful act committed with his maidservant etc., though he seem, from the bottom of his heart to be sorry for his offence, yet to give to the poor namely to David Glover 3s 4d to pray for him upon pain of

---

[13] NLW, Chapter Act Book 'A', 89.

deprivation of his stall and living thereunto belonging to the which article he did assent.[14]

It is perhaps some measure of the high professional regard in which Tomkins was held that he was not dismissed by the cathedral authorities for what, in their eyes, was clearly a sin and not merely an error. Indeed, within a few years of this episode Tomkins was appointed master of the choristers and organist at St David's in succession to Thomas Eliot. But what of Margaret? Had she fled back to Cornwall on discovering her betrayal? The word 'procure' suggests that to bring her home would have required some effort on Tomkins's part, but he apparently succeeded, for in the following year, 1572, a third and last child, a boy, arrived. Confusingly, this boy, destined to become the greatest and most gifted member of his musical family, was, like his elder brother, baptized Thomas. Even allowing that in adult life the younger Thomas was to acknowledge as correct a family tree showing Margaret Poher as his mother, and that she undoubtedly accepted him as her own, there is no escaping the possibility that this boy could have been the love child of Thomas Tomkins *père* and his Welsh maidservant.

No sixteenth-century registers of births at St David's have survived. Many of the cathedral records for the period have deteriorated badly as a result of water damage and the resultant damp moulds, and several that have survived are no longer legible. It is impossible to prove that the composer Thomas Tomkins was not Margaret's child. However, it is at least odd that she and Thomas *père* should choose to name both of their sons Thomas, giving neither of them a second name to distinguish one from the other. Is it too fanciful to suppose that this name was the obvious choice of a girl who had loved her employer and, with a heavy heart, had given up her child for his sake? It seems more than possible that Thomas Tomkins's mother was, like the place of his birth, Welsh, and that Tomkins himself remained unaware of his father's transgression.

That Thomas Tomkins the elder was a well-educated man is beyond question, albeit that he does not appear to have gained a university degree. In the middle of the sixteenth century a grammar school was established at St David's. The first recorded master was Harries Jackson, and the pupils were young vicars choral and choristers who were ordered to attend school daily at six in the morning. In 1573 Tomkins the elder was appointed master,[15] holding the post for two years in tandem with his duties as a vicar choral at the cathedral. It seems probable that he then relieved Thomas Eliot as master of the choristers and organist, at least partially, taking over completely by 1577. As David Evans has explained:

---

[14] NLW, Chapter Act Book 'A', 236.
[15] George W. Middleton (1977), *The Streets of St Davids,* St David's.

St David's 23

A list of the cathedral's staff found in the Chapter Act Book 'A' and dated 1573, indicates that Tomkins was at that time a 'Vicar Choral and master of the children.' In a slightly amended list for the same month he was said to be merely a vicar choral. Thomas Eliot's name does not appear in either list and there is no record of his resignation or death in the cathedral's extant records. John E West, in his *Cathedral Organists* (1899), stated that Eliot's period of office ended in 1577 but he seemed unaware of Tomkins's presence at the cathedral for he makes no mention of him.[16] The information on St David's was given to West by Dr Codner, cathedral organist there in 1894–6. It may well be that Codner had been unable to find the dates for Eliot's stay in Wales from cathedral documents which at that time were readable … Many of the pages for the period 1576–86 are now totally illegible even under ultra-violet light. It is clear however, that until the early years of this century certain passages from the affected pages must have been decipherable. As late as 1918, Sir Ivor Atkins in his well-known study of the organists of Worcester Cathedral[17] quoted passages which now cannot be found in the damaged pages. Unfortunately, none of the rescued references to musicians provides information about Eliot, and the omission of his name from the two 1573 lists casts serious doubt upon the accuracy of West's date for the end of Eliot's period of office, supplied by Codner. It could be argued from the evidence of one of the transcribed extracts found in Atkins's book that Tomkins must have been acting as the master of the choristers and organist well before 1577.[18]

The 1573 entry in the Chapter Act Book, describing Tomkins as 'master of the children', probably referred, unusually, to his role as master of the grammar school. The changeover from Eliot to Tomkins as organist and master of the choristers may well have been gradual, especially if Eliot was becoming incapacitated due to illness, but by 1577, the transfer completed, Tomkins was finding it difficult to make ends meet and was seeking a pay rise. He clearly knew his worth, and had already threatened to take a better-paid post elsewhere before making application to the commissioners of the archbishop of Canterbury, who included Richard Davies, bishop of St David's. His plea was considered on 29 April 1577:

> Whereas Thomas Tomkins, Master of the Choristers and Organ Player in this Church, as well by his own report as by the testimony of others, declareth that he hath not so great wages as others have had who occupied his place and office heretofore; and also credibly affirmeth that he is not able to live and continue a member of this Church upon such wages and commodity as he now enjoyeth, but must of necessity be obliged to leave this Church, and to accept such place, as with greater commodity, wages and living, is elsewhere offered unto him. It is therefore ordered, constituted and appointed by the Reverend Father in God Richard, Bishop of St. Davids and Mr. Lewis Gwyn, deputies unto the Most Reverend Father in God Edmund [Grindale], by God's Providence Archbishop of Canterbury and Metropolitan of England, in His Grace's Visitation within the Diocese of St. Davids, executed by the foresaid Deputies or Delegates, that Thomas Tomkins the younger, Son unto the foresaid Thomas Tomkins the elder, now being one of the Choristers of this Church, shall from henceforth, to the end

---

16 John E. West (1899), *Cathedral Organists past and present*, London, 76.
17 Atkins, *Early Occupants.*
18 Evans, 'A Cornish Musician in Wales', 21.

that his poor Father, at whose finding he is, may thereby the rather be relieved, have a Vicar's Stall in the said Cathedral Church of St. Davids which one Richard Johnson lately held, and is now void, and from the Feast of the Nativity of St. John the Baptist next coming, shall and may enjoy all profits and commodities belonging to the same stall and place of Vicar Choral, without defalcation, according to the custom of the Church. And it is further appointed, constituted and decreed by the foresaid Delegates or Deputies that there is now but one chorister in this Church, besides the said Tomkins the younger (the Statute requiring six in all) two other children of years, voice and aptitudes, likely to do God's service, as appertaineth to a Chorister of the foresaid Church, shall be appointed by the Chanter and Chapter, so that at least there may be three of them continually kept and maintained.[19]

Given that the elder Tomkins's two sons were both named Thomas, one aged about 10 years and the other 5 in 1577, it is clear that it must have been the older boy who was given a post as vicar choral. The incident concerning William Huett in 1565, a vicar choral still subject to the discipline of his schoolmaster, and the fact that the pupils at the grammar school at St David's were young vicars choral, demonstrate that boys could be granted paid stalls, albeit that the usual convention was for such posts to be awarded only to adult singers. It seems possible that the employment of such young paid appointees was deemed necessary in a remote location where, even before young Tomkins's promotion, the number of choristers had dwindled from the required six to just two boys.

The cathedral authorities, clearly anxious to retain the services of Thomas Tomkins the elder, were able to offer him a little extra money by employing his son rather than increasing the basic rate of pay for the master of the choristers and organist. All organists were expected to compose music as part of their duties, and although no music by him survives, it is possible that Tomkins had already more than proved his worth by providing music for use in services at the cathedral. The device chosen to reward and retain Tomkins leaves no doubt about his value to the chapter, and especially so as it was approved only six days after the organist's elder son had been reprimanded for bad behaviour:

1577. April 23. The said Commissioners (the Lord Bishop of St. David's and the Archdeacon of Cardigan, Commissioners to my Lord of Canterbury) decreed and directed that if Thomas Tomkins (a chorister) did not appear before them on Monday next, here in the Chapter House, he should not be accepted, reputed and counted a Chorister or member of the Church, nor have any allowance of living allowed during his absence.[20]

Why had young Thomas absented himself? Was he unhappy at home as well as disillusioned by his cathedral duties? His rebellion came to a head in 1586, the year in which his father, by then a widower, had announced his

---

[19] Atkins, *Early Occupants*, 39–40.
[20] Ibid., 39.

intention to remarry. A Chapter Act book entry for 22 January noted curtly that 'Thomas Tomkins, junior, having grossly misbehaved, is expelled, and his stall having been declared vacant, is given to David Thomas'.[21]

In these years England was constantly harried by Spanish sea power. Thomas, a youth of 19 years, left his home at St David's and enlisted in the navy. Whether or not he served in action against the unsuccessful Spanish Armada of 1588 is not known, but three years later he was aboard the *Revenge*, one of six royal galleons under the command of Lord Thomas Howard and Sir Richard Grenville dispatched to the Azores. After more than three months at sea, they anchored off Flores to take on supplies and to allow their men, half of whom were sick, to recover on land. Totally unprepared, they were surprised by a Spanish fleet of fifty-three galleons. Howard was able to get away with five ships, but Grenville, on the *Revenge*, had embarked only about one hundred men, including Tomkins, when the Spanish attack began. Bravely deciding to cut through the Spanish ships, Grenville engaged in an action that lasted throughout the night and in which two of the huge Spanish galleons were sunk. At dawn, dying of his wounds, Grenville wanted to blow up the *Revenge*, but the remnants of his crew forced him to surrender. Grenville died on the deck of the *Felipe*, the largest Spanish warship, and among the many others who lost their lives in that heroic action was the firstborn son of Thomas Tomkins the elder.

> And the sun went down, and the stars came out far over the summer sea,
> But never a moment ceased the fight of the one and the fifty-three.
> Ship after ship, the whole night long, their high-built galleons came,
> Ship after ship the whole night long, with her battle-thunder and flame;
> Ship after ship, the whole night long, drew back with her dead and her shame.
> For some were sunk and many more shatter'd, and so could fight us no more –
> God of battles, was ever a battle like this in the world before?
>
> (Tennyson, *The Revenge*)

---

[21] Ibid., 40.

Chapter 3

Menevia Sacra

Throughout his long years at St David's, Tomkins *père* appears to have taken at least as much interest and pleasure in the history of the cathedral and in the countryside around it as in its musical life. When Richard Fenton published his book *A Historical Tour Through Pembrokeshire* in 1811, he referred to a 'MS History of St David's in Latin by one Tomkyn, 1610', and quoted from it a description of the windows of the chantry, endowed by Bishop Adam Houghton at St Mary's College, St David's: 'We find that those magnificent windows were decorated with painted glass representing the most memorable occurrences in the prelate's [Houghton's] life; amongst others, Pope Clement the Sixth's excommunication of him, and, in return, the bishop's excommunication of the pope.'[1]

In a footnote, Fenton quotes the Latin passage setting out the description of the windows, and also gives the source of the quotation as 'Tomkyn's MSS Bodl. Lib.': 'Hic a Papâ, Clement.6, excommunicatus fuit, et postea ipsum papam excommunicavit, ut in fenestris vitriis ejusdem collegii ejusque picturis ostenditur, ac etiam ejusdem tumba inscriptum apparebit.'[2]

Unfortunately, no trace remains at the Bodleian Library of either the MS History of St David's or of the Tomkyn manuscripts; they had already vanished when Sir Ivor Atkins, searching for material on the Tomkins family, visited the Bodleian in 1945. 'Nevertheless', he wrote, 'it is hardly likely that Fenton, who himself had been educated at St David's Cathedral Grammar School, invented the work, and if it existed there can be no doubt that its author was Thomas Tomkins, the one-time vicar choral of St David's. The late Mr Francis Green of St David's, a high authority on matters relating to West Wales, some years ago assured me that Tomkins was not a Welsh name and was only found in West Wales in the sixteenth and seventeenth centuries in connection with this St David's family.'[3]

There is every possibility that the author of the manuscript once held by

---

[1] Richard Fenton, *A Historical Tour Through Pembrokeshire* (facsimile by Dyfed County Council, 1994), 39.

[2] Ibid.

[3] Sir Ivor Atkins (1946), 'The Authorship of the XVIth Century Description of St David's Printed in Browne Willis's "Survey" (1717)', *National Library of Wales Journal*, 4, (3–4), Summer.

28 *The Lives and Times of Thomas Tomkins and his Family*

the Bodleian was indeed Thomas Tomkins the elder, and even though the original had been lost Atkins was convinced that a large part of it was copied in a narrative description of St David's Cathedral and the surrounding countryside reproduced in a document by Browne Willis: *A Survey of the Cathedral Church of St David's and the Edifices belonging to it as they stood in the year 1715* (London, 1717), a work described by Atkins as 'of great value now so rare as to be quite unattainable'.

> In the Prefatory Epistle to the *Survey* Browne Willis gives his reasons for undertaking the work, and enumerates the difficulties under which it was carried through. He tells us that he himself had never been to St David's, but had felt it urgent, in view of the wretched condition of the Cathedral at that time, that some careful record should be made of what was still left of it, before further decay should set in. Accordingly, he prevailed upon a friend then living not far from St David's to do this. That friend, we now know, was Dr William Wotton (1666–1727), the well-known scholar. To Willis's work Wotton made two important contributions. We are concerned only with the second, entitled *Memoirs relating to the Cathedral-Church of St David's and the Country as it was in the latter End of Queen Elizabeth's Reign.*
>
> These *Memoirs*, Wotton tells us, were entirely based upon a manuscript which had been put into his hands by his friend Mr Havard, 'Vicar of Aber-Gwily in Carmarthenshire', who himself had received it from Mr William Lewes of Llwyn Derw, its former owner. The manuscript he describes as written at the end of Queen Elizabeth's reign, but who its author was he did not know. He did not print the whole; but such portions as he used (which comprise pages 42–87 of Willis's *Survey*) he left unaltered. Its literary style he thought 'uncorrect and verbose'. 'For which Reason', he says, 'I have chosen rather to give an exact Abstract of every Thing that I could judge to be material in the MS than to transcribe the Whole'. In spite of Wotton's judgement upon the style it is probable that most people today will find the account of St David's and its surrounding country of fascinating interest, and the narrative fresh, vivid and racy.[4]

Wotton added notes of his own to the original manuscript, setting them in square brackets, and these, it has to be said, are infinitely more 'verbose' than the original. Where, for instance, the writer describes the grain exports of the peninsula in 'thousands of bushels', Wotton expends thirty lines in explaining the difference between a South Wales tel and an English bushel! None the less, contemporary accounts of cathedrals in Elizabethan times, as well as of topography, are rare, and this description of St David's, minus Wotton's additions, remains an extremely valuable record. Eager to refute Giraldus Cambrensis's view of St David's as the most barren place in the kingdom, the writer 'tells us, at his first setting out, that he knew many places both in England and Wales, to which St David's is to be preferred for fertility of soil, and several other valuable things of life':

> The country about it is open and flat, consequently exposed to the sea-wind,

---

[4] Atkins, 'The Authorship'.

Menevia Sacra

being surrounded by sea every way, except towards the east. It is wholly destitute of wood, the sea-coast is very rocky and dangerous, and in winter-time, especially, may give a stranger a very horrid notion of the place: and yet in that part of Dewisland which is near St David's, it bears all sorts of grain without any of those helps of lime, marl and ouze [seaweed] which is used in other parts of the country; and has no other sort of compost, than what the best ground in England has. There is land belonging to the bishop, near St David's, which was never known in any man's memory to lie fallow. No place in Wales has more or better barley, though that is, of all other grain, the daintiest for growth. They have, indeed, but few beans, but of wheat, barley, oats, rye, and peas, there is plenty, and many hundreds, nay thousands of bushels are exported every year from thence.

Though the greater part of the ground is employed in tillage, yet they make butter and cheese sufficient for their use. They have indeed but little hay, but that is supplied by the straw of peas and oats for their horses, and other straw for their other cattle. Of other provisions in this country, there is great variety and plenty; their beef and mutton is very sweet and fat, goats-flesh they want not, which may well be termed venison (as it is) for its sweetness; and Dewisland hogs are famous to a proverb. Their seas produce as good fish as upon any coast about this country, such as plaice, gurnets, whiting, lobsters, mackerel, and within the last two years, God hath sent a blessing to St David's, not before bestowed, though common upon the neighbouring coasts, which is, herrings in great abundance. The fresh rivers yield good trout and eels, and the water is extremely good; so that it may be questioned at St David's, which contributes most to make their ale so celebrated, the malt or the water.

Wood is what they want most in this country; to remedy which, they have coal about seven miles off, and furze and fern for burning, and turf for fuel of the poorer sort: that they dig out of several commons which lie near the town, particularly out of one which is three miles long, and comes up to the town's end, and was given to that parish by Rhees ap Tudor, who lies in that church; to which he was, no doubt, a good benefactor. It is called Crûg-glâs-y-ddyfrog [i.e. the watery green hillock]. This common not only supplies them with turf but is the great support of their cattle in winter. It is said formerly to have been a forest, and they conclude so, because butts of trees are daily found in the ground there, as they dig for turf.

The air here is extremely pure, and the people live long, and are very hardy. Few strangers that have ever come hither have complained of it. The winters are not so cold as in the more inland parts; frost and snow never continue long, and the snow generally melts as it falls.

Concerning the city or town of St David's, there will not be much expected by way of commendation, and it needs no discommendation, it is of itself so bad. It seems to have been of some largeness formerly, by the number of streets yet remaining; of which there are five that still retain their ancient names; the chiefest is High Street, where the Cross stands, St Nuns Street, New Street, Ship Street, and Pit Street, which leads into the Valley, or precincts of the church. The town stands up on a hill above the bottom in which the church stands, which is called the valley. Here are the vicars' houses, the Bishop's Palace, and the canon's houses, all or most of them in good repair; and indeed, if we take away the church, and those houses in the valley, the whole town besides is scarce worth the naming. The valley is enclosed with a very high wall, by which, and the gates, when looked to, the churchmen could formerly have defended themselves against a whole country that should have come against them with swords and shields.

The Bishop's Palace I note from all the rest of the buildings there is the most

30 *The Lives and Times of Thomas Tomkins and his Family*

excellent, with very large rooms in it, so that the King and Bishop have formerly kept their several courts there. It had been maintained to this day in good repair if Bishop Barlow (who lived in the time of Henry VIII and Edward VI) had not uncovered the roof of the house for the lucre of the lead. Since that time, part of it was covered with slate, and the rest is open. Twelve years revenue of the bishopric will not repair the rest, as it has been.

Besides these houses of the canons and prebendaries, there was a college of priests, which belonged to the vicars choral of the church, which, in Edward VI's time, was dissolved, and (as it was said) was betrayed by one Green, sub-chantor and master of the college at that time. It is now altogether ruinous.

This place is called in Latin, *Menevia*; for which name several reasons are given. Some derive it from *Man-Yw* [small yews] as if it had its name from several small yew trees, which did anciently grow there. Others say it comes from *Menyw*, which signifies a woman; and for this, they tell us the following story: that in the time of the Arch-Flamins, there was a great company of votaries, addicted wholly to a solitary life, in this place, who abandoned the company of women entirely. Now it so happened, once upon a time, that there was an invasion, in which all the men in the country being killed, the women being destitute of husbands, came to the monks for relief, who hearing of their approach, shut the gates against them and cried out *Menyw! Menyw!* [a woman! A woman!] From which the place has been called Menevia ever since.[5]

There were formerly several chapels about St David's, which all belonged to the mother church, dedicated to several saints, and were commodiously seated to draw the devotions of the pilgrims. The first and principal of these is St Nun's Chapel, so called from St Nun, who is said to have been St David's mother. There is a fine well beside it, covered with a stone roof, and enclosed within a wall, with benches to sit upon round the well. Some old simple people go still to visit the saint at some particular times, especially on St Nun's Day (March 2) which they keep holy, and offer pins, pebbles, *etc.* at this well.

Westwards of the town, about a mile distance, near the key, stands *Capel-y-Pistyll*, which has its name from a spring that runs under it, into a cistern at the east end, under the pinion [gable-end].

Capel Stinian [St Justinian's Chapel] lies next. This has been a very fine strong building; I know but few churches in Wales of a better kind of building, with battlements round it, and a tower at one end, in which there were bells formerly. The walls are still very strong, though there has been no covering upon it these many years. There is a well by this chapel. It is something above a mile west of St David's.

Not far off is *Capel Patrick* [St Patrick's Chapel], full west of St David's and placed as near his country, *viz.* Ireland, as it could well be. It is now wholly decayed. All these chapels are near the sea side, and adjoining to the places where those that came by sea commonly landed. They were placed here to draw the devotion of the seamen and passengers when they first came ashore; other pilgrims used likewise to come to them. What was there offered, was carried to the cathedral, and divided every Saturday among the canons and priests. Some yet living, that belong to the church, can remember since the offering money was brought on Saturdays to the chapter house, and there divided by the dishfuls, the quantity not allowing them leisure to tell [count] it. That the devotion to this church was very great in popish times is certain, and how meritorious they

---

[5] Wotton describes this explanation as 'impertinent'. Edward Lhwyd, writing in Camden's *Britannia* (1698), suggested that the word Menevia signified a narrow sea, e.g. the channel between Caernarvonshire and Anglesey is called Abermeneu.

Menevia Sacra 31

accounted it appears by this old verse: *Roma semel quantum, bis dat Menevia tantum.* [It was esteemed as meritorious to visit St David's twice, as to visit Rome once.] Which has been answered thus: *Mercedem similem reddit uterque locus.* [It is as meritorious to visit one, as the other.]

The last is *Capel-y-Gwrbyd* [i.e. the Chapel of the Fathom] where they show St David's fathom [the length of his extended arms] upon an arch of the chapel, which is about three yards and a half long. He is described in the old chronicles to have been a very tall man [!]. These were the chapels formerly standing near St David's.

The roads or harbours near St David's are these: 1. *Solfa*, about 3 miles to the east of the church. A ship of a good burthen may come in, when it is high water, but it does not flow far. 2. *Porth-Clais* [i.e. the road of the peak] St David's key is there. It is a little mile from the town. The tide comes in here a good way; it is a very safe harbour by reason of a defence of stone made across it near the haven's mouth, with a place only on one side for boats to pass. Here no doubt the merchants did formerly load and unload, as they do still. 3. The next is the *Sound*, which is the current that runs between the mainland and the Isle of Ramsey. It is about half a league over and may be crossed when the weather is fair in about three quarters of an hour in a boat with oars, and in an hour easily, unless the sea be tempestuous. This is the largest harbour of them all. A ship may lie here safely in any weather, if it can once get in; but the entrance is very dangerous at both ends; for to the southward, near the mouth, there are several rocks, one particularly, which they call 'The Bitch and her Whelps'. It is a craggy rock that begins on the island side, and crosses the Sound half way over. To the northward there are divers rocks, besides 'The Bishop and his Clerks'; and in the middle of the Sound is one rock more dangerous than the rest, which is called the 'Horse' or 'Mare'. At high water this rock cannot be seen; so that a stranger cannot well perceive whereabouts it lies, and may be upon it before he is aware, by reason of the great number of currents which run in on both sides. These currents are caused by the rocks, which are narrow in this passage, and break the main tide, which flows in north and south. Sometimes one may discern six or seven of these currents, or eddies, which must be all crossed between St David's and Ramsey; nay, some say there are nine of them. This makes it very dangerous for a stranger to attempt to come in, though the seamen thereabouts make it their common passage to and from North Wales, it being their directest way. The chief landing place in this road is called Port Stinian, from the adjoining chapel; and here they take boat to cross over to Ramsey.

Ramsey is an island that is a mile and a half long and three quarters of a mile broad. There is an old wall that crosses the island, but for what reason it is so divided, is not remembered. Formerly it was tilled; but that was long ago. It is now wholly employed in pasture for sheep and for breeding of horses. The mutton there is always fat; and they have a great number of conies [rabbits], which are all black. The fern, which grows there in great abundance, is very tall; and it produces thorns of a good bigness, and great store of juniper. 'Till within these eight or nine years, there was an eyrie of excellent hawks upon this island, which were highly valued 'till the old falcon was stolen. The tassel [male hawk] was seen thereabouts within these two or three years, whereupon Sir John Wogan asked leave to cast off an old falcon of his, in hopes of some breed; but they went away. Great numbers of fowls breed upon the island, and in the rocks to the south-west there are vast numbers of puffins, which living upon fish, have a very fishy taste, and were always allowed to be eaten in Lent.

There are two chapels in this island, one at the south end, called *Capel Stinians*; the other to the north, called *Capel Divanog* [i.e. the chapel upon a plain flat ground]. Each of these chapels has a fine spring of pure water running by it. At the south end of this island are two smaller islands, one called *Carreg Cantor* [Chanter's Rock], which belongs to the Chanter of St David's; the other, *Carreg Ynis y Pyrry*, which belongs to the archdeacon of Caermarthen. These islands are very small, and turn to little account. *Carreg Ynis y Pyrry* is the biggest of the two, and of late has caused some discourse upon the account of a claim which Sir Francis Meyrick makes to it, by virtue of his lease of *Kanryan*, which he holds from the archdeacon of Caermarthen. In caves about these islands, seals, or sea-calves, breed, which are taken about Michaelmas by the seamen, who go out for them in boats and kill them in their caves with clubs. They observe when they strike at these sea-calves, that if they do not hit them upon the snout, the blow goes for nothing; and when they run away, they throw great stones behind them with their hind feet, which are very dangerous, if those that hunt them do not take heed.

North-west of Ramsey lie 'the Bishop and his Clerks', six rocks so called, which compass the island on that side, one by one in rank. The first that points to southward is called *Carreg Escob* [Bishop's Rock]; the second, *Carreg Rossom*; the third, *Gwen Carreg* [White Rock]; the fourth, *Divech*; the fifth, *Carreg Hawloe*; the sixth, *Emscar*. This last lies at the north end of the Sound, with divers other young novices that appear not. It were good for mariners to keep aloof of these fellows; for they are very stout and will not budge a foot. I think they (I mean the bishop and his clerks) are able to resist the King of Spain's great navy, and put her Majesty to no charge at all.

The next noted place upon this coast is *Port Mawr* [i.e. the great bay]. It is no road for ships, being in a manner dry when the tide is out: but then the country people throw their *Sayns*, or large nets, in summertime along this bay, and catch what fish there are within that compass. The chiefest fish they catch are *Suens*. This bay is near *Capel Patrick*. A mile and a half west and by north of St David's, and southward of 'the Bishop and his Clerks', lies St David's Head. It is a huge rock, and visible far off at sea; though what is commonly called the Head is a small rock near it, round at the top like a head. The sea is said to be very deep by St David's Head, so that a boat may come to the side of a rock without danger, unless the sea be very boisterous. They have a tradition of one Adam Samson, a pirate in Henry VII's time, who was taken in St George's Channel, after having done much mischief thereabouts, by one of the King's ships. This ship, with him on board, was accidentally driven this way, upon which, Samson, taking his opportunity, persuaded the master to go close by the rock, and then leaped upon it and saved himself. On top of the rock above the Head there are remains of an old fortification; and hard by, there is a round broad stone turned edgewise, and leaning upon another stone, which they call 'Arthur's Quoit'.

In the rocks by the sea side, above the Head, grow a sort of diamonds. They lie in the veins of the rocks, and must be picked out with an iron tool. They have a blackish earth about them, which makes them the more discernable, and the points appear forward. They excel the stones of St Vincent's Rock by Bristol, both in hardness and colour; and when well set with a good foil, they make a fine show. Some of them, when first taken out of the rock, are of the colour of amethyst, but with handling and rubbing, the colour fails, and they become white like other stones.

About a quarter of a mile from hence is the famous stone, which they call here 'the Shaking Stone', *Ymaen figl.* It is so large that 20 yoke of oxen will not remove it from its place, and yet it lieth upon a bank; and notwithstanding its hugeness, (they say) a child of eight years will shake it; but I can move it, though six men should stand upon it, with less than the strength of one of my hands, so much

Menevia Sacra

33

that a man that stands upon it would be afraid of falling. These two verses describe it fully.

Concutit hunc lenis Motus, quem non movet ullus

Cumque minus moveas, tum movet ecce magis.

In a house near this stone, which is the farthest stone that way, and is called *Porth Mawr*, from the Bay, there goes out of a chamber, a passage underground that leads into the sea; it is almost a quarter of a mile long. Why it was made is not known.

Upon a rock in a township, called *Clegr fwyaf* [i.e. the biggest rock] something above a mile from St David's, there is a spring, which is said to ebb and flow with the sea, which is half a mile from it.

On the burrows near the sea, there is a stone pitched in the ground, which they call 'Arthur's Stone'. Formerly, in the memory of man, it lay flat, and with an inscription upon it, as it is said … but why placed there is not known. The bishop has 12d. a year for ten acres of ground, which he holdeth by that stone in that place.

Eastward of St David's, about a mile by the sea side, at *Carn Ochr* [i.e. a heap of stones upon the side of a bank] they find a sort of ore in the veins of the rocks, which glisters like copper; it lies within the rocks as diamonds do, but more plentifully: a good quantity of it may be gathered in a reasonable time: it is in the bishop's lands.

Upon the road to Haverfordwest, about a mile and a half from the town, not far from the place called *Llandridion* [i.e. Druid's Church], there are nine wells within five or six paces of one another. They spring all severally; and from those wells, the place is called the Nine Wells.

There is said to have been a town formerly near the burrows, called *Caer Leon*, which has its name from old *Caer Legion*, or *Caer Len*, in Monmouthshire, from whence St David removed the See to St David's.

I was shown some walls at the end of the town, where they say there was once an almshouse. But it is now wholly destroyed. Indeed the whole town seems to be little better than a collection of almshouses, where every man is more apt to take than to give.

From this point, the writer transfers his attention from the topography of the area to observations on the cathedral itself:

In the chapel called Our Lady's Chapel, which is the uppermost part of all the church, are two tombs of two bishops, as their effigies show. One, by the inscription, is known to be Bishop Martin's, who gave to the vicars choral 12d. apiece yearly for dirge-money, which they now call distribution-money, payable every 9th of March. Whose the other is, is not known. In the new chapel, called the Bishop's Chapel, lies Bishop Edward Vaughan, who is supposed to have founded it. It lies between Our Lady's Chapel and the chancel. Over the grave is a marble stone, with his picture cut in brass, and fastened thereto [the inscription from the tomb is then quoted].

In the two aisles beside the chancel lie two of the Wogans. Those monuments seem to be very ancient, being cut cross-legged in their armour.

In the chancel there are two monuments of bishops; they are in coffins of stone, placed near together, with coverings of marble, but the coffins are empty. The pictures of the bishops are carved out of the said stones. One of these is known, by the title over his head, to be Anselmus. This Anselmus (as is said) gave to the vicars choral 6d. apiece yearly, payable April 1. The other, that lies by him,

34 *The Lives and Times of Thomas Tomkins and his Family*

is not known. Some think it should be Silvester. These lie on the right hand near the quire, as you go out of the quire into the chancel.

Over against these two coffins, on the other side, is St David's shrine, between two pillars of the chancel, within a fair arch of timber-work painted. St David himself is painted in his *Pontificalibus*; and on each side of him, is a bishop saint; one, by the inscription, is known to be St Patrick; the other is somewhat defaced.

On the right side of the chancel, under the altar, just above Anselmus's tomb, between the two middle pillars, lies Rhees ap Tudor, in complete armour in free stone, very artificially [i.e. skilfully] cut; and on the other side, lies his son, after the same fashion, called Rhees y gryg.

In the middle of the chancel stands a fair monument of marble of the Earl of Richmond's, great grandfather to her Majesty that now is. He is engraved in brass in his armour. At the entrance to the quire, out of the body of the church, lies Bishop Gower [the inscriptions from both tombs are quoted].

In the body of the church, by the pulpit, is Bishop John Morgan's tomb. This bishop gave to the vicars choral all the small tithes of the parish. There are no more monuments of bishops that have been buried in St David's Church, of which any memory now remains: but there are several monuments of canons, friars, monks, *etc.*, still visible, of whom there is little or no remembrance of their names.

There follows an illustrated description of the heraldic escutcheons that were formerly visible in many parts of the cathedral, but which have been lost for several centuries, information in itself of great interest. 'I was very glad', wrote Wotton, 'to find this collection, made by so very considerable a man.' But was this 'considerable man' Thomas Tomkins the elder? During his work of transcribing and editing the manuscript, Wotton observed that 'by this author's care in registering the donations of so many several bishops to the vicars choral, I was tempted to think he himself was a vicar choral of this church. But upon farther enquiry, Mr Lewes of Llwyn-Derw, assured me, that from the hand-writing, he judged it to have been written by Mr George Owen, Lord of Kemys, a Hundred in Pembrokeshire, whose assistance Mr Camden [of Camden's *Britannia* (1698)] owns with so much gratitude, in his account of that county.' However, the perceptive Wotton clearly remained unconvinced that Owen was the anonymous writer. 'Mr Lewes is a man of that exactness that I know not how to disbelieve him', he wrote, ' especially as he has seen other MSS of this Mr Owen's writing. But Mr Lhwyd quotes a MS History of Pembrokeshire, as written by Mr Owen, in which there is a description of the Shaking Stone, which does not entirely agree with that above related out of this MS. It is on page 638 of his Additions to Camden's *Britannia*. Our author says it lies on a bank. Mr Owen says it is mounted upon divers other stones, above a yard in height, and so equally poised, that a man may shake it with one finger. Our author speaks as an eyewitness, which the other does not. All that I can gather from this is that either the same person did not write both these accounts, or that the account which Mr Lhwyd saw, was written before this.'[6]

---

6 Browne Willis (1717), *A Survey of the Cathedral Church of St David's*, London, 71–2.

Menevia Sacra   35

There are other discrepancies also between the two accounts, and Atkins was confident that Wotton's doubts were justified:

> Our examination seems to show that the manuscript used by Wotton was not written by George Owen, but more probably by some one living at St David's who had first hand knowledge of the country round about it. And it is probable that Wotton's conjecture that the writer was a vicar choral will prove correct.
>
> To the reasons which Wotton gave for his conclusion, much could be added. We notice that though somewhat disdainful of the little city, the anonymous writer delights in its ancient remains. The cathedral fascinates him, and, like the typical 16th century antiquarian that he is, he proceeds to blazon its heraldry. We notice that in addition to the special interest in all matters affecting the vicars choral which Wotton noticed, the writer shows himself intimately acquainted with the life of the cathedral and can tell us much of its traditions. He can recall the College of Priests which belonged to the vicars choral … He can tell us exactly what happened to the offerings which the numerous pilgrims made at the chapels near the sea … He knows that of the two little islands lying to the south of Ramsey one belongs to the chantor [precentor] the other to the archdeacon of Carmarthen. He knows, too, which are the bishop's lands, and what payments he receives for them … Everywhere, in fact, we seem to find confirmation of Wotton's conjecture.[7]

Atkins also noted several clues in the manuscript that point to the probable date of its composition. References to Sir John Wogan and Sir Francis Meyrick suggest a date within the last five years of the sixteenth century. Wogan was very probably the Sir John Wogan of Wiston, who was one of the signatories to a petition addressed to the Lord Keeper, dated 8 November 1595; Meyrick was knighted by Essex at Dublin on 2 August 1599. Atkins believed that the clearest indication of date given by the anonymous writer was contained within his humorous allusion to 'the Bishop and his Clerks' being able to 'resist the King of Spain's great navy, and put her Majesty to no charge at all': Elizabeth must have been alive at the time of writing, setting a date before her death in 1603. 'It is much more likely, however, that it lies nearer to 1588, for its whole tone suggests that the threat of the Spanish Armada is still ringing in the ears of the writer. If we may take this vivid reference to the Armada as the governing factor in arriving at the date of the manuscript in its original form, it would seem natural to assign it to about 1588, and to regard the later passages as due to a later recension'.[8] But of course, hostilities between the English and Spanish fleets continued for some years after the Armada of 1588, and a date for the manuscript of the 1590s remains entirely possible.

Wotton makes no reference to the manuscript in his possession as having been written in Latin, nor do his extracts include the passage about stained glass windows, Bishop Houghton and Pope Clement VI, quoted by Fenton

---

[7] Atkins, 'The Authorship'.
[8] Ibid.

from the lost Bodleian MS. It is also obvious that whereas the Bodleian papers were clearly attributed and dated 'Tonkyn, 1610', the manuscript that passed from Lewes to Havard and then to Wotton was neither signed nor dated. None the less, this narrative is almost certainly the work of an educated man who could well have served as a vicar choral at St David's, who has learnt his local knowledge by far more than casual acquaintance, and who was possessed of a charming wit. That man is more likely to have been Thomas Tomkins the elder than any other, and it is very possible that the anonymous manuscript used by Wotton was a preliminary draft of a document written by Tomkins, and later expanded and translated into Latin by him to add academic respectability to his work.

The tone of the narrative suggests that the writer had already left St David's when it was written, and Tomkins *père* had certainly left there by 1594. But ultimately, even if it could be proved that the manuscript is not in Tomkins's hand but in the hand of George Owen or some other writer, it remains a remarkably vivid description of the place in which Thomas Tomkins the elder spent over twenty years of his professional life, and in which his son, Thomas, destined to become arguably the finest of all Welsh composers, grew to adulthood.

In September 1572, news spread in Pembrokeshire of the discovery by three teenagers of a great quantity of ancient treasure, gold and silver, contained in a brass crock at Spittal.[9] Struggling to make ends meet, Tomkins *père* would have welcomed even a little gold and silver, and it seems probable that in that same year, the year in which his second and most gifted son was born, Tomkins the elder took holy orders. Perhaps he chose to do this from a true sense of vocation, perhaps partly in contrition for his adultery, but probably also in order to gain an extra income so as to make better provision for his family. It seems unlikely that he would have been appointed master of the St David's Grammar School in 1573 had he not been ordained by that time. None the less, as we have seen, even after his subsequent appointment as master of the choristers and organist, he was, by 1577, still in great financial difficulty.

The condition of cathedral music at St David's appears to have gone from bad to worse after 1577. Recruitment of choristers and vicars choral continued to falter, and by 1581 the organ was worn out after more than a century of use. Added to this, the cathedral was without a full-time precentor from about 1571 when Archbishop Parker granted Thomas Huett a dispensation from residing for more than two months in every year at St

---

[9] BL Lansdowne MS 14, fol. 33. See B.E. Howells (1972), *Pembrokeshire Life: 1572–1843*, Haverford West, Pembrokeshire Record Society, 1.

David's. 'He had an estate at Llanavon Vawr in the county of Brecon, where was a stately habitation called Ty Mawr, or ye Great House, in which he died in 1591.'[10]

No doubt in response to Tomkins's appeals, Bishop Richard Davies, in the last year of his life, directed that a new organ should be built *ad usum divini servitii*.[11] But nothing was done: a chapter order of 1586 or 1589 describes the organ as 'worn out so that it cannot be used for divine service'.[12] This must have been the last straw for Tomkins, whose income had been cut in 1586 by the expulsion of his eldest son from a vicar choral's stall, and whose ability to continue as cathedral organist was stifled by loss of both an instrument and an adequate number of choristers: but an escape route now presented itself. In 1586 he married Anne Hargest of Penarthur, a farm very close to St David's Cathedral.

Anne's family, from Hargest in Radnorshire, was comfortably off, and it seems probable that the money that she brought to the match gave Tomkins some financial independence for the first time since he had left Cornwall. Fourteen years earlier, one of Anne's relatives, Richard Argas (or Hargest), a vicar choral at the cathedral, had been hauled over the coals by the chapter for indulging himself and others to excess: 'Richard Argas. Also upon the same day Argas by Mr. Chantor and chapter aforesaid is admonished that he shall not permit the vicars nor any of them to use unlawful games in his house, as card tables, and extraordinary drinking and spending, etc., and the said Argas assented thereunto.'[13]

This rare glimpse into the recreational life of a pleasure-loving Elizabethan vicar choral highlights the gulf between the spiritual ideal expected of their servants by the cathedral authorities and the rather more worldly reality of the few men available to them in that remote peninsula. It also shows that at least one member of the Hargest family had more than adequate means to gamble, to drink and to spend. None of this of course was of any consequence to the liaison between Tomkins the elder and Anne Hargest. The marriage was a happy one, and within a year of their union the first of Anne's seven children, John, was born. It was time for Tomkins *père* to move on and seek his fortune elsewhere.

Thomas Tomkins the elder's Uncle Edward, as we have seen, sold out his property in Cornwall in 1571, and by then both Thomas and his brother John

---

[10] Francis Green (ed., 1927), *Menevia Sacra* by Edward Yardley, Archdeacon of Cardigan, 1739–70, London.

[11] NLW, Chapter Act Book 'B', 104.

[12] Atkins, *The Authorship*.

[13] NLW, St David's Chapter Act Book 'A', 241.

38 *The Lives and Times of Thomas Tomkins and his Family*

had also left the county of their birth. By the mid-1580s a certain John Tomkins had established himself as a successful clothier in Worcester. He was married at St Nicholas's Church, Worcester, on 15 April 1588, to Elizabeth, a daughter of Richard Wheeler, a prosperous landowner and one of the wardens of the company of Weavers and Walkers. John and Elizabeth Tomkins had three sons, John, Robert and Edward, and three daughters, Elizabeth, Sara and Margaret. On 25 January 1594, John Tomkins was elected a member of the 'forty-eight' city councillors; ten years later he had risen to membership of the 'twenty-four' aldermen; and in 1599 he held a lease from the dean and chapter of a house in Northgate in the city. In 1607 and 1608 he was bailiff of Worcester, the king's representative in the city, and his name appears in a list of those fined for not taking knighthood in 1625.

The departure from Lostwithiel of Edward Tomkins and the arrival soon afterwards in Worcestershire of a Tomkins family with sons named John and Edward seems to be more than mere coincidence. John Tomkins the clothier died in November 1634 leaving money in his will[14] 'to the poore of the parish of yearlly where I was borne' – 'yearlly' probably being Yardley, then in Worcestershire. A possibility therefore remains that John's father was Edward Tomkins of Lostwithiel; that Edward, his prosperity founded upon the cloth trade, had removed from Lostwithiel to Yardley and re-established his family in Worcestershire; and that Edward's son John went on to set up his own successful clothing business in Worcester.

Traces remain of the lives of two of John the clothier's sons. Young John sang in the choir at Worcester Cathedral and was probably the only known Worcester chorister named Tomkins (1608) to move to the Chapel Royal as a chorister (in 1611). Edward was elected constable of St Nicholas ward in 1636, and became a member of the forty-eight in 1641; he died on 10 May 1651 at the age of 63, and he too seems to have had a son, James, who was elected constable of St Clement's ward in Worcester on 25 August 1623.[15]

It seems very probable that there were family links between John Tomkins the clothier and Thomas Tomkins *père*, and it is certain that Thomas Tomkins *fils* retained a close lifelong interest in the clothing trade. In at least one instance of his charitable giving, as we shall see, he went so far as to stipulate that 'clothiers before others are to be preferred' as beneficiaries of his money, thus demonstrating generously a lasting affinity with his family roots and, perhaps, acknowledging a personal debt to that trade.

The heirs of John Tomkins the clothier continued to prosper in Worcestershire. A post-Restoration indenture dated 4 December 1663 between 'John Tomkins of Pendock, gentleman, Jane Tomkins of Pendock,

---

[14] TNA, PROB 11/167.

[15] See Shelagh Bond (1974), *The Chamber Order Book of Worcester 1602–1650*, Worcester (WHS).

Menevia Sacra   39

widow [his mother], and John Cox of Ledbury, a clothier', settles a country house, Morecourt in Pendock, and property elsewhere in Pendock, Longdon, Birtsmorton and Castlemorton, on Tomkins's son John and John Cox's daughter Mary prior to their marriage.[16]

Thomas Tomkins the elder could not hope to match the wealth and influence of John Tomkins the clothier, an eminent citizen, respected among the cathedral community in Worcester. But there was yet another John Tomkins who had a connection with Worcester Cathedral, who, like Thomas *père*, was a clergyman, and who might well have been his brother. In the year 1590, 'at the motion of Mr John Tomkins', the dean of Worcester, Francis Willis, gave the sum of £4 for the old organ of St Mary's Church, Shrewsbury,[17] where John Tomkins was the incumbent. An entry in the St Mary's churchwarden's accounts for 1590 record the sale: 'Note that the Dean of Worcester, who bought the said organs [for £4] gave at the motion of Mr John Tomkins and us the churchwardens to the Church of St Mary's, a communion book worth [ ]s 4d.'[18]

It is therefore more than possible that Thomas Tomkins the elder had family connections in Worcestershire and Shropshire. Maybe it was the wealthy clothier, John Tomkins, who persuaded the Worcester dean and chapter to use their influence with colleagues in a neighbouring diocese to obtain a cathedral post in England for Thomas. Perhaps, too, Thomas and Anne named their firstborn son 'John' in gratitude for this kindness. But, in any event, on leaving St David's it was to the city of Gloucester that Thomas and his family made their way.

---

[16] Worcestershire Record Office (WRO), BA 8397, 705: 139, Parcel 4, No. xl. Other indentures filed in this same box detail Tomkins family involvement with Morecourt and other lands and property in Pendock, Longdon, Birtsmorton and Castlemorton from 1600 onwards.

[17] Atkins, *Early Occupants.*

[18] Shropshire CRO, 1041/Ch/1 fol.128R. I am grateful to Dr Richard Newsholme for bringing this entry to my attention.

Chapter 4

Gloucester

By 1594, Tomkins *père* was installed as a minor canon at Gloucester Cathedral, and it would be easy to make the assumption that this was the year in which he had left St David's. However, all records at Gloucester Cathedral of appointments before 1594 have been lost, and it is probable that he and his family had removed from St David's to Gloucestershire in 1586, the year after which all mention of Thomas Tomkins *père* in the chapter records of St David's ceases and in which William Huett was appointed master of the choristers in his place. Huett, that same young man who, in 1565, had caused so much trouble to the chapter and to Mr Morgans, the cathedral schoolmaster, now took over the reins of a stumbling team.

St David's was losing the services of a distinguished organist, and possibly the chorister skills of Thomas Tomkins *fils* too. Aged 14, Thomas had, throughout his childhood, breathed Pembrokeshire air, probably accompanied his father around the peninsula on horseback, or on boat trips to Ramsey Island, and learnt the art of music at his father's side. He might also have taken his rightful place in the cathedral choir. Through financial necessity, Tomkins the elder was now obliged to forsake any personal ambition in music and to accept a minor canon's post in Gloucester whilst undoubtedly, at the same time, wishing the best possible future as a church musician for his gifted elder son.

'But what say I, Music? One of the seven liberal sciences? It is almost banished this realm', wrote John Bossewell in 1572, 'If it were not the Queen's Majesty did favour that excellent science, singing-men, and choristers might go a begging, together with their master the player of the organs.'[1] Most composers of ecclesiastical music had received their training and early inspiration as choristers, and yet the Church was disinclined to pay adequately for the men who by their compositions would add to its glory. Without the active support of the sovereign, the greatest patron of music in the land, neither sacred nor secular music-making in England could have survived into the late seventeenth century.

The parsimony of the cathedral authorities at St David's towards Tomkins the elder was reflective of the situation throughout the Church in England; so

---

[1] John Bossewell (1572), *Workes of Armorie*, 3rd book, fol. 14.

The Lives and Times of Thomas Tomkins and his Family

much so as to prompt one anonymous churchman to write that for a man 'to bring up his son in a cathedral church is to make him a beggar by profession'.[2] In sixteenth-century England Tomkins's ambition for his son could only be satisfied by finding him membership of a choir close to the court: in Westminster, in St Paul's, in Windsor, or, above all, in the Chapel Royal, and probability points to this last as Tomkins's goal.

Exactly when Tomkins junior might have arrived in London is a matter for conjecture but, if he became a Chapel Royal chorister, this could have been by 1586, when his father resigned his post at St David's and transferred to Gloucester, or possibly even earlier. Equally, since boys' voices remained unbroken for longer then than is common today, he could have continued as a chorister until his late teens.

From at least the fifteenth century a custom had existed in the Chapel Royal of pressing men and boys with good voices for service in the choir. Richard III had granted a licence to John Melyonek, one of the gentlemen of the Chapel, giving him authority 'that within all places in this our realm, as well cathedral-churches, colleges, chapels, houses of religion, and all other franchised and exempt places, as elsewhere, our College Royal at Windsor reserved and except, may take and seize for us and in our name all such singing men and children, being expert in the said science of music, as he can find, and think sufficient and able to do us service'.[3] A similar warrant was granted in 1550 to Philip Van Wilder, gentleman of the privy chamber, 'in any churches and chapels within England to take to the King's use, such and as many singing children and choristers, as he or his deputy should think good'.[4]

This custom was still very active in Tomkins's childhood, and if not subject to pressing himself, he will certainly have known other boys and men who were. What is certain is that Tomkins became a pupil of the great William Byrd (1543–1623), as proved by his dedication of the fourteenth of his *Songs* of 1622, *Too much I once lamented*, inscribed by Tomkins 'To my ancient, and much reverenced Master, William Byrd', and it is even possible that a known link between Byrd and Gloucestershire could have resulted in Tomkins becoming his pupil.

In his own boyhood Byrd is believed to have been one of the children of the Chapel Royal and a pupil of Thomas Tallis (*c.*1505–85), who had already been organist there for some years when Byrd was born. Appointed organist of Lincoln Cathedral in 1563, Byrd was sworn in as a gentleman of the Chapel Royal in February 1570, finding himself once more in close

---

[2] Walter L. Woodfill (1969), *Musicians in English Society from Elizabeth to Charles I*, Princeton, 144.

[3] BL Harley MS 433.

[4] *Cheque Book*, viii.

Gloucester 43

association with his old master. Byrd shared the duties of organist of the Chapel with Tallis, and it seems possible that it was Tallis who had arranged for Byrd to come to his assistance.

Tallis and Byrd became partners in a printing venture, and in 1575 were granted a licence by Elizabeth that gave them a virtual monopoly over the printing of music and music paper in England. It is no surprise to discover that this privilege was deeply resented by many of London's printers and stationers, but Tallis and Byrd were able to demonstrate that they were gaining no profit from the licence and furthermore that they were finding it almost impossible to live on their incomes from the Chapel Royal. Consequently, in 1577 Elizabeth granted them both leases on property, possession of which was intended to give each of them a yearly rent of 30 pounds. The lease granted to Byrd was that of the Manor of Longney, situated on the River Severn, just seven miles south-west from Gloucester.

This lease, yielding the profit from rich farmland, represented a major part of Byrd's income and, some thirty years later, was to involve him in a troublesome lawsuit. No doubt he visited Longney from time to time in order to keep a watch on the activities of his tenants, and it is inconceivable that when only a short distance by river from Gloucester he would not have visited the cathedral there. If so, and if Tomkins junior had not already moved to London directly from St David's, Byrd might possibly have discovered the talented son of a talented minor canon at Gloucester Cathedral and brought him back to the court to serve as a chorister at the Chapel Royal and, in due course, to become his pupil.

In his 1577 petition to the queen, Byrd had complained that 'being called to your Highness service from the cathedral church of Lincoln, where he was well settled, is now, through his great charge of wife and children come into debt and great necessity, by reason that by his daily attendance in your Majesty's said service he is letted from reaping such commodity by teaching as heretofore he did and still might have done to the great relief of himself and his poor family'.[5] Presumably authority was granted for Byrd to continue taking private pupils in addition to his official duties at the Chapel Royal, and since Tomkins junior was one of these it is probable that his father was required to find Byrd's tuition fees from his very limited income. Tomkins *père* was not a wealthy man, and it would surely have been beyond his means to pay also for the accommodation, food, education and travelling expenses of any of his sons in London. On the other hand, the maintenance and education of children accepted as choristers at the Chapel Royal were funded from an allowance paid by the Crown to the master of the children. Thomas Tomkins junior is known to have been a pupil of Byrd, a gentleman and

---

5 Hatfield House MSS, CP 160, 134.

44 *The Lives and Times of Thomas Tomkins and his Family*

organist of the Chapel Royal; since Byrd's professional life at this time was based in London, and until 1593 his home was nearby at Harlington, it is likely that Tomkins junior was in London too.

The Chapel Royal was never a fixed building; it was an institution, the origins of which date back to at least the twelfth century, and was subject entirely to royal command. Travelling with the monarch from palace to palace and on royal progresses, it was the responsibility of the clergymen and musicians of the Chapel Royal to arrange and perform divine service in the sovereign's presence. By Elizabeth's time the Chapel Royal regularly accompanied the queen to her palaces at St James, Greenwich and elsewhere, but the majority of services were held in the magnificent chapel at Whitehall (destroyed by fire on 4 January 1698), and this, even though documentary proof is lacking, must surely have been young Thomas Tomkins's most probable destination.

Tomkins *père* remained a minor canon at Gloucester for the rest of his professional life.

> The Patent of King Henry the Eighth appointed six Minor Canons; reduced at the Restoration to four (out of whom are chosen the Precentor, Sacrist, Deacon and Sub-deacon); a chief School-master and Usher; each of whom has a house and stipend. They are also presented to small livings, rejected by the Prebendaries, in the patronage of the Chapter. An Organist, or Master of the Choristers; six Lay-clerks, or Singing-men; eight choristers; four Alms-men; two Sextons, or Vergers; an Auditor, Chapter-clerk, and two Sub-sacrists.[6]

The 'small livings' were permitted provided that the benefices concerned were not more than twenty-four miles distant from the city of Gloucester. Those enjoyed by Tomkins as incumbent from 1594 were at the Church of St John the Baptist, Tredington, a small village two and a half miles south-east of Tewkesbury, where he remained until 1609,[7] and at St Catharine's Church in the city of Gloucester, which he held until 1597; but for a much longer period, from 1596 to his death in 1627, he was vicar of yet another city church, St Mary de Lode.[8]

On the preferment in 1594 of Anthony Rudd, dean of Gloucester, to the bishopric of St David's, Dr Lewis Griffith was appointed dean and remained at Gloucester until his death in 1607.[9] It is possible that Tomkins's appointment as a minor canon resulted from discussions between Rudd and Griffith, following a recommendation from Francis Willis, the dean of

---

[6] Thomas Dudley Fosbrooke (1819), *An Original History of the City of Gloucester*, London (repr. Stroud, 1976), 115.

[7] Ralph Bigland (ed. Brian Frith, 1992), *Historical, Monumental and Genealogical Collections, relative to the County of Gloucester*, 1348, II.

[8] Fosbrooke, *An Original History*, 161 and 173.

[9] David Welander (1991), *The History, Art and Architecture of Gloucester Cathedral*, Stroud, 345.

Gloucester 45

Worcester. It is also possible that Griffith sought Tomkins's assistance in breathing new life into the music of the cathedral, sadly neglected throughout Rudd's tenure. The first recorded organist and master of the choristers of the cathedral, Robert Lichfield, who appears to have been at Gloucester from about the year 1562, died on 6 January 1582, but no official replacement was found for him until the appointment of John Gibbes in or about the significant year of 1594.[10]

These were turbulent times in relationships between bishops and deans at Gloucester, and Tomkins must have encountered an atmosphere soured by animosity and suspicion. In 1580 an archiepiscopal visitation had revealed 'a scandalous state of affairs, presumably due to the dean's constant absence. There was great slackness, absenteeism, inefficiency and even dishonesty in the financial affairs of the chapter … the dean, Dr Laurence Humphrey, had refused "on account of the reverence due to his dignity" to appear before Archbishop Grindal's commissary at the archiepiscopal visitation. They were all "pronounced contumacious" and suspended.'[11] Soon after Griffith's arrival at Gloucester in 1594 he was summoned to an episcopal visitation but failed to appear. 'Even at the session the following November when the bishop was present in person, only two prebendaries turned up to answer questions. On 4 March 1595, after a summons had been affixed to the dean's stall in the choir, he came with the prebendaries and a bitter wrangle ensued about the statutes … However, in the end, all promised to observe the statutes as they stood, and the servants of the dean and chapter, the schoolmaster and usher, the minor canons and organist, the almsmen and bell-ringer's deputy all agreed to carry out their duties faithfully.'[12]

The living of St Mary de Lode provided Tomkins's income with a small but significant boost. At this time minor canons at the cathedral were paid £10 per annum, lay clerks £6. 13*s*. 4*d*., and choristers £3. 6*s*. 8*d*. The earliest available Cathedral Treasurer's Accounts[13] record that between 1609 and 1627, the year of his death, in addition to the £10 paid annually to Tomkins as a minor canon, he received a further £2. 2*s*. 8*d*. as incumbent of St Mary de Lode, so by any standards he was far from well off.

Built over two substantial Roman buildings, St Mary de Lode still stands in St Mary's Square, opposite to the western gate that leads into the cathedral precincts. As he made his regular way between St Mary de Lode and the cathedral, Tomkins senior would have passed a mound of earth known as 'St Mary's Knapp', and been aware of its dreadful significance as the scene, little

---

[10] Brian Frith (1973), 'The Organists of Gloucester Cathedral', *The Organs and Organists of Gloucester Cathedral*, Gloucester.

[11] Welander, *History, Art and Architecture*, 345.

[12] Ibid.

[13] Gloucester Cathedral Treasurer's Accounts, 1609–1634. GRO, D936 A.1/1.

46 The Lives and Times of Thomas Tomkins and his Family

more than thirty years before his arrival in Gloucester, of Bishop John Hooper's agonized death.

Hooper's fiery Old Testament intolerance had been legendary, and that he made enemies is unsurprising, given the vitriolic nature of his vengeful spirit. For instance, his desired prescription for 'hypocrites and dissemblers' who were discovered to have secreted holy relics in the high altar of a certain church was that they should be 'put to death in the church, upon the same altar wherein this relic was hid', and that 'the bones of these traitorous idolaters, with the relic', should be 'burnt there ... as Jehoiada did all of the false priests, 4 Reg. xxiii. And the doing thereof should not have suspended the church at all, but have been a better blessing thereof than all the blessings of the bishops of the world: for God loveth those that be zealous for his glory.'[14]

In 1549 Hooper had been an accuser of Bishop Bonner, who, as a result, had lost his bishopric. On the accession of Mary Tudor, Bonner and his fellow bishop, Gardiner, resolved that Hooper would be one of the first to suffer for his reformed doctrines. On 15 March 1554, he was condemned to the Fleet Prison by an order from the queen, and three days later his bishopric was declared void. On 28 January 1555, he was brought before Gardiner at Southwark and, refusing to recant, was condemned to be burnt as a heretic. Deprived of his priesthood by his old enemy Bonner, he was sent to Gloucester under guard and lodged in a house opposite St Nicholas Church. Allowed an interval of just one day, on Saturday 9 February, a market day, Hooper was led to St Mary's Knapp, chained to an oak stake, and burnt with three successive fires made of green wood. He survived this torment for about three quarters of an hour during which, it is said, both Gardiner and Bonner looked down with satisfaction from the windows above the western gate.

Another of Bonner's many victims was one Thomas Tomkins, a weaver of Shoreditch, who might just conceivably have been distantly related to the Cornish family of cloth traders. Bonner imprisoned this man because he 'hath believed and doth believe, that in the sacrament of the altar, under the forms of bread and wine, there is not the very body and blood of our saviour Jesus Christ in substance, but only a token and remembrance thereof, the very body and blood of Christ being in heaven and nowhere else'.[15] Imprisonment and beating failed to persuade Tomkins to recant. Eleven days after the martyrdom of Bishop Hooper he was examined at Fulham by Bonner, who took hold of Tomkins's hand and thrust it into the flame of a 'candle of three or four wicks ... supposing that by the smart and pain of the fire, being terrified, he would leave off his defence of his doctrine'.[16] This too failed, as did subsequent

---

[14] Bishop Hooper (1846), *Early Writings of Bishop Hooper*, Cambridge, Parker Society, 202.
[15] John Foxe (1583), *Book of Martyrs*, London.
[16] Ibid.

Gloucester 47

interrogation by Bonner. On 9 March Tomkins was brought before Bonner for the last time, but still he refused to recant. Seven days later he was taken to Smithfield and burnt at the stake.

The family of Tomkins *père* and his second wife, Anne, grew steadily in the years following their move from St David's. Six more children were born: Robert, Nicholas, Giles, Peregrine, Margaret and Elizabeth. The boys, in addition to their elder brother John, probably sang in the choir at Gloucester Cathedral. John was to become a fine musician, second only in eminence to his half-brother, Thomas, progressing as organist from King's College, Cambridge to St Paul's Cathedral and the Chapel Royal. Robert became a viol player in the King's Musick and a composer of anthems. Nicholas, although musical, did not choose music as his career, but like his brothers found a place at the court of Charles I, where he was one of the gentlemen of the Privy Chamber.[17] Giles followed John to the post of organist at King's College, Cambridge, going on to become organist of Salisbury Cathedral. He appears to have found particular favour with Charles I and, with his brother Robert, was one of the musicians for the lutes, viols and voices in the King's Musick. The fifth of Tomkins the elder's sons by his second marriage, Peregrine, does not appear to have been particularly musical, and of Margaret and Elizabeth, nothing is known.

The statutes of Gloucester Cathedral directed that one of the minor canons 'older than the rest and more eminent, both for his behaviour and for his learning' was to be elected precentor. His task was 'handsomely to direct the singing men in the church, and as a guide, to lead them by his previous singing, that they make no discords whilst they sing; whom the rest shall obey', a position for which Tomkins the elder was quite clearly eminently well suited and to which, by 1605, he was appointed,[18] receiving an extra £1. 6s. 8d. annually for his additional responsibilities until his death, when Richard Marwood was elected to take his place.[19] Tomkins also played an active part in the proceedings of the Gloucester consistory court; his signature appears on many court documents.

Human weakness among the lay clerks proved to be just as much a headache for the Gloucester dean and chapter, and for the precentor, as it had been for their fellow clergy at St David's in their dealings with the vicars choral. For example, at the visitation in 1613 it was presented that 'Bridget, wife of William Dowghton, a singing man of our Church, hath been suspected to live incontinently with one Abell Sparkes of Gloucester, and as we have heard, they have been entertained in ye house of Richard Broadgate

---

[17] A Latin verse by 'N. Tomkins', presumably Nicholas, is among the prefatory poems to Ferrabosco's *Ayres* of 1609. In it, Tomkins hails Ferrabosco as 'leader and king of the lyrical race, master of the heavenly lyre'. I am grateful to Dr Pamela Coren for drawing this verse to my attention.

[18] Frith, 'Organists of Gloucester Cathedral', 48.

[19] Gloucester Cathedral Treasurer's Accounts, 1609–1634. GRO, D936 A.1/1.

a singing man'. At the same visitation, Richard Broadgate (a witness to Tomkins the elder's will) was also presented 'for laying violent hands on Richard Sandy [presumably the whistle-blower] at the choir door'![20]

As at St David's, Tomkins *père* continued to pursue his antiquarian interests; he completed a detailed 'Account of the Bishops of Gloucester', the manuscript of which, now lost, was used by Browne Willis in writing his *Survey of the Cathedrals* (1727).

Thomas Tomkins the elder died in March or April 1627. His will, proved on 19 April, is preserved among the Records of the Diocese of Gloucester:

> Memorandum that in the month of March 1626 according to the computation of the Church of England Thomas Tomkins *Clerke* one of the petty canons of the cathedral church of Gloucester and chanter of the same being sick and weak in body but of perfect memory being asked how he would dispose of his estate and goods said divers and sundry times all that I have I give unto Anne Tomkins my wife to dispose thereof as she sees good and her I make my executrix. Witnesses present: Richard Broadgate, one petty canon of the cathedral church of Gloucester, Elizabeth Chapman.[21]

His wife, Anne, followed him to the grave just six months later, and her will, dated 29 November 1627 and proved on 14 December, is also to be found among the same diocesan records:

> I, Anne Tomkins of the city of Gloucester Widow being of whole mind and good and perfect remembrance [bequeath] unto my son John Tomkins, unto my son Robert, unto my son Nicholas, unto my son Giles, unto my son Peregrine, unto my daughter Margaret, and unto my daughter Elizabeth Smith mine own natural children a piece of gold of 11s. a piece to make each of them a ring for motherly remembrance. Also I give unto my late husband's son Thomas Tomkins and unto his daughter Ursula 10s. a piece. The residue of my goods ... I give unto my daughter Bridget Tomkins whom (in regard she is not altogether unprovided-for) I make my sole executrix of this my last will and testament.[22]

Anne, who, like nine out of ten women at that time, had never learned to write, made her mark on the will in a shaky hand and in the presence of three witnesses, including John Merro, a singing man at the cathedral who had been a close colleague of her husband and a family friend for many years. In leaving the residue of her estate to Bridget, the second of the three children born of the marriage of Tomkins the elder and Margaret Poher, and acknowledging her as 'my daughter', Anne makes a clear distinction between Bridget and Thomas Tomkins junior, to whom she does not accord the same loving honorary status. Her choice of the expression 'my late husband's son' certainly appears to suggest the possibility that Tomkins junior was born out of wedlock, but none the less,

---

[20] See Suzanne Eward (1985), *No Fine but a Glass of Wine: Cathedral Life at Gloucester in Stuart Times*, Norwich, 16.

[21] GRO, Gloucester Diocesan Records, Will 1627/196.

[22] GRO, Gloucester Diocesan Records, Will 1627/2.

Gloucester 49

in remembering him and his daughter Ursula in her will, Anne makes her affection for them both self-evident. Her 'late husband's son' had already expressed his own deep affection for his father in music: *Our hasty life away doth post*, the exquisite first madrigal in Tomkins junior's *Songs of 3, 4, 5 and 6 parts*, published in 1622, is inscribed to 'My deare Father, Mr Thomas Tomkins'.

The cathedral records reveal that after the death of her husband, the dean and chapter had agreed to grant the sum of £1 10*s*. 0*d*. to Anne Tomkins 'upon condition of her departure' from her house. So speedy and insensitive an eviction of an elderly and ailing lady seems, unsurprisingly, to have angered Bridget deeply. So great was the intensity of her bitterness that she took it upon herself to deface the property, whereupon the dean and chapter promptly withheld their benevolence, choosing instead to transfer the money towards the cost of making good the damage she had caused.[23]

John Merro clearly stood by Anne in those last, sad months of her life, and may well have given her shelter. A remarkable man, he was one of the most significant music copyists of the early seventeenth century. His work has attracted the attention of several scholars,[24] including Pamela Willetts, who was the first to identify Merro as a music copyist,[25] Philip Brett,[26] Andrew Ashbee[27] and Craig Monson.[28] Merro's repository of purely instrumental music is to be found in the Bodleian Library (MSS Mus.Sch. D245-7), whereas manuscripts in the British Library (Additional MSS 17792-6), and in the New York Public Library, the largest and oldest of Merro's sets of partbooks (Drexel MSS 4180–5), contain both instrumental and vocal music. Brett suggests that this last, 'a large collection of motets, anthems, madrigals and instrumental music [was] compiled between about 1600 and 1620. Most of it is in the hand of John Merro. Like Additional MSS 17992-6, it may have subsequently belonged to Matthew Hutton, since it contains annotations which appear to be in his hand.'[29]

Monson has shown that Add. MS 17792 was probably begun after the completion of Drexel MSS 4180–5 in 1622–25, although there is evidence to suggest that both anthologies were in progress in the 1630s.[30] Pamela Willetts described Merro's careful calligraphy:

---

[23] See Eward, *No Fine*, 13.

[24] See John Irving (1989), *The Instrumental Music of Thomas Tomkins 1572–1656*, New York and London, 124 *et seq.*

[25] Pamela Willetts (1961), 'Music from the Circle of Anthony Wood at Oxford', *British Museum Quarterly*, 24: 71–5.

[26] Philip Brett (ed., 1967), 'Consort Songs', *Musica Britannica*, XXII, London, 173.

[27] Andrew Ashbee (1967), 'Lowe, Jenkins and Merro', *Music and Letters*, 48: 310–11.

[28] Craig Monson (1982), *Voices and Viols in England, 1600–1650: The Sources and the Music*, Ann Arbor, 138–58.

[29] Brett, 'Consort Songs'.

[30] Monson, *Voices and Viols*, 137, 138 and 144. Monson provides a valuable list of the contents of Drexel MS 4180–85 and Add. MS 17795.

Fig. 4.1   MS page of a Fantasia *a* 3 by Tomkins, in the hand of John Merro.

Gloucester 51

> Both music and text ... are skilfully written although there are a few spoiled pages
> and deleted passages. Those who have endeavoured to copy out music will know
> that considerable practice is needed to acquire a consistent musical calligraphy;
> the regularity in these books shows that they were not the work of a novice. For
> the accompanying texts this writer uses both secretary and italic hands, usually
> keeping one style for the whole of one item, but sometimes writing the beginning
> of the text and words such as 'Alleluia', in italic and the rest in secretary style.[31]

In a prose fragment at the back of D245, Merro refers to a book by Samuel Hoard, *God's Love to Mankind*, published in 1633, an attack on the theology of predestination, central to the beliefs of Calvinists. He says that in this book 'the comfortless dangerous and desperat doctrine of absolute reprobation is most plainelie and soundlie confutid'. His collections include works by London-based composers well known to Thomas Tomkins the younger, pieces by Tomkins himself, and works by a number of west countrymen, including John Okeover, organist and master of the choristers at Wells, who was appointed to the same duties at Gloucester in 1640. Okeover seems to have been a visitor to Gloucester even before his appointment to the cathedral there. His signature appears as witness to the will of Richard Marwood, 'Clerke of the colledge in Gloucester', dated 12 August 1635.[32] The three partbooks D245–7 were presented to the Oxford Music School in 1673 by William Isles, who was probably a relative of Dr Thomas Isles, a canon of Christ Church and a former prebendary of Gloucester Cathedral.

Merro's anthologies were presumably used at musical gatherings in Gloucester. The availability to him of composers' autographs, easily accessible to the younger Tomkins, suggests that the latter may well have been a frequent visitor to Gloucester during the first three decades of the seventeenth century, bringing with him manuscripts from the Chapel Royal.

We may also see John Merro as pedagogue, passing his musical knowledge down to a younger generation. Two years after the death of Anne Tomkins a rather more generously minded dean and chapter paid him 10 shillings 'for a room which he rented of John Beames to teach the children to play upon the viols'. John Merro died on 23 March 1636 and was buried in the Lady Chapel of Gloucester Cathedral beside his wife Elizabeth, who had died in November 1615; upon his tombstone was inscribed:

> I once did sing in this,
> Now in the choir of Bliss.

---

[31] Pamela Willetts, 'Music from the Circle of Anthony Wood', 71.
[32] Frith, 'Organists of Gloucester Cathedral', 51.

Chapter 5

Her Majesty's Chapel

Friend of Ben Jonson, or if not friend, equal
In his great strength, but with tougher and less plastic
Material – and no instruments like to the English sense
Of words to use ... Byrd master and squarer of sound.

(Ivor Gurney, *William Byrd*)

Elizabethan London was dynamic, exciting, noisy, and surely, to a teenager such as Thomas Tomkins, a confusing place. He arrived in the midst of a half-century of rapid expansion. In 1550 the population of the capital stood at about 12,000; by 1600 it had risen to over 200,000, resulting in ever-increasing overcrowding, especially for the very poorest citizens, struggling to survive in teeming, filthy alleys. The stench of sixteenth-century London's open drains and mid-street gutters may easily be imagined; the clatter and din aptly described by Tomkins's contemporary, the first literary artist of London street life, Thomas Dekker (*c.*1570–*c.*1637):

> In every street, carts and coaches make such a thundering as if the world ran upon wheels; at every corner, men, women and children meet in such shoals, that posts are set up of purpose to strengthen the houses, lest with jostling one another they should shoulder them down. Besides, hammers are beating in one place, tubs hooping in another, pots clinking in a third, water-tankards [water-carts] running at tilt in a fourth. Here are porters sweating under burdens, there are merchants' men bearing bags of money. Chapmen [pedlars] (as if they were at leap-frog) skip out of one shop into another. Tradesmen (as if they were dancing galliards) are lusty at legs and never stand still. All are as busy as country attorneys at assizes.[1]

To this general hubbub must be added the tuneful but competing street cries of an army of hawkers: fish-wives, costermongers, blacking men, knife-sharpeners, water-sellers, vendors of brooms, hats, padlocks, rugs, flowers, fruit and every conceivable type of produce, all vying for the attention and the cash of the populace. Still familiar to Londoners in the nineteenth century, and lingering into the twentieth, over 150 cries of London have been collected. Tomkins's fellow composers Thomas Weelkes (*c.*1576–1623) and Orlando Gibbons (1583–1625) incorporated musical cries into their works; in Chelsea in 1911 Ralph Vaughan Williams (1872–1958) noted a lavender-

---

[1] Thomas Dekker (1606), *The Seven Deadly Sinnes of London*, London.

54 *The Lives and Times of Thomas Tomkins and his Family*

seller's cry and embodied it into the magical *Lento* second movement of his 'London' Symphony; and from Luciano Berio (1925–2003) we have *The Cries of London*. In Elizabethan London, and therefore in young Tomkins's ears, such cries would have been everywhere.

It is always instructive to see ourselves as others see us. When Paul Hentzner, a counsellor to Duke Charles of Münsterberg and Oels, visited London in 1598 he observed with surprise that 'the English excel in dancing and music, for they are active and lively, though of thicker make than the French', adding that 'they are vastly fond of great noises that fill the ear, such as the firing of cannon, drums, and the ringing of bells; so that in London it is common for a number of them, that have got a glass in their hands, to go into some belfry and ring the bells for hours together for the sake of exercise'.[2] Four centuries later, another German, Oscar Schmitz, would charge that England was a 'Land without Music' (*Das Land ohne Musik*), but under the Tudors and Stuarts, music in England was both internationally famous and acknowledged to be the equal of any in Europe.

Foreign visitors were especially impressed by the outstanding quality of the music and singing in the Chapel Royal. Henry Remelius, ambassador from Denmark in 1584, heard the Office at Greenwich 'so melodiously sung and said … as a man half-dead might thereby have been quickened'.[3] A French ambassador, Champigny, said of the service at Eltham, 'in all my travels in France, Italy and Spain, I never heard the like … a concert of music so excellent and sweet as cannot be expressed'.[4] And when His Serene Highness Duke Frederick of Württemberg, Count Mümppelgart, Knight of the Garter, visited Elizabeth at Windsor in 1592, his private secretary, Jacob Rathgeb, was equally moved by the music in St George's Chapel:

> The castle stands upon a knoll or hill; in the outer or first court there is a very beautiful and immensely large church, with a flat even roof, covered with lead, as is common with all churches in this kingdom. In this church his Highness listened for more than an hour to the beautiful music, the usual ceremonies, and the English sermon. The music, especially the organ, was exquisitely played [the organist at St George's Chapel, Windsor in 1592 was Nathaniel Giles]; for at times you could hear the sound of cornets, flutes, then fifes and other instruments; and there was likewise a little boy who sang so sweetly amongst it all, and threw such charm over the music with his little tongue, that it was really wonderful to listen to him. In short, their ceremonies were very similar to the Papists … with singing and all the rest.[5]

Elizabeth had effectively saved English music from the threat of Puritan

---

[2] Quoted in William Brenchley Rye (1865), *England as Seen by Foreigners in the Days of Elizabeth and James I*, London.

[3] Quoted by Ian Dunlop (1962), *Palaces and Progresses of Elizabeth I*, 'Greenwich', London.

[4] Quoted by John Buxton (1965), *Elizabethan Taste*, London, 195.

[5] Rye, *England as Seen by Foreigners*, 15–16.

Her Majesty's Chapel 55

destruction. Like her father before her she was a lover of music. Like him she maintained a sizeable band of court musicians, and she could, according to Camden, play 'handsomely' upon the lute. She was also a good performer on the lyre and the virginals. Tallis and Byrd, in dedicating their *Cantiones Sacrae* to her in 1575, praised not only her playing but also her elegant voice; her delight in dancing was renowned. The importance of music to the queen, both as a source of pleasure and as an adjunct to diplomacy, is well illustrated by Jacob Rathgeb's description of the reception accorded to his master on their arrival in Berkshire, which preceded by three days their attendance at the above service. The queen was 59 years old at the time:

> On the morning of [Thursday] the 17th August … we arrived about noon at Reading, where her Majesty has her court residence in England, and we were lodged at the house of the Mayor of that place: from thence to London is barely thirty-two miles. Hardly had his Highness undressed and put on other apparel, when the Earl of Essex [Robert Devereux, Earl of Essex], one of the most distinguished lords in England, also one of the Queen's Council, Master of the Horse, and Knight of the royal Order called the Garter, visited his Highness at his lodging, welcomed him in her Majesty's name, and invited him to take dinner in his, the Earl's apartments. To which his Highness, after returning due thanks, was conveyed in a coach, and was feasted most sumptuously, when the Earl entertained his Highness with such sweet and entertaining music (which in all probability belonged to the Queen), that he was highly astonished at it.
>
> After the repast was ended, his Highness was again accompanied by the same distinguished lord to his lodging; but early in the afternoon he was summoned by her Majesty and fetched by others, and was conducted to the Queen's own apartments [where he was granted an audience] … in the afternoon of 18th August he had another audience of her Majesty, on which occasion she herself made and delivered an appropriate speech, in the presence of Monsieur de Beauvois, in the French language, which together with many others, her Majesty understands and speaks very well; and since … her Majesty held Monsieur de Beauvois in especial favour, after he had been conversing with her Majesty very lively and good-humouredly, he so far prevailed upon her that she played very sweetly and skilfully on her instrument, the strings of which were of gold and silver.[6]

The palace of Whitehall, more than any other of Elizabeth's many palaces, castles and manor houses, was equipped for the display of power and royal ceremonial; its chapel, adjoining the east side of the great hall, renowned for the very finest church music in the land.

Many of the musicians and composers employed at court were Catholics, including Tallis and Byrd, who, in spite of their recusancy [refusal to attend Anglican services], were protected by Elizabeth. The queen's love of music was almost certainly an important factor in determining her religious policy, and men of genius or talent, provided that they were prepared to accept the status quo quietly, could expect not only to be tolerated but positively encouraged

---

6 Ibid., 11–12.

in the pursuit of their art, an art both dear to the queen's heart and vital to her ideal of ritual expression.

The organization of the Chapel Royal was tightly controlled, and from about 1585 until the death of Elizabeth was under the direction of the lord chamberlain. Before that time, and again following the accession of James I, a dean (usually a bishop) was appointed by the monarch to take charge. Chaplains and singing men appointed to the Chapel Royal were all called gentlemen of the Chapel, and one of their number, designated sub-dean, exercised the actual daily supervision. Next in order of seniority to the sub-dean was the master of the children, whose foremost responsibility was to ensure that the twelve singing boys (choristers) were fully prepared to sing their parts. He was also responsible for the boarding, lodging, clothing and welfare of the boys.

One of the gentlemen was appointed episteller, whose duty it was to intone the epistle at the communion service; another, responsible for intoning the gospel, held the office of gospeller. One of the gentlemen was appointed clerk of the cheque, with responsibility for the day-to-day financial administration of the Chapel, including the maintenance of a list of attendance. 'Should any of the gentlemen fail to attend his appointed services, the clerk of the cheque administered "the penalty of a check for every one absence from any in his appointed monethe". "Check" or "cheque" meant "fine" and it is perhaps easier to understand the title "clerk of the cheque" as "clerk of the fines".[7]

By the middle of the sixteenth century the customary number of gentlemen, besides the sub-dean but including chaplains, singing men, the master of the children, and the clerk of the cheque was thirty-two. In addition, the serjeant of the vestry, with duties equating roughly to those of a churchwarden, was, along with the yeoman and groom of the vestry, responsible for the sizeable collection of Chapel Royal sacramental plate, books, vestments and other ornaments and furnishings. Given that the Chapel was frequently on the move, the work of these officers often involved a great deal of hard manual labour and the assistance of several carters.

Sadly, most of the pre-eighteenth-century records of the clerks of the cheque have been lost, probably burnt in the fire that destroyed the Whitehall chapel in 1698. However, the most important document, the *Old Cheque Book of the Chapel Royal*, has survived. A selection from it was published in 1872 by the Camden Society in an edition prepared by Edward Rimbault, and a modern, comprehensive edition, compiled by Andrew Ashbee and John Harley, was published in 2000. With the exception of the period from 1640 to 1660, the Cheque Book contains documents of the Chapel Royal from 1561 to 1744, entries having been made by various members of the Chapel

---

[7] David Baldwin (1990), *The Chapel Royal: Ancient and Modern*, London, 296.

Her Majesty's Chapel 57

Royal community, but principally by the clerk of the cheque. The book is by no means an accurate ledger or history. 'A few entries refer to [it] as "our booke of record" or "remembrance" and it is clear from the format that the intention is to provide reference material (incorporating chapter or verse of authority granted) for all aspects of the Chapel's activities and development'.[8]

> The MS is written on large folio paper, measuring 16 and _ inches by 11. It is in the original binding, much dilapidated, with an ornamental device on each side of the covers, and the letters 'E.R.' stamped in gold. On the fly-leaf is written 'Old Cheque-Book of the Chapels Royal'. It consists of 87 leaves folioed, the last leaf being pasted down on the cover. Out of these folios, 30 are entirely blank, one leaf has been torn out (probably blank), and many pages are only partly written upon. It has also 4 preliminary pages (not folioed), three of which are written over … The utmost irregularity is displayed with regard to the various entries, chronology, and subject-matter being equally set at defiance.
>
> From the miscellaneous character of the MS rendering it something like a common-place book, and the manner in which the entries were made from time to time, the clerk evidently sometimes opening the book at random, and only seeking for a vacant space to make his note, it seemed undesirable to print it page for page. Believing that a certain classification or arrangement of the materials would make the work more generally useful and interesting, I have entirely recast the matter, placing it under the various heads in which it seemed naturally to arrange itself.[9]

Much important information not recorded elsewhere, concerning church musicians whose names are still revered and many others who would otherwise be unknown, is owed to this invaluable source document. For example, we learn that on 25 January 1569, Robert Parsons, a gentleman of the Chapel, was drowned at Newark, and William Byrd from Lincoln was sworn gentleman in his place on 22 February 1570; and that on 13 November 1581, William Edney died of the plague, and Thomas Woodson of Poules [St Paul's] was sworn in his place on 25 December following. All entries are written in the same dispassionate style:

> Tho. Tallis died the 23rd of November, and Henry Eveseed sworne in his place the last of the same. Childe there.
>
> Jo. Bull sworne the [?] of Januarie in Mr. Bodinghurst['s] place. Childe there.

The phrase 'childe there' indicated that the musician appointed as gentleman had received his boyhood training in the Chapel Royal. However, the entries for Thomas Tallis and William Bodinghurst are the only two in the Cheque Book to include such a qualification, suggesting that the convention had been dropped almost as soon as it had started. In later years, the appointment of such gentlemen of the Chapel as Pelham Humfrey, John Blow

---

[8] Andrew Ashbee and John Harley (eds, 2000), *The Cheque Books of the Chapel Royal*, Aldershot, xix.

[9] *Cheque Book*, xi–xii.

58   *The Lives and Times of Thomas Tomkins and his Family*

and William Croft, all of whom had been Chapel boys, were recorded in the Cheque Book without the addition of 'childe there'. Similarly, when Tomkins's appointment as a gentleman of the Chapel was listed in 1621, no mention was made of him having been a 'childe there'. None the less, the strongest possibility remains that he was a chorister there soon after 1585, the year of Tallis's death, going on to serve his apprenticeship under Byrd, probably before 1593 when Byrd, then aged 50, sold his house in Harlington and removed to Stondon in Essex. By this time Tomkins was 21 years old and Byrd had probably retired from the Chapel Royal.

In addition to the master of the children, a master of the grammar school was employed for the choristers of the Chapel Royal and other children of the court. Choristers therefore benefited both from instruction in music and what, in that day, was termed a learned education, but their diet was frugal and their domestic conditions lacking in cheer. In 1583 William Hunnis, dually gifted as poet and musician, whose work found inclusion in Richard Edwards's miscellany of verses *The Paradise of Daynty Devises* (1576), and who was master of the children from 1566 until his death in 1597, had made a heartfelt plea for an increase in his allowances:

> 1583 November The humble petition of the master of the children of her Highness' Chapel
>
> May it please your honours, William Hunnis, master of the children of her Highness' Chapel, most humbly beseech to consider of these few lines.
>
> First, her Majesty alloweth for the diet of twelve children of her said Chapel daily six pence apiece by the day, and forty pounds by the year for their apparel and all other furniture.
>
> Again there is no fee allowed, neither for the master of the said children nor for his usher, and yet nevertheless is he constrained, over and besides the usher still to keep both a man servant to attend upon them and likewise a woman servant to wash and keep them clean.
>
> Also there is no allowance for the lodging of the said children, such time as they attend upon the court, but the master to his great charge is driven to hire chambers both for himself, his usher, children, and servants.
>
> Also there is no allowance for riding journeys when occasion serveth the master to travel or send into sundry parts within this realm, to take up and bring such children as be thought meet to be trained for the service of her Majesty.
>
> Also there is no allowance nor other consideration for those children whose voices be changed, who only depend upon the charge of the said master until such time as he may prefer the same with clothing and other furniture, unto his no small charge.
>
> And although it may be objected that her Majesty's allowance is no whit less than her Majesty's father of famous memory therefore allowed: yet considering the prices of things present to the time past and what annuities the master then had out of sundry abbeys within this realm, besides sundry gifts from the king, and divers particular fees besides, for the better maintenance of the said children and office: and besides also there hath been withdrawn from the said children since her Majesty's coming to the crown twelve pence by the day which was allowed for their breakfasts as may appear by the treasurer of the chamber his account for the time being, with other allowances incident to the office as appeareth by the ancient accounts in the said office which I here omit.

Her Majesty's Chapel 59

> The burden hereof hath from time to time so hindered the masters of the children *viz.* Master Bower, Master Edwardes, myself and Master Farrant: that notwithstanding some good helps otherwise some of them died in so poor case, and so deeply indebted that they have not left scarcely wherewith to bury them.
>
> In tender consideration whereof, might it please your honours that the said allowance of six pence a day apiece for the children's diet might be reserved in her Majesty's coffers during the time of their attendance. And in lieu thereof they to be allowed meat and drink within this honourable household for that I am not able upon so small allowance any longer to bear so heavy a burden. Or otherwise to be considered as shall seem best unto your honourable wisdoms.[10]

Although Hunnis's petition met with no success, his financial difficulties were relieved two years later by the grant to him of crown lands, and the daily allowance for each chorister was at last increased from 6 pence to 10 pence during the time of Hunnis's successor, Nathaniel Giles (*c.*1558–1634). Giles, a close friend of Tomkins, who dedicated to him his madrigal *Come, shepherds, sing with me*,[11] had been organist of Worcester Cathedral from 1581 to 1585, after which he was appointed organist and choirmaster of St George's Chapel, Windsor, and also, in 1596, of the Chapel Royal. He took over as master of the children at the Chapel Royal on the death of Hunnis in 1597. When Giles died in 1634, William Child, who had been standing in for him for some time, took his place at Windsor.

One means by which the master of the children could and did increase his income was to employ the boys under his charge as actors. The age-old tradition of boy players in the early history of the theatre reached its apogee in the latter half of the sixteenth century, by which time the bond between Chapel Royal and stage was at its strongest. Drama had appeared set on a divided course: 'courtly drama acted by young gallants and choir children in halls and noble houses, and popular drama acted by common players in the yards of inns and later at The Theater, the first London playhouse, erected in 1576. The literary men from Oxford and Cambridge took the drama as their special province. They drew a sharp distinction between the civilized theatre of the Court and the common playhouse of the vulgar.'[12] In the 1580s the children of the Chapel Royal were acting in the old refectory at Blackfriars, where John Lyly (1544–1606) was producing courtly dramas such as *A most excellent comedie of Alexander, Campaspe and Diogenes* and *Sapho and Phao*, both based on slight themes suggested by stories of classical deities, and both first presented in 1584. In the following year, Lord Hunsdon (Henry Carey), the illegitimate son of Henry VIII and Mary Boleyn, sister of Anne, became lord chamberlain to Elizabeth I and therefore in overall control of the Chapel

---

[10] TNA, MS SP 12/163, 88, quoted in E.K. Chambers (1923), *The Elizabethan Stage*, Oxford, II, 37–8.

[11] *Songs of 3.4.5. and 6. parts* (1622).

[12] G. Sampson (ed., 1945), *The Concise Cambridge History of English Literature*, Cambridge, 248.

60 · *The Lives and Times of Thomas Tomkins and his Family*

Royal. Hunsdon had formed his own company of players as early as 1564, and, unconscious of any conflict of interest, in 1590 leased the Blackfriars premises where the Chapel Royal boys played. The 'Lord Chamberlain's Men', which Hunsdon founded in 1594, formed an indoor theatre at Blackfriars, and, in 1598, moved across the Thames to the open-air Globe theatre,[13] but the children of the Chapel Royal continued to act in the Blackfriars theatre, where, in 1602, the duke of Stettin-Pomerania attended one of their plays:

> The Queen keeps a number of young boys, who are taught to sing and to play on all sorts of musical instruments – they are also expected to continue their school studies at the same time. These boys have special instructors in the various arts, and especially in music. As part of their education in courtly manners they are required to put on a play once a week, and for this purpose the Queen has provided them with a theatre and with a great deal of rich apparel. Those who wish to see one of the performances must pay as much as eight shillings of our Pomeranian money. Yet there are always a good many people present, including ladies of the highest repute, since the plots are always well developed and of a suitably elevated character. All the performances are by candlelight and the effect is indeed spectacular. For a whole hour before the play begins there is a concert of music for organs, lutes, pandoras, citterns, viols and recorders. When we were there a boy cum voce tremula sang so charmingly to the accompaniment of a bass viol that with the possible exception of the nuns at Milan, we heard nothing to equal him anywhere.[14]

Playwrights other than Lyly who wrote for the children of the Chapel Royal included John Fletcher, Thomas Middleton, John Marston, George Chapman and Ben Jonson. Not all of the boys saw the opportunity to act as a beneficial 'part of their education in courtly manners', and it was not unknown for boys to be impressed by the master of the children for nothing better than, as one father complained to the queen, 'to exercise the base trade of a mercenary interlude player, to his utter loss of time, ruin, and disparagement'. Nathaniel Giles and his assistants responded that 'if the queen would not bear them forth in that action, she should get another to execute her commission for them' as 'they had authority sufficient so to take any noble man's son in this land' and 'were it not for the benefit they made by said playhouse [Blackfriars], who would, should serve the Chapel with children for them'.[15]

It is diverting to imagine Thomas Tomkins treading the boards at Blackfriars, delivering his lines in an attractive South Pembrokeshire accent. But although many of his fellows were obliged to act, it is probable that a prodigy such as Tomkins, under Byrd's tutelage, would have been spared such duties.

---

[13] See Baldwin, *The Chapel Royal*, 112–15.

[14] G. von Bülow (1892), *The Diary of Philip Julius, Duke of Stettin-Pomerania*, Transactions of the Royal Historical Society, VI.

[15] C.W. Wallace (1912), *The Evolution of the English Drama*, Berlin, 209. Quoted by Baldwin, *The Chapel Royal*, 120.

Her Majesty's Chapel 61

Royal policy provided that all qualified former choristers of the Chapel Royal should be found a place at university, at Oxford or Cambridge.[16] In Tomkins's case the choice seems to have been in Oxford's favour. *The Registers of the University of Oxford* give a brief account of Tomkins's affiliation: 'Thomas Tomkins, Magdalen College. 14 years student in Music; supplicated BMus 6 June, admitted 11 July 1607.'[17]

An account by the Oxford historian Anthony à Wood, who had met Tomkins's son Nathaniel in Worcester around 1670, concurs with these details:

> This eminent and learned musician was son of Thomas Tomkins Chauntor of the Choir at Gloucester, descended from those of his name at Lostwithiel in Cornwall, educated under the famous musician William Byrd and afterwards for his merits was made Gentleman of His Majesty's Chapel Royal, and at length Organist of the Cathedral Church at Worcester.[18]

As Denis Stevens has pointed out, 'residence was not required at that time for a degree of this nature, although membership in a college was necessary in order to supplicate for the degree'.[19] Noting that Tomkins was a 'student in music' for fourteen years, i.e. since 1593, may indicate that his studentship with Byrd began in that year, as believed by Sir Ivor Atkins, and that his affiliation to Magdalen College followed thereafter. However, it seems more probable that he had completed his studies with Byrd by 1593, following this period of private tuition by an affiliation to Magdalen College of fourteen years ending in 1607. Although the precise sequence cannot be ascertained, it would have been remarkable if his studies with Byrd had begun no earlier than 1593, given that his reputation was already sufficiently established by 1596 for him to have taken over as organist and master of the choristers at Worcester Cathedral and to be recognized as a composer soon afterwards.

As we have seen, the wealthy clothier John Tomkins had been living in Worcester for some years by 1593. It seems very likely that Thomas could have left London in or before that year, have moved to Worcester to live with his prosperous relative and to continue his studies with Nathaniel Patrick, the organist of Worcester Cathedral, and have begun his affiliation to Magdalen College in 1593. It is also entirely possible that he was resident at Magdalen between 1593 and 1596. However, in a document dated 17 June 1650, the Worcester mayor and aldermen certified that Tomkins was then 'of the age of 78 years' and had 'lived here very near 60 years',[20] thus confirming that Tomkins was born in 1572 and supporting the proposition that he had arrived

---

16 See Woodfill, *Musicians in English Society*, 145.
17 J.R. Bloxam (1853), *Registers of the University of Oxford*, Oxford, II, part I, 147.
18 A. Wood (1813–22), *Athenae Oxonienses; Fasti Oxonienses*, ed. P. Bliss, London, I, 799.
19 Stevens, 31.
20 TNA, SP 23/124/233.

62   *The Lives and Times of Thomas Tomkins and his Family*

in Worcester some few years before his official appointment to the cathedral in 1596.

In addition to the thirty-two gentlemen of the Chapel Royal who received wages, there were a few others whose appointment was purely honorary. These 'gentlemen extraordinary' were appointed by the monarch, the dean, or on the vote of a majority of the gentlemen in ordinary either to honour their outstanding skill or because they had helped the Chapel in some remarkable way. In 1592, for example, William Phelps, a musician of Tewkesbury, was elected a gentleman extraordinary because he 'did show a most rare kindness to Mr Doctor Bull in his great distress, being robbed in those parts'.[21] Tomkins was probably honoured in this way long before his official appointment as a gentleman in ordinary in 1621. His name first appears in the Cheque Book in 1620 when he witnessed the appointment of another gentleman, Thomas Piers, in June of that year. 'It is more than likely, however, that he had been a gentleman extraordinary for some considerable time before that – perhaps even from 1603 or thereabouts.'[22]

During the years of Tomkins's musical education, Elizabeth I faced two of the greatest challenges to her throne: the Babington conspiracy of 1586, in which Mary Stuart, queen of Scotland, a prisoner in England for nearly eighteen years, was implicated in a plot to effect her freedom by the assassination of Elizabeth, thus bringing her to the executioner's block at Fotheringay Castle on 8 February 1587; and the threat of Spanish invasion, culminating in the defeat of the Armada in 1588. The gentlemen and children of the Chapel Royal will have witnessed the contrast in their queen's demeanour at prayer before and after these momentous events: anguish perhaps after the first, and prayers of joy and thanksgiving after the second. The Old Cheque Book records the details of a single royal ceremony in the Chapel Royal during Elizabethan times: that of *The Princely coming of her Majesty to the Holy Communion at Easter*, on 15 April, 1593:

> The most sacred Queen Elizabeth upon Easter day, after the holy gospel was read in the chapel at St James, came down into her Majesty's travess [private closet]: before her highness came the gentlemen pensioners, then the barons, the bishops, London and Llandaff, the earls, and the whole council in their colours of state, the heralds at arms, the lord keeper bearing the great seal himself, and the Earl of Hereford bearing the sword before her Majesty.
>
> Then her Majesty's royal person came most cheerfully, having as noble supporters the right honourable the earl of Essex, master of her Majesty's horse, on the right hand, and the right honourable the lord admiral on the left hand, the lord chamberlain to her Majesty (also next before her Majesty) attendant all the while.
>
> Dr. Bull was at the organ playing the offertory. Her Majesty entered her travess

---

[21] *Cheque Book*, 32.

[22] Peter Le Huray (1967), *Music and the Reformation in England 1549–1660*, London, 275.

Her Majesty's Chapel   63

most devoutly, there kneeling: after some prayers she came princely before the table, and there humbly kneeling did offer the golden obeisant, the Bishop the hon. Father of Worcester holding the golden basin, the sub-dean and the epistoler in rich copes assistant to the said Bishop: which done, her Majesty returned to her princely travess sumptuously set forth, until the present action of holy communion, continually exercised in earnest prayer, and then the blessed sacrament, first received of the said Bishop and administered to the sub-dean, the gospeller for that day, and to the epistoler, her sacred person presented herself before the Lord's table, royally attended as before, where was set a stately stool and cushions for her Majesty, and so humbly kneeling with most singular devotion and holy reverence did most comfortably receive the most blessed sacrament of Christ's body and blood, in the kinds of bread and wine, according to the laws established by her Majesty and Godly laws in parliament. The bread being wafer bread of some thicker substance, which her Majesty in most reverend manner took of the Lord Bishop in her naked right hand, her satisfied heart fixing her semblant eyes most entirely upon the worthy words sacramental pronounced by the Bishop, etc., that with such an holy aspect as it did mightily add comforts to the goodly beholders (whereof this writer was one very near): and likewise her Majesty received the cup, having a most princely linen cloth laid on her cushion pillow and borne at the four ends by the noble Earl of Hereford, the Earl of Essex, the Earl of Worcester, and the Earl of Oxford: the side of the said cloth her Majesty took up in her hand, and therewith took the foot of the golden and now sacred cup, and with like holy reverend attention as before ... did drink of the same most devoutly (all this while kneeling on her knees) to the confirmation of her faith and absolute comfort in her purged conscience by the holy spirit of God in the exercise of this holy communion, of her participation of and in the merits and death of Jesus Christ our Lord, and the perfect communion and spiritual food of the very body and blood of Christ our Lord Saviour: and so returning to her said travess, there devoutly stayed [until] the end of prayers, which done her Majesty royally ascended the way and stairs into her presence, whom the Lord bless for ever and ever. Amen.

Anthony Anderson, Sub-Dean[23]

John Bull, who 'was at the organ playing the offertory' on this occasion, had been a Chapel Royal chorister as a boy and became organist of Hereford Cathedral in 1582. He was appointed a gentleman of the Chapel in 1586, taking over as organist following the death of William Blitheman in 1591. Bull's keyboard music exercised a keen influence upon Tomkins, who, recognizing that not all of Bull's pieces were of equal quality, was to preface one of his anthologies: 'These especially: and none but lessons of worthe: to be prickt [i.e. copied] ... All doct. Bulls offertories and In nomines the choice of them'.[24]

The service attended by the queen at Easter in 1593 was just one of the many that constituted the established rhythm of worship at court, a rhythm that was customary to the organists, gentlemen and choristers of the Chapel Royal. Tomkins had become fully familiar with the demands, disciplines and

---

[23] *Cheque Book*, 150–51.
[24] Paris, Bibliothèque Nationale, MS Rés. 1122. See also Irving, *Instrumental Music*, 35.

protocols of this rarefied world, and in the years ahead would return to the Chapel many times, crossing England from Worcester to London in the service of Church and State.

Chapter 6

Worcester

Thomas Tomkins took up his appointment as master of the choristers at Worcester in 1596. The cathedral treasurer recorded in his accounts that Tomkins's employment would attract remuneration of £11. 6s. 8d. per annum, and no doubt the dean and chapter heaved a collective sigh of relief. After the premature death of Nathaniel Patrick in March 1595 they had invited John Fido (or Fideau) to take his place, possibly as a temporary measure pending the availability of Tomkins. It was a decision that they would soon come to regret.

Fido had been the organist at Hereford Cathedral for only fifteen months before his transfer to Worcester, but in that short time had shown himself to be hopelessly insubordinate, and in 1594 had been reprimanded for using 'slanderous words against the custos and vicars [choral]'.[1] One can imagine that the Hereford dean and chapter were only too pleased to pass this troublesome organist on to Worcester, where, unfortunately, his defiance of authority went from bad to worse. Fido left Worcester, was accepted back, perhaps reluctantly, at Hereford late in 1596, admitted as organist there on 7 January 1597 subject to a year's probation, was granted permanent status on 14 May 1597,[2] but then left to take up an appointment as master of the boys at Christ Church, Dublin, in May 1600. Later, he took holy orders and returned to Worcester, becoming a minor canon in 1611 and, from 1615 to 1636, rector of St Nicholas Church, but even after ordination it seems that his behaviour failed to improve. In 1625 he was 'admonished for negligence and contempt', and finally, in 1633, was suspended in respect of 'many misdemeanours'.

Nevertheless, Fido was an able organist and composer. He also maintained his contact with Hereford, visited other cathedrals and academic institutions, and had a keen eye for business. The Hereford Cathedral claviger's accounts of 1612–13 record that 40s. was paid 'to Mr Fidoe of Worcester for Songe

---

[1] Sir Ivor Atkins (1918), *The Early Occupants of the Office of Organist and Master of the Choristers of the Cathedral Church of Christ and the Blessed Virgin Mary, Worcester*, WHS.

[2] H. Watkins Shaw (1991), *The Succession of Organists*, Oxford, 135.

See also William Reynolds (2002), 'A Study of Music and Liturgy, Choirs and Organs in Monastic and Secular Foundations in Wales and the Borderlands, 1485–1645', unpublished Ph.D. thesis, University of Wales, Bangor, 183.

Fig. 6.1   Internal view of Worcester Cathedral, drawn and engraved by James Ross for Valentine Green's *A History of Worcester* (1794).

Worcester

bookes'; and at Lincoln Cathedral on 27 December 1599 'Magister Fido' received from the chapter 40s. for various song books.[3] He also appears to have visited King's College, Cambridge, for a period of nine weeks in 1605/6, 'but was never a formal member of that institution: "Item: paid to Fido for books in the same use and for [playing upon organs] for 9 weeks, 30s."'.[4]

A seventeenth-century bassus partbook in the library of Gloucester Cathedral (MS 101) includes, in the main, examples of the works of composers from the cathedrals of Gloucester, Hereford and Worcester, including Fido (*Deliver me from mine enemies; Hear me, O Lord, and that soon,* and *I call with my whole heart*). 'The provenance of [MS 101] can be positively identified as that of Gloucester Cathedral immediately prior to the Commonwealth. Inside the back cover a list of names is inscribed showing the "quiristers of decani side 1641", which may be confirmed by cross-referencing with the treasurer's accounts for that year.'[5]

> The manuscript is divided into four clear-cut sections – firstly, Preces and Festal Psalms, then, services and full anthems, and lastly verse anthems. Originally one of a carefully planned set, it has been suggested by Morehen that the absence of full services in the bassus book implies that a second set of books would once have existed to correct this deficiency, in addition to providing a further selection of anthems. Its date of compilation may be put at between 1622 and 1641, with a limited number of subsequent additions in a different hand. The condition of the book suggests that it would have been written shortly before the latter date, it would then have received limited use until it was stored away during the Commonwealth.[6]

A manuscript of particular significance with regard to both Fido and Tomkins, a Southwell Minster tenor partbook (Tenbury MS 1382), is to be found in the Bodleian Library, Oxford. This anthology, comprising items by several Chapel Royal composers, such as Bull, Morley, Tye, William Mundy, John Mundy, Parsons, Tallis, Nathaniel Giles, Weelkes and John Tomkins's *Have mercy upon me*, also contains fifteen anthems by Byrd, and an equal number by Thomas Tomkins, including both anthems and verse anthems:

Anthems

Almighty God, the fountain of all wisdom
Holy holy holy, Lord God
Lord, enter not into judgement
O God, the proud are risen up
O Lord, wipe away my sins
O sing unto the Lord a new song

---

[3] I. Payne (1993), *The Provision and Practice of Sacred Music at Cambridge Colleges and Selected Cathedrals c.1547–c.1646*, London, 76.

[4] Reynolds, 'A Study of Music and Liturgy', 231.

[5] John Morehen (1981), 'The Gloucester Cathedral Bassus Partbook MS 93', *Music and Letters*, 62: 189–97. See also Reynolds, 'A Study of Music and Liturgy', 261–3. The Catalogue reference number of this partbook has been revised from MS 93 to MS 101.

[6] Reynolds, 261–2.

68   *The Lives and Times of Thomas Tomkins and his Family*

Verse Anthems

Behold, I bring you glad tidings
Death is swallowed up
Glory be to God on high
Know you not
O Lord, let me know mine end
The Lord bless us
The Lord, even the most mighty
Thou art my King, O God
Turn thou us, O good Lord

Tenbury MS 1382 also contains music by three purely 'provincial' composers: Nathaniel Patrick, Nicholas Strogers and John Fido. Originally one of a set of eight partbooks with an organ book, the manuscript includes a preface, dated 1617, showing that the original set of books was 'bestowed on the quire of the Collegiate Church of Southwell of the bountiful and friendly gift of Mr Jarvis Jones of Oxford, one of the sons of Walter Jones, sometime Prebend Resident[iar]y of the Prebend of Normanton within the said Church'.

> In common with Gloucester MS 101, a strong link is evident with Worcester and Hereford Cathedrals. Furthermore, Thomas Tomkins and Nathaniel Giles both have associations with Worcester Cathedral and the Chapel Royal in addition to having anthems contained in MS 1382. A grouping of nine verse anthems by Thomas Tomkins enjoys pride of place at the beginning of the manuscript and similarly, the first five of the section of full anthems are also by Tomkins. Nathaniel Giles's full anthem *O Lord Almighty, thou God of Israel* is unique to this source, while his verse anthem *O Lord turn not away thy face* had wider appeal. Also, John Bull, a onetime organist at Hereford Cathedral, has two anthems in MS 1382 – *Deliver me, O God* and *Almighty God, which by the leading of a star* – but these were widely known and exist in many sources.
>
> John Fido may be seen as the lynchpin in the compilation of this manuscript. Although there is a preponderance of anthems by Chapel Royal composers, John Fido himself has six verse anthems:
>
> > *O Lord, in thee is all my trust*
> > *If the Lord himself*
> > *Hear me, O Lord and that soon*
> > *I call with my whole heart*
> > *O King of heaven*
> > *Deliver me from mine enemies*
>
> Three of these are unique to this source (*O Lord, in thee is all my trust*; *If the Lord himself* and *O King of heaven*), while two others are found only in the Gloucester bassus book (*Deliver me from mine enemies* and *I call with my whole heart*). John Morehen suggests that John Fido (although not the actual scribe) may in some way have been directly involved in the compilation of the manuscript. This hypothesis is given strength by the use of Fido's name without the prefix Mr or Dr, the composer always being referred to simply as 'John Fido'. The only other composer whose Christian name is given in the partbook was Thomas Tomkins (referred to as Mr Thomas Tomkins or Mr Th: Tomkins).
>
> Morehen continues his argument by seeking to establish a possible link

between John Fido and Jarvas Jones 'of Oxford', the donor of the set of partbooks to Southwell Minster. He reveals that Thomas Fido, a brother of John, received an Oxford BA degree from Magdalen College on 27 May 1606, a year prior to Thomas Tomkins receiving a BMus from the same college. This could help to explain the deliberate positioning of the verse anthems by Tomkins at the front of the partbook. The significance of Oxford is further established in that four brothers, William,[7] John, Robert and Thomas Fido and a possible fifth, Edmund, all studied at Oxford around this time. Morehen proposes that Jarvas Jones (who himself had graduated with an Oxford BA in 1615) consulted one of the Oxford Fidos, most likely Thomas or Edmund, with a view to secure music from their brother John at Worcester.

An alternative solution is also offered by Morehen who considers the possibility that Walter Jones, father of Jarvas Jones, may have retired to Worcester from Southwell. A man of that name is recorded as having been granted an almsroom at Worcester, and if this identification is true, then Jarvas may well have procured the set of partbooks for Southwell directly from his father, who could well have known John Fido personally.[8]

Tenbury MS 1382 is the earliest of the datable sources of English liturgical music of the first half of the seventeenth century. As well as demonstrating the combination of standard repertoire, some drawn from the Chapel Royal, with items of local interest, it also provides important proof that the fifteen anthems by Tomkins that it contains were composed before 1617, i.e. within the first two decades of his appointment to Worcester.

Atkins suggested that Fido might well have acted as an assistant to Tomkins, 'no doubt taking Tomkins's place during the latter's absence upon his Chapel Royal duties ... There always seemed high hope that he would mend his ways, but it does not appear that he ever did; indeed his appearances in the Chapter Books are generally punctuated by admonitions ... As he reappears as a minor canon in 1639 he must evidently have been a person of some resilience.'[9] But in spite of any shortcomings in his behaviour, John Fido, who died about 1640, was clearly a talented and energetic man who, in disseminating songbooks widely, made a significant contribution to English church music. And the Gloucester bassus partbook (MS 101), including Fido's contribution to it, demonstrates a musical link, long before the Civil War, between the cathedrals of Gloucester, Hereford and Worcester. These links were to flower early in the eighteenth century into an annual music meeting of all three, held in each city in turn: the Three Choirs Festival. That the bassus partbook survived at all is little short of miraculous: it was rescued in the early 1950s from the Gloucester Cathedral incinerator, where it had been consigned with other items of 'rubbish'! An empty leather music binder

---

7 The will of William Fido (dated 1613, London, TNA, B 11/122, q.68 (PCC 68 Capell), yeoman of The Phowse, Stockton, Worcestershire, has bequests to his brothers John, Robert and Thomas.

8 Reynolds, 264–5.

9 Atkins, *Early Occupants*.

70   *The Lives and Times of Thomas Tomkins and his Family*

in the cathedral library, embossed 1642, is the only remnant of other pre-Civil War music treasures destroyed in those flames.

By the end of the sixteenth century, Worcester was the twelfth largest city in England. The population doubled between 1563 and 1646, when it had reached around 7,000, and records of the period mention that its citizens were engaged in at least one hundred different occupations,[10] but the mainstay of the economy was the cloth trade. In common with other cities, Worcester was an insanitary place. Open latrine pits and shared privies provided a perfect breeding ground for rats – and with rats came plague. There were several outbreaks throughout the years in which Tomkins lived in the city, and it is said that no less than 1,551 citizens died in the epidemic of 1637 alone, but there were outbreaks in 1609, 1610, 1617, 1625 and 1630 too, and again in 1644–5. Tomkins had been organist at Worcester for barely a year when, in 1597, following a disastrous harvest, the malnourished citizens fell easy prey to plague.

Dominating the skyline, then as now, was the cathedral, within it every type of architecture from Norman to Perpendicular. The crypt is Norman, the choir early thirteenth century, and the nave in the Decorated style of English architecture. To the late fifteenth century belongs the chantry chapel raised above the tomb of Prince Arthur (1486–1502), the eldest son of Henry VII, whose early death at Ludlow resulted in the accession of Henry VIII to the throne and the resultant political and ecclesiastical dislocation. In addition to the cathedral there were ten other churches within the city walls, each with a community ethos of its own. Five gates pierced the walls, beyond which lay a largely rural county dotted about with small market towns: Fore Gate, leading to the north; St Martin's Gate, leading to the east; Friar's Gate, leading from that street to the east; Sidbury Gate, to the south; and Water Gate or St Clement's Gate, near the old bridge. On the centre of the bridge a strong stone tower stood to command the pass. The roads out of the city and throughout the county, as elsewhere, were in a deplorable condition, little more than muddy tracks that turned rapidly to quagmire in wet weather. Tomkins's many journeys to London, with night-stops at inns *en route*, each an expedition of at least seven days, must have been strenuous and wearisome in the extreme.

By 1596 English national confidence was riding high. 'The danger from both Spain and France was over; the defeat of the Armada had crippled Spain; Henry of Navarre had defeated the Leaguers at Ivry and was king of France. Elizabeth could now attack the papists with impunity. The year 1592 marked

---

[10]   See Keith Wrightson (2000), *English Society 1580–1680*, London, 36.

Fig. 6.2   Worcester Cathedral.

the beginning of the Recusant Rolls, and in 1593 all recusants not having goods and lands to a certain amount were ordered to leave the country or be deemed felons.'[11] The cruel butchery of Catholics became a common sight in many a market square, and these were especially dark days for many in Worcestershire, a county suspected of being a hotbed of popery. Most of the notable county families were Catholics: the Windsors, the Throckmortons, the Talbots, the Blounts of Kidderminster, the Sheldons of Beoley, the Habingtons of Hindlip, the Lyttelton of Hagley, the Actons of Ribbesford, the Berkeleys of Spetchley, and the Pakingtons of Westwood. 'Throughout the county Mass was being said in secret, and many local people were implicated in plots, culminating in the Babington Conspiracy of 1586.'[12] But not all recusants were to be found in the ranks of the gentry, and not all were Catholics: many of those who chose to absent themselves and their families from the services of the established Church were yeomen, husbandmen or tradesmen, and many were Puritans, a term of abuse without official meaning,

---
[11] *Victoria County History of Worcestershire*, II, 54.
[12] A. MacDonald (1943; 2/1969), *Worcestershire in English History*, London, 84.

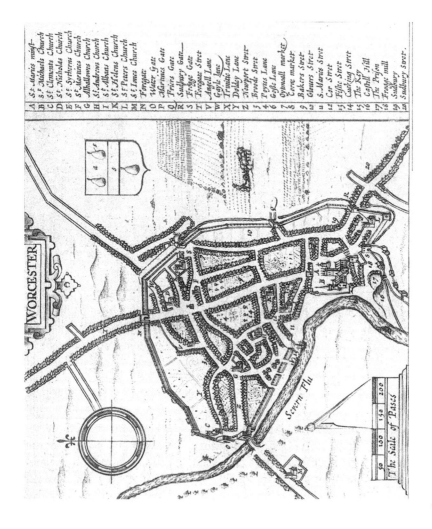

Fig. 6.3 Map of Worcester, c.1610.

Worcester 73

used to describe not only the followers of Calvin but also those Protestants who looked askance at the revival of any Romish practice, such as the wearing of surplices, within the Anglican Church.

Tomkins, orthodox in his beliefs, a convinced Royalist and church musician, held a profound dislike for Puritans and recorded his view of them more than once, jotting down stanzas of satirical verse or political comment in his anthologies:

> A learned Bishop of this land, thinking to make Religion stand
> in Equall poise on every side, to make a mixture thus he tried:
> An ownce of protestant he singles & with a dram of papist mingles:
> A scruple adds of puritan: And works them all in his brayne pan.
> Now when he thinks they should digest, the scruple troubles all the Rest.

And:

> If lyes, if slanders, if debate; if privat mallice perfect hate
> If contumacy; then Bold Checkmate to government of Church and State
> Characters bee of Sanctity: the Puritan a saynt must bee.[13]

At the time of his appointment to Worcester in 1596 Tomkins would have found his colleagues in the cathedral community both alarmed by the danger of recusancy and relieved by the appointment, in April, of a new bishop, Thomas Bilson, after the See had remained vacant for almost two years. The tenure of Bilson's predecessor, Richard Fletcher, who had acted as chaplain at the execution of Mary Stuart, queen of Scotland, had lasted barely twelve months when he was translated to London in 1594. By then, the See was so impoverished that it had proved difficult to find anyone who was willing to become bishop of Worcester in Fletcher's place. When Elizabeth I offered the office to William Day he had turned it down, writing on 14 January 1594 to the lord treasurer, William Cecil, 'it would utterly beggar me to take it … I pray you to move her highness to be gracious unto me and in my old age not to put me to seek another county air, new acquaintance, and another living without sufficient maintenance.'[14] In July 1596 Bilson wrote to Cecil concerning recusants in the county. He had been shocked to find that Worcestershire was as dangerous a place as any he knew, and contained 'nine score recusants of note besides retainers, wanderers and secret lurkers, dispersed in forty parishes'. Of these about forty were 'families of gentlemen where either themselves or their wives absent themselves from church'. He named thirty-two of the 'wealthier sort', and eighteen gentlewomen who 'refused the church, although their husbands did not', besides 'fourscore and ten

---

[13] BL Add. MS 29996, fol. 152.
[14] Historical Manuscripts Commission, *Rep. on Cecil MS*, V, 79, quoted in *The Victoria County History of Worcestershire* (1926), II, 54, n. 4.

74 *The Lives and Times of Thomas Tomkins and his Family*

several households of the meaner sort where man or wife or both are recusants, besides children and servants'.[15]

As appalling as the roads out of Worcester might have been, there was one way in which a traveller of the sixteenth or seventeenth centuries might journey in comparative ease between that city, Gloucester, Tewkesbury, and even Bristol: the Severn, a river of infinite delights. Flowing, as it does, through the heart of Worcester, the Severn passes close by the west end of the cathedral, where once boatmen gathered to pick up passengers, and where their successors still tie up to take on board customers for sightseeing trips. Tomkins would have known the river well, perhaps knew the boatmen by their first names, and undoubtedly sailed down this wide, peaceful stream to visit his father and family in Gloucester. But there was another riverside destination to which he must have been drawn time and time again.

A dozen miles south of Worcester, where the river meanders between Upton-on-Severn and Tewkesbury, a winding brook to the west of the Severn flows north through Longdon Marsh, and, turning east near the village of Longdon, empties itself into the river just beyond an impressive mansion, now the home of Bredon School. This is Pull Court, a large and picturesque stone building in the Elizabethan style with curved gables and square-headed mullioned windows, built between 1836 and 1839 to replace a much older house, already described as 'ancient' in 1628, which was demolished in 1798.[16] Pull Court, formerly known as Poole Court, stands on land listed in the Domesday Survey of 1086 as Lapule, where 'three virgates of land belonged to Langedune [Longdon], the manor of Earl Odo', and where 'a man of the monks of Lire [the Norman abbey of La Vieille Lyre] held one virgate of land'.[17] Pull Court is set in countryside of outstanding beauty, close to the southern border of Worcestershire, cradled between Bredon to the east, and, dominating the western skyline, the ancient Malvern Hills, rising abruptly from the lowlands to a height of nearly 1,400 feet, magnificent in their bare grandeur. Sadly, the M50 motorway now disturbs the Longdon peace, but at Pull Court it is still possible to forget that the busy world exists, and here it was that Tomkins composed his light and playful keyboard piece *A Toy made at Poole Court*.[18] Here was a pastoral retreat away from cathedral cares and city

---

[15] See *The Victoria County History of Worcestershire*, II, 54.

[16] See ibid., IV, 45/7.

[17] See *Domesday Survey of 1086 for Herefordshire*, where Lapule is listed 'In Wirecestre Scire'.

[18] It has generally been assumed that Poole Court was near Lostwithiel in Cornwall, where the Trelawney family owned a house at Pool Menheniot, and that Tomkins therefore revisited his ancestral county. However, I am grateful to Mr Henry Sneyd, a Trelawney descendant, for advising me that he has never seen any reference to Pool Menheniot as Poole Court. Furthermore, he advises that it is most unlikely that any Cornish house had the suffix 'Court' attached to its name in the seventeenth century.

Fig. 6.4a Old Pull (Poole) Court House, 1538 to 1798.

Fig. 6.4b Pull Court today.

76   *The Lives and Times of Thomas Tomkins and his Family*

clatter, that self-same area which, three centuries later, was to provide a sanctuary for Edward Elgar, who would cycle out to Longdon Marsh to find peace and inspiration. And there was a good reason why Longdon and the area around it held a very special place in Tomkins's heart.

Alice Patrick had been married to her husband, Nathaniel, Tomkins's predecessor at Worcester, for less than two years when, in 1595, she suffered a double blow: both her husband and her first child died within a few months of each other. Her family home in Tewkesbury was close to the place of her birth, Longdon, where, on 18 April 1563, she was baptized in St Mary's Church. Alice's family, the Hassards, had been yeomen farmers in Longdon and the nearby parish of Castlemorton for many generations:

> Alice's grandfather died a few years before she was born and his probate inventory shows that he was modestly well-off, although he must have lived simply, as most of his assets were tied up in stock and crops. Her father, John, may at first have followed the family tradition in husbandry and farming; certainly he inherited much of his father's stock after his death, and six children were born and baptised at Longdon, of whom Alice was the second. In about 1580 the family moved to Tewkesbury, and more siblings were born so that Alice became one of at least twelve. John Hassard prospered, and by 1584, the year of his death, he was living in Oldburye Street in a house held of the Crown and had also purchased property elsewhere in the town. In his will he styled himself 'gentleman' indicating his rise in social status.[19]

Alice would naturally have introduced Tomkins to her friends and relations in and around Tewksbury and Longdon, and the owners of Pull Court, the Childe family, may well have been on good terms with the Hassards. But in addition, the Childes would certainly have been familiar with the family of Tomkins's prosperous and influential relative, John Tomkins, who also owned property in the Castlemorton area.

William Childe, of Northwick and Pensax in Worcestershire, had purchased Pull Court in 1575. The house remained in his family's possession until 1609, when his grandsons, William, John and Thomas, sold it to Sir John Rous, who in 1628 sold it to Roger Dowdeswell. Tomkins probably knew all three families. Dowdeswell, a lawyer, died in 1633, leaving Pull Court to his eldest son, Richard, a staunch Royalist who, in 1644, was to suffer severely in the cause of the king.

John Aubrey had probably been a guest at Pull Court. Writing in his *Brief Lives* about Sir Walter Ralegh (1552–1618), he recalled that 'in his youth for several yeares he was under streights for want of money. I remember that Mr

---

[19] Richard Newsholme (1996), 'Thomas Tomkins: Domestic Life at Worcester', *Leading Notes* (Journal of the National Early Music Association), 5 (2): 22–5. Details of Hassard wills drawn from Tewkesbury parish registers (GRO); Longdon parish registers (WRO); John Hassard [senior] probate: WRO 1560/237; John Hassard [junior] probate: TNA, PROB 11/84/106LH.

Thomas Child, of Worcestershire, told me that Sir Walter borrowed a Gowne of him when he was at Oxford (they were both of the same College) which he never restored, nor money for it.'[20]

It is possible that the family of the composer William Child, who was born in Bristol in 1606/7 and became organist at St George's Chapel, Windsor, in 1632, was related to the Worcestershire Childes. The Severn flows from Worcester to Pull Court and continues its journey to Bristol, making an easy link between all three places. Tomkins would almost certainly have known William Child, whose compositional style shows some affinity with his own, and it is intriguing to conjecture that he might have taught the younger man, possibly at Pull Court.

Alice Patrick and Thomas Tomkins were destined to wed; she was 34 and he 25. Irrespective of the difference in their ages the match would certainly have satisfied the yardstick considered by contemporary opinion to represent the ideal basis for marriage: equality of rank and religion, and a firm conviction that prudence was of more lasting worth than passion. Thomas Tomkins and Alice Patrick were married in Tewkesbury Abbey on 24 May 1597, and there is no doubt that their lives together were entirely happy.

In addition to 'an old virginal and an old recorder', books, candlesticks, pots and pans, beds and bedding, fire irons, other household items and land in the city of Worcester, Alice inherited £10 'marriage money' from Nathaniel Patrick. This was Alice's dowry, promised to Nathaniel by Alice's mother but never received; it was still owing to him when he made his will.[21]

The couple moved into a house close to Worcester Cathedral known as the Song School, or Choristers' School, situated at the east end of College Green, so-called because of its dual purpose as organist's home and rehearsal room for the cathedral choir. The house comprised 'a hall, a parlour, a cellar, a chamber below and two chambers over, with a little buttery', and here, in 1599, their only son, Nathaniel, named in memory of Alice's first husband, was born.

If growing resistance to conformity was troubling the minds of churchmen, the years embraced by the defeat of the Armada in 1588 and the first three decades of the sixteenth century were to prove a 'golden age' for English musicians. The removal of the threat of invasion from Spain and the snuffing out of conspiracies to dethrone Elizabeth ushered in a period of relative political and religious calm. Composers formerly preoccupied with the necessity of providing newly minted music for Anglican services were, by the latter part of Elizabeth's reign, able in addition to turn their thoughts and talents to secular music intended purely for pleasure: to the composition of madrigals and instrumental music.

---

[20] John Aubrey, *Brief Lives*, ed. Oliver Lawson Dick (London, 1949; 2/1971), 253.
[21] WRO. See E.A. Fry (ed., 1904), *Calendar of Worcester Wills 1451–1600*, London, 69.

It was the work of the Italian school of madrigalists, men such as Luca Marenzio (1553–99) and Costanzo Festa (*c*.1490–1545), which afforded the most important influence on English composers of madrigals. The Italians, in turn, had been influenced by Flemish composers, including Adrian Willaert (*c*.1490–1562) and Jacob Arcadelt (*c*.1505–1568), both of whom were well acquainted with Italy. Willaert had visited Venice, Rome and Ferrara, and Arcadelt had been a singer at the court of the Medici in Florence before being appointed singing master to the boys at St Peter's in Rome and then a member of the college of papal singers. In 1588, a collection of works in the Italian style, *Musica Transalpina*, edited by Nicholas Yonge (d. 1619), was published in London, but instead of retaining the familiar Italian texts, these songs were, for the first time, translated into English. In that same year there followed a collection by Byrd entitled *Psalmes, Sonets and Songs*, only the second collection after *Cantiones sacrae* to be published under Byrd's exclusive licence for printing and selling music.

The full title of Byrd's madrigal set was 'Psalmes, Sonets, & songs of Sadnes and pietie, made into Musicke of five parts: whereof, some of them going abroade among divers, in untrue coppies are heere truly corrected, and th'other being Songs very rare and newly composed, are heere published for the recreation of all such as delight in Musicke: By William Byrd, one of the Gent of the Queenes Maiesties honorable Chappell'. It was in this first set of madrigals that Byrd appealed to his countrymen and women to take up singing:

> Reasons briefly set downe by th'auctor, to perswade every one to learne to sing.
>
> First it is a Knowledge easely taught, and quickly learned where there is a good Master, and an apt Scoller.
>
> 2. The exercise of singing is delightfull to Nature & good to preserve the health of Man.
>
> 3. It doth strengthen all the parts of the brest, & doth open the pipes.
>
> 4. It is a singular good remedie for stutting and stammering in the speech.
>
> 5. It is the best meanes to procure a perfect pronunciation & to make a good Orator.
>
> 6. It is the onely way to know where Nature hath bestowed the benefit of a good Voyce: which guift is so rare, as there is not one among a thousand, that hath it: and in many, that excellent guift is lost, because they want Art to expresse Nature.
>
> 7. There is not any Musicke of Instruments whatsoever, comparable to that which is made of the voyces of Men, where the voyces are good, and the same well sorted and ordered.
>
> 8. The better the voyce is, the meeter it is to honour and serve God there-with: and the voyce of man is chiefly to be imployed to that ende.
>
> *omnis spiritus laudet Dominum.*
>
> Since singing is so good a thing
> I wish all men would learne to sing.

A further volume of madrigals, edited by Thomas Watson and published in 1590, contained a set of 'Italian madrigals Englished not to the sense of the original ditty, but after the affection of the note', i.e. the English words were fitted to the music, contrary to the usual convention of fitting music to words. Thomas Morley (1557–1602), recognized this and promptly set about the composition of madrigals in which English music, albeit still Italian in style, was set to English words – and there could have been no finer time to find such words.

One of England's richest musical periods coincided with an equally golden age of English literature. English poetry and drama of the sixteenth century had moved progressively and magnificently forward, from the imitation of the Italian sonnet by courtier poets such as Sir Thomas Wyatt (1503–42) and Henry Howard, Earl of Surrey (c.1517–47), to the full flowering of works by Sir Philip Sidney (1554–86), Christopher Marlowe (1564–93), Edmund Spenser (1552–99), Ben Jonson (c.1572–1637), John Donne (1572–1631) and, of course, William Shakespeare (1564–1616); English words, and words of quality at that, were everywhere for composers to set, many of them written with exactly that purpose in mind.

Morley, who shared Byrd's Catholic faith and, like Tomkins, was trained by him, published five volumes of canzonets, madrigals and balletts[22] between 1593 and 1597. His most popular works were light-hearted in character, and many English madrigalists, amongst them Orlando Gibbons, Thomas Weelkes, John Wilbye and Thomas Tomkins, were inspired to follow his example. Morley described the madrigal as 'next unto the motet, the most artificial [i.e. artistic; made by art], and to men of understanding most delightful. If therefore you will compose in this kind you must possess yourself with an amorous humour ... so that you must in your music be wavering like the wind, sometime wanton, sometime drooping, sometime grave and staid, other while effeminate ... and the more variety you show the better shall you please'.

It was Morley who wrote the first comprehensive treatise on composition printed in England, the *Plaine and Easie Introduction to Practicall Musicke* (1597), dedicated to Byrd, from whom he took over the patent for the printing of music and music paper in 1598. A copy of the *Plaine and Easie Introduction* was purchased by Tomkins which, thanks to the care of successive owners, has survived without damage. This precious volume, complete with annotations by Tomkins, and bearing his signature upon the title page, is

---

[22] A composition for several voices, generally with a refrain to the words *fa-la*, associated particularly with the name of Giovanni Gastoldi (c.1550–1622). The name 'ballett' (from the Italian *balletto*) indicates that the rhythm was suitable for dancing.

Fig. 6.5   Frontispiece of Thomas Tomkins's own, signed, copy of Morley's *Plain and Easy Introduction to Practical Music*.

preserved in the library of Magdalen College, Oxford, having been left to his Alma Mater by the late Edward Meyerstein (d. 1953); it had previously been in the possession of Arthur Mann (1850–1929), a former organist and choirmaster at King's College, Cambridge, and in a note affixed to the fly-leaf in 1909, Dr Mann explained that:

> This book was formerly in the possession of *WH Monk*, the well known editor of 'Hymns Ancient & Modern'. It came into my possession shortly after his death. I regard this example of a famous book as one of the most valuable copies in existence. Certainly up to the present moment I have not seen one anywhere, to compare with it in any way whatsoever.[23]

In addition to Tomkins's many comments on the text, four canons written by him in the margins of pages 100 and 101 are of particular interest, as are his additions to Morley's list of theorists and composers included on the last page of the *Plaine and Easie Introduction*, purporting to be the 'authors whose authorities be either cited or used in this booke'. Tomkins obviously considered Morley's list of English composers to be lacking: he added the names of Bevin, Mudd, Blitheman, Mundy, Bull, Hooper, Carleton, Gibbons, Warwick, John Tomkins and Morley himself. The name of Thomas Tomkins was added by a later hand.

By 1601 the long reign of Elizabeth I was drawing to a close. In that year Thomas Morley printed a volume containing probably the best-known English madrigal collection, *The Triumphs of Oriana*, twenty-five madrigals by twenty-three English composers dedicated, surprisingly, not to Elizabeth, the 'fair Oriana' addressed, but to her cousin, Charles Howard, lord admiral and earl of Nottingham. Each madrigal closes with a variant of the refrain

> Then sang the shepherds and Nymphs of Diana:
> Long live fair Oriana.

This couplet is actually a translated adaptation of lines from Giovanni Croce's madrigal *Ove tra l'herbe e i fiori*, which had appeared in the second volume of *Musica Transalpina* (1597). The notion of writing a set of madrigals in praise of a single subject, in this case the queen, was itself borrowed from an Italian model of 1592, *Il Trionfi di Dori*, the gift of an Italian gentleman, Leonardo Sanudo, to his bride, in which twenty-nine composers each contributed a single

---

[23] Both Meyerstein and Mann noted, additionally, that Tomkins had been a chorister of Magdalen College in his youth. J.R. Bloxam (1853), in the *Registers of the University of Oxford*, Oxford, I, 27, had listed Tomkins as a chorister of the College, but later realized that this was a mistake, suggesting instead that the person who was a chorister in 1596, clerk in 1604–6, and usher in 1606–10 was in fact Thomas Tomkins's son, Nathaniel. This too was a mistake: Nathaniel Tomkins was not born until 1599 and was, in any case, a graduate (BD) of Balliol College. Denis Stevens has pointed out that the student and usher of Magdalen College who was in residence from 1604 until 1610 'was a Northamptonshire Tomkins, and so far as is known, was not related to the Tomkins family of Cornwall'. See Stevens, 31 and the corrections in the notes to Bloxam's *Registers*, VIII, 139.

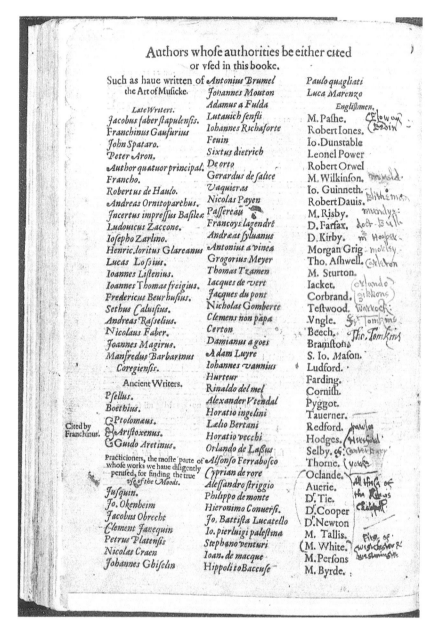

Fig. 6.6 Additions, mostly in the hand of Thomas Tomkins, to his own copy of Morley's *Plain and Easy Introduction to Practical Music*. The names added by Tomkins are those of Bevin, Mudd, Blitheman, Mundy, Bull, Hooper, Morley, Carleton, Gibbons, Warwick and John Tomkins.

Worcester 83

madrigal. Amongst the better-known contributors to *The Triumphs of Oriana* were Thomas Weelkes (*c.*1576–1623); John Wilbye (1574–1638); John Bennet (fl.1599–1614); John Milton (*c.*1563–1647), the father of the poet; and Thomas Morley himself. Tomkins contributed one madrigal, *The Fauns and Satyrs tripping*, the text of which is in a style characteristic of the collection:

> The Fauns and Satyrs tripping,
> With lively Nymphs of fresh cool brooks and fountains,
> And those of woods and mountains,
> Like roes came nimbly skipping,
> By signs their mirth unripping.
> My fair Queen they presented
> In Peace's arms with Amaltheas twenty,
> Brimful of wealthy plenty;
> And still to give, frequented,
> With bare gifts not contented,
> The demi-gods pray to the gods supernal
> Her life, her wealth, her fame may be eternal.
> Then sang the shepherds and Nymphs of Diana:
> Long live fair Oriana.

The Triumphs of Oriana collection sold well and was undoubtedly performed with enjoyment in the homes of the educated classes. Whether it was ever performed before Elizabeth I is unknown, and within two years of its appearance, it was clear that her life was drawing to a close.

On 14 January 1603, in the wind and rain of a dark winter's day, the queen made her final journey from Whitehall to her palace at Richmond. It is likely that the gentlemen and choristers of the Chapel Royal accompanied her, and Tomkins, presumably a gentleman extraordinary by then, may well have been with them. If so, it could have been then that he met for the first time a man who was to play a major part in his life at Worcester: Henry Parry, a favourite chaplain of the queen.

Parry was noted for his sagacity. Elected a scholar of Corpus Christi College, Oxford, in 1576, he graduated BA in 1581, gained his MA in 1585, and became a fellow in 1586. He went on to graduate BD in 1592 and DD in 1596, and soon earned a reputation for great learning, endowed, according to his epitaph, *multiplici eruditione, trium linguarum cognitione*. On Archbishop Whitgift's presentation Parry had held three benefices, all in Kent;[24] whilst in that county he married, and his wife, Elizabeth, gave birth there to her first child, Henry, in 1593. Three other children followed: Richard, George and Pascha.

---

[24] Monkton in 1591–94; Great Mongeham in 1594–96; and Chevening and Sundridge in 1596–1610.

84   *The Lives and Times of Thomas Tomkins and his Family*

Elizabeth I greatly disliked the notion of married priests. It was one step too far from an ancient tradition to which she remained emotionally linked, along with her fondness for vestments, crucifixes and other symbols of the Old Faith. Henry Parry was a clever and ambitious man. No priest was closer to the queen, a queen still pictured in official portraits as a clear-eyed woman with Titian-coloured hair but who, in reality, was now 'aged, toothless, bald and irascible'. A notice that used to stand upon Parry's tomb at Worcester declared that 'he was a bachelor', possibly a nineteenth-century error rather than evidence of a chaplain too nervous to explain his departure from celibacy to a mercurial and quick-tempered sovereign. Certainly Elizabeth cared for Parry to the extent of making him expensive gifts: a china teapot and a silver canister.[25] And it was he who was called to her side during her last sickness.

By the end of February, weak and emaciated, Elizabeth had withdrawn into a private chamber where, barely capable of movement, she lay upon the floor cocooned in cushions. Visited by Sir Robert Carey, she took his hand:

> And wrung it hard, and said: 'no Robin, I am not well', and then discoursed with me of her indisposition, and that her heart had been sad and heavy for ten or twelve days, and in her discourse she fetched not so few as forty or fifty great sighs … The next day … she had cushions laid for her in the privy chamber, hard by the closet door, and there she heard service. From that day forwards she grew worse and worse.[26]

On 21 March the queen was at last persuaded to undress and go to bed. In his memoirs, the Abbé Vittorio Siri related how, as she lay dying, the queen called for her musicians to play around her bed so that 'she might die gaily as she had lived, and that the horrors of death might be lessened'. From then on, wrote the barrister John Manningham, 'she began to lose her speech, and from that time, ate nothing, but lay on one side, without speaking or looking upon any person'. Two days later Henry Parry preached at a service in the chapel at Richmond, 'a very learned, eloquent, religious and moving sermon' on the subject of vows. Whitgift, Manningham, Egerton, Nottingham, Shrewsbury, Worcester, Grey, Sir William Knollys and Sir Edward Wotton were present to hear Parry, 'whose prayer, both in the beginning and conclusion, was so fervent and effectual for her Majesty that he left few eyes dry'.[27]

Manningham, who had arrived that day, 23 March, dined with Parry and three other senior clerics. Over the cooked meats and wine they told him that the queen

> hath been by fits troubled with melancholy some three or four months, but for

---

[25] See J. Chambers (1820), *History of Worcester*, Worcester. Chambers notes that a Mr Nash of Sidbury, whose wife claimed that, by her mother's side, she was a descendant of Parry, had a china teapot and silver canister, given by Elizabeth I to Parry.

[26] Sir W. Scott (ed., 1808), *Memoirs of Sir Robert Carey, Written by Himself*, Edinburgh.

[27] John Manningham (1868), *Diary*, London (Camden Society), 145–6.

Worcester 85

this fortnight extreme oppression with it, in so much that she refused to eat anything, to receive any physic, or admit any rest in bed, till within these two or three days. She hath been in a manner speechless for two days, very pensive and silent since Shrovetide sitting sometimes with her eye fixed upon one object many hours together, yet she always had her perfect sense and memory, and yesterday signified by the lifting of her hand and eyes to heaven, a sign which Dr Parry entreated of her, that she believed that faith which she had caused to be professed, and looked faithfully to be saved by Christ's merits and mercy only, and by no other means.[28]

To Parry, then, fell the lot of reassuring the hierarchy of the established Church that their sovereign did actually adhere to the Protestant faith. Semi-comatose as she was, the slightest flicker of the eyes was counted proof enough.

Elizabeth died on 24 March 1603. Whitgift had remained to pray until late at night when everyone departed, except Parry and a few ladies-in-waiting. Between 2 and 3 o'clock in the morning, 'mildly like a lamb, easily like a ripe apple from the tree' she took Death's hand. Parry 'sent his prayers before her soul', wrote Manningham, 'and I doubt not but she is amongst the royal saints in heaven in eternal joys'.[29]

---

[28] Ibid.
[29] Ibid.

Chapter 7

Awfull Majestie

James I rode south from Scotland in 1603 to an ecstatic welcome from his new English subjects. There is no evidence that Tomkins had written any music for the funeral of Elizabeth I but it is probable that his full anthem for seven-part choir *Be strong and of good courage* (the *Confortare*), published in *Musica Deo sacra*, was composed for the coronation of James I, and this is supported by the inclusion of an anthem beginning with these words in the order of the coronation.[1] Denis Stevens has pointed out that there is some indication that Tomkins's anthems for more than six voices were all early works:

> Certainly *O God the proud are risen* (*a* 8) and *O sing unto the Lord* (a 7) may be dated before 1617, for they are both found in the tenor partbook copied by Jarvis Jones of Oxford in that year.[2] The one other anthem a 7 is *Be strong and of good courage* ... appearing in the list of anthems used at the coronation of James I in 1603. It may well be identical with the one composed by Tomkins, who was then 31 years old. The music for this coronation was in the very capable hands of Nathaniel Giles, a former organist of Worcester, and John Bull, whose name Tomkins had added to the list in his copy of *A Plain and Easy Introduction*. Two of the gentlemen of the Chapel were William Byrd and John Stevens: the former had taught Tomkins, and the latter had befriended him during his early years in London. Both appear as dedicatees in the *Songs* of 1622, and it is therefore not impossible that these four men, Giles, Bull, Byrd and Stevens, who either knew Tomkins personally or were conscious of his growing reputation as a composer, may have been influential in having him invited to compose one of the coronation anthems. Certainly the music is worthy of a great occasion and a fine performance.[3]

Another coronation anthem by Tomkins, *O Lord grant the King a long life*, also published in *Musica Deo sacra*, which does not appear among the anthems sung at the coronations of James I or Charles I, may well have been written specially for national celebration or for local use at Worcester. But there is no doubt that Tomkins's skill had been noticed at court, if not especially so by the new king, who lacked any interest or ability in music, and who, in his treatise on kingly duties, *Basilikon Doron*, had endorsed a widely held view that gentlefolk lowered themselves by excelling in such an activity.

---

[1] J.W. Legg (ed., 1902), *The Coronation Order of King James I* (edited from the Lambeth MS), 10 ff. See also Stevens, 30 and 84.
[2] Bodleian Library, Tenbury MS 1382.
[3] Stevens, 30–31 and 84.

88   *The Lives and Times of Thomas Tomkins and his Family*

Hopes were running high among English Catholics that in James I they would find a monarch more tolerant of their faith. Although he had been brought up as a Presbyterian, James was known not to have any sympathy with Low Church principles. Then, at the Hampton Court conference in January 1604, by which he had intended to isolate the Puritan position, he proclaimed his general satisfaction with the state of the Church, albeit that the English bishops were seeking further reformation.[4] James was prepared to show toleration towards Catholics provided that they would transfer their political loyalty from pope to king, and that their numbers did not increase. 'His remission of the recusancy fines, however, at the start of his reign, soon showed that neither condition was likely to be fulfilled. The fines were renewed and a proclamation issued ordering all Roman Catholic priests out of the country. This was the immediate cause of the Gunpowder Plot.'[5]

Worcestershire, having a high proportion of Roman Catholics among its county families, occupied a central position in the Gunpowder Plot of 1605. The originator of the plot, Robert Catesby, was a cousin of Robert and Thomas Wyntour of Huddington Court, near Worcester. In the aftermath of the failed plot orders were given for a thorough search for Catholic priests and conspirators, and it was in Worcestershire that most of the conspirators 'lay hid in barns and poor men's houses'.[6] The poisoned atmosphere may easily be imagined; neighbours becoming informers; rumour, calumny and gossip filling the air; fugitives and their families cowering in dark holes, seized by terror.

Such profoundly disturbing and scandalous events must have made an immense impact upon Tomkins and the cathedral circle. The bishop of Worcester, Gervase Babbington, was zealous not only as bishop but as magistrate:

> His activity as a magistrate may be seen from the fact that in 1601 there are 51 recognizances of persons bound over in the whole county to appear at Sessions, and of these 12, nearly a quarter, were taken before the Bishop. It was at first difficult to account for this great activity, and I was inclined to put it down to the fact that living in Worcester the Bishop was the nearest available magistrate, and so did most of the work, but as it did not appear that his successors worked in the same way, I discarded this idea, and the true explanation, I think, is the following: There was a court which sat at Ludlow called the Court of the Marches of Wales, a sort of West Midland Star Chamber, which administered, not the law as it was, but the law as its members thought it ought to be. This court was always trying to extend its jurisdiction over Worcestershire ... Among its officers was Babbington. He was Queen's Counsel in the Court of the Marches of Wales. I have not been able to find if the counsel were paid by fees for each case, but it

---

[4] The conference agreed to a new biblical translation, resulting in the Authorized Version of 1611.

[5] MacDonald, *Worcestershire*, 85.

[6] TNA, *Calendar of State Papers Domestic*, James I (1603–10), 283.

Awfull Majestie 89

seems to me that this fact of being counsel accounts for the Bishop's great activity as a magistrate. He was, to use a present day phrase, 'touting' for work in his court.[7]

In Babbington's favour, he does not seem to have actively enforced the law against Roman Catholics or Puritans for not attending church, but his preoccupation with matters legal as well as episcopal at a time of general unrest can have left him little time to take much interest in the music of the cathedral. Things were very different under his successor, Henry Parry.

In 1605, the year of the Gunpowder Plot, Parry had been appointed dean of Chester, remaining there for only two years before being translated to the bishopric of Gloucester, where he will have been aware of the work of Tomkins the elder and John Merro, and where he made 'the pulpit in the body of the church at his own charge'.[8] In 1610 he was appointed bishop of Worcester 'to the great grief' of his former diocese, in which, especially in the cathedral city, he had 'bestowed much on the poor'.[9] He had proved his ability as a preacher in the closing days of Elizabeth's reign, and James I considered him one of the best he ever heard. When James's brother-in-law, Christian IV of Denmark, visited England in 1606 – an occasion for much drunken revelry at court – the Danish king presented Parry with a valuable ring in appreciation for a sermon that he heard him preach at Rochester.

With the accession of James, the long years of maritime war with Spain finally and formally came to an end. The Treaty of London in 1604 gave new impetus to British expansion overseas and the establishment of the first permanent English colonies. Parry took a close interest in these exciting developments, particularly the settlement founded at Jamestown in Virginia in 1607. His name appears in the third charter granted to the new colony by James I on 12 March 1612; he was one of the subscribers to the undertaking, giving the sum of £13. 6s. 8d.

Henry Parry was even more generous to his Alma Mater, Oxford, where in 1602 the Bodleian Library had been opened:

> Sir Thomas Bodley having begun to build the east part of the public library ... the sages of the university considered among themselves, the adding of three more sides to what would make a complete quadrangular pile, wherein the schools of the superior and inferior arts, as also of tongues, might be contained; yet how to bring their minds to pass they knew no other way (Sir Thomas Bodley having been at great charges already to restore the library) than to obtain contributions from those persons that had formerly been of the university.[10]

---

[7] J.W. Willis Bund (1899), 'Religious Life in Worcestershire in the Seventeenth Century, shown by Sessions Records' – a lecture read on 20th January 1899, *Associated Architectural Societies Reports and Papers*, 24 (2): 574–93.

[8] Welander, *History, Art and Architecture*, 351.

[9] *DNB*, 375 (quoting Browne Willis, *Survey*, II, 723).

[10] Anthony à Wood (1792–6), *The History and Antiquities of the University of Oxford*, ed. John Gutch, Oxford, II, 375.

Parry contributed the princely sum of £40, and the dean and chapter, probably at his prompting, added a further £26. 3s. 4d. to the fund. From Tomkins's point of view, by now a composer at the peak of his powers, Parry was exactly the right man in the right place at the right time. Parry's name, unlike that of Babbington, barely features in the Sessions records; he was more devoted to the pulpit than to the bench. Not only was he supportive of the arts but also imbued with vision and an ability to infuse others with his own enthusiasm for worthwhile schemes, one of which, the realization of Tomkins's great desire to have at Worcester an organ built to his own design and worthy of his talents, now became reality. Sixteenth-century reformers such as Hooper had attempted to expel organs from the service of the church. That they failed is affirmed by the flowering of both English organists and organs in the century that followed. Men of the stature of Orlando Gibbons and John Bull earned reputations in Europe as well as in their homeland, and great new organs were built at Durham, Salisbury, and elsewhere.

In 1612 the dean of Worcester, Arthur Lake, and the chapter, authorized the purchase of a new organ, and in the following year the renowned organ builder Thomas Dallam was commissioned to build it. Among Dallam's previous achievements were the organ for King's College, Cambridge (1606) and a mechanical organ, operated either by keys or by a clock, which Elizabeth I sent as a gift, with Dallam himself as escort, to the Sultan of Turkey.[11] At Worcester he created a great organ, a magnificent instrument to rival any in the land. The antiquary Thomas Habington (1560–1647) knew it well, and in 1639 described its appearance on the screen in his *Survey of Worcestershire*:

> At the west and highest ascent into the Choir is mounted aloft a most fair and excellent organ adorned with imperial crowns, red roses, including the white fleurs-de-lis, pomegranates, being all Royal badges. Toward the top are two stars, with the one, 'H. Parry, Episcopus'; with the other, 'A. Lake, Decanus'; and written about the organ: 'By the meditation and mediation of Thomas Tomkins, Organist heere unto the Righte reverend Bishop and venerable Deane, who gave theise munificent guiftes and invited their fryndes by the industry of the said Thomas Tomkins'.

Habington continues at length, giving a comprehensive description of the extensive and colourful heraldry with which the organ was decorated; following this with a long list of the arms of 'honourable and worshipful gentlemen' who subscribed towards the cost of the organ, painted 'on the front of the choir and seat of the organ'.[12] There were over a hundred contributors to the organ fund, Henry Parry and Arthur Lake heading the list

---

[11] For Dallam's diary of his journey to Constantinople see J.T. Bent (ed., 1893), *Early Voyages and Travels in the Levant*, London, Hakluyt Society.

[12] Thomas Habington (1899), *A Survey of Worcestershire*, Worcester (WHS), II, 462–7.

Fig. 7.1 Bishop Henry Parry (1561–1616). A portrait by an unknown artist.

with a donation of 20 pounds each. This list, along with costs and details of the organ are given in a document in the Worcester Cathedral Library.[13]

Anno Dñi 1613

	li	s	d
All the materialls and workmanship of the newe double Organ in the Cathedrall Church of Worcester, to Thomas Dallam organ maker came to … … …	211	00	00
The Case and Joyners worke about the loft to Robert Kettle … … … … … … … … …	68	14	8

---

[13] D248.

92   *The Lives and Times of Thomas Tomkins and his Family*

The floore and loft in Carpenters work about   13   00   00

The guilding and painting to William Peacey   77   08   00

The particulars of the great Organ

Two open diapasons of mettall CC fa ut: a pipe 10 feet long[14]
Two principals of mettal
Two smal principals or 15ths of mettal
One twelfth of mettal
One recorder of mettal, a stopt pipe

In the Chaire Organ
One principal of mettal
One diapason of wood
One flute of wood
One small principal or fifteenth of metal
One two and twentith of mettal
ffor painting the Escutcheons about the loft to
Jo: Davis of Worcester ... ...   <u>11</u>   <u>00</u>   <u>00</u>

                                 381   02   08

The Chair Organ is the small organ in front of the larger one in the view of the Organ on the Screen taken from the Quire. The origin of the name is not clear. The organist sits between the Great and the Chair Organs, with his back to the latter. We tend to think of an organist sitting on a bench rather than a chair, but he could quite well have used a chair when the organ had no pedals. This little organ, a miniature Great, has developed into what is now called the Choir Organ, containing stops suitable for accompanying the choir, though no one would normally confine himself to one manual in his accompaniment. There is no evidence to suggest that the word 'chair' is a corruption of 'choir'. It is clearly and intentionally written as 'chair' or 'chayre'.[15]

Robert Kettle, responsible for the 'case and joyners worke about the [organ] loft', was a versatile man. Not only had he undertaken various tasks in the cathedral in 1611, including working on the bishop's seat and mending the cathedral chimes, he was also retained in that year to look after the clocks and

---

[14] For further information about the term 'CC fa ut' and the pitch of the Worcester organ, see Le Huray, *Music and the Reformation*, 112–13.

[15] Vernon Butcher (1981), *The Organs and Music of Worcester Cathedral*, Worcester, 9.

Awfull Majestie 93

to pump the bellows of the organ, receiving 6*s.* 8*d.* each quarter for each office.[16] More than this, Kettle had also been a lay clerk at the cathedral from 1610; he died in 1627. The nave face of the organ loft was destroyed when a new choir screen was installed in the early nineteenth century, and Kettle's fine workmanship in the cathedral might have been lost altogether when, in 1864,

> remaining panels from the choir side were removed ... with other later woodwork, by an architect, A. E. Perkins, preoccupied with the liturgical correctness of Early English Gothic. Sir Gilbert Scott deplored their removal and they were stored and eventually found a home in Holy Trinity Church, Sutton Coldfield, on the south side of the Vesey chapel. The work uses a wide range of different decorative motifs and displays great vigour and skill.
>
> It is possible that the seventeenth-century overmantel in the Commandery [Worcester] is also the work of Kettle as there is considerable similarity, particularly in the handling of flowers and leaves. The pulpit at Ipsley Church also has similar detail.[17]

The Worcester Cathedral organ used until 1613 had been in place since 1556, when 'a pair of organs was set up on the north side of the quire'.[18] For the visit of Elizabeth I to Worcester in 1575, the Sunday service at the cathedral included 'a great and solemn noise of singing ... in the quire both by note and also playing with cornetts and sackbuts', and cornetts continued to be used in the cathedral well into the seventeenth century.

Although Tomkins now had access to a splendid organ, he continued to encourage the performance of verse anthems,[19] and even full anthems, with instrumental accompaniment. Thomas Myriell, a great friend of Tomkins, and, like John Merro at Gloucester, a skilful music copyist, compiled an anthology in 1616 under the title *Tristitiae Remedium,* now housed in the British Library.[20] Two of the compositions included in the collection were later printed in *Musica Deo sacra* as verse anthems:

> and though Myriell's partbooks contain no organ score, it is perfectly clear that strings or wind instruments, or a mixed consort of both, were expected to play along with the voice parts ... One of the full anthems in this anthology is the justly famous *When David heard,* which appeared in the *Songs* of 1622 with a dedication to Myriell, and again in *Musica Deo sacra.*[21]

---

[16] Worcester Cathedral Library (WCL), A26. See also Patricia Hughes (1990), 'Buildings and the Building Trade in Worcester 1540–1650', unpublished Ph.D. thesis, University of Birmingham.

[17] Ibid.

[18] Butcher, *The Organs,* 7, quoted from Valentine Green (1764), *A Survey of the City of Worcester,* enlarged into *The History and Antiquities of the City and Suburbs of Worcester* (1796), 2 vols. The word 'pair' formerly often meant a set of things, as in a pair of stairs, meaning a flight of stairs, or, as in a pair of trousers, a single item. 'A pair of organs' therefore means 'an organ'.

[19] Anthems in which important sections are assigned to one or more solo voices with independent accompaniment.

[20] BL Add. MSS 29372–7, *Tristitiae Remedium. Cantiones selectissimae diversorum tum argumentorum labore et manu exaratae.* Thomas Myriell. A.D. 1616.

[21] Stevens, 35–6.

94   *The Lives and Times of Thomas Tomkins and his Family*

It was this version of *When David heard* that so arrested the attention of Charles Butler when he heard it in the Music School at Oxford in 1636 and was hard put to it to determine whether he 'should more admire the sweet well-governed voices, with consonant instruments, of the singers, or the exquisite invention, wit, and art of the composer'.[22]

Myriell, a clergyman, was for long thought to have been archdeacon of Norfolk and precentor of Chichester Cathedral. However, Pamela Willetts has been able to identify him positively as having served as rector of St Stephen's Walbrook from 19 September 1616 until his death late in 1625.[23] This appointment, in the heart of London, explains the more easily how it was that Myriell came to be part of Tomkins's circle of close friends, and also how he made the acquaintance of Thomas's half-brother John. Both John Tomkins and Thomas Myriell had been at Cambridge, Myriell matriculating at Corpus Christi College *c.*1596, and receiving his BA degree in 1600–1601, John Tomkins, a scholar of King's College and, in 1606, organist of the chapel, remaining in Cambridge until 1619, when he made his way to London, becoming organist at St Paul's, close to St Stephen's Walbrook.

Myriell included a consort song by John Tomkins, *O thrice-blessed earthbed,* in one of his anthologies, now in the British Library collection (Add. MS 29427), where a full anthem by Thomas Tomkins, *It is my well-beloved's voice,* and one of his verse anthems, *O Lord let me know mine end,* are also to be found. All three men, Myriell and the Tomkins brothers, would also have known Nicholas Yonge, editor of the *Musica Transalpina* anthology of Italian madrigals and lay clerk at St Paul's, and may well have been amongst those who visited his house in Cornhill to make and to enjoy music; as Yonge himself explained in the foreword to his publication:

> Since I first began to keep house in this city, it has been no small comfort unto me, that a great number of gentlemen and merchants of good account (as well of this realm as of foreign nations) have taken in good part such entertainment of pleasure, as my poor ability was able to afford them, both by the exercise of music daily used in my house, and by furnishing them with books of that kind yearly sent me out of Italy and other places.[24]

Jacobean gentlemen soon came to realize that in their Scottish king they had a sovereign who was, in every way possible, different from the fiery, noble, courageous and popular Elizabeth. An account of James I's appearance and behaviour written by a courtier, Sir Anthony Weldon, paints an unattractive picture:

---

[22] Charles Butler (1636) *The Principles of Music,* London (repr. New York, 1970 with an introduction by Gilbert Reaney), 5.

[23] Pamela Willetts (1968), 'Musical Connections of Thomas Myriell', *Music and Letters,* 49: 36–42.

[24] See Monson, *Voices and Viols,* 7.

Awfull Majestie

He was of a middle stature, more corpulent through his clothes than in his body … his clothes ever being made large and easy, the doublets quilted for stiletto-proof … He was naturally of a timorous disposition … his eyes large, ever rolling after any stranger that came into his presence … His beard was very thin; his tongue too large for his mouth, which made him speak full in the mouth and made him drink very uncomely, as if eating his drink, which came out of the cup at each side of his mouth. His skin was as soft as taffeta sarsnet [a thin silk], which felt so because he never washed his hands, only rubbed his finger ends slightly with the wet end of a napkin; his legs were very weak, having had, (as was thought), some foul play in his youth … that weakness made him ever leaning on other men's shoulders; his walk was ever circular, his fingers ever in that walk fiddling about his cod piece … He was very liberal of what he had not in his own grip, and would rather part with £100 he never had in his keeping than one twenty shilling piece within his own custody … A very wise man [allegedly King Henry IV of France] was wont to say that he believed him the wisest fool in Christendom, meaning him wise in small things, but a fool in weighty affairs.[25]

Admittedly, Weldon was a notorious hater of the Scots, dismissed from his post at court for having written a gross libel against the Scottish nation. King James was made to endure much similar and largely unjustified slander. Even so, he had many faults and they were well known. Although an intelligent, well read and learned man, he was constitutionally lazy. He was careless of dress, hating to change his clothes; he drank to excess, particularly in later life, as did his queen, Anne, second daughter of King Frederic of Denmark; and his extravagance was legendary.

Between 1603 and 1612 James spent £185,000 on jewels; pensions given as rewards to courtiers rose by £50,000 to £80,000 a year; expenditure on the household doubled by 1610 and the queen and Prince Henry, James's elder son … had their own lavish households which swallowed up more royal revenue. Elizabeth had spent less than £300,000 a year in peace time. Under James this figure rose immediately to £400,000 and reached a peak of £522,000 in 1614.[26]

He was not greatly interested in women, preferring the company of handsome young men – so it seems hardly surprising that Queen Anne should have turned to alcohol:

[She] was a dull, lazy, frivolous, and at times a somewhat domineering woman with few thoughts for anything more substantial than fine clothes, court balls and masques, and drink; it was on the alcoholic level alone that she had any true meeting-point with her husband. With such a neurotic king and such a hare-brained queen the court inevitably became a byword for sin and sordidness, a vastly different place from what it had been in the time of the great Elizabeth. What had England done, men mused nostalgically, to merit the replacement of their beloved Gloriana with this unworthy Scot?[27]

Many in the kingdom were pinning their hopes for the future upon James's

---

25 Sir Anthony Weldon (*c.*1640), *The Character of King James*, repr. in *Secret History of the Court of King James I*, II, 1–13.

26 Katherine Brice (1997), *The Early Stuarts 1603–1640*, London, 26.

27 Tresham Lever (1967), *The Herberts of Wilton*, London, 73–4.

Fig. 7.2 Henry, Prince of Wales (1594–1612). A portrait drawing by William Hold.

elder son, Henry, prince of Wales, a young man of action, intelligence and discernment who, having been granted his own court by an entirely inartistic father, chose to purchase fine Italian paintings and to engage Alfonso Ferrabosco II as his instructor in music. The French ambassador to the English court, De La Broderie, described something of the character of the prince in a letter of 1606:

> None of his pleasures savour the least of a child. He is a particular lover of horses and what belongs to them, but is not fond of hunting; and when he goes to it it is rather for the pleasure of galloping than that which the dogs give him. He plays willingly enough at tennis, and at another Scots diversion very like mall [probably golf]; but this always with persons older than himself, as if he despised those of his own age. He studies two hours, and employs the rest of his time in tossing the pike, or leaping, or shooting with the bow, or throwing the bar, or vaulting, or some other exercise of that kind; and he is never idle ... He is already feared by those who have the management of affairs, and especially the Earl of Salisbury, who appears to be greatly apprehensive of the prince's ascendant; as the prince, on the other hand, shows little esteem for his lordship.[28]

---

[28] Thomas Birch (1760), *The Life of Henry, Prince of Wales, eldest son of King James I*, 75–6.

Awfull Majestie 97

Although James I would have his elder son pursue only martial arts, Henry was a lover of music and patron of composers. He maintained a large and expensive establishment of musicians at his St James's Palace court, which soon became more popular than that of the king himself. Henry was also, like Elizabeth I, an accomplished and enthusiastic dancer. In 1604, Juan Fernandez de Velasco, duke of Frias and constable of Castile, was sent to England by Philip III as ambassador to negotiate and conclude a peace between this country and Spain. James, whose principal preoccupation was in hunting, was seventy miles from London, engaged in his favourite diversion, when the duke arrived in London. With reluctance he was compelled to break off his hunting and return to the capital. A few days later a ball was held in the duke's honour at which Prince Henry demonstrated his youthful prowess as a dancer:

> There were present at this ball more than fifty ladies of honour, very richly and elegantly dressed, and extremely beautiful, besides many others who, with the noblemen and gentlemen that were present at the dinner, were already engaged in dancing. After a little while the Prince [Henry] was commanded by his parents to dance a galliard, and they pointed out to him the lady who was to be his partner; and this he did with much sprightliness and modesty, cutting several capers in the course of the dance. The Earl of Southampton then led out the Queen, and three other gentlemen their several partners who all joined in dancing a *brando*. In another, her Majesty danced with the Duke of Lennox. After this they began a galliard, which in Italy is called a *planton*; and in it a lady led out the Prince, who then led out another lady whom their Majesties pointed out to him. After this a *brando* was danced, and that being over, the Prince stood up to dance a *correnta*, which he did very gracefully.[29]

Clearly, Michael Drayton had expressed the view of many in the introductory stanza to his long narrative poem *Poly-Olbion*, dedicated to the prince of Wales:

> Britaine, behold here portray'd, to thy sight,
> Henry, thy best hope, and the world's delight;
> Ordain'd to make thy eight great Henries, nine:
> Who, by that vertue in the treble Trine,
> To his owne goodnesse (in his Being) brings
> These severall Glories of th'eight English Kings;
> Deep Knowledge, Greatnes, long Life, Policy,
> Courage, Zeale, Fortune, awfull Majestie.
> He like great Neptune on three Seas shall rove,
> And rule three Realms, with triple power like Jove;
> Thus in soft Peace, thus in tempestuous Warres,
> Till from his foote, his Fame shall strike the starres.

But Henry was not to fulfil his promise. In the autumn of 1612 he began

---

Quoted by David R.A. Evans (1983) in 'Thomas Tomkins and the Prince of Wales', *Welsh Music*, 7 (4): 58.

[29] Rye, *England as Seen by Foreigners*, 123.

to suffer from headaches and tiredness, shrugged these off as trivial, and insisted upon playing a game of tennis 'without wearing sufficient clothing'. Shortly afterwards he became much worse; drop by drop his life ebbed away, and on 6 November, the 18-year-old heir to the throne died of typhoid fever, probably the result of ingesting sewage-contaminated water whilst swimming in the Thames. Thus the nation's future was shackled to the destiny of a flawed prince, Henry's younger brother, Charles (1600–1649).

Giles Fletcher, John Donne and other poets, articulating the sense of overwhelming loss felt by a whole nation, composed elegies on the untimely death of Henry. 'O dearest prince how many hearts were known / To save thy life, that would have lost their own?' asked Fletcher.[30] John Coperario (c.1575–1626)[31] paid homage to Henry in his *Songs of Mourning*, setting words by Thomas Campion (1567–1620), and Thomas Tomkins, John Ward (1571–?1638), Coperario and other prominent musicians of the time, were called upon to write anthems for the prince's funeral. 'When the body of the prince was brought to the Chapel Royal, the choir sang "several anthems to the organs and other wind instruments".'[32] *When David heard* may well have been one of these anthems, and another 'was undoubtedly the highly chromatic and expressive *Know you not*, which Tomkins had hurriedly but devotedly composed for the occasion',[33] setting words provided by Arthur Lake, the dean of Worcester:

> Great Britain mourn, let every family mourn; O family of David, O family of Levi, sorrowing for him as for thy first-born, sob and sing, sigh and say: Ah, Lord, ah, his glory!

---

[30] Giles Fletcher, 'Upon the most lamented departure of the right hopeful, and blessed Prince Henry, Prince of Wales'.

[31] John Cooper, lutenist, violist and composer who studied in Italy and on his return, c.1604, adopted the Italianized name of Coperario.

[32] Birch, *The Life of Henry, Prince of Wales*, 362.

[33] Stevens, 32.

Chapter 8

The Greatest Maecenas

The years of Henry Parry's episcopate in Worcester were also years which saw the publication of the collected works of Ben Jonson, Shakespeare's Sonnets, *King Lear, Troilus and Cressida* and *Pericles*, the writing of *Macbeth, The Tempest* and John Donne's *An Anatomy of the World*. Unlike Thomas Morley, who contributed a setting of *It was a lover and his lass*, and possibly more music, to the production of *As You Like It*, Tomkins, in his search for secular texts, does not seem to have been drawn to the work of England's greatest poet. Morley lived in London in the same parish as Shakespeare – both men appealed against their assessment for taxes, and may well have been acquainted with each other. Tomkins, on the other hand, based in Worcester and when in London busy with duties at the Chapel Royal, chose many of his lyrics from the miscellanies of Elizabethan and Jacobean poetry, gathered together in anthologies long before copyright laws were imposed, and written by persons whose names are unknown to this day.

Among the poets known personally to Tomkins was one who became an especial friend, both to him and to his half-brother John: Phineas Fletcher (1582–1650), whose poem *An Hymn* ('Drop, drop, slow tears, /And bathe those beauteous feet') was set not only by Orlando Gibbons but, with striking originality, by the 15-year-old William Walton in 1917, and in an equally remarkable setting from 1962 by Kenneth Leighton. Both Phineas and his brother Giles (1588–1623) were steeped in the poetry of Edmund Spenser (1552–99), continuing to write in the Spenserian tradition, and both were brothers in holy orders. 'Giles's *Christs Victorie, and Triumph in Heaven and Earth* (1610) is written in 265 eight-lined stanzas, containing many passages of individual beauty and dramatic power. The vigour of his phrase and the loftiness of his aim combine to make him a worthy link in the chain which connects his great master Spenser and his great successor Milton. Phineas wrote much more, and, though just as serious, had a lighter touch. *Brittains Ida, or Venus and Anchises* (1628) is a pretty poem in the style of Shakespeare's *Venus and Adonis*. His immense poem *The Purple Island: or the Isle of Man* (1633) in seven-lined stanzas is colossal in scope, for it proposes to explore man's nature.'[1] John Tomkins and Phineas Fletcher met

---

[1] G. Sampson (ed., 1945), *The Concise Cambridge History of English Literature*, Cambridge, 196.

99

100   *The Lives and Times of Thomas Tomkins and his Family*

at Cambridge; David Evans has written of their friendship, a bond that could not have been closer:

> John's prodigious talent was publicly recognised when at the age of only twenty he was appointed organist at King's College ... It was most unusual for an undergraduate to be given such a position and he fulfilled his duties at King's for the next two years in addition to completing his studies for the degree of Mus.Bac. He graduated in 1608 and probably composed his seven-part motet Cantate Domino for the degree ceremony.

> John spent thirteen years in his post at King's College. During that time he became a close friend of Phineas Fletcher, who was a Fellow there.[2] Fletcher had been born into a literary family and was educated at Eton. In 1600 he entered King's College and by 1608 had secured both his B.A. and M.A. degrees. Success in obtaining his B.D. was rewarded when he was given a fellowship at the college in the summer of 1611. He soon acquired a reputation as a poet among his Cambridge friends, one of whom was John Tomkins. A poem of his entitled 'To Mr. Jo. Tomkins' identifies the composer as Thomalin in *Piscatoriae Eclogues* and *The Purple Island* (both published in 1633).[3]

> Thomalin my lief, thy music strains to hear,
> More wraps my soul, than when the swelling winds
> On craggy rocks their whistling voices tear;
> Or when the sea, if stopped his course he finds,
> With broken murmurs thinks weak shores to fear,
> Scorning such sandy cords his proud head binds:
>   More than where rivers in the summer's ray
>   (Though covert glades cutting their shady way)
> Run tumbling down the lawns, and with the pebbles play.

It seems that Fletcher rated Tomkins's musical abilities highly, and there are a number of references to the King's College organist's prowess scattered throughout his longer poems. The following lines from *The Purple Island* seem to imply that Tomkins was also a capable performer on a string instrument, either a lute or a viol.

> Young Thomalin, Whose notes and silver string
> Silence the rising Lark and falling Swan.

The mention of the 'falling Swan' may well be an oblique reference to a composition by Orlando Gibbons, whose most famous madrigal, *The Silver Swan*, describes the death of this noble bird.

> The silver Swan who living had no note,
> When death approached unlocked her silent throat;
> Leaning her breast against the reedy shore
> Thus sung her first and last, and sung no more.

Fletcher's *Piscatoriae Eclogues* is a lengthy dialogue poem which is divided into seven sections. Only three of the characters are clearly identifiable. 'Thelagon' is Fletcher's father, 'Thirsil' is Fletcher himself, and 'Thomalin' in Eclogues II, VI and VII refers to the young Tomkins. The setting for the poems is the banks of

---

[2] *DNB*, XIX, 316–17.

[3] A.B. Grosart (ed., 1869), *The Poems of Phineas Fletcher*, I–II ; F.S. Boas (ed., 1909), *Giles and Phineas Fletcher, Poetical Works*, II.

The Greatest Maecenas 101

the Cam, where the young men are obviously intent on enjoying themselves in the company of friends both male and female. One of their main pastimes was fishing and there are numerous references to Tomkins's liking for the sport.

> Thomalin, forsake not thou the fisher-swains,
> Which hold thy stay and love at dearest rate:
> Here mayst thou live among their sportfull trains,
> Till better times afford thee better state.

In 1616 it appears that an intrigue forced Fletcher to give up his Fellowship at King's. He took holy orders and served as private chaplain to Sir Henry Willoughby at Risley in Derbyshire for the next five years. In his poem 'To Thomalin', probably written at the time he left Cambridge, Fletcher makes it clear that he was unhappy about the situation. The six stanzas tell how Thirsil, in the depths of despair, was to be parted from his dearest friend.

> Thomalin, since Thirsil nothing has to leave thee,
> And leave thee must: pardon me (gentle friend)
> If nothing but my love I only give thee;
> Since then to other streams I must betake me,
> And spiteful Chame[4] of all has quite bereft me:
> Since Muses selves (false Muses) will forsake me,
> And but this Nothing, nothing else is left me.

During his time at Cambridge he made frequent visits to London, particularly after his half-brother Thomas began to find favour at court as a result of writing his wonderful anthem *Know you not* for the funeral of Prince Henry in 1613. The Tomkins brothers were able to see something of the musical activity of the city and court … In Fletcher's 'To Mr. Jo. Tomkins', presumably written to mark John's departure from Cambridge to London in 1619, the poet gently chides the composer regarding his frequent visits to the capital over the preceding years. The permanent loss of his friend obviously caused Fletcher considerable anguish.

> To thee I here bequeath the courtly joys,
> Seeing to court my Thomalin is bent:
> Take from thy Thirsil these his idle toys;
> Here I will end my looser merriment:
> And when thou sing'st them to the wanton boys,
> Among the courtly lasses' blandishment,
> Think of thy Thirsil's love that never spends;
> And softly say, his love still better mends:
> Ah too unlike the love of court, or courtly friends!

In the third stanza there is a clear reference to one of Tomkins's compositions.

> How oft have I, the Muses bower frequenting,
> Missed them at home, and found them all with thee!
> Whether thou sing'st sad Eupathus lamenting,
> Or tunest notes to sacred harmony.

A second mention of the piece occurs in 'To E.C. in Cambridge'.

> And when me list to sadder tunes apply me,
> Pasilia's dirge and Eupathus complaining;

---

4 The River Cam.

102 *The Lives and Times of Thomas Tomkins and his Family*

The work to which Fletcher refers is surely *O thrice-blessed earthbed,* John Tomkins's only surviving consort song.[5] It is likely that Fletcher himself wrote the words.

O thrice-blessed earthbed,
Under whose happy pressure
All in a sheet more blessed
Lies fast my sleeping treasure.
Pasilia, awaken!
Leave death's cold, too cold pleasure;
No love in death is taken.
But thou with death, aye me,
Aye me, art ever living,
And I in death still live,
In love am dying.
But death's hand is but vain,
Souls to dissever:
We'll live in heav'n again,
We'll live for ever,
No chance shall there pursue
Souls here distressed.
Till then, till then adieu,
Adieu most blessed.

Although it seems John Tomkins had ambitions to be a gentleman of the Chapel Royal, one of the most prized musical posts in the land, he had to content himself with a position as singer at St Paul's Cathedral. The post of organist at the cathedral was not an official one at this time, and those singers who were able to play the organ were obliged to take their turn at the instrument. It is generally believed that he shared the duties of organist there with the composer Adrian Batten. From 1619 onwards John Tomkins's name is regularly mentioned in the cathedral records, which fortunately survived the Great Fire of London in 1666. During Tomkins's period of service at St Paul's the dean was none other than John Donne. It was not long before John Tomkins was making his presence felt in London's musical life. The composer Thomas Ravenscroft included John's psalm-tune *Gloucester* in his *Whole Book of Psalms,* first printed in 1621.[6]

Thomas Tomkins's collection of twenty-eight madrigals, the *Songs of 3, 4, 5 and 6 parts,* was steadily building throughout these years, each a tribute to a friend, relation or colleague. John Tomkins contributed a short dedicatory poem to the collection, a eulogy in praise of Thomas:

Yet thou were mortal: now begin to live,
And end with only Time. Thy Muses give
What Nature hath denied, Eternity:
Gladly my younger Muse doth honour thee,
But mine's no praise. A large increase it has
That's multiplied through strong affection's glass.

---

[5] P. Brett (ed., 1967), *Musica Britannica,* XXII: *Consort Songs,* 32–3.

[6] David R.A. Evans (2002), '"Cerddor euraid": lle John Tomkins ym marddoniaeth Saesneg yr ail ganrif ar bymtheg'. ('"The Golden Pair": John Tomkins: his place in English seventeenth-century verse'), *Taliesin,* 114: 58–68 (published in Welsh).

The Greatest Maecenas 103

> Yet is thy worth the fame, and were no other
> Though as a Judge I spake, not as a Brother.
> This comfort have, this Art's so great, so free,
> None but the good can reach to censure thee.

Thomas's own tribute to his half-brother, John, is in the dedication of the twenty-sixth *Song*, a sacred madrigal, *Woe is me*, based on a text taken from Psalm 120:

> Woe is me! That I am constrained to dwell with Mesech;
> and to have my habitation among the tents of Kedar.

The choice of text is no accident. It is a coded message expressing regret that Thomas is unavoidably parted from his half-brother. The work is thought to have been written in 1619, the year when John moved from Cambridge to his new appointment in London and Thomas was still working full-time at Worcester Cathedral.

The twenty-first madrigal in the collection proves that Fletcher's connection to the Tomkins family was still intact until 1622. *Fusca, in thy starry eyes* is dedicated 'To Mr. Phineas Fletcher' and its text has a link to one of his poetic characters.

> Fusca, in thy starry eyes
> Love in black still mourning dies,
> That among so many slain,
> Thou hast loved none again.

Fusca was the name given by Fletcher to his cruel 'dark lady', of whom in his poem 'To Thenot' he says

> There may I safely sing, all fearless sitting,
> My Fusca's eyes, my Fusca's beauty dittying.

In Thomas's madrigal collection the texts for numbers 12, 16, 22 and 25 have similarities of phrase and rhyme scheme with Fletcher's work, and may well, along with the Fusca madrigal, be by him.[7]

In November 1616 James I conferred the impoverished deanery of Gloucester on William Laud (1573–1645), a dignity which nearly five years later was described by James as 'a shell without a kernel'. Laud, diminutive, red-faced and often bad-tempered, was president of St John's College, Oxford. Already 43 years of age, he had not been honoured by any previous promotion in the Church, but was now given a mandate by the king to set right much that was amiss at Gloucester. No doubt having seen for himself the splendid instrument that had been built at Worcester, Laud turned to Tomkins for advice on achieving a similar standard at Gloucester. Thomas Dallam, probably accompanied by Tomkins, visited Gloucester and found the organ there 'very mean and very far decayed'. On his advice, Laud decided to follow Worcester's example and to appeal for funds, and on 12 March 1616 wrote to

---

[7] Ibid.

104 *The Lives and Times of Thomas Tomkins and his Family*

'the right worshipful our very worthy and loving friends the gentry and others of the county and city of Gloucester':

> We are at this time repairing the decays of the church, and by that charge are utterly disinabled to provide a new organ without the help of such worthy gentlemen and others well disposed as shall approve and endeavour herein within the county and the city. We are led on upon this adventure by the example of our neighbour church of Worcester, which (though it be far better able than our is, yet found this burthen too heavy for them) and therefore took this course with good success to the great honour of the gentry and other inhabitants of that shire. The county of Gloucester is far larger, and we have no cause to doubt but that this county and city will be as forward and bountiful as their neighbours have been.[8]

The appeal failed, the old organ was patched, and nothing more was done about it for more than twenty years. And this is not surprising. From the moment of his arrival in Gloucester, Laud had stirred up a hornet's nest of controversy as a result of his reforming zeal.

> There was not a church in the kingdom which exhibited in more ample measure, the peculiarities of the Calvinistic discipline. Everything was in a state of scandalous disorder. The cathedral was falling into decay: the worship was assimilated, as nearly as it might be, to the service of a conventicle. So notorious, in short, were the irregularities which had long prevailed, that they had excited the attention and displeasure of the King ... The first measure of Laud was to assemble the Chapter, to lay before them His Majesty's instructions, and to procure their consent to two acts, the one, for a speedy reparation of the fabric; the other, for removing the communion table to the east of the choir ... He further recommended to the clergy and to the subordinate officers of the church, the practice of a reverent obeisance on entering the choir; a custom which, at that period, was generally observed in the chapels of the King and of many among the first nobility of the land. But notwithstanding the acquiescence of the clergy, the difficulties which Laud had still to encounter were numerous and formidable.
>
> The Bishop of Gloucester, at that time, was Dr Miles Smith, who owed his advancement to his reputation for Hebrew learning, and to his useful labours as one of the translators of the Bible ... one who had such substantial claims to public respect, was in bitter opposition to the redress of the abuses which deformed his own cathedral – he was an inflexible Calvinist; and so fierce was his resistance to the restoration of order, that, when he heard of the directions, given by Laud, for the removal of the communion table, he vowed that, if the Dean should persist in these innovations, he would never more enter the walls of the church. And, to this resolution, it is said, he faithfully adhered to the day of his death.
>
> It appears that the Bishop had a chaplain, named White, who was quite as intractable as himself, and much more openly turbulent. This man, in the plenitude of his zeal, took upon himself to address an inflammatory letter to the chancellor of the diocese, in which he bitterly complained of the proceedings of the Dean and the tame submission of the Chapter; and expressed his astonishment that not one among them should be found, with a spark of the spirit of Elias in his bosom, to speak a word in God's behalf. The letter soon got

---

[8] See Henry Gee (1921), *Gloucester Cathedral its Organs and Organists*, London, 7–8.

The Greatest Maecenas 105

abroad; a copy of it was thrown into the pulpit of St Michael's Church, where the Sub-Dean usually was the preacher. The parish clerk, having found it there, placed it in the hands of the curate. By the curate it was communicated to others. Copies of it were speedily multiplied. The paper thus became divulged all over the city, which then swarmed with Puritans. A cry against popery was raised, and such was the tumult and confusion, that it became necessary for the magistracy to commit the most violent to prison, to threaten others, with the exaction of security for their peaceable behaviour; and even to take measures for strengthening the local authorities by a reference to the Court of High Commission. In this stage of the matter, the Dean wrote to the Bishop requesting his aid in the control of 'such tongues and pens as knew not how to submit to any law but their own', and stating that, if such outrages were not instantly suppressed, it would become his duty to represent the whole of these transactions to the King. He had but little expectation, however, that the Bishop would be very active in the redress of mischiefs, of which his own chaplain had been the prime mover. He therefore wrote to the Bishop of Lincoln, requesting that he assist him (the Dean) to vindicate the insulted discipline of the Church.

It was some time before the firmness of Laud was rewarded by the restoration of peace and order. In the course of less than a twelvemonth, however … the disorders were effectually reformed. But then, the reformer went forth more indelibly branded than ever with the mark of an incorrigible and malignant papist![9]

Laud was no papist; his first literary work, published in 1624, was as an anti-Roman controversialist. The book in which his views were expressed became the standard defence of Anglicanism against Rome, and, as such, was recommended by Charles I to his children. Laud also held a lifelong commitment to important aspects of Arminianism, a doctrine based upon the teaching of the Dutch Protestant theologian Jacobus Arminius (1560–1609). Calvin had insisted that God preordained the salvation or damnation of an individual, even before his birth. Arminius challenged this, teaching that election to salvation was conditional; atonement universal; that men could achieve nothing good without the Holy Spirit; and that Grace was sufficient for victory over sin, although once gained it could still be lost.[10] Laud totally rejected the notion of predestination. 'My very soul abominates this doctrine', he wrote, 'for it makes God, the God of all mercies, to be the most fierce and unreasonable tyrant in the whole world.'[11]

Arminianism was the antithesis of Puritanism. As early as the 1580s the name 'Arminian' had been given to clergy opposed to Calvinist doctrines, but their principal focus was less upon predestination than upon reviving Catholic ceremony and a sense of continuity within the Church. As Laud advanced along the path of his career, as bishop of St David's in 1621, of Bath and Wells

---

[9] Charles Webb le Bas (1836), *The Life of Archbishop Laud*, London.

[10] Frederick Platt (1908), 'Arminianism', *Encyclopaedia of Religion and Ethics*, Edinburgh, I, 807–16.

[11] W. Scot and J. Bliss (eds, 1847–60), *The Works of the Most Reverend Father in God, William Laud*, Oxford, III, 304–5.

106 *The Lives and Times of Thomas Tomkins and his Family*

from 1626, of London from 1628, and archbishop of Canterbury from 1633, so the Arminian faction in the English Church gained in power, both ecclesiastical and political. Determined to impose conformity on the Church, Laud, never prepared to compromise or to seek reconciliation with his opponents, chose instead, by the use of Star Chamber and High Commission, to impose savage penalties upon those who stood in his way. His removal of the communion table to the east end of the choir at Gloucester in 1616 was, to Laud, no more than a first step in the realization of his vision of an English Catholic Church free from Roman or Puritan influences, a vision that he pursued relentlessly and styled 'Thorough'. Turbulent times lay ahead, the consequences of which, in 1616, would have seemed inconceivable, either to him or to the doughtiest of his enemies.

The music of the Church was a fundamental element in Laud's ideal of Catholic ceremony, essential if the flock were to be brought to faith by beauty as well as by the word. 'It is true', he wrote, 'that the inward service of the heart is the great service of God, and no service is acceptable without it; but the external worship of God in the sanctuary is the great witness to the world that our hearts stand right in that service to God'. At Gloucester, lack of money denied Laud an organ to equal that at Worcester, but Tomkins was soon to find himself in regular contact with this diminutive martinet.

In March 1617 James I set out on a royal progress to Scotland. Laud accompanied him, as did the newly appointed dean of Worcester, Joseph Hall (1574–1656). The royal party arrived in Edinburgh on 16 May and remained in Scotland for three months. The Scots, convinced that James intended to foist Anglican worship upon them, treated the visit with great suspicion. Laud managed to upset local sensitivities by his tactlessness, made worse by his insistence upon wearing a surplice at the funeral of one of the king's guards, but the king, wisely deciding not to press the issue of religious uniformity in the land of his birth, sent Laud home early.

Orlando Gibbons composed a secular verse piece for this royal visit, *Do not repine fair sun*, the text for which was written by Joseph Hall, a churchman who was also a writer of pastoral poems and satires, and who had served as chaplain to Prince Henry. John Merro copied this work into one of his manuscript collections,[12] and its presence there emphasizes once again a connection between the Chapel Royal, Worcester, and Gloucester. Both Hall and Tomkins were Worcester-based, the latter with strong connections of family and friendship in Gloucester. Tomkins seems the most likely link between this courtly composition and Merro, but it also seems possible that he might have travelled to Scotland with his dean and his king.

Already in regular attendance at the Chapel Royal as a gentleman

---

[12] New York Public Library, Drexel MSS 4180–85.

The Greatest Maecenas

extraordinary for some years, Tomkins was among the gentlemen present on 29 June 1620, when Thomas Peirs was sworn gentleman in place of James Davies.[13] In the following year he was appointed as one of the organists of the Chapel, a 'junior' partner to his good friend Orlando Gibbons: '1621. Edmund Hooper, Organist, died the 14th day of July, and Thomas Tomkins, Organist of Worcester, was sworn in his place the second day of August following'.[14]

Laud, who, after initial distrust, enjoyed the confidence of James I, was frequently invited to preach in the Chapel Royal. Tomkins must have heard him there on many occasions; have seen the understanding looks that passed between Laud and his patron, George Villiers, marquess and later duke of Buckingham (1592–1628); and have seen too the more suggestive glances that passed between Buckingham and the man upon whose love his career was built, the king. A very different kind of courtier gained Tomkins's admiration: William Herbert, earl of Pembroke (1580–1630). Both Clarendon in his *History of the Rebellion* and Aubrey in his *Brief Lives*[15] claim that Pembroke was the most universally loved and esteemed young man of his age. He was, wrote Aubrey, 'the greatest Maecenas to learned men of any peer of his time: or since'.

> He was well bred, well educated, a graceful speaker, a ready wit, mild-mannered, affable and charming. He was long at court, yet so disinterested that he was greeted with regard and affection by his fellow courtiers, most of whom were continually clamouring for place. But it must be admitted that his disinterestedness was that of a wealthy, unambitious man with nothing to gain for himself. He liked an easy life; anything, or almost anything, for peace was his motto. He preferred to swim with the tide than strike out manfully upstream against the flow of measures of which he did not approve.[16]

Pembroke held many offices of State; he had been a companion to Prince Henry; chancellor of Oxford University from 1617 (Pembroke College being named after him), and he took an active interest in worldwide voyaging and the colonies in Virginia and Bermuda. He and his brother Philip, 'the incomparable pair of brethren', were nephews of Sir Philip Sidney, joint dedicatees of Shakespeare's First Folio, patrons of poets and friends of letters. Pembroke was himself a poet, albeit that nothing of his was published in his lifetime; a friend of Philip Massinger, Inigo Jones, and John Donne, whose son published a volume of his poetry in 1660; Henry Lawes and Nicholas Lanier set his poems to music; and he was the dedicatee of the Elizabethan anthology *A Poetical Rhapsody*, issued by two brothers, Francis and Walter

---

[13] *Cheque Book*, 47.

[14] Ibid., 10.

[15] Edward Hyde, Earl of Clarendon (1702–4), *The History of the Great Rebellion*, Oxford, I, 71–3; Aubrey, *Brief Lives*, ed. Dick, 144–6.

[16] See Lever, *The Herberts of Wilton*, 74–5.

Fig. 8.1 William Herbert, 3rd Earl of Pembroke (1580–1630). A portrait by Anthony Van Dyck.

The Greatest Maecenas 109

Davison, in 1602. It was to this 'Hamlet of the court'[17] that Tomkins dedicated his *Songs of 3, 4, 5 and 6 parts* in 1622:

MY VERY GOOD LORD

Though it may seem a presumptuous and improper thing for me to present your Honour with a Song, who are daily busied in the great and weighty Counsels and affairs of the King and Kingdom: yet have not my thoughts been wound up to this height, without an appearing reason to myself, of excuse, and pardon at the least, if not of fittingness, and hope of acceptation.

For though your Lordship's employments be daily, yet hath the Day many hours, and if you should bestow all of them on sad and serious matters, you might shorten them, and deprive us too soon of the benefit both of your Counsels and Actions. Besides (if I may presume to give your Lordship any account of my poor self) I first breathed, and beheld the sun, in that Country, to which your Lordship gives the greatest lustre, taking the Title of your Earldom from it, and even therefore have always (I know not by what secret power of natural affection) ever honoured and wished your Lordship's prosperity. To which considerations may be added that goodness of nature, eminent in your Lordship, was ever a friend to Music, and the known virtues of your mind, which seems to be best in tune, in those who love Music best, as being least distracted by low cogitations, and your often frequenting and favourable attention to the Music in the Chapel, which useth sometimes to raise the soul above her Companions, Flesh and Blood; as also the place which you hold under His Majesty, which consequently renders you, a Patron and Protector of Music.

Concerning the Songs, if they shall be found answerable to the desire and affection of their indulgent parent: I beseech your Honour to consider, that as there are few men absolutely perfect, save only in contemplation; so neither is more clearness to be expected in the rivers, than in the spring, not more perfection, in imperfect men's contemplations, or works of this kind.

For the lightness of some of the words I can only plead an old (but ill) custom, which I wish were abrogated: although the Songs of these books will be even in that point, suitable to the people of the world, wherein the rich and poor, sound and lame, sad and fantastical, dwell together.

Lastly, I do again most humbly beseech your Lordship to pardon my presumption, and to accept of these my imperfect offers, who will offer my prayers to God for your Lordship, that you may enjoy a happy and blessed Harmony in the whole course of your life, (between yourself and your friends, your body and mind) to the end that you may have content (which is the best kind of Music) here, and the Music of the Angels hereafter.

> This is, and shall be, the prayer of
> Your Honour's most humbly devoted
> in all observance and duty,
> THOMAS TOMKINS

In seeking an aristocratic patron, and in common with his contemporaries Shakespeare, Jonson and Donne, Tomkins was clearly hoping for something well beyond mere financial support. An overriding motive for any creative artist seeking such a seal of approval had, ever since the patronage of Virgil

---

17 S.R. Gardiner (1893), *History of England, 1603–42*, VII, 133.

110   *The Lives and Times of Thomas Tomkins and his Family*

and Horace by Caius Maecenas, been the desire for widespread personal recognition. Tomkins must have been hoping that the reflected glory of Pembroke would boost his own reputation in a way not to be expected from long years of service to the Church; he desired fame and knew himself to be worthy of it.

As we have seen, Tomkins dedicated each of the twenty-eight *Songs* to individual members of his family and to friends, as well as collectively to the earl of Pembroke. He was the only English madrigalist to do this, albeit that the practice was well established in Italy. The first song in the collection is dedicated to Tomkins's father; the last to his son, Nathaniel. His five half-brothers – Giles, John, Nicholas, Peregrine and Robert – are all included, as are the composers John Coperario, William Byrd, Orlando Gibbons, John Ward, and two great lutenists, John Danyel and John Dowland. Worcestershire friends are there too: Humphrey Withy, Henry Moule, Nicholas Carlton and Nathaniel Giles.

Tomkins would have known Giles at the Chapel Royal, but he was also a Worcester man and, as we have seen, one of his predecessors as organist at the cathedral; his son, Nathaniel Giles, came to Worcester as a minor canon in 1626. Many members of the Chapel Royal appear as dedicatees of the songs; in addition to Byrd and Gibbons we find the names of William Cross, Thomas Day, John Stevens and Thomas Warwick.

It may be that Cross was familiar with Monteverdi's seventh book of madrigals, published in 1619, and had introduced Tomkins to it. One of Monteverdi's madrigals, *Con che soavità*, a setting of a text by Guarini, is paraphrased by Tomkins in his own madrigal *How great delight*, dedicated to Cross.

> Cross was associated with the gentlemen of the Chapel Royal as early as 1603, when he signed an admonition prepared by the sub-dean, and his name is found again, along with that of Thomas Tomkins, in a document dated June 29, 1620. Day's name is appended to the same document: he seems to have joined the choir in 1615, after having been in the establishment of Prince Henry. He served as organist of Westminster Abbey from 1625 until 1632, becoming master of the children of the Chapel Royal in 1636. John Stevens was one of the senior members of the choir. He was sworn in place of Thomas Wiles, in 1590, and is often named 'Recorder of Songs', which means that he copied much of the music used in the Chapel.[18]

Tomkins dedicated the madrigal *When I observe* to Thomas Warwick, a gentleman by birth, descended from a leading Cumberland family. Rimbault tells us that in Sir Edward Bysshe's Visitation of Kent, Warwick's father, Thomas, is styled 'of Hereford', where the son was probably born. John Davies of Hereford (1565–1618), in his *Scourge of Folly* (1611), has a short

---

[18] Stevens, 41–3.

The Greatest Maecenas   111

poem 'To my dear friend, countryman and expert master in the liberal science of music, Mr Thomas Warwick'.[19] He was one of the royal musicians for the lute in 1625, and Wood maintains that he composed a song of forty parts, which, about 1635, was performed before Charles I by members of the royal band and their friends. He was elected an organist of the Chapel Royal in 1625, where he worked with Tomkins and befriended him.

Thomas Myriell, the compiler of *Tristitiae Remedium*, takes his place in the collection of *Songs*, as does William White of Durham, two of whose anthems were included by Myriell in his anthology. White was a member of the choir of Westminster Abbey at the time of Queen Elizabeth's funeral, and he and Tomkins might have met on that or some other occasion of state when both were in London. The dedication of *Fusca, in thy starry eyes* to Phineas Fletcher has been mentioned above. A particularly fine five-part ballett, its quality reflects the high esteem in which Tomkins held the man whose friendship was as important to his half-brother John as to himself. Fletcher wrote a play for the visit of James I to King's College, Cambridge, in 1615 but the king left before the play was staged, leaving the poet distraught; he became rector of Hilgay, Norfolk, in 1621 and spent the rest of his life there.

Two of the dedicatees, William Walker and Robert Chetwode, have yet to be identified conclusively; they might have been among Tomkins's London friends, or even members of the Worcester business community. Two others remain: William Heather and Theophyllus Aylmer. Tomkins dedicated the ravishing *Music divine* to Heather, and drew upon the Song of Solomon 2: 8 for the sacred madrigal *It is my well-beloved's voice* for Aylmer.

> 'Mr. Doctor Heather', as Tomkins calls him, was a native of Harmondsworth, Middlesex, and he perpetuated his name in the professorship of music at Oxford, which he founded in 1626, the year before his death. Although Heather was not formally admitted to the Chapel Royal until 1614, his connection with it must date from the early part of the century since he signed a document prepared by the sub-dean in 1603.[20] Aylmer, like Heather, enjoys the prefix 'Mr. Doctor', but his doctorate was in divinity, not music. Theophilus Aylmer was a son of John Aylmer, bishop of London (the family name is variously spelt Ailmer or Aelmer). A prebendary of St. Paul's in 1583, he served for a short time as rector of Much Hadham in Hertfordshire before coming to London as archdeacon. He was a prominent figure in the city for nearly thirty-five years, and although his connection with Thomas Tomkins is not a particularly direct or musical one, it is clear that the two were well acquainted.[21]

Tomkins was clearly self-conscious about setting texts that he considered somewhat frivolous: 'an old (but ill) custom, which I wish were abrogated'. His inclusion of sacred madrigals in the 1622 *Songs of 3, 4, 5, and 6 parts* (*It*

---

[19] *Cheque Book*, 207.
[20] *Cheque Book*, 70.
[21] Stevens, 44.

112   *The Lives and Times of Thomas Tomkins and his Family*

is my well beloved's voice, *Turn unto the Lord*; and *Woe is me that I am constrained*) hints at an insistence upon embodying, whilst a rare opportunity for publication was available to him, at least a representative selection of his best sacred work in a collection designed for secular use. *When David heard* is alone amongst his sacred madrigals in appearing in both the 1622 *Songs* and the posthumous *Musica Deo sacra* of 1668, suggesting that a piece written for secular use, and dedicated to Thomas Myriell, had also found a liturgical setting.

In his search for suitable texts for sacred works, Tomkins almost always turned to Holy Writ: the Psalter, the Prayer Book, or less frequently, the Bible. In only three of his sacred works did he choose to set devotional verse. The text of *Not in the merits of what I have done* is by an anonymous writer, but the words of *Leave, O my soul* and *Above the stars* might well have been written by Joseph Hall during his time as dean of Worcester. The composition of music for the church remained Tomkins's first concern; in 1621 his psalm tunes *Dunfermline* and *Worcester* had been published in Ravenscroft's *The Whole Book of Psalms*, but he was to see nothing more of his large output of anthems and services committed to print in his lifetime.

It has been generally accepted that the *Musica Deo sacra* anthology, full title *Musica Deo sacra et ecclesiae Anglicanae: or Music dedicated to the Honor and Service of God, and to the Use of Cathedral and other Churches of England*, was edited and brought to publication by Tomkins's son, Nathaniel. Research by John Milsom has now established this beyond doubt, and also that the set of *Musica Deo sacra* at Christ Church, Oxford (Mus. 698–707), was Nathaniel's master copy. Dr Milsom has revealed that Nathaniel not only corrected the printed pages of the Christ Church *Musica Deo sacra*, but also added four verse anthems in manuscript at the end.[22] One of these, *Know you not*, is Thomas Tomkins's funeral anthem for Prince Henry; the other three, which are incomplete, are almost certainly by him, although for long thought to be Anonymous Anthems[23] – *Have mercy upon me, O God*; *O Lord, let my mouth be [filled with thy praise]*; and *O God, the heathen are come into thine inheritance*.

The *Musica Deo sacra* collection contains the First, Second, Third (the 'Great' Service), Fourth and Fifth Services, a set of Preces and Psalms (15 and 47) and 94 anthems, 53 of which are 'full', and the remainder of which are 'verse' anthems.[24] It is in five volumes, four of which are voice parts; the fifth

---

[22] John Milsom (2001), 'Tracking Tomkins', *Musical Times* (Summer), 54–63.

[23] Nos 150, 267 and 296 in Ralph T. Daniel and Peter Le Huray's catalogue *The Sources of English Church Music 1549–1660* (Early English Church Music, Supplementary vol. 1 (London, 1972)).

[24] Seventeenth-century 'full' anthems were written like the continental motet, i.e. for a number of voices with or without organ doubling, or 'verse', in which sections for solo voice or voices alternated with the full chorus.

The Greatest Maecenas   113

is the Pars Organica, or organ part. This last contains the independent accompaniments to the solo voice parts in the verse anthems and, as typically found in manuscript organ books of the time, incomplete sketches of the full vocal scores. In addition, there is a quantity of surviving sacred music by Tomkins that is not included in *Musica Deo sacra*. This comprises eight full anthems, four of which are fragmentary; ten verse anthems (in addition to the three attributed to Tomkins by John Milsom and listed in the previous paragraph), seven of them fragmentary; two verse services, one of which is incomplete; Preces and Responses; two Litanies; and the two metrical psalm tunes published by Ravenscroft.

Editors have sometimes criticized the lack of accuracy in Nathaniel Tomkins's editing of *Musica Deo sacra*, especially his lapses of precision in the correct underlay of text to music, but it is entirely to Nathaniel's credit that the lion's share of his father's sacred music has been preserved. Because of Nathaniel's selfless labour of love, a greater number of compositions for the English Church have been left by Thomas Tomkins than by any other composer of the sixteenth and seventeenth centuries.

Chapter 9

Sceptre and Crown

> He was the author of his line –
> He wrote that witches should be burnt;
> He wrote that monarchs were divine,
> And left a son who – proved they weren't!
>
> (Kipling, *James I*)

Bishop Henry Parry and William Shakespeare died in the same year, 1616, Parry suffering a fatal stroke at his palace in Worcester on 21 December. During the six years of his episcopate he had, as at Gloucester, proved himself a generous benefactor to the poor, and not only in the city: his influence was felt throughout the county and at least as far north as Alvechurch, where he was lord of the manor. A measure of the affection in which the people of Worcestershire had held him was to be found perhaps in the magnificence of his tomb in the north-west transept of their cathedral: a splendid memorial, which, sadly, was removed during restoration work in the nineteenth century. His effigy lay under a semicircular arch, enclosed by pillars and surmounted by a classical cornice. In the spandrels were emblems of Time and Death, and in the centre the arms of the see, impaling argent the arms of the Parry family.[1] On the right pillar were the arms of the See, and on the left the arms of the See of Gloucester.

Parry's successor, John Thornborough, was a man of a very different stamp. Like Parry, Thornborough had been one of the chaplains to Queen Elizabeth I. His zeal in upholding the rights of the Crown when he was bishop of Limerick from 1593 to 1603 had gained him the reward of an English bishopric. He was translated to Bristol in 1603 and then, after Parry's death, to Worcester, in spite of fierce opposition from the king's favourite, the duke of Buckingham, who coveted Worcester for his relative, Henry Beaumont. William Laud, frequently haunted by vivid dreams, was, on one occasion,

---

[1] A fesse between three Lozenges Azure, on the fesse an Annulet Or for difference (Parry). A brass plaque in the north wall of the north-east transept at Worcester records that the remains of Henry Parry's effigy were removed in 1872 to a medieval recess in the south side of the nave, where it remains. However, since it is the custom that effigies lie with the feet towards the east, the transfer from the north to the south side of the cathedral resulted in the only substantial fragment of Parry's effigy being concealed against the wall.

116 *The Lives and Times of Thomas Tomkins and his Family*

terrified by a nightmare in which Thornborough appeared to him, his head and shoulders draped in shroud-like white linen. Thornborough remained at Worcester until 1640.

> To him more than to anyone else is to be attributed the dislike that arose in the West Midlands to episcopacy. He was an out-and-out supporter of the policy of 'Thorough'. As he had enforced the royal will in Ireland, so he enforced it in Worcester. The result of the change is well shown by two entries in the rolls [of Quarter Sessions]. In 1618 Robert Briggs was committed for trial at the Sessions for 'speaking certain words against the Bishop of Worcester'. Again in 1620 William Hunter was committed to Sessions for 'that he used opprobrious words against the Bishop of Worcester'. These charges were brought under the Statute of Richard II, against speaking evil of the great men of the realm. No trace of anything of the kind appears under either of the episcopates of Babbington or Parry.
>
> To make matters worse, in 1629 Thornborough appointed his son [Edward] Archdeacon of Worcester, and so obtained a hold over the diocese that enabled him to work out his policy of supporting the royal power.[2]

Nepotism brought Edward Thornborough to his position, but he appears to have spent very little of his time in Worcester. He attended his installation as archdeacon in person, but his stipend there seems to have been invariably signed as received by someone else on his behalf. Edward Thornborough's brother, Giles Thornborough, was a canon at Salisbury Cathedral, and at Laud's visitation there in 1634, Article 15 is answered, 'Mr Gyles Thornborough and Mr Edward Thornborough … reside and keep continuall hospitality at the Cathedrall Church'. Tomkins's brother Giles was organist at Salisbury by 1630, and there is evidence to suggest that the Thornborough brothers and the Tomkins brothers were friends. Edward Thornborough was probably, in addition, a fair virginals player. Three of Tomkins's *Verses* (or *Voluntaries*) for keyboard, dedicated to Edward, survive.[3] Perhaps these were performed at musical evenings in Salisbury, but it is also possible that on his rare visits to Worcester Edward Thornborough was an occasional member of a group of Thomas Tomkins's musician friends, a group that included Humphrey Withy and his younger brother, John, both of whom trained under Tomkins as choristers at the cathedral.

The Withy brothers were descendants of Jasper and Joane Withy of Claines, a village some three miles north of Worcester, now a suburb of the city. Humphrey Withy (1596–1661), who seems to have been a particularly close friend of Tomkins, was the dedicatee of the madrigal *Sure there is no god of love*. He had been a chorister at Worcester Cathedral, remaining there as a lay clerk until his death in 1661. He also acted as sub-deacon and librarian,

---

[2] J.W. Willis Bund (1899), 'Religious Life in Worcestershire in the Seventeenth Century, shown by the Sessions Records', *Associated Architectural Societies Reports and Papers*, 24 (2).

[3] Bodleian Library, MS Mus. Sch. C93. The dedication 'For Mr Arc Thorneborgh' is in Thomas Tomkins's hand; the more informal 'for Edward' is not.

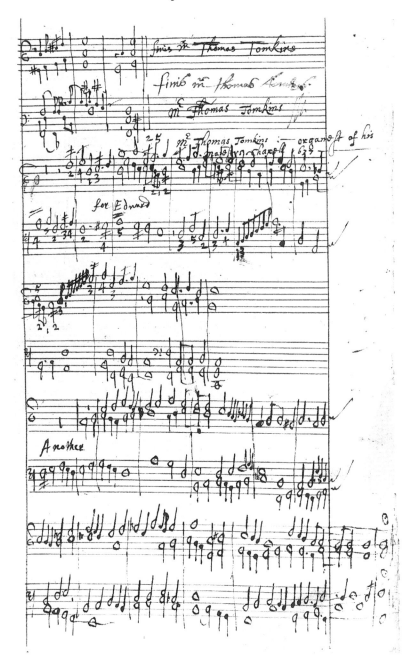

Fig. 9.1 The ending of the *Offertory*, signed 'Mr Thomas Tomkins:– organist of His Majesty's Chapel, 1637'. Two short pieces 'for Edward' – Edward Thornborough, archdeacon of Worcester.

118 *The Lives and Times of Thomas Tomkins and his Family*

deacon and sub-treasurer, and eventually clerk of works and verger. In 1631 the Oxford clergyman Samuel Fell was appointed master of St Oswald's Hospital in Worcester's northern suburb. The building had fallen into ruin after the Reformation, but Fell was successful in restoring the property and generating sufficient rents to fund the building of a new almshouse and chapel. Humphrey Withy was the steward of the project, responsible to Fell for overseeing the construction work and administration of the hospital. Erection began in 1633 and continued until 1642. Samuel Fell went on to become dean of Christ Church, Oxford, and vice-chancellor of the university.

John Withy (*c.*1600–1685), on the other hand, devoted his entire life to music. Anthony à Wood wrote that he was 'excellent for the lyra viol and improved the way of playing thereon much', a view confirmed by John Playford who, in his *Musick's Recreation on the Viol, Lyra-way* (London, 1669), described John Withy as a 'famous master' of the instrument. A number of lyra viol pieces by John Withy are known, some of them published by Playford, and a set of parts of fantasias and dances composed by Withy, Facy, Gibbons, Jenkins and Tomkins is preserved in an anthology once in Withy's own possession: 'John Withie his Booke'.[4]

Wood also described John Withy as 'a Roman Catholic and sometime teacher of music in the citie of Worcester'.[5] This surprising divergence from his Anglican roots is perhaps consistent with Withy's presence in London in the late 1630s and his composition of a song for one of Richard Brome's plays of romantic intrigue, *The English Moore*, performed in 1637 or 1638 by Queen Henrietta's Company at the Salisbury Court Theatre. A company bearing the name of a Roman Catholic queen, who herself delighted in appearing in amateur dramatics, may well have shown favour by giving employment to a songwriter of the same religious persuasion. Music was an integral part of several of the plays performed by the Queen's Company, and John Withy may have provided much of it. None the less, he appears to have left London by the early 1640s and returned to Worcester, where he resumed his life as a music teacher and his association with Tomkins, and where, described as a 'popish recusant', his name appears frequently in churchwardens' and constables' presentments of the 1660s. Towards the end of his life, probably weary of social smear and religious persecution, he appears to have returned to the Anglican fold.

John Withy's son, Francis (*c.*1645–1727), continued the musical tradition. A string player, music copyist and composer, he was a singing man at Christ Church, Oxford, from 1670 until his death.[6] Another prominent member of the family,

---

4 Rochester (New York), Sibley Music Library. (See List of Works.)

5 Bodleian Library, MS Wood D19 [4], fol. 136.

6 See Robert Thompson (1991), '"Francis Withie of Oxon" and his Commonplace Book, Christ Church, Oxford, MS 337', *Chelys* (journal of the Viola da Gamba Society), 20.

Sceptre and Crown 119

Richard Withy (1607–*c.*1669), a successful and prosperous lawyer, became attorney to the city council at Worcester, where, in former times, the Withys were honoured by the naming of a street: Withy Walk (now St Paul's Street).

In an incomplete set of instrumental partbooks from Worcester, possibly in Humphrey Withy's hand and passed down to his nephew Francis,[7] the names of Thomas Tomkins, Humphrey Withy and John Withy are to be found along with the dates 1641 and 1642. All three clearly performed in a consort of viols, and it may be assumed that Tomkins and his musician friends would have met informally in each other's houses for the relaxing pleasure of making music together; perhaps some of their wives were instrumentalists too; and maybe these friends also entertained a wider public.

Henry Moule (or Molle, or Mowle, pronounced 'Mole'), a close friend of Tomkins, was the usher, i.e. second master, at the King's School, Worcester, until he succeeded to the mastership (headmastership) in 1627, serving the school for well over half a century in total. Four years older than Tomkins, he had matriculated at St Mary Hall, Oxford (now united with Oriel College), in 1584, aged 16, and took his BA from All Souls in 1589, the year of his arrival in Worcester. By this time he had changed his name from Randall or Randolph to Moule. Humphrey Withy's first wife, Margaret Moule, may well have been Henry Moule's daughter. Tomkins dedicated *Phyllis, now cease to move me* to Moule, who, in addition to his school duties, 'held the combined livings of Knightwick and Doddenham, near Broadwas, from 1598, and added that of Fladbury, near Evesham, in 1619, holding them both with the mastership till he died, about seventy-five years old, in 1643'.[8] In his poem 'Upon losing his Way in a Forest', the dramatist and poet Thomas Nabbes, a King's scholar from 1616 to 1620, poked gentle fun at one who, it has been suggested, was his one-time teacher:

> Thou cunning Moule that knowst to work thy way
> Through thickest mysteries to the cleerest day
> Of radiant knowledge, was not this dayes fate
> Writ in thy booke of Moones predestinate
> For grief or danger? Yes thou know'st was writ;
> And by prevention couldst have hindered it.
> But 'twas my error onley: had she shone
> I could have read it plainly in the Moone:
> For such thy powerful art is, it can bind
> The starres in characters to speake thy mind.

In a footnote, Nabbes explains that the 'cunning Moule' was 'an astrologer in the company that maintained a *nuncius inanimatus* to bee effected by the beames of the Moone, and many other ridiculous things'. Amongst Nabbes's

---

[7] Bodleian Library, MS Mus. Sch. E415–18.
[8] Alec MacDonald (1936), *A History of the King's School Worcester*, London, 113–14.

poems is an 'Encomium on the Leaden Steeple at Worcester', in which he celebrates the detached belfry, demolished in 1647, which stood just outside the Bishop's Chapel to the north of the cathedral. His plays included *Hannibal and Scipio,* an historical tragedy, and *The Unfortunate Mother,* a tragedy that failed to find a place in any theatre, whereas his three comedies, *Covent Garden, Tottenham Court* and *The Bride,* all of which belong to the 1630s, are acknowledged to have included his best work.

Tomkins and Nabbes may well have been acquainted through the Moule connection, and have met in both Worcester and London. After some time in the employment of a nobleman near Worcester, Nabbes settled in London, but in his 'Encomium on the Leaden Steeple' he expressed a wish to be buried in Worcester Cathedral. It seems, however, that he was buried in the Temple Church in London. At the time of his death in 1909, Swinburne was engaged in an essay on Nabbes, but the Stuart playwright's work is all but forgotten now.

Thomas Nabbes was among numerous contributors of dedicatory verses prefixed to *Worcester's Elegie and Eulogie,* the work of his fellow pupil at the King's school, John Toy, a minor canon who became master of the school following the death of Henry Moule's successor, Thomas Taylor. Toy, like Moule before him, was to become a close friend of Thomas and Alice Tomkins. A mild and scholarly man, Toy was the author of a few books, all of which are wholly forgotten. Even so, Anthony à Wood afforded him space in his *Athenae Oxoniensis:*

> John Toy, son of John Toy, was born and bred in Grammar Learning within the City of Worcester, became either a Servitor or Batler of Pembroke College in 1627, aged 16 years, took one degree in Arts, entered into Orders, and became Chaplain to the Bishop of Hereford; under which title he took the degree of Master of Arts in 1634. Afterwards he was made Master of the Free, then of the King's School within the place of his nativity; which last he kept for twenty years space, and furnished the Universities with several hopeful youths.[9]

Humphrey Withy, Henry Moule and John Toy were all, at various times, near neighbours to the Tomkins family in College Green. Other friends, such as the Childes of Poole Court, lived further afield, and among these was the composer Nicholas Carlton, dedicatee of Tomkins's madrigal *Phyllis, yet see him dying,* whose home was at Beoley in the north of the county. Tomkins included Carlton's name among those that he added to the list of composers printed on the last page of Morley's *Plain and Easy Introduction to Practical Music,* an indication of the high regard in which he held his friend's music. Carlton wrote one of the earliest known examples of a keyboard duet under the title *A Verse for two to play on the Virginal or Organ,* which Tomkins copied out in his own hand into one of his anthologies[10] along with pieces by other

---

[9] Wood, *Athenae Oxoniensis,* II, 223.
[10] BL Add. MS 29996.

Sceptre and Crown 121

contemporaries, including Byrd, Gibbons, Ferrabosco, Farmer and Morley. Inspired by Carlton's innovative work, Tomkins added 'another of the like' of his own to the same manuscript, the *Fancy: for two to play*, and it is not difficult to imagine the two friends sitting side by side at the virginals, good-humouredly making music together. Carlton died in 1630, naming Thomas Tomkins in his will as his 'singular and esteemed good friend' and nominating him as co-executor of his estate in Beoley.

Tomkins was fortunate in his friends and in his happy marriage. Both must have been strained by the nature of his dual responsibilities to both Worcester and London, and after his appointment as an organist of the Chapel Royal in 1621 it is probable that he would have been required to spend an even greater proportion of his time at court than in former years. He was already in his fiftieth year, but, with energy apparently undiminished and in good health, he continued to face the long and tiring journeys across country.

By the end of January 1625 the health of James I was in steep decline. On 27 March, William Laud, by then the bishop of St David's, was preaching the mid-Lent Sunday afternoon sermon to a large gathering of courtiers in the Chapel Royal at Whitehall. Suddenly, he was aware that his congregation had been distracted by some news brought into the Chapel, a look of anguish spreading across their faces. The king was dead. Laud broke off his sermon and stepped down into the nave, the better, he later claimed, to be able to comfort the bereaved.[11]

To Tomkins, as organist, now fell the double responsibility of attending to the music for two royal occasions: the funeral of the king on 7 May, and subsequently for the coronation of Charles I on 2 February 1626. In both of these major undertakings he was assisted by three senior members of the Chapel, all of whom were, as we have seen, his close personal friends and dedicatees of madrigals in his *Songs* of 1622: William Heather, John Stevens and Nathaniel Giles. Heather was a singer in the Chapel; Stevens, the recorder of songs; and Giles, master of the children. Although present as senior organist at the funeral of James I, Orlando Gibbons seems not to have composed any music for this most important occasion of state, an indication perhaps that his health was poor, thus adding considerably to Tomkins's burden.

A full account of the order of the funeral, written by the sub-dean of the Chapel, Stephen Boughton, is preserved in the Cheque Book, but unfortunately, although Tomkins would have composed much of the music, no record of it remains. However, Peter James has suggested that the verse

---

[11] Peter Heylyn (1668), *Cyprianus Anglicus, or the History of the Life and Death of William Laud*, London, 131–2.

122   *The Lives and Times of Thomas Tomkins and his Family*

anthem *Death is swallowed up* (not included in *Musica Deo sacra*) might have been written on the death of James I, and this remains a distinct possibility (see Chapter 18).

> [The king's] dead corpse were [*sic*] brought from Theobalds to Denmark House … where all his officers attended and waited during the time that his corpse lay there, except the Chapel, who waited upon King Charles at Whitehall.
>
> At Denmark House the hall there was made a chapel for the time, where the confessor read morning prayer daily, and upon Sundays one of the chaplains preached: the desk was covered with black cloth …
>
> Two days before the day of the funerals the corpse was brought into the said Chapel in great solemnity with an anthem, and set under a hearse of velvet, and the gentlemen of the Chapel from that time waited there, and performed solemn service with the organs brought thither for the purpose; they also waited with the corpse by course night and day: by night first decani side, and next cantoris side, and twice in the night, *viz.* at nine of the clock and at midnight, they had prayers with a first and second chapters, and ended with an anthem.
>
> King Charles resided all the time that the corpse lay at Denmark House at Whitehall, being attended by his officers and servants as he had while he was Prince, and there the gentlemen of the Chapel waited.[12]

In addition to receiving quantities of valuable cloth as extra 'fees' for their services, Boughton tells us that he and ten other clergymen were given a clothing allowance of 'nine yards apiece of blacks for themselves, and two yards apiece for their servants'; that Giles, Heather, Stevens and Gibbons each received nine yards of black cloth for themselves also, and that their servants had two yards apiece; and that the rest of the gentlemen, seventeen in number, including Tomkins, 'had for their blacks every one seven yards, and for every of their servants two yards apiece'. Lesser dignitaries received lesser amounts, and even the organ blower received four yards.[13] Elsewhere, in contrast to this all-pervading inky blackness, others were to be seen flaunting their wealth and status in glittering attire.

On May Day 1625, one week before his father's funeral, Charles I had been married by proxy at Notre Dame, Paris, to Henrietta Maria, sister of King Louis XIII of France. The duke of Chevreuse acted as Charles's proxy. Louis, 'looking like the glorious sun outshining the other stars', escorted his sister. She wore a diamond crown, and a dress of gold and silver cloth embroidered with gold fleur-de-lis beset with diamonds and precious stones. Three weeks later, Buckingham, eager to maintain the hold over monarchy that had seemed his right under James, arrived in Paris to escort Henrietta across the channel to meet the husband whom she had never seen. Leaving his funereal black in the wardrobe, Buckingham had purchased twenty-nine suits for the journey: 'one of purple satin embroidered with pearls, another of white satin and velvet "set all over both suit and cloak with diamonds, the value whereof

---

[12] *Cheque Book*, 154–5.
[13] Ibid., 156.

Sceptre and Crown 123

thought to be fourscore thousand pounds". He had also had a new hat made with diamond-studded band and a diamond-encrusted feather, and had arranged to be accompanied by nearly seven hundred attendants, and to be driven to Paris in a coach upholstered in crimson velvet and covered with gold lace.'[14]

On 31 May Charles set out from London to Canterbury to await the arrival of his 16-year-old bride at Dover. Henrietta Maria was known to be travelling in great grandeur with a retinue of up to 4000 souls; Charles, anxious to match this magnificence, summoned a large entourage to surround him at Canterbury, including the whole of the Chapel Royal. Vestments, plate, candlesticks, ornaments and books would once again have been piled into horse-drawn carts, whilst other wagons would have been provided for the organists, gentlemen, singing boys, clerics, Chapel servants and their bags, baggage and paraphernalia – a lumbering cavalcade setting out from Whitehall ahead of their sovereign, all to the single end that the daily choral services in Canterbury Cathedral might be performed, probably in combination with the cathedral choir, in a manner fitted to the king's dignity.

The Chapel Royal party would have arrived in Canterbury in the last week in May. But the combined stresses of James's funeral and this latest excursion following so soon in its wake had placed too great a strain upon Orlando Gibbons. On Whit Sunday, 5 June, he suffered a sudden seizure and died, his passing recorded, with the usual lack of emotion, in the Cheque Book of the Chapel Royal:

> Mr Orlando Gibbons, organist, died the 5th of June being then Whitsunday at Canterbury where the king was then to receive Queen Mary who was then to come out of France, and Thomas Warwick was sworn in his place organist the first day of July following and to receive the pay of a pistoler [episteller].[15]

Gibbons had been celebrated as the finest keyboard player in the country. His death, in his forty-second year, a great shock to all of his fellow musicians, would have affected Tomkins especially deeply. Gibbons had been both a valued colleague and a close family friend. About the year 1606 Gibbons had married Elizabeth, daughter of John Patten, a one-time yeoman of the vestry of the Chapel Royal who, in 1607, became keeper of the King's Closet. When Patten made his will in February 1622, nominating Gibbons as his sole executor, one of the witnesses to his signature was Tomkins's half-brother, Peregrine. Gibbons proved the will on 17 September 1623, but had but little time left in which to enjoy the residuary estate bequeathed to him by his father-in-law.

Thomas and Peregrine Tomkins mourned the passing of Gibbons, but in

---

14 Christopher Hibbert (2001), *Charles I*, London, 87.
15 *Cheque Book*, 11.

124 *The Lives and Times of Thomas Tomkins and his Family*

court circles it was anxiety that the great musician might have been suffering from plague that gave the greatest cause for concern. Writing to Sir Dudley Carleton on 12 June 1625, John Chamberlain admitted 'that which makes us the more afraid is that the sickness increaseth so fast … Orlando Gibbons the organist of the Chapel (that had the best hand in England) died the last week at Canterbury not without suspicion of the sickness'.[16] Well might Chamberlain have been afraid, for during 1625 the bills of mortality recorded 35,428 dead from plague in London alone, with up to 5000 being buried every week. But on the day of Gibbons's sudden illness two doctors, Poe and Domingo, had attended him. After his death they were called upon by 'Mr Secretary Morton' to make a report 'touching the musician that died at Canterbury and suggested to have the plague'. They reported:

> We whose names are here underwritten: having been called to give our counsels to Mr Orlando Gibbons; in the time of his late and sudden sickness, which we found in the beginning lethargical, or a profound sleep: out of which, we could never recover him, neither by inward nor outward medicines, & then instantly he fell in most strong, & sharp convulsions: which did wring his mouth up to his ears, & his eyes were distorted, as though they would have been thrust out of his head & then suddenly he lost both speech, sight and hearing, & so grew apoplectical & lost the whole motion of every part of his body, & so died. Then here upon (his death being so sudden) rumours were cast out that he did die of the plague, whereupon we together with Mr Major's appointment caused his body to be searched by certain women that were sworn to deliver the truth, who did affirm that they never saw a fairer corpse. Yet notwithstanding we to give full satisfaction to all did cause the skull to be opened in our presence & we carefully viewed the body, which we found also to be very clean without any show or spot of any contagious matter. In the brain we found the whole & sole cause of his sickness namely a great admirable blackness & syderation in the outside of the brain. Within the brain (being opened) there did issue out abundance of water intermixed with blood & this we affirm to be the only cause of his sudden death.[17]

In other words, poor Gibbons had suffered a fatal stroke, and a modern reader of this *post mortem* report cannot but admire the accuracy of the diagnosis arrived at by Poe and Domingo. Orlando Gibbons was buried in Canterbury Cathedral on the day after his death, 13 June, and on that same morning Charles, hearing that his wife's ship had at last arrived in England, galloped to Dover to meet her.

Within a week Charles was back in London, addressing his first parliament. He had chosen William Laud to preach the opening sermon; within weeks another Arminian, Richard Montague, was appointed as royal chaplain; and over the next several months Calvinists were removed from positions of influence, their places filled by Arminians. In terms of religious observance,

---

[16] TNA, *State Papers Domestic*, Charles I, 1625, III, 60.
[17] Ibid., III, 37.

the royal will, which was also the will of the king's closest adviser, Buckingham, could not have been clearer. Unfortunately, that will did not command widespread support amongst members of the House of Commons, the majority of whom were of a decidedly Puritan insistence: Calvinist and fiercely anti-Catholic. They were also in favour of an active Protestant foreign policy, as was the king, but Crown and Commons were not to see eye to eye over ways and means. Asked by Charles for money to fight the Spanish, parliament refused to grant tonnage and poundage (subsidies and customs dues) for more than one year instead of for the king's life, as was customary.

With plague raging in London, MPs removed to Oxford in August 1625. Buckingham's abuse of power had taken root at the heart of their disillusionment, and when members mounted attacks upon his favourite, Charles dissolved parliament. An expeditionary force to Cadiz in the following October, planned by Buckingham as lord admiral, ended in a costly and shameful disaster, but undeterred, he and Charles began to plan yet another expedition.

Charles had been drawn, partly by family ties, into foreign adventures that he could not afford. His sister Elizabeth, to whom he was deeply attached, had married a Protestant prince, Frederick, the Elector Palatine. In 1619 the Protestants of Bohemia revolted against the Catholic Habsburgs. Frederick accepted the throne of Bohemia. A Spanish army invaded the Palatinate, and in November 1621 the Protestants were decisively crushed by their Habsburg overlords at the Battle of White Mountain. Protestantism was banned in Bohemia, and Frederick and Elizabeth forced to flee into exile in Holland. Frederick had upset the delicate balance between Catholic and Protestant powers in Europe, effectively triggering the Thirty Years War, a bloody conflict that was not to end until 1648 with the Treaty of Westphalia. The war had become a political issue in England, firstly because James I had adopted an entirely non-interventionist approach to it, and then, when Charles did decide to go to war, because of Buckingham's failure as a military leader. The plight of his sister and his impotence to influence the outcome of the war would continue to preoccupy Charles for the rest of his life. But as 1625 drew to a close his thoughts were much concentrated upon the coronation, already long delayed.

The appalling death toll from plague necessitated a postponement of Charles's coronation until 2 February 1626, 'a very bright shining day'. Tomkins will have been grateful for the extra time that the epidemic had afforded him, if not for its cause. Once again, as at the funeral of James I, he was assisted by William Heather, Nathaniel Giles and John Stevens in the preparation of the music. All concerned in planning the service would have been well aware of Charles's deep concern for the proper observance of ritual, and an added frisson of apprehension would have been added by the king's

126   *The Lives and Times of Thomas Tomkins and his Family*

insistence that William Laud took the place of Bishop John Williams (1582–1650), the dean of Westminster, at the ceremony. Williams had previously enjoyed royal favour, becoming chaplain to James I in 1617; he was installed as dean of Westminster in 1620, and in the following year was appointed privy counsellor, lord keeper, and bishop of Lincoln. But even though it was Williams who had been Laud's benefactor, recommending him to the See of St David's in 1621, he now stood in the way of a ruthlessly ambitious cleric. Laud set about undermining Williams with the king, and the two became implacable enemies.

Charles was not accompanied by his queen as he set out by barge at nine o'clock that morning from Whitehall to Westminster: Henrietta Maria had refused to accept that the Protestant archbishop of Canterbury, and not her own confessor, a Catholic bishop, should place the crown of England upon her head. Earlier that morning, all the personnel of the Chapel Royal had met at the College Hall in Westminster:

> Where they had breakfast at the charge of the College; from thence they went by a back way to the church, and so into the vestry, where together with the choir of Westminster they put on surplices and copes and went into Westminster Hall, and there waited until the king came thither, who came from Whitehall by water, and landing at the Parliament stairs came into the Great Hall, where was a great scaffold covered all with cloth, and upon it a throne and chair of estate, where the king sat until the whole train were marshalled in their order. The Chapel followed the knights of the Privy Council, who went next after the knights of the Bath, the sergeant porter with his black staff and sergeant of the vestry with his verger going before them; next the choir of Westminster, then the Chapel, who went singing through the Palace yard and round about the church, through the Great Sanctuary till they came to the west door of the church: when all the Chapel were within the church they began the first anthem.[18]

During the first anthem, *I was glad*, the king, seated upon a throne raised up on a platform just below the altar, received the acclamation of the people. The choir then sang *Strengthened be thy hand*, after which Bishop Senhouse of Carlisle preached a sermon on the text, 'Be faithful unto death and I will give you the crown of life'. The sermon ended, Archbishop Abbot administered the oath, the king kissed the Bible, and the choir sang *Come, Holy Ghost, eternal God, proceeding from above*. Two bishops then sang the Litany, the choir singing the Responses; Charles's magnificent robes were removed, revealing clothing of white satin; and while the choir sang the fourth anthem, *Sadock the Priest*, the archbishop anointed the king's shoulders, head, arms and breast with sacramental oil, and adorned him with the robes of St Edward the Confessor, the royal sword and spurs. The crown having been set upon the king's head by Abbot, the choir sang *The King shall rejoice*. As Charles made his way back from the altar to his throne, the choir sang the *Te Deum*; once

---

[18] *Cheque Book*, 157.

Sceptre and Crown 127

seated, he accepted the homage of the nobility; and as the archbishop prepared to begin the communion, the choir sang *Behold, O God our Defender*. At communion, Abbot administered the bread and Laud the wine; the epistle and gospel were read by the bishops; the choir sang the Nicene Creed and, after the offertory verse, the anthem *Let my prayer be set forth in thy presence*. The organist, presumably William Cross, played until the offertory was ended, and after communion the choir sang a last anthem, *O hearken then unto the voice of my calling*.

> After all the ceremony in the church was ended, the king returned back again into Westminster Hall in the same manner as he went, the Chapel going in their former order, and singing all the way till they came to Westminster Hall door, and there they stayed, making a lane for the king and all the lords to pass betwixt them, and continued singing till the king was within the Hall: and from thence they returned back into the church, where in the vestry they put off their copes and surplices, and came to Whitehall, where they had some allowance of diet for their suppers.
> All the way, from the scaffold in the Great Hall, through the Palace yard and the street in the Great Sanctuary, unto the scaffold in the choir of the church, was strewn with rushes, and upon the rushes, covered with blue broad cloth.[19]

Tomkins had composed most, if not all, of the eight anthems sung by the combined choirs of the Chapel Royal and Westminster Abbey. *Behold, O God our Defender* (the second part of the verse anthem *O Lord of Hosts*) and the text of *Sadock the Priest* survive, the latter preserved in a manuscript collection of words and anthems used in the Chapel.[20] It is inconceivable that he would not have poured the very finest fruits of his inspiration into these works, and the loss of any of them is regrettable. It also seems highly likely that Tomkins's huge contribution to the service would, at the very least, have been marked by the painting of his portrait but if so, the canvas appears not to have survived.

The six-hour coronation, the single most important event of his entire career, will have required several weeks of preparation and rehearsal; the composition of the music, very many exhausting hours; and yet the Cheque Book simply records that Tomkins was paid £2 'for composing many songs against the coronation of King Charles', whilst John Stevens received three-quarters as much, £1. 10*s*. 0*d*., 'for pricking [copying] these songs'.[21] Chapel Royal duties associated with the funeral of James I and the coronation of Charles I would undoubtedly have detained Tomkins in London for a continuous period of at least a year, and after the death of Orlando Gibbons there would have been no opportunity for him to escape the court. Thomas Warwick had been elected to replace Gibbons, it is true, but he was also busily employed as one of the royal musicians for the lute, a duty that would have

---

[19] Ibid., 159–60.
[20] BL Harley MS 6346.
[21] *Cheque Book*, 58–9.

128 *The Lives and Times of Thomas Tomkins and his Family*

occupied the lion's share of his time. But help was close at hand: early in 1626, probably in time for the coronation, Tomkins's half-brother John, organist of St Paul's, was appointed a gentleman extraordinary of the Chapel 'for the next place of an organist there, or the place of Anthony Kirby, which of them shall first fall void'.[22] That 'next place' presented itself on 28 October 1626, following the death of Francis Wiborowe, and two other gentlemen were accepted into the service of the Chapel at the same time: Richard Boughton, and Henry Lawes (1596–1662), brother of John Tomkins's friend and colleague William Lawes (1602–45).[23]

In that same month, October 1626, the control of the Chapel Royal passed into the hands of a new dean, a disciplinarian whose authority was soon to prove absolute: the newly appointed bishop of Bath and Wells, William Laud.

---

[22] Ibid., 11.
[23] Ibid.

Chapter 10

Sacred and Profane

By the time of William Laud's appointment as dean of the Chapel Royal in 1626 Thomas Tomkins was already 54 years old; his finest church music had been written, and after 1622 he was to compose no more madrigals. He had given of his best in the service of his sovereign and in 1628 it appeared that the court would at last give formal recognition to his skill and devotion to duty. Alfonso Ferrabosco II, who had served James I, composed the music for several of Ben Jonson's masques, been music master to the royal princes, and was made 'Composer of King's Music' by Charles I in 1626, died in March 1628. Consequently, Sir Francis Windebank, Secretary of State, drew up the following document in accordance with orders issued by Laud:

> Charles by the grace of God &c. To all men to whom &c. Greeting. Know ye that we for certain good causes and considerations us hereunto especially moving of our especial grace certain knowledge and mere motion have given and granted and by these presents for us our heirs and successors do give and grant unto our wellbeloved Thomas Tomkins the room and place of composer of our music in ordinary. And him the said Thomas Tomkins composer of our music in ordinary we do make nominate and appoint by these presents, Which said room and place Alfonso Ferrabosco deceased late had and enjoyed, To have and to hold and enjoy the said room and place of composer of our music in ordinary to the said Thomas Tomkins during his natural life. And further of our more ample grace we have given and granted and by these presents for us our heirs and successors we do give and grant unto the said Thomas Tomkins for his attendance in the exercise of the said room and place the wages and fee of forty pounds by the year, To have receive and take the said wages and fee of forty pounds by the year to the said Thomas Tomkins and his assigns from the time of the death of the said Alfonso Ferrabosco during the natural life of him the said Thomas Tomkins out of the treasure of us our heirs and successors at the receipt of the exchequer of us our heirs and successors by the hands of the Treasurer and Under-treasurer of us our heirs and successors there for the time being, At the four usual feasts or terms of the year, that is to say at the feasts of the Annunciation of our Blessed Virgin Mary, the Nativity of St. John Baptist, St. Michael the Archangel and the Birth of our Lord God by even and equal portions quarterly to be paid together with such other entertainments as the said Alfonso Ferrabosco late had and enjoyed or ought to have had and enjoyed for the same. Although express mention &c. In witness &c. witness &c.

Saving the king the boredom of having to actually read this tedious prolixity, Windebank added a brief explanatory note:

> This containeth Your Majesty's grant to Thomas Tomkins during his life of the room and place of composer of music in ordinary with the fee of forty pounds by

Fig. 10.1 Warrant of Charles I for the appointment of Thomas Tomkins as Composer-in-Ordinary.

Sacred and Profane   131

the year from the death of Alfonso Ferrabosco. And is done by the order of the Lord Bishop of Bath and Wells.[1]

WINDEBANK

Charles I rarely troubled to read more than a tiny proportion of the many state papers and documents that found their way daily to his desk, choosing instead to farm them out to appropriate ministers, whose decisions he invariably accepted. His handwritten annotations, where they do appear, betray a troubling lack of interest or knowledge in many subjects, rarely rising above 'Do it if you find it suit my service',[2] or some such shallow comment. He once went so far as to confess to Windebank, 'I have not the patience to read them all'.[3] Inherently lazy and heavily dependent upon his ministers, Charles was probably unaware of much that was done in his name.

The king never doubted for a minute that his authority to rule was ordained of God, but unlike Elizabeth I or even his own father, was never able to grasp the reality of his situation: that the successful exercise of political power, like the cultivation of a garden, was dependent upon constant daily effort. His ministers also believed firmly in the divine right of their sovereign, but recognized that the Almighty needed a great deal of assistance if the garden of State was not to run to weeds. Charles's profound reliance upon the unpopular duke of Buckingham, for instance, was in large measure a product of his laziness. Buckingham not only exercised a powerful control over the king's emotions but, unlike him, was prepared to give of his all to the business of government.

Tomkins was soon to discover the weakness and malleability of his monarch at first hand. Even though the king had affixed his signature to the grant it was revoked soon afterwards; the title Composer-in-Ordinary snatched away from Tomkins because, it was said, that place had already been promised to Ferrabosco's son.[4] This disappointment came hard on the heels of the deaths of Tomkins's father and step-mother, and would have been particularly hurtful, not only because a royal pledge had been broken, but because the letter of revocation, sent to Sir John Coke, was written by the lord chamberlain, Philip Herbert, earl of Montgomery, brother of William Herbert, earl of Pembroke, dedicatee of his *Songs* of 1622.

How different was the younger brother from the elder. Philip Herbert had little to commend him beyond his looks. He was ill-educated. He was foul-tempered and foul-mouthed, with a nasty streak of malice, and with few

---

[1] TNA, SP 39/23/53.

[2] TNA, SP 16/312/12.

[3] R. Scrope and T. Monkhouse (eds, 1767–86), *State Papers Collected by Edward, Earl of Clarendon*, 3 vols, Oxford, I, 302.

[4] Historical Manuscripts Commission, 12th Report, I, 341 (Coke MSS).

132 *The Lives and Times of Thomas Tomkins and his Family*

interests beyond 'hunting and hawking, the bowling alley, the tiltyard, and the gaming table'.[5]

A boorish peer had defeated Laud's ambition for an important and valued member of the Chapel Royal establishment, but there is no possibility that the king would have taken any personal interest in this rebuff – by the spring of 1628 he was preoccupied by rising turmoil in parliament.

In 1626, in the aftermath of the disastrous expedition to Cadiz, MPs, seeking a scapegoat, attempted to impeach Buckingham. To save his favourite, Charles dissolved parliament. With no parliament to approve revenues, the king levied forced loans on all subsidy payers, an action seen by many as an abuse of a fundamental liberty – that subjects held sole rights over their property and for the king to take it without consent was theft. By April 1628 Charles, again with no money, was unwillingly obliged to recall parliament. At the suggestion of Sir Edward Coke, the Commons and Lords presented the king with a Petition of Right, seeking to bring non-parliamentary taxation, imprisonment without cause, billeting and martial law to an end. The Commons no longer trusted the king, and he, deeply hostile to any curbs on his power, felt alienated from parliament.

Then, in August 1628, Charles suffered a devastating blow. Claiming to have been inspired by the Petition of Right, John Felton, a disaffected army officer, walked from London to Portsmouth, made for the house in the high street where the duke of Buckingham was staying, and stabbed him to death. Crowds in the streets received news of the assassination with jubilation. The king, utterly distraught, shut himself in his room for two days, refusing food or company. Perhaps Nicholas Tomkins, a gentleman of the Privy Chamber, was amongst those who stood close by, distressed by the uncontrollable sobbing of their king. Two lines by James Shirley said it all:

> Here lies the best and worst of fate,
> Two kings' delight, the people's hate.

Thomas Tomkins had observed the manner in which two kings had been bewitched by this diligent, charismatic dandy. The spell was broken at last, but no pavan in lamentation for the loss of Buckingham came from his pen or to his heart. Doubtless reflecting deeply on all that he had seen and heard of the late duke, Tomkins scribbled a feeble epitaph into one of his anthologies[6] and returned to his work at the Chapel – where Laud's authority was beginning to make its mark.

Orders for the gentlemen of the Chapel, setting out their annual

---

[5] Lever, *The Herberts of Wilton*, 76.
[6] BL Add. MS 29996, fol. 184.

Sacred and Profane   133

obligations for attendance, had been formally drawn up a decade earlier, and for his first three years as dean Laud seems to have been prepared to watch and wait. Following his translation to the See of London in 1628, he began to tighten the disciplinary screw, and between 1630 and 1632 regulations were imposed 'for rectifying and settling of divers orders' upon vestry staff for the proper performance of their duties. Admonitions were handed out to certain yeomen of the vestry for 'uncivil speeches and misbehaviour' and for 'going in and out so often into the vestry (without command)'. Two of the gentlemen, Richard Sandie and Nathaniel Pownall, were admonished 'to be more industrious and studious, for the better increase of knowledge and performance of their duty in their faculty for the king's service in the Chapel', and 'admonition was given to all the gentlemen in general that at all times of waiting they bring their psalters into the Chapel and sing at the Psalmody, and not be silent when it is their duty to use their voices'.[7]

Charles I was the first monarch to be born into the Church of England. Devout in his Anglicanism, punctilious in his observances and insistent upon strict ceremonies, his vision for the Church chimed exactly with Laud's concept of 'the beauty of holiness'. If that vision was to become the ideal, perfection must first be achieved in the Chapel Royal, the example of which would become a paradigm for the whole Church. How could this be achieved if one single member of the Chapel staff failed to pull his weight? Even Thomas Warwick was not spared, his pay having been stopped for the whole month of March 1630 'because he presumed to play verses on the organ at service time, being formerly inhibited by the dean from doing the same, by reason of his insufficiency in that solemn service'.[8]

A picture emerges of gentlemen of the Chapel riding to Whitehall through mud and mire, perhaps arriving at night and bedding down in the vestry, or perhaps galloping up, minutes before the beginning of a service, and marching into the Chapel in riding boots and spurs. Laud, not surprisingly, was having none of it. Orders were issued that 'the gentlemen of the Chapel shall (at all such times as they do attend that service) come in decent manner in their gowns and surplices, and not in cloaks and surplices, nor with boots and spurs. The like observation to be used by all others that come to approve their voices, or to be suitors for places there', and that 'Secondly it is ordered that no man shall have his lodging in the vestry, or a key to the vestry door, without the consent of the sergeant of that office for the time being.'[9]

All of these rulings seem to be entirely reasonable, but another, more controversial measure, introduced at Laud's insistence, went beyond the formal control of the salaried male servants of the Chapel. A bachelor who was

---

[7] *Cheque Book*, 77–8.
[8] Ibid., 78.
[9] Ibid.

134   *The Lives and Times of Thomas Tomkins and his Family*

never comfortable in the presence of women, Laud must have alienated many a courtly lady when he ordered the yeomen to 'take care that the king's cushions be not made common [i.e. none other than the king was to sit upon them] at communions, and not [to] suffer women to be in the Chapel in seats or otherwise at communion time but such as receive the sacrament'![10]

Thomas Tomkins and his half-brother John, both now serving as organists at the Chapel Royal, would undoubtedly have seen a good deal of each other since John's arrival at St Paul's in 1619. John Donne had been appointed dean of St Paul's in 1621, and the two Tomkins brothers must from time to time have been amongst the great crowds gathered at St Paul's Cross to hear the sermons that had made Donne famous throughout the land. Donne was 'High Church'; he preached at the Chapel Royal on a number of occasions, was much esteemed by the king, and may even have been known socially as well as professionally to Thomas and John Tomkins – he certainly came to know of their brother Giles.

Giles had followed in John's footsteps, succeeding Matthew Barton as organist of King's Chapel, Cambridge, in 1624. In 1629 he went to Salisbury Cathedral as organist and choirmaster, and in the following year, although retaining his post in Salisbury, joined Thomas and John at court, succeeding Richard Dering as 'Musician for the Virginals' to Charles I.

The musical reputation of Salisbury was, like the stately spire of that magnificent building, rightly celebrated. Over long years the cathedral had been served by a succession of great organists and composers, and by singing men and boys of distinction. Both John Farrant senior and his more renowned son, also John, had served there, the younger becoming a chorister under his father, and organist from about 1598 until his death in 1618. Farrant *fils* appears to have been a particularly inspiring teacher, contributing greatly to a long tradition of excellence in the musical education of Salisbury choristers. John Aubrey was to write that 'the quire of Salisbury hath produced as many able musicians, if not more than any quire in this nation',[11] and two of the most gifted of those musicians, Henry and William Lawes, close friends of Giles's brother John, may well have received their earliest instruction in music from Farrant – they grew up in the Close at Salisbury, where their father, Thomas, was a lay vicar from 1602.

Giles Tomkins, well acquainted with Thomas Lawes, his neighbour in the Close, would surely have met his two sons there. William Lawes was a pupil of John Coperario. Both he and Alfonso Ferrabosco II, the leading innovators of early Baroque English instrumental and vocal music, would have been familiar with Thomas Tomkins, and Coperario, the dedicatee of Tomkins's madrigal *Oyez! has any found a lad?*, seems to have been a close friend. This

---

[10]   Ibid., 76.
[11]   John Aubrey (1847), *The Natural History of Wiltshire*, ed. John Britten, London, 80–81.

Sacred and Profane   135

song, based on the jargon of the town crier, suggests experience of London and its streets shared by companions to whom the cries of the city were as familiar as birdsong. One can imagine the Tomkins brothers, Thomas, John and Giles, perhaps in company with Henry and William Lawes, Coperario and other court musicians ambling down Cheapside from St Paul's Churchyard on their way to the Mermaid Tavern at the top of Bread Street, where Shakespeare had once supped, and where Ben Jonson and his cronies were still regular customers.

Coperario, like Thomas and Giles Tomkins, divided his life between town and country. John Aubrey, sometimes unreliable but always entertaining, tells us that Coperario and Ferrabosco 'lived most in Wiltshire ... at Amesbury and Wulfall, with Edward [Seymour], earl of Hertford, who was the great patron of musicians'.[12] Equally close to Salisbury is Wilton House, ancestral home of the earls of Pembroke. Hertford took William Lawes into his household and placed him under the tutelage of Coperario; and Philip Herbert, earl of Montgomery, who succeeded his brother William as fourth earl of Pembroke in 1630, had taken Alfonso Ferrabosco II into *his* house as lutenist. 'He sang rarely well to the theorbo lute. He had a pension in Baynard's Castle [Pembroke's London House]',[13] and must presumably have been a frequent performer at Wilton also.

All of which leads one to suspect that the revocation of Thomas Tomkins's Composer-in-Ordinary grant, the highest honour available to an English musician, resulted less from an unfortunate loss of memory on the part of the king than from the deliberate manipulation of an unscrupulous lord chamberlain on behalf of the son of his favourite musician.

Soon after this shabby treatment of Thomas Tomkins, his half-brother Giles was also obliged to face a particularly unpleasant attempt at manipulation, finding himself, from the moment of his arrival in Salisbury, at the centre of an unholy row between bishop and dean. Fortunately, Thomas Shuter, Salisbury chapter clerk at the time, recorded the proceedings relating to Giles Tomkins in a rough notebook known as Shuter's Memorials, the register into which he would have transcribed them having been lost. 'The Memorials are written or rather scrawled in the most appalling handwriting which it is possible to imagine, with blots and crossings out. They are in a mixture of dog Latin and English, and are only partly legible.'[14] None the less, they give a vivid insight into contemporary church politics.

John Holmes, tutor of the choristers at Salisbury from 1621, died on 30

---

[12] Ibid.

[13] Ibid., 88.

[14] Dora H. Robertson (1938), *Sarum Close, A Picture of Domestic Life in a Cathedral Close for 700 years and the History of the Choristers for 900 years*, London; republished Bath, 1969, 196–7.

January 1629 leaving a wife, Dulcibella, three sons and two daughters. One of these daughters, Alice, had married a vicar choral, James Clark, in 1627, and following the death of her father, Clark, having been appointed as temporary tutor of the choristers pending the selection of a permanent replacement, promptly moved into the Choristers' House. Dulcibella, equally promptly, suggested that her son Thomas should succeed his father; a proposal readily supported by John Davenant, the Calvinist bishop of Salisbury, and three members of the chapter, Dr Barnston, Dr Seward and Mr Lee. Davenant felt so strongly about this matter that he demanded the right to a vote on the chapter, basing his claim on the fact that he held the prebend of Potterne. John Bowle, the dean, however, was equally determined that Giles Tomkins should be appointed to the post, and was backed in this by three other members of the chapter, one of whom was Giles Thornborough, the brother of Archdeacon Edward Thornborough of Worcester. Votes within the chapter were therefore equal, resulting in deadlock: battle lines were drawn for a struggle that was to rage for close on two years.

Bowle's next strategy was to propose Giles Tomkins as a lay vicar. Davenant countered that this was inadmissable because Tomkins had not appeared for a voice trial, in spite of three days' notification. Holmes supporters argued variously that a lay vicar could not be appointed without the approval of the vicars choral, that Holmes had proved his suitability, and that he could play the organ. The custos of the choristers, Dr Barnston, went so far as to say that Giles Tomkins was neither suitable for singing the psalms nor for 'the artifice of singing called prick-song singing', but where and when he had ever heard Tomkins attempting either was not revealed!

The arguments in chapter, begun on 14 April, remained unresolved after three whole days of bitter debate. Then, on 16 April, Giles Tomkins himself arrived. Still the dean and his supporters avowed that Tomkins was lawfully elected; still the bishop's party declared for Holmes. Without more ado, the dean took unilateral action, administered to Tomkins the oath of allegiance and royal supremacy to the king and of fidelity to the Church, then the oath of canonical obedience to the dean and chapter, and immediately afterwards admitted him to the place of a lay vicar. Davenant and Barnston were furious, remonstrating that 'it was void in law and by rights none', but their protests were in vain, the dean had achieved his aim, conceding only that the question of the other post, that of instructor of the choristers, would be referred to the archbishop of Canterbury for decision. Now followed a scene that bordered on farce.

The dean and his three supporters escorted Giles Tomkins to the Choristers' House, with the clear intention that he should take possession of it. The bishop and *his* trio of supporters seem to have followed in hot pursuit:

> The [chapter clerk's] writing is so bad at this point that it is only possible to

Sacred and Profane 137

gather an outline of what happened ... The nine men must have arrived outside the house to be met by the redoubtable Dulcibella, who was still in possession, supported by her son, Thomas Holmes, and her son-in-law James Clark. While the dean commanded her to clear out, the bishop exhorted her to stay on. Tempers would run high on both sides, and the scene was certainly a stormy one. Dulcibella was a tigress fighting for her young: she wanted to keep a home for her children. She stood her ground successfully, for we are told that the house was not given to Tomkins. This woman became a legend in her family, and the name, which her character belied, was handed on to the third generation of her descendants. Beautiful she may have been: gentle she certainly was not.[15]

The clerical spat continued back in the chapter house until, with all thoughts of unanimity or even harmony cast aside, the warring parties adjourned to lick their wounds and to await a response to their appeal to George Abbott, the archbishop of Canterbury. Instead of simply dictating the outcome, however, Abbott appointed a committee consisting of the bishops of Ely, Llandaff, Norwich and Winchester, and the dean of St Paul's – John Donne. The chairman was Abbott himself, but even this elevated group, in spite of finding in favour of Giles Tomkins, was strangely reluctant to resolve the matter, and on 22 June 1629 wrote to the king from Lambeth Palace:

> May it please your most excellent Majesty according to your gracious reference we whose names are underwritten have several times met and endeavoured to accommodate the differences between the Bishop on the one side, and the Dean and Chapter of Salisbury on the other side but not being able to prevail with both parties as we desired we have held it our duty to certify your Majesty that upon the whole hearing of both sides we find not reason to think otherwise than that Giles Tomkins was lawfully elected unto the places now in question and that he ought to be admitted into the possession of the same yet notwithstanding we submit all unto your princely pleasure.[16]

Charles's reply, drafted by his secretary, Viscount Dorchester, arrived six days later:

> His Majesty having seen the report whereof this is a true copy doth require that the within-named Giles Tomkins be admitted by way of provision into the place now in question. But for the validity of the election and right of voice in the Chapter with their dependencies his Majesty leaveth the same unto a trial at law in such course as is accustomed in cases of like nature, not ... by the order ... the pretensions and right of either part to it. [Partly illegible].[17]

The king, characteristically unwilling to make a clear-cut decision, had added confusion to an already intractable problem. Davenant immediately saw that those ambiguous words 'by way of provision' opened to question any assumption that Tomkins's appointment should be of a permanent nature. The wrangling started all over again; Tomkins remained in some sort of

---

15 Ibid., 179.
16 Ibid., 180–81.
17 Ibid., 181.

138 *The Lives and Times of Thomas Tomkins and his Family*

professional limbo, so Giles Thornborough, acting as dean in Bowles's absence, sought the agreement of the vicars choral that Tomkins should at least be paid for the last quarter as a lay vicar and be admitted to a lay vicar's house; but the vicars choral, as divided as the chapter, could not agree amongst themselves.

In the following October the dean, by an ingenious masterstroke, caused himself to be appointed custos of the choristers in place of Barnston and, in exercising his double authority, again ordered that Tomkins should be paid his salary as a lay vicar and given access to the Choristers' House – but the fiery Dulcibella, the power behind James Clark, still refused to quit. By this time the cathedral, according to Bowle, was completely 'destitute of all choristers', forcing him to propose the recruitment of local boys to sing in their surplices and gowns; Clark was 'admonished canonically, one two and three times to remove his family out of the Choristers' house … upon pain of expulsion out of this place', a threat that he (and Dulcibella) ignored.

The petition presented by Bowle in the 'trial at law' prescribed by the king finally came to court on 5 November 1630.[18] In the following month James Clark was evicted from the Choristers' House and given possession of another property. For almost two years a puerile quarrel amongst senior churchmen had denied Giles Tomkins both his position in the cathedral and his right to occupy the house tied to that position, and his troubles were still not at an end.

The difficulty of balancing his responsibilities between cathedral and distant court inevitably placed Giles Tomkins in an unenviable position. He had been in post at Salisbury for only a little over three years when, in Laud's Visitation Articles of 1634, his absences fuelled a complaint concerning the cathedral choristers:

> One Giles Tomkins hath the charge of instructing them in the art of singing, which he protesteth he doth carefully, and I believe he doth. He hath been blamed lately for leaving them without a guide and teacher once or twice when he went to wait at court, but he promiseth he will do no more so, yet protesteth that they all save two sing their parts perfectly, and need no teacher in his absence.[19]

It is inconceivable that Giles ever had any intention of relinquishing his highly lucrative post at court. His salary there of 40 pounds per year, plus allowances for liveries, was at least four times the amount paid to a church musician; and this valuable income had enabled him, in 1630, the year of his appointment to the King's Musick, to marry. A family man, Giles, who had a wife and three children to support, could not possibly have lived on what he could earn at Salisbury alone. Two of his sons were born within three years of

---

[18] TNA, Chancery Proceedings, C2. Ch I, S. 9.9.22.
[19] Stevens, 19, quoting *Wiltshire Notes and Queries*, March 1893.

Sacred and Profane 139

his marriage, Thomas (b. 1631) and Giles (1633–1725), and then after the death of his first wife, probably in childbirth around 1635, Giles remarried, and another son, John, was born in 1637.

The duties of the King's Musick embraced not only state and public occasions, such as the accompaniment of masques and the giving of concerts, but also private consort performances in the king's chamber, and attendance at the king's table during dinner.

In spite of his promise to 'do no more so', Giles *père* continued to leave his choristers at Salisbury to their own devices from time to time, remaining in the king's service as a virginals player with the 'lutes and voices' of the King's Musick from 1630 to 1642, sharing his duties with Thomas Warwick. During these years the strength of the King's Musick reached more than sixty players, including 'perhaps nineteen viols and violins, nine hautboys and sackbuts, seven flutes, three to five recorders, eight cornetts (who also played other instruments), eighteen or more lutes and voices, two virginals, and a harp. Many of the men played more than one instrument, of course.'[20] There was also an organ keeper and tuner, and in addition Queen Henrietta Maria maintained her own, separate musicians who numbered a master, fourteen men and two boys.

This impressive assembly of liveried musicians was under the overall direction of the virtuoso master of the Musick, Nicholas Lanier (1588–1666), a formidable musician – composer, flautist and lutenist, and also a painter. In 1613, along with Coperario and others, Lanier composed a number of masques, including one for the marriage of the earl of Somerset; four years later he not only set Ben Jonson's *Lovers made Men*, but also sang in it and painted the scenery. Charles, the first monarch fully to appreciate paintings as art, even sent Lanier to Italy in 1625 to buy pictures for his extensive collection.

By 1640 the instrumentalists and singers assembled under Lanier in the King's Musick included representatives of several leading families of musicians, amongst them Lanier's own sons, Andrea, Jerome, Clement and John Lanier II; the three sons of Alfonso Ferrabosco II, John, Henry and Alfonso; Davis and Leonard Mell; Thomas and Theophilius Lupo; Anthony and Henry Bassano; William and Henry Lawes; and Giles and Robert Tomkins.

Robert, like his brother Nicholas, was a bachelor, and both were much favoured by the king. He was one of up to a dozen violists in the 'lutes and voices', appointed on 28 March, 1633, in place of Robert Kyndersley.[21] He seems to have composed no consort music, though the organ parts of three

---

[20] Woodfill, *Musicians in English Society*, 185.
[21] H.C. de Lafontaine (1909), 'The King's Musick', *Proceedings of the Musical Association*, 36th session, 29–45.

140   *The Lives and Times of Thomas Tomkins and his Family*

anthems are to be found in Batten's manuscript,[22] these titles (*Thou art fairer; Hear me, O God;* and *Like as the hart*) occurring also in the Chapel Royal anthem book. Six further anthems are attributed to Robert Tomkins in the latter source, and it is a pity that the words only are preserved. Batten's organ parts, interesting as they may be to the historian, give us no idea of the quality of Robert's music.[23]

All of the Tomkins brothers would almost certainly have gathered together in Gloucester in 1627 for the funerals of Thomas *père* and Anne Tomkins. Perhaps on rare occasions in the 1630s it was possible for Thomas, John, Giles, Robert and Nicholas to be together in London, and possibly they were joined there by Peregrine, who had been made rich in 1623 by his marriage to Jane, daughter of Sir Henry Hastings, a wealthy landowner whose four farms at Humberstone in Leicestershire had yielded him a handsome dowry.

John Tomkins had also made rapid progress since being appointed as organist of St Paul's in 1619. He was sworn a gentleman extraordinary of the Chapel Royal in 1625, was promoted to episteller on 28 October 1626, gospeller on 30 January 1627, and gentleman on 19 July of that same year. Professional success was soon followed by marriage – to Margaret Griffiths, daughter of Sylvanus Griffiths, dean of Hereford – and the union was blessed by the birth of three sons during the succeeding decade: John, Sylvanus and Thomas.

Since leaving Scotland as an infant, Charles I had largely ignored the land of his birth. He showed no affection for the Scots, whom he did not understand, and it was not until 1633, when he travelled to Edinburgh for his coronation as king of Scotland, that he crossed the border for the first time as an adult. Both Giles and John Tomkins travelled with the royal party as joint organists of the Chapel Royal, setting out from London on 8 May and making a deliberately slow progress via Royston, Huntingdon, Althorp, Stamford, Grantham, Welbeck Castle, York, Richmond, and on in triumph through the Lowlands. The coronation itself, presided over by John Spottiswood, archbishop of St Andrew's, lasted for four hours, after which the king threw specially minted crowns to the enthusiastic crowds. A fortnight later Charles and his entourage returned to England.

Giles and John will have described the whole glorious itinerary to their half-brother Thomas: the lavish entertainment laid on by the earl of Newcastle at Welbeck Castle; the two hundred liveried men who had escorted the king into Durham, where he had touched the sick for the king's evil; the

---

[22] Bodleian Library, Tenbury MS 791. Adrian Batten followed John Tomkins as organist at St Paul's in 1624.

[23] Stevens, 15.

Sacred and Profane 141

amazing scenes in Edinburgh, the fifty-four gun salute, tableaux, triumphant arches, the coronation service itself, and their own profound involvement in the music.

But perhaps the Tomkins brothers also mentioned the other, tarnished, side of this golden coin: the protestations of Presbyterians, incensed by the bishops' wearing of surplices and the use of the Anglican Prayer Book at the coronation – a worrying hint of greater troubles yet to come.

Chapter 11

A Faithful City

Worcestershire is a pleasant, fruitfull, and rich countrey, aboundinge in corne, woods, pastures, hills and valleys, every hedge and heigh way beset with fruits, but especially with peares, whereof they make that pleasant drinke called perry ...

(Nehemiah Wharton, Worcester, 1642)

Spared the tiring journey to Scotland in 1633, the coronation of Charles I at Westminster in 1626 was the apogee of Tomkins's professional life. The following year marked a turning point in his domestic affairs at Worcester. Although he had received only a negligible inheritance from his step-mother's will he was now financially secure, and it seems probable that, in addition to his income from the Chapel Royal and the little extra money he had been paid for the coronation music, the patronage of the earl of Pembroke might have been generous. So much so that in 1627 Tomkins felt sufficiently affluent both to set about building a substantial house in the cathedral close and to make a generous charitable donation to the city of Worcester, the purpose of which is carefully recorded in the City archives:

Thomas Tomkins Organist of the Cathedrall Church of Christ and the blessed Mary the virgin of Worcester out of his zeale and pious disposicion and to the glory of Almighty god hath Given and delivered unto the Maior, Aldermen and Cittizens of the Cytty of Worcester, the some of fifty pownds to bee lent unto two younge Trades men of the said Cytty That are yong beginners in their trades, whereof Clothiers before others are to bee preferred, And the said Two yonge men Are from tyme to tyme for ever by the Chamber and Common Councell of the said Cytty to bee elected And to have the said fiftie pownds by equall porcions, vizt Twenty and five pownds apeece for one Two or three years as yt shall please the Chamber and Common Councell aforesaid, The said Two yonge men severally giveinge good securitie unto the said Corporation for the repayment of the said severall some of Twenty and five pownds, and Allsoe each of them Twenty shillings yearley upon the day before the feast of All Saints unto the Corporacion, which said fourty shillings the said Thomas Tomkins hath appointed shall be given to equally To four aged honest and devout people, such as are most observed to frequent the divine service of god by hearing of the praiers of the Church and the word of god reade out of the holy bible and booke of Common praier. The said four poore to be Chosen by the Maior and Aldermen of the said Cytty for the tyme beeinge or the greatest parte of them, And the distribucion of the said Fourty shillings to bee alwaies upon the day before the feast of All Saints.[1]

---

[1] WRO, Record of Benefactors of Worcester Charities 1627, fol. 15.

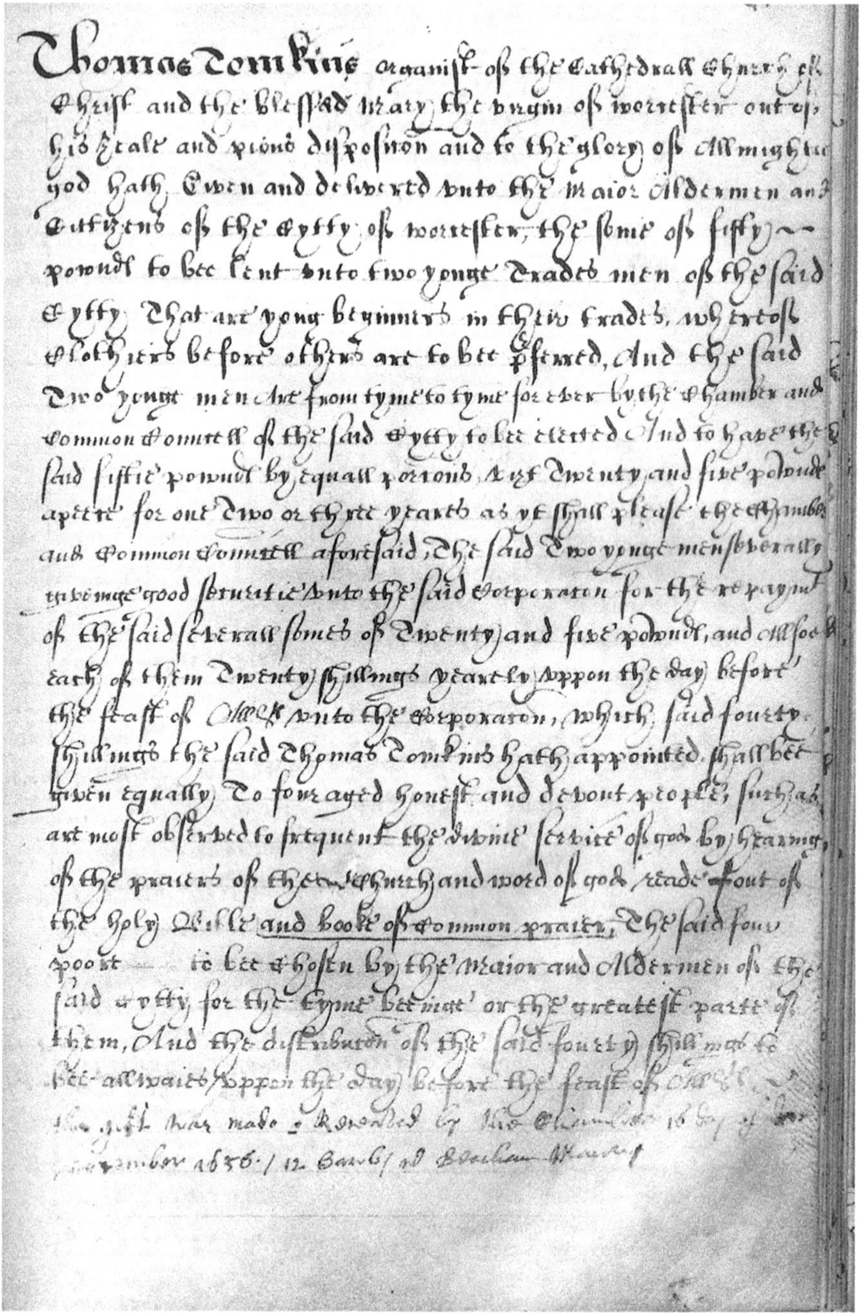

Fig. 11.1 Record of Benefactors of Worcester Charities, 1627, fol. 15r.

City records show that nine years later the fund established in 1627 was still serving Tomkins's charitable purpose:

16th December 1636

At this chamber yt is likewise agreed that the gift of Thomas Tompkins, gent. Organist of the cathedrall church of Worcester, being the some of fiftie pownds in such manner and forme as hee hath proposed the same to this house, shall bee accepted of and that the cittie shall acknowledge the receipt thereof under the common seale.

Att this chamber yt is likewise that Samuel Kings shall have £25 parte of the said fiftie powndes given by the said Mr Tomkins according to the true meaning of the said guift, to hould the same for three yeares paying the interest for the same yearely on All Saintes even to be disposed of according to the meaning of the said Mr Tomkins; James Taylor, Nicholas Wildie, sureties.

Att this chamber it is likewise agreed that John Wild shall have the other £25 of Mr Tompkins guifte paying the interest att the same time for the said three yeares to bee disposed of as aforesaid; Henrie Phillips, Richard Juce, sureties.[2]

Both Samuel Kings and John Wild made good use of Tomkins's scheme, going on to become well-known Worcester clothiers.

Loan funds were a common form of charity in seventeenth-century England and this one was to help new freemen, having served their seven-year apprenticeship, to set up in business. Twenty shillings a year represented an interest rate of 4% compared with the more normal usurer's rate of 8%. For the broad plan of the gift Tomkins seems to follow a similar presentation of the previous year by Maurice Hillier, also a parishioner of St Michael in Bedwardine [the cathedral stood in the parish of the nearby church of St Michael in Bedwardine], who allowed the same capital sum, the same interest and also specified two young clothiers; but perhaps his thoughts went back to the deathbed of a young colleague, Henry Goldsborough, over twenty years before. Goldsborough had dictated the details of a similar charity gift[3] in Tomkins's presence; although his bequest was to benefit poor scholars at the City Free School. At the age of twenty-three his death must have been a tragic one. His father had been a canon of Worcester and bishop of Gloucester, and Henry himself had studied at Oxford and acted as cathedral manciple. The will was dictated in the presence of various cathedral dignitaries and relatives, and he added codicils with Thomas Tomkins and others acting as witnesses as the day wore on.

Goldsborough's gift has fared better than Tomkins's and survived to modern times. Tomkins's can only be traced as far as 1642 and at some date after this the fund was not repaid to the Corporation and so was lost.[4]

The generosity of Tomkins and his wife was acknowledged by a grateful community. It was said of Alice that 'she bred up orphans, sent often meat, and money to sick neighbours, her servant hath been seen to distribute good

---

[2] Shelagh Bond (ed., 1974), *The Chamber Order Book of Worcester 1602–1650*, Worcester (WHS), 311.

[3] WRO, Worcs. probate 1613: 74.

[4] Richard Newsholme, 'Thomas Tomkins: Some Reflections on his Personality', *Leading Notes* (Journal of the National Early Music Association), 5 (1): 14–18.

146   *The Lives and Times of Thomas Tomkins and his Family*

pieces of money to many poor families from year to year, from house to house'.[5]

> Legislation in 1563 and 1573 had compelled parishioners to contribute to the relief of 'impotent paupers' in their parish and the accounts of the overseers for the poor of St Michael's record Alice's care for the child of one John Heekes who seems to have come into this category. Heekes's wife died in January 1615/16 and left him with two small children (one would have been aged about two as her baptism is recorded in March 1613/14). The family was poor and had received alms and bread money on several occasions. After their mother's death Alice contributed clothing:
>
>> Item for making a wastecote given by Mres Tomkins for one of the children ijd [two pence]
>
> and also took a turn in fostering one of the children:
>
>> Itm paid to Mr Tomkins for keepinge one other of Heekes his Children fiftie weekes at vjd [six pence] the weeke ended the xijth this April 1619— xxvs [twenty-five shillings][6F]

The dean and chapter granted Tomkins two leases, both dated 25 November 1627. The first of these was for eleven acres of pastureland in the parish of St Clement's, and extended over a period of twenty-one years.[7] The second was a lease of forty years on four bays and a half of old, decayed buildings at the east end of College Green, granted on condition that 'the same be converted to some good and necessarie uses at their proper coste & charge within three years next following the date hereof'. Tomkins obviously intended to restore or rebuild these ruinous properties, and a clause in the lease makes it clear that should he be dispossessed through no fault of his own, the dean and chapter would repay him 'the value of all timber, boards, bricks, tiles, iron, lead, tin, sand, clay, and other building stuff whatsoever, bestowed or to be bestowed in reparation or new building of the said houses or buildings, also all charges of workmanship'.[8]

> Two houses were built. Tomkins and his family lived in one of them, a fine residence that survives, much altered, as 9 College Green. Before Tomkins's restoration the properties had been divided into three tenements, sublet separately. By this time they were described as 'ruinous' and rebuilding over the next few years gave him a substantial property with a hall, kitchen, buttery, five chambers [above stairs], a garret, and a high turret or study on the third floor. [Also a garden, 34 ft by 42 ft, including a water pump, woodhouse and

---

    [5] From a sermon preached by John Toy at the funeral of Alice Tomkins, 2 February 1642. See Stevens, 54–6, and also full text of eulogy in Chapter 12, p. 171.

    [6] Richard Newsholme, 'Thomas Tomkins II: Domestic Life at Worcester', *Leading Notes*, 5 (2): 22–5, quoting WRO Churchwardens' accounts of St Michael in Bedwardine, Worcs., fols 23 and 38.

    [7] WCL, A7 (10), fol. 123.

    [8] Ibid., fol. 133.

A Faithful City 147

coalhouse.] The Old Song School continued to be known as the organist's house for many years with the rent accruing from it being paid to the organist.[9]

The reasons for needing such a large house are not immediately apparent. A letter of 1638 suggests that Tomkins was not expecting to be lodging visitors – this was left to his son [Nathaniel] whose prebendal house was even larger, and who in any case was required to offer hospitality by Henry VIII's statutes. It is possible, however, that the extra space was needed to board choristers. This was quite a common seventeenth-century practice, and at Windsor, for example, the Master of the Choristers was required as part of his employment to see to their 'teachinge, keepinge, Dyetinge, aparelinge, orderinge and lodginge'.[10]

In 1629 Nathaniel Tomkins graduated from Balliol College, Oxford, with the degree of BD and immediately returned to Worcester as one of ten prebends, taking his place as canon of the tenth stall in the cathedral that had always been – and would remain – at the centre of his life. As a boy, in 1610, Nathaniel had been a bible clerk at the cathedral, and in the following year became a chorister. Unsurprisingly, music played a dominant role in his life, too dominant in the minds of some; one commentator was to remark that 'he could make better music upon an organ than on a text'.[11] None the less, the presence in Worcester of so talented a musical son must have been of enormous support to his ageing father, and doubtless Nathaniel found himself seated in the organ loft at least as often as in a prebendary stall.

No doubt he was welcomed back as a valuable additional member of his father's circle of musician friends, and he was soon closely involved with the life of the King's School, where he encouraged the choirboy plays that had been a legacy from Tudor times.[12] Marriage to his sweetheart, Theodosia Broad, added the finishing touch to Nathaniel's contentment, but there were those who suspected that slippery intrigue had eased Nathaniel's smooth passage to Worcester – and that no less a figure than William Laud had lubricated it!

In his *Scrinia Reserata*, John Hacket, faithful chaplain to John Williams, bishop of Lincoln, later archbishop of York, and lord keeper of the great seal of England, recounts how the reputation and power of his master had been eroded by Laud. Williams, who has been compared to Wolsey in the pomp and plenty with which he was surrounded, was bound to engender the hostility of an austere prelate such as Laud and to give rise to deep unease in

---

[9] Newsholme, 'Tomkins: Some Reflections on his Personality', quoting WCL A7 (10) fol. 123 [1627 lease]; sublet by Edw. Archbold – see WRO probate 1618/154; T. Cave and R. Wilson (1924), *Parliamentary Survey of the Lands & Possessions of the Dean and Chapter of Worcester*, Worcester (WHS), 176; Song School lease to Thomas Oliver 1712, WCL A7 (22) fol. 51.

[10] Newsholme, 'Tomkins: Domestic Life'.

[11] I.G. Smith and P. Onslow (1883), *Diocesan History of Worcester*, London, 266.

[12] W.M. Ede (1925), *The Cathedral Church of Christ and the Blessed Virgin Mary of Worcester*, Worcester, 136.

148   *The Lives and Times of Thomas Tomkins and his Family*

the mind of his young sovereign. From the outset of his reign Charles increasingly sidelined Williams, turning more and more to Laud for advice. 'Of all men', wrote Hacket, 'Bishop Laud was the party whose enmity was most tedious and spiteful against his great benefactor Lincoln. He battered him with old and new contrivances fifteen years.'[13] Laud was also successful in throwing discredit upon Williams in his conversations with the king's favourite, the powerful but ill-fated duke of Buckingham, whose mother revealed as much to Williams, telling him that Laud 'would underwork any man in the world that he himself might rise'.[14]

On 23 October 1625 Charles ordered Williams to surrender his great seal of office to Sir John Suckling, comptroller of the Household. Although virtually banished from court, Williams remained bishop of Lincoln and dean of Westminster, and for the first fifteen years of Charles's reign held fast to his country house at Buckden on the Great North Road, receiving frequent visitors from among the great and the good. Here there were stables, barns, granaries and dairies, houses for doves and for brewing, and 'outward courts which were next to them', which the bishop had 'cast into fair alleys and grass-plots. Within doors, the cloisters were the trimmest parts of his reparations: the windows of the square beautified with storeys of coloured glass; the pavement laid smooth and new: and the walls on every side hung with pieces of exquisite workmanship in limning, collected and provided long before.' Williams maintained a staff of sixty and entertained royally in these palatial surroundings. 'The Bishop's fancy', wrote Hacket, 'was marvellously charmed with the delight of music, both in the chapel and in the chamber: as Solinus says of Alexander, the son of Amyntas, *Voluptati aurium indulgentissimi erat deditus* [he was dedicated to the tender pleasure of the ears]. Which was so well known that the best for song and instrument and as well of the French that lodged in London, as of the English, resorted to him chiefly in the summer quarter, to whom he was not trivial in his gratifications.'[15]

Williams, both a lover and a maker of music, learned the art whilst he was 'a poor subsizar in St John's College in Cambridge of little regard or learning'.[16] His delight in singing continued throughout his life, and it was not uncommon for him to take the tenor part in his own services at chapel. He had, according to Hacket, 'such favour and countenance from the nobility … that they vouchsafed their presence at his feasts, but chiefly for his music-

---

[13] John Hacket (1693), *Scrinia Reserata, A Memoriall Offer'd to the Great Deservings of John Williams, D.D., who sometime held the Place of Lord Keeper of the Great Seal of England, Lord Bishop of Lincoln and Lord Archbishop of York*, London, II, 65. See also Paul Vining (1992), 'Nathaniel Tomkins: A Bishop's Pawn', *Musical Times* (October), 538–40.

[14] Hacket, *Scrinia Reserata*, 19.

[15] Ibid., 29–30.

[16] David Mathew (1951), *The Age of Charles I*, London, 112, quoting J.O. Halliwell (ed.), *Autobiography of Sir Symonds D'Ewes*, I, 204.

A Faithful City   149

sake, which was the banquet they came for; and he was furnished very well both for voices and instruments in his own family. It was sumptuous, I confess, for one of his level in those days.'[17] Buckden provided Williams with a sanctuary, far from his accusers at court, but a 'sanctuary [which] afforded him no more shelter than an arbour in the winter against a shower of rain'.[18] Not all of Williams's guests were worthy of his hospitality.

Nathaniel Tomkins, theologian and musician was, it seems, among those welcomed by Williams to share in the luxuries of both his table and his music-making but who abused that privilege. He had an ulterior motive for his visits to Buckden, a motive that eventually resulted in his being cashiered by Williams for treachery, but which, at the same time, served to further his career. He had agreed to become, as Hacket put it, 'one of those spies and state-rats that are set to run and scent in every corner'.[19]

'It was Mr N.T.' wrote Hacket, 'a musician and a Divine' whose duplicity was uncovered. 'He had leave to use the whole house, to go into the bishop's bedchamber or study … the organist transcribed some letters which he found and sent them to an enemy, who compassed this bishop about with such toils … So this enchanter thought it feasible to draw intelligence out of closets and cabinets by such as wanted fortune, and that he could force open anything with the petard of preferment. He missed not his aim with this false brother, upon whom he caused a prebend to be conferred in the church of Worcester.'[20]

So Nathaniel Tomkins became a spy on behalf of John Williams's arch-enemy, Laud – for surely the 'petard of preferment' was his and his alone. But how was Nathaniel recruited? It is inconceivable that Laud would have made a personal approach to a student. Could it be that Thomas Tomkins had spoken of his gifted son to Laud, perhaps in conversation at the Chapel Royal, mentioning that Nathaniel was at Oxford and that he was among those musicians who frequented the bishop of Lincoln's mansion? Could the father even have been an intermediary between his ambitious son and the many times more ambitious bishop of London? The questions remain forever open. But there could have been no more effective cover for a cuckoo in the Buckden nest than that of a musician, one amongst many, alert to any snippet of incriminating conversation, free to wander at will.

Williams, a Calvinist, stood between Laud and his ultimate goal: the See of Canterbury. After the assassination of Buckingham, the king treated Laud, the newly installed bishop of London, as though he were already Primate of All England, leaving Williams, dismissed from office, to lament that 'a cashiered courtier is an Almanack of the Last Year, remembered by nothing but the

---

17 Hacket, *Scrinia Reserata*, I, 35.
18 Ibid., II, 62.
19 Ibid., II, 33.
20 Ibid., II, 38.

150   *The Lives and Times of Thomas Tomkins and his Family*

Great Eclipse'.[21] Nathaniel Tomkins, secret agent, had assisted Laud in his campaign to undermine a rival; perhaps he had no choice, but was made an offer that he could not refuse. Whatever the facts of the matter, Nathaniel was spared the stepping-stone of a poorly paid living on leaving Oxford, moving instead to a large house in College Green, Worcester, a fitting residence for Mr Tomkins the prebendary. 'This musician', concluded Hacket, 'would not have abused so kind a master if he could have got a prebend by an honester cause.'

The cathedral to which Nathaniel returned had, from 1627, been in the care of a new, exceptional dean, William Juxon. Coming to Worcester from Oxford, Juxon had been elected president of St John's College six years earlier. Within six years more he was to be consecrated bishop of London and appointed dean of the Chapel Royal, and following the death in 1636 of Sir Richard Weston, earl of Portland, the king chose Juxon to replace him as lord high treasurer, the first cleric to hold that great office since the reign of Edward IV.

Like Laud, Juxon was a High Churchman and an Arminian, but in personality the difference between the two could not have been more marked. Juxon was 'a gentle, tactful and tolerant man … the delight of the English nation, whose reverence was the only thing all factions agreed on, by allowing that honour to the sweetness of his manners that some denied to the sacredness of his function, being by love what another is in pretence, the Universal Bishop'.[22] John Aubrey recalled that 'My Lord Falkland was wont to say that he never knew any one that a pair of lawn sleeves had not altered from himself, but only Bishop Juxon'.[23] For relaxation, Juxon liked nothing better than the thrill of the chase, and it may be that Thomas Tomkins's keyboard *Hunting Galliard*, more a musical description of the hunt than a typical galliard, was composed with him in mind. It is also possible that Tomkins himself shared Juxon's enthusiasm for hunting with hounds, just as the dean took pleasure in music and composition: at Peterhouse and Durham there is an *Easter Anthem* by Juxon. The arrival of this deeply spiritual, approachable and popular figure must have gone some way towards offsetting the profound animosity felt by many in the Worcester community towards their religious leaders, and especially the steely bishop, John Thornborough, who, in the year of Juxon's arrival, erected a handsome tomb for himself in the cathedral – fourteen years before his death.

Under the Act of Uniformity church attendance on Sunday was not an

---

[21] Ibid., II, 26.

[22] Bertram Green (rev. 1979), *Bishops and Deans of Worcester*, Worcester, 45, quoting W.H. Hutton.

[23] Aubrey, *Brief Lives*, 313.

A Faithful City   151

option; absence was treated as a criminal offence, and Thornborough tightened the enforcing screws with unprecedented severity. He also claimed the right of granting licences to sell beer and ale:

> Instructions, it would seem, were given to the constables to report, or to speak technically to 'present,' those who failed to attend ... During the time of Thornborough's episcopate the presentments for not attending church became a regular thing, and they are made in the same way as any other infraction of the law. For instance, one at Fladbury, in 1640. Presentment that 'Richard Walter and Dorothy Nares sell ale without a licence, and Mary Banner, the wife of William Banner, does not go to church'.[24]

But life in Worcester was not all gloom and doom. Since 1618, when, much to the horror of Puritans, James I had ordered the public reading from every pulpit in the land of the 'Declaration of Sports', the king's subjects felt safe to enjoy time-honoured games on Sundays. Charles I had the good sense to order the same declaration repeated in 1633. Single-stick, boxing, wrestling, sword-fighting, bull and bear baiting, cock-fighting and battle-like games of football were all enjoyed hugely by a populace not yet disgusted at the sight of pain inflicted upon man or beast. Less violent pleasure was to be found in country dancing, maypoles 'with garlands graced', morris dancing, and in the stately pavan and lively galliard. Tomkins evokes a popular dance of the times in his keyboard *Worcester Brawls*, not, as might be assumed, drunken fisticuffs. The character Guerino in John Marston's play *The Malcontent* (1604) describes a brawl:

> Why, 'tis but two singles on the left, two on the right, three doubles forward, a traverse of six round; do this twice, three singles side, galliard trick of twenty, coranto pace; a figure of eight, three singles broken down, come up, meet two doubles, fall back, and then honour [i.e. bow or curtsy].

What could be simpler?

From the time of Mary Tudor, Worcester had been a market town; separate streets were set aside as the market for specific animals and produce on market days, and Thomas and Alice Tomkins will have known this bustling street scene well, sending their female domestic servants to purchase provisions every week. 'Broad Street was set aside for cattle; Edgar Street for horses; Angel Street for sheep; Dolday for pigs; St Swithin Street (Goose Lane) for poultry; Mealcheapen Street for meal; Queen Street for corn; Church Street for crockery; St Nicholas Street for vegetables; The Cross and High Street for meat; and Fish Street for fish'.[25]

Throughout his Chapel Royal years the correspondence between Tomkins and his wife, Alice, must have been extensive. Provincial carriers' carts called at several London taverns once or twice each week, and the letters that they

---

[24] Willis Bund, 'Religious Life', 581.
[25] Hubert A. Leicester (1935), *Worcester Remembered*, Worcester, 132.

152   *The Lives and Times of Thomas Tomkins and his Family*

carried between the capital and Worcester, had they survived, would surely have told an absorbing tale of social and domestic life in both centres. Without them we are left to piece together our impressions of their lives and personalities from the historical record, from national and local archives, and from Tomkins's own annotations to autograph music manuscripts.

As we have seen, the Chapel Royal acted as a centre for the dissemination of music to provincial cathedrals. Doubtless, when parcelling up individual manuscripts or bound anthologies of music to dispatch to faraway colleagues, Tomkins would have included a letter filled with the latest news and gossip from court. The good humour that these might have contained may be guessed at from annotations made in his distinctive, probably left-handed, script in surviving anthologies. Weaving his words around the manuscript of a madrigal by John Farmer, *Take Tyme while tyme doth last*, Tomkins warns of the difficulty of the piece, giving 'The Solution How to Sing it' at length and, with characteristic waggishness, he adds: 'This Tenor part is made purposely only to Fright & dismaye the Singer. By driving od Chrotchets through semibrifes brifes & longs ... This hard Tenor part Being the playnsong.'[26]

Elsewhere, Tomkins's critical comments are addressed to a contemporary, such as John Merro in Gloucester, his son Nathaniel in Worcester, or his brother Giles in Salisbury, each having responsibility for teaching music to boys. Of a set of 'Fancies for the vyolls in 4 parts' by Alfonso Ferrabosco he writes: 'All of them excellent good. But made only for the vyoll & organ which is the reason that he takes such liberty of compass, which he would have restrayned: If it had bin made for boyes only.'[27]

Tomkins, in recommending a set of songs in four parts by Byrd, writes that 'The following are all within the compass of the hand & so most fitt to be played with ease',[28] and he delights in another piece by Byrd, a ground, *The leaves be green*, with the comment 'a most excellent piece'.[29] Such remarks pepper the manuscripts revealing Tomkins as a perceptive critic, his most commonly used expressions being 'good', 'very good' and even 'excellent good'!

In that same anthology useful recipes and prescriptions are to be found interspersed between the music, copied out neatly in another hand. It is possible to imagine Tomkins, perhaps whilst spending a night at some country inn, or perhaps in London, meeting with a friendly apothecary and asking his advice about the treatment of a troubling skin condition that will not heal, his own or Alice's perhaps. The apothecary agrees to write a prescription; the only paper to hand is one of the composer's treasured anthologies of music;

---

[26] BL Add. MS 29996, fols 146–7.
[27] Ibid., fol. 72.
[28] Ibid., fol. 109.
[29] Ibid., fol. 153.

A Faithful City

153

Tomkins slides the book over the table, selects a blank page, and the apothecary writes:

Rec:
verdigris	5 drachms
of good honey	14 drachms
of strong vinegar	7 drachms

and boil all these together over a slow fire until it be of red colour and of the thickness of an ointment. This ointment is good against old wounds, fistulas and for taketh away dead flesh and dryeth very much.

The drachms are expressed in the symbols of an apothecary, which suggests a professional hand, but the writer does not end with that prescription. He goes on to write down methods of making conserves from flowers, and two ways to preserve quince. The quince was widely used in former times, not only to flavour jams and jellies, etc., but as a remedy for constipation, coughs, burns, chapped skin and haemorrhoids. No doubt several uses were found for this versatile fruit in the Tomkins household!

At a national level, the mounting distrust between Crown and Commons was to come to a head at a parliamentary session on 2 March 1629. Two issues dominated the debate: religion and tonnage and poundage. When it became obvious that the Commons were unwilling to grant him revenues, the king decided to adjourn parliament. Before the speaker was able to announce this to the Commons he was pinned down in his chair by two MPs. Sir John Eliot then shouted out three resolutions. These condemned as 'a capital enemy to the king and commonwealth' anyone who promoted popery or Arminianism, advised the king to levy tonnage and poundage without parliamentary consent, or who voluntarily paid customs dues. The king promptly resolved to dispense with the services of parliament in future, thus embarking upon a Personal Rule of eleven years.

By this time the Arminians had begun to establish a dominant role within the Church: Laud was installed as bishop of London, second only in importance to the archbishop of Canterbury, and other key Sees including York, Winchester, Norwich and Chichester were filled by leading proponents of Arminianism, this in spite of the fact that the overwhelming majority of English Protestants disliked its doctrines. A split was being driven between the king and many of his most influential subjects, a split, as some historians have expressed it, between 'court' and 'country'.

Throughout the 1630s Laud and his allies, with the full backing of the king, pursued Arminian policies, seemingly oblivious to the resentment that was being stoked by their good intentions. The anti-Calvinist mission of the Arminians was to bring people to God by the 'beauty of holiness', expressed

154 *The Lives and Times of Thomas Tomkins and his Family*

in an emphasis on the ceremonial and sacramental aspects of worship rather than on preaching. Little wonder, then, that Laud's critics should accuse him and his fellow Arminians of popery, no matter how baseless the charge; the outward show *seemed* indistinguishable from popery. Furthermore, the gulf between the people and the hierarchy of the Church was increasingly widened by antagonism to the involvement of bishops in secular affairs. Memories went back to the days before the Reformation when princes of the Church had wielded enormous power in the political arena. Laud, elevated to archbishop of Canterbury in 1633, strode into the Privy Council as one of its most influential members; three years later Juxon took up his appointment as lord treasurer. Critics of the Church feared the worst: the rise of an English Richelieu.

After Juxon's departure from Worcester, his place was taken by a controversial figure: Roger Mainwaring, a former scholar of the Worcester King's School and an Arminian who, as chaplain to Charles I, had maintained in a sermon preached before the king in 1627 that 'the authority of parliament was not necessary for the raising by the king of aids and subsidies'. Unsurprisingly MPs, outraged by this, sentenced Mainwaring to be imprisoned during the pleasure of the House, fined him £1000 and suspended him for three years. At the beginning of the Personal Rule, Charles ordered that Mainwaring should be pardoned, and appointed him dean of Worcester in 1633; later in the same year he was consecrated bishop of St David's, resigning the deanery in 1636. But his troubles were by no means over, and the memory of Mainwaring's efforts to implement Laud's policies at Worcester would come back to haunt him.

There seems to be little doubt that choral standards at Worcester declined markedly during the years of Tomkins's long absences at the Chapel Royal in the 1620s and early 1630s; years in which, it may be supposed, John Fido was *locum tenens* before being suspended in respect of 'many misdemeanours' in 1633; and years in which the low salaries paid to Tomkins and his team had fallen well behind rises in the cost of living. Then as now, this cannot have helped the dean and chapter in the recruitment and retention of high-quality lay clerks and others, and at a chapter meeting held on 23 June 1632 Juxon decided to do something about it by diverting a proportion of parish corn rents towards the upkeep of the choir:

> Whereas the quoire of this Cathedral Church of Worcester consisting of many ministers, a gospeller and pisteler, organist, lay clerks and choristers are three times in the day employed in the services of God and in common prayer for the king and the whole state of this kingdom when all the parish churches in the land are silent, except certain days in the week, and for their salary hath been very mean (by ancient institution) and for that the rate of all things are highly

A Faithful City 155

inhaunced since the pecuniary salaries were instituted. And also that some other inferior members of the said Cathedral Church (as namely the schoolmaster) take great pains in the breeding of the King's scholars and others for small pensions. Therefore we do appoint that the eighth part of every pecuniary rent shall be laid upon the rent reserved over and above the ordinary rent to the benefit of the quoire.[30]

Little improvement seems to have been achieved over the next couple of years. Further additional income from the corn rents of the parishes of Broadway and Overbury were allotted to the choir in November 1634, but at a Visitation of the County of Worcester in 1635 Laud's agents were far from satisfied, warning Mainwaring and the chapter 'that none be admitted to any place of your choir before he be first approved of for his voice and skill in singing by such of your church as are able to judge thereof, and that the places there, as they fall void, be supplied with men of such voices as your statutes require'.[31] The choristers were to be 'duly and diligently catechised, which hath been formerly too much neglected'. Even the exterior of the cathedral was in an appalling condition, and the dean and chapter were ordered to put it to rights:

Item that your churchyard be decently and without prophanation kept and that you take care that the bones of the dead may not lie scattered up and down, but that they be gathered together and buried. And that the chapel called Capella Carnarie situate in the entry of your cathedral, now prophaned and made a hay barn, be restored and employed to the wonted use.[32]

Mainwaring had been appalled at the state of affairs that he had found in Worcester. At the end of 1635 he sent a letter to Laud explaining that 'The King's scholars, being 40 usually coming tumultuously into the choir, I ordered to come in *binatim*, and to do reverence toward the altars'.[33] In fact, Mainwaring had issued an order on 25 November 1635:

It is decreed that the schoolmasters shall diligently observe that the King's scholars do decently come into the Church by 2 and 2, doing their reverence towards the East, and that when that prayer is done that likewise they pass out 2 by 2 doing the like reverence towards the East.[34]

And it was probably Mainwaring, as zealous as Laud, who had pointed out many of the cathedral's shortcomings personally to the Visitors, including the shameful condition of the Carnary Chapel. It fell to Mainwaring's successor, Christopher Potter, to restore this charnel house chapel and put it to 'the wonted use', which, in his interpretation of the Visitors' instruction, was as

---

30 WCL, Chapter Acts, A 74.
31 Historical Manuscripts Commission 3, House of Lords MSS, 158.
32 A.F. Leach (1913), *Documents Illustrating Early Education in Worcester, 685–1700*, Worcestershire (WHS), 246.
33 TNA, *Calendar of State Papers, Domestic*, Charles I, 1635, 395.
34 WCL, Chapter Acts, A 75; Leach, *Documents*, 246.

156   *The Lives and Times of Thomas Tomkins and his Family*

the appropriate building for the King's School. The dean instructed Nathaniel Tomkins to make the necessary arrangements, and he had duly obeyed, moving the school out of the College Hall and into the Carnary Chapel. Unfortunately, the man who had allowed the chapel 'to be prophaned and made a hay barn' was none other than the fiery nonagenarian bishop of Worcester. Thornborough was absolutely furious, expressing his protest in writing to Laud on 13 January 1637:

> I let your Grace understand, that the decayed chapel standing over the charnel house, not within, but without the Church, was used by the bishops for a house to put hay in ever since the dissolution, they having none other. Nevertheless in obedience to your Grace's order, I delivered the same to Mr Tomkins the Prebendary, who promised that the same should be converted to a pious use, viz., for prayers at six in the morning. But now he removeth and breaketh down all things of the old spacious School into this little chapel, joining on the Church of the Bishop's Palace, who will be much disquieted, and disturbed with the noise of the boys, who are in number near 200, the place being little more than half as big as the former School: in this chapel there is an ancient monument of some great personage, and I am persuaded there will be more prophanation of the place by swearing, and lying amongst boys, than when hay was laid in it.[35]

Nathaniel had taken the opportunity to eject both the school and the private house of the master, Henry Moule, from College Green. There does not appear to have been a soul in Worcester, apart from the dean, who supported the prebendary's action. Both clerics had earned for themselves the loathing of the King's scholars, aggrieved at their eviction from the spacious College Hall, and the hatred of Bishop Thornborough, who found himself supported, perhaps for the first time, by a majority of the citizens. It was now the turn of Dean Potter to write complainingly to Laud on 25 January:

> The Bishop's anger we have deserved by 2 things. 1. By rescuing a charnel house from his prophanation who passionately desired to keep it still for his hay house (keeping his own chapels not so cleanly as now we keep that).
>
> Now I humbly beseech your Grace to hear our grievances. His Lordship ... denies us our land belonging clearly to our charnel house and necessary to us for our School, and says we shall have it when we have sued for it in law, but not before ...
>
> ... He hates and speaks most unworthily of Mr Tomkins our Prebend, who is as worthy, honest and truehearted a churchman as any is of his quality in England. And the Bishop's hatred has so inflamed the citizens, that this good and worthy man is made amongst them the matter of sport and contempt, all the injuries and affronts possible put upon him by their very boys, nay by our own School boys, to whom we give exhibition [maintenance]. Very lately, coming out from quire service as he was doing his adoration to God, purposely to hinder him in that action, the boys came thrusting and thronging upon him (who was then senior at home and had my authority) in such an insolent fashion that he was forced to hit one a box on the ear. The town triumphs at this, and the boy's father

---

[35] TNA, *Calendar of State Papers Domestic*, Charles I, 343/77; Leach, *Documents*, 247. The Bishop's Palace was used as the Deanery from 1842; it is now known as the Old Palace.

A Faithful City

means to sue him for striking in the Church. If our Bishop have the hearing of this business it will be a heinous matter. But I know that your Grace will relieve him, if there be need. In the mean while, I will do justice upon that saucy lad, and turn him out of his exhibition.[36]

Although only obeying orders, it is difficult to avoid the impression that Nathaniel might have relished his task of converting the bishop's hay barn. The result of the lawsuit, if it ever came to court, is not known, but the townspeople of Worcester and the dean and chapter of their cathedral seemed, in any case, to be set on a collision course. Signs on the stone tower of the old bridge over the Severn proclaimed Worcester to be *Civitas Fidelis* (a faithful city) and *Deo et Rege* (for God and King), but many of her citizens were totally opposed to the Arminianism being thrust upon them by both archbishop and king.

Civic hackles rose when, following the Visitation in 1635, Dean Potter had denied the use of the cathedral pulpit to the city lecturer (preacher), John Halciter. Lectureships were an ancient tradition, endowed by town corporations such as that at Worcester from as early as the mid-sixteenth century. By the 1630s the main features of the Worcester Cathedral service on Sunday afternoons were a sermon by a lecturer, after which the organist, choir and a packed congregation joined in the singing of metrical psalms. 'It was said that no greater congregation could be seen anywhere except at St Paul's.'[37] Laud and his fellow Arminians considered the institution of city lecturers to be a threat to their reforms, running counter to the archbishop's absolutely unequivocal views on the relative importance of pulpit and altar. 'The altar is the greatest place of God's residence upon earth. I say the greatest,' wrote Laud. 'Yea, greater than the pulpit, for there tis *Hoc est corpus meum* [this is my body], but in the pulpit tis at most but *Hoc est verbum meum* [this is my word].'

Even though more than fifteen hundred citizens had died like flies in the great plague of Worcester in 1637, the mayor, the bishop and the dean found time to pursue a lengthy correspondence with Laud relating to the lectureship controversy, a correspondence that did not end until December 1639. The bishop supported the corporation against his own dean:

> Corporations tended to be Puritan, or at least anti-Laudian … The mayor and his brethren were accused by the Dean of attending the lecture only, and not divine service, but defended themselves by saying they had already been to their own churches. The Dean accused the Bishop of encouraging 'factious ill spirits' among the citizens, allowing them 'to sit covered in our Church in their gay and gaudy seats', and favouring the lecturers, Hardwick and Halciter: 'Hardwick, no graduate, an ignorant ass, talking false Latin'.[38] The corporation petitioned Laud

---

[36] TNA, *Calendar of State Papers Domestic*, Charles I, 344/107; Leach, *Documents*, 248.

[37] Woodfill, *Musicians in English Society*, 157.

[38] TNA, SP16/344/107, quoted by Bond, *Chamber Order Book*.

158   *The Lives and Times of Thomas Tomkins and his Family*

> that they might continue to have sermons in the cathedral from their lecturer ...
> The king wrote to the mayor and chief officers that they were to attend the
> cathedral services.[39]

The king ordered that his letter, dated 13 March 1637, was to be entered
amongst the acts and orders of the city, but this was not done. The
corporation had spent £80 in fitting up the west end of the cathedral as an
auditorium, with raked seating rising 'by degrees as high as the bottom of the
west window. There the senators and their wives sat in pomp, and more state
than in their Guildhall',[40] listening to the lecturer, whose pulpit was also at the
west end. The dean had ordered the removal of this elaborate seating structure
and the transfer of the pulpit to the west end of the quire, much to the chagrin
of the mayor and leading citizens, many of whom objected to choral services.
In 1639 they petitioned Laud, complaining that the new arrangements were
totally inadequate for the large numbers attending and that many people were
now obliged to stand 'to the great hazard of their healths'.

Presumably, Dean Potter had hoped that in abolishing separate facilities for
sermons the lecturers would be silenced and that the people would, instead,
be drawn to the choral services. But the corporation had determined that
lecturers' fees and expenses would continue to be paid by the city. Potter,
seeking a compromise, wrote to Laud on 18 November: 'The times are crazy
and I hope your wisdom and goodness may, for our peace and quiet, in that
place, yield a little to their folly ... The complying of our weak silly bishop
and these silly weak ones of my company ... has put [the townspeople] into
such a fury and malice against me, Mr Boughton and Mr Tomkins, as is
hardly to be imagined.'[41]

Stephen Boughton, canon of the third stall, and Nathaniel Tomkins were
Potter's strongest allies. If Bishop John Thornborough, once a firebrand, had
become weak and silly it might have had something to do with the fact that
he was approaching his 93rd year; in his view it was Nathaniel who was 'the
only incendiary between the bishop and the church'. So it fell to one of the
'silly, weak ones', William Smyth, recently appointed as canon of the first stall,
to hint at the real problem – pride – in a letter that he sent to Laud on the
same day as that written by his dean. He sympathized with the citizens, 'mere
neighbours, but now so distant in their better affections', and suggested that
they should be allowed to return to the west end of the cathedral; not as
before, with 'fixed seats and with degrees exalted', but moveable seats, 'equal
for height, unless the mayor's seat and some few were a little more eminent'.[42]
Laud seized upon this, agreeing that 'there against the dead wall [of the west

---

[39] Ibid.

[40] TNA, SP16/432/26 and SP16/432/80.

[41] TNA, SP 16/432/80.

[42] TNA, SP 16/432/81.

A Faithful City 159

end] shall be set moveable seats, decent, handsome, and easy for the mayor and his brethren'.[43] But as 1639 came to an end Potter was obliged to report to the archbishop that 'our citizens are highly displeased' at not having been granted 'their secret desires, which they dared not express, *viz.* their gay and lofty seats, the ruins whereof remain with us'.[44] Moreover, the corporation threatened to petition the king for a refund from the cathedral of the considerable sum that they had laid out on the fixed seating.

In the midst of this turmoil, ghastly for Nathaniel and Theodosia, and upsetting for his parents, news came to Worcester of the death of Thomas Tomkins's half-brother John on 27 September 1638. John Tomkins's wife Margaret was left with three small children: John, aged 7; Sylvanus, aged 3; and Thomas, less than a year old.[45] Only two years earlier, Charles Butler, in his book *The Principles of Music*, had honoured Thomas and John Tomkins as the 'Golden Pair of Music':

> Let him heedfully examine, observe, and imitate the Artificial works of the best Authors, such as Clemens non Papa, Horatio Vecchi, Orlando di Lasso, Alfonso Ferrabosco, Luca Marenzio, G. Croce, Doctor Fayrfax, Doctor Tye, Mr. BYRD, Mr. White, Mr. Morley, and now excelling Mr. Thomas and John Tomkins (that Aureum par Musicorum).

The country had lost one of its finest musicians, and it is sad that so few of his compositions have been preserved. Apart from the psalm tune *Gloucester*, published by Ravenscroft, all that remains are the words of six anthems in a Chapel Royal anthem book,[46] a single part of *Have mercy upon me*, dated 1617, in a partbook in the Bodleian Library,[47] the madrigal *O thrice-blessed earthbed* in Myriell's anthology,[48] a setting of *Cantate Domino*,[49] and a single keyboard piece, probably a solo for the virginals, entitled *John come kiss me now*.[50]

John Tomkins was buried in the north aisle of St Paul's Cathedral beneath a memorial tablet bearing the following epitaph:

> Johannes Tomkins, Musicae Baccalaureus, Organista sui temporis celeberrimus, postquam Capellae regali, per annos duodecem, huic autem Ecclesiae per

---

43 TNA, SP 16/433/30.

44 TNA, SP 16/436/50.

45 As Denis Stevens has pointed out (Stevens, 14, n. 1), Rimbault (*Cheque Book*, 209) talks of 'another son, Robert, who was one of the Royal Musicians in 1641', and this (in spite of Eitner's guarded statement – "Seine Verwandtschaft ist unsicher" – in R. Eitner (1899–1904), *Quellenlexicon der Musiker und Musikgelehrten*, Leipzig, IX, (425) misled Fellowes so far as to list this mysterious son as Robert (6) in Grove's *Dictionary*, 5th edition, VIII, 497. Robert (6) and Robert (9) should combine to form one person.'

46 BL Harley MS 6346.

47 Bodleian Library, Tenbury MS 1382.

48 BL Add. MS 29372–7, also in 29427.

49 BL Add. MS 29366–8, 18936–9.

50 BL Add. MS 29996.

160 The Lives and Times of Thomas Tomkins and his Family

novemdecem sedulo inservisset, ad coelestem chorum migravit Septembris 27, Anno Domini 1638. Aetatis suae 52. Cujus desiderium mœrens uxor hoc testatur Marmore.[51]

In half-a-dozen heartfelt lines, William Lawes paid glowing tribute to one who had been colleague and friend, one whose artistry had perhaps provided inspiration for his own superb and highly original music. Lawes's valediction to John Tomkins was published by his brother Henry in the *Choice Psalms put into Musick for Three Voices* of 1648. But by 1648 William Lawes was dead, killed in the service of his king, and England was in turmoil.

ELEGY ON THE DEATH OF JOHN TOMKINS

Musick, the master of thy art is dead,
And with him all thy ravished sweets are fled:
Then bear a part in thine own tragedy,
Let's celebrate strange grief with harmony;
Instead of tears shed on his mournful hearse,
Let's howl sad notes stol'n from his own pure verse.

---

[51] William Dugdale (*c*.1680), *Old St. Paul's*, 101: 'John Tomkins, Bachelor of Music, the most celebrated organist of his time, departed to the celestial choir on 27th September in the year of our Lord 1638 at the age of 52, after serving the Chapel Royal with great devotion for twelve years and this church for nineteen years. His grieving wife bears witness to her love of him with this marble memorial.'

Chapter 12

Distracted Times

> The gods did not reveal, from the beginning,
> All things to us; but in the course of time,
> Through seeking, men find that which is better.
>
> But as for certain truth, no man has known it,
> Nor will he know it; neither of the gods,
> Nor yet of all the things of which I speak.
> And even if by chance he were to utter
> Finality, he would himself not know it;
> For all is but a woven web of guesses.
>
> (Xenophanes)

Throughout the 1630s Archbishop Laud, supported by the king, increasingly imposed Arminianism upon the Church. Unyielding in his determination to succeed, Laud never flinched from using the power of the courts both to enforce his religious policies and to express his own wrath against those who would oppose him.

In January 1630, at Laud's instigation, Dr Alexander Leighton was charged before the dreaded Star Chamber for writing a pamphlet in which he called bishops 'Sataned', 'enemies of the State', and 'Men of Blood'. And as though to prove Leighton right, Laud voted that he be imprisoned during His Majesty's pleasure, pilloried, whipped, have his ears cut off, and have the letters SS branded on his cheek, thus stigmatizing Leighton as a 'Sower of Sedition'.[1]

Not all of Laud's punishments were so severe. At the same time as the Leighton case was proceeding, Giles Tomkins's detractor at Salisbury, Bishop John Davenant, became involved in a dispute concerning the blinkered perception of religious art. Recorder Henry Sherfield, leader of the city's Puritan elite, had noticed a group of women making low curtsies in St Edmund's Church. He asked them why they did it; they replied 'that they made them to their Lord God, and to God the Father in the glass window'. Sherfield thought the window idolatrous because it depicted God as the creator of the world, and obscene because it showed 'a naked man, and the

---

[1] John Rushworth (1659–1701), *Historical Collections of Private Passages of State*, London, II, 55–7.

161

Fig. 12.1 Archbishop William Laud (1573–1645). A portrait by an unknown artist, after van Dyck.

woman naked in some part'.[2] Davenant instructed that the window was to remain in place, but Sherfield took up a pikestaff, climbed a ladder, and smashed it. He too was brought before Star Chamber, committed to prison, awarded a fine of £500, ordered to apologize to the bishop, and to pay for the window to be repaired. Even then, Laud considered that the court had dealt too leniently with him.

The Court of Star Chamber, the King's Council sitting as a court of law, had its origins in the fifteenth century. The court, which assembled in the Star Chamber, a room in the palace of Westminster (so called because of the painted stars which adorned its ceiling) was for much of its life respected as an instrument of just and decisive action. Under Charles I, however, Star Chamber became an ecclesiastical weapon, the focus of persecution against

---

[2] H. Shortt (1957), *The City of Salisbury*, London, 70; and *Victoria County History of Wiltshire* (1957), V, 131.

Distracted Times   163

the opponents of Arminianism, feared for the severity of its punishments. That the bishops, thought by many to be lowborn upstarts, should be invested with secular power was a cause of considerable resentment. That they should also be permitted to thrust themselves into the King's Council gave offence to noble and commoner alike. Anonymous handbills containing threats to the archbishop's life began to appear all over London.

Laud had no interest in conciliation. Elaborate ritual, ornate services and ecclesiastical discipline were to be imposed without appeal. But, like Juxon, he was a man of genuine musical sensitivity; an anthem by him is to be found in the Peterhouse partbooks and in the collection of anthems and services that Thomas Tudway (*c.*1650–1723) compiled for Lord Harley.[3] In his will, he bequeathed his organ at Lambeth to the See; and he left the organ at his country house in Croydon, his harp, chest of viols, a harpsichord and 50 pounds to John Cob, who was probably his household musician.

Laud espoused principles that, as far as the good order of church music was concerned, were absolutely essential. Those principles finally prevailed, and remain in place to this day. That Tomkins fully approved of them is not to be doubted but, faced with widespread accounts of the gruesome proceedings in Star Chamber, it seems unlikely that this deeply spiritual man would have condoned Laud's methods. Could a hint of aversion, a *double entendre* that came unbidden to his mind, be found in Tomkins's setting of 'Above the stars my saviour dwells, I love, I care for nothing else'?

In July 1637 the doors of Star Chamber swung open for the trial of Laud's old enemy Bishop John Williams. The archbishop voted that he should be fined £10,000, stripped of all his offices and imprisoned during His Majesty's pleasure. But the best-known and most far-reaching case that Laud heard in Star Chamber concerned William Prynne (1600–1669), a lawyer, moral fanatic, and the prolific author of tedious texts. In 1633 Prynne published a vituperative tract of eleven hundred pages entitled *Histriomastix, a Scourge of Stage Plays*, in which, amongst other things, he took a swipe at the theatrical profession as a source of immorality, condemning 'women actors' in particular as 'notorious whores'. Laud was angered and shaken by this thinly disguised attack upon both himself – as a student he had enjoyed taking part in amateur theatricals – and upon Queen Henrietta, whose delight in appearing in lavish theatrical productions was well known. In *Histriomastix* Prynne attacked the queen's faith and accused her of lowering the social tone at court. Laud, already fearful of assaults upon the establishment and possible assassination attempts upon himself and his fellow bishops, said that the book was scandalous, 'against the State in an infamous manner', and its author guilty of 'infamous treason'.[4]

---

[3] BL Harley MSS 7337–42.
[4] W. Scot and J. Bliss (eds, 1847–60), *The Works of the most Reverend Father in God, William Laud*, Oxford, VI, 234–7.

164   *The Lives and Times of Thomas Tomkins and his Family*

Prynne was sentenced to lose his ears, to stand in the pillory, to pay a fine of £5,000, to lose his Oxford degree and membership of the bar, and to be perpetually imprisoned.

The Prynne hearing of June 1637 and of others like it, such as the equally famous trials of John Bastwick and Henry Burton, outspoken enemies of episcopacy, must have carried a chilling message to musicians of the court and the church; where would their future lie should the Puritans ever prevail over the bishops? To men such as John Withy of Worcester, a Roman Catholic composer employed by Queen Henrietta's Company, professional life in London was approaching an inescapable twilight.

To impose Anglican ritual and Prayer Book upon England was one thing; to impose them upon Presbyterian Scotland was quite another. Betraying just how little he understood of his Scottish subjects, Charles insisted that they accept the English Prayer Book, soon known as 'Laud's prayer book', and all that it implied. 'For a man who prized uniformity and the maintenance of royal authority above all else, and saw these values primarily in religious terms, the introduction of the English Prayer Book into the land of his fathers was as characteristic as his insistence that, come what may, the Scots accept it.'[5] Rumours spread in Scotland that the book was full of 'popish rites', and a petition of 1637 condemned it for sowing 'the seeds of divers superstitions, idolatry and false doctrine, contrary to the true religion established within this realm'.[6] When the new Prayer Book was used at St Giles's Cathedral, Edinburgh, in July of that year the service was halted by a riot. Scotland wanted rid of episcopacy; resistance grew; Laud told the king to 'risk everything rather than yield a jot'; and in February 1638 Charles banned all future protests against the Prayer Book on pain of treason. Hundreds of thousands of Scots, forced to choose between faith and king, signed the 'Covenant', a pledge to resist to the death any innovations in religion. A fuse had been set to the so-called Bishops' War.

The king rode north on 27 March to crush 'the Scottish Covenanting rebels'. Having assembled at Berwick, his ragbag of an army proved incapable of engaging the Scots. On 23 July, Charles, back in London, summoned Thomas Wentworth, his devoted lord deputy in Ireland, to return to England – and rewarded him with a long-awaited earldom. The new earl of Strafford persuaded the king to end his Personal Rule, to call a parliament, and, with the support of his confidant Laud, urged Charles to embark upon a second Scots war. Wentworth had enjoyed considerable success in Ireland by his ability to control the Irish parliament, and believed that it was equally within his power to persuade the English parliament to fund a campaign against the Scots.

---

5   Charles Carlton (1995), *Charles I, The Personal Monarch*, London, 196.
6   Brice, *The Early Stuarts*, 104.

Distracted Times 165

Thomas Tomkins, returning to London in 1639, will have travelled through a country gripped by war fever. In this, possibly his last journey to the capital, he was fulfilling a small secondary task on behalf of the Worcester dean and chapter, the nature of which is recorded in the cathedral treasurer's accounts: 'Paid for carriage of the old plate to London and bringing down the new, according to Mr Thomas Tomkins's bill, 19s.7d.'[7]

His return to Worcester was delayed, and it appears that he was still in London on 20 February 1640 when a delegation of commissioners from Scotland, led by Lord Loudoun, arrived at court to plead with the king. They were seeking acceptance of legislation put forward by the Scottish parliament and a new method of choosing the Lords of the Articles, the intermediary body between king and parliament. 'The Scots, on the way to London, had distributed copies of their own account of the Pacification of Berwick, the account which the king had had burnt in the previous August. In open conversation they had compared the king to a truant schoolboy who had promised them everything when his schoolmaster Laud was not by, and had taken it all back again when the archbishop resumed his sway.'[8]

The waters of diplomacy, already turbulent, were not calmed by the meeting, and it was probably the substance of this difficult encounter that Tomkins recorded in one of his anthologies as 'The English Lords' Answer to the Proposition of the Scots Lords'; he may even have been present at Whitehall to hear the frosty royal rejection of the Scots' demands:

> That the proposition as much concerns a conformity of religion [and] of church government in both kingdoms ... no alterations or innovations [are to be made] against that which is passed by the laws of each kingdom, which are dangerous to either.
>
> That the government of the Church of England is titled and Established by the laws of this kingdom. That both the Houses of Parliament have now in consideration all things conducing to them touching the peace of the Church of England, will do therein that in their wisdoms they shall think fit.
>
> That although you may be commanded by those which sent you to make this proposition: yet for ambassadors of any foreign prince, much less for commissioners, his majesty's subjects, to insist upon a thing that is destruction to the government established by the laws of this kingdom, and to accompany these propositions with discourses and arguments in prejudice of the settled government: is both unusual and unfit.
>
> Therefore his majesty expects that according to your many professions and that which is contained in your own paper: you will not meddle with the Reformation here in England ... as likewise that you would not publish nor divulge any discourse by which the Subjects of this kingdom may be stirred up against the Established laws of this kingdom. But that you will acquiesce with this answer.[9]

---

7 WCL, Treasurer's Accounts (1639), A26, 66.

8 C.V. Wedgewood (2001), *The King's Peace 1637–1641*, London, 273, quoting *Calendar of State Papers, Domestic*, Charles I, 1639–40, 446–7 and 557.

9 BL Add. MS 29996, fol. 182.

166   *The Lives and Times of Thomas Tomkins and his Family*

Charles had no intention of making a peaceful agreement with the Scots. They were his subjects; Scotland was a part of his kingdom; he was king by divine right; therefore an affront to the king was an affront to God. Even whilst the arguments with Loudoun and his companions were under way, he wrote secretly to the royalist commander of Edinburgh Castle with instructions to make ready to fire on the city should he think the situation warranted it.[10]

The Scottish bishops had already fled to England, and north of the border anti-royalist protest was growing in intensity. The king had hoped that the recalled parliament of Easter 1640 would agree speedily to his demands for cash and supplies to crush the rebels. Handicapped by a speech impediment, Charles left it to the arrogant and pompous lord keeper, John Finch, to set out his policy. Finch warned the house that the king did not require their advice, but an immediate vote of supplies. His words served only to irritate the Commons, already thoroughly alienated and in no mood to give immediate approval to anything. Under the leadership of John Pym the king's opponents began to air at length their long-held grievances: the infringement of parliamentary liberties, innovations in religion, and violations of property. The tail was wagging the dog, but the defiance of members of both the lower and the upper houses resulted directly from their perception that the traditional political liberties and the Protestant religion as established by Elizabeth I and maintained by James I was under direct threat from Charles's policies. 'Neither Speaker Glanville, nor the two Secretaries of State, nor the various court nominees and supporters, could force the debate back into the narrow channel mapped out for it in the king's interest by Lord Keeper Finch.'[11] Utterly frustrated, Charles dissolved parliament after only three weeks.

The business of the so-called 'Short Parliament' may well have been in Tomkins's mind when he set down in pithy allegorical verse his fears for the instability of the times:[12]

> *The game at Chess*
>
> The pawnes make all the play
> Have all the say
> The Rookes looke on
> & yet they make no play.
>
> The knights dare not Remove
> The Bishops bee
> Some fast. Some chased
> From place to place we see.

---

[10] TNA, *Calendar of State Papers, Domestic*, Charles I, 1639–40, 558.
[11] Wedgewood, *The King's Peace*, 282.
[12] BL Add. MS 29996.

Distracted Times

167

> Let thother looke to't,
> Er't be too late.
> They have had sufficient check
> Beware the mate.

Whatever Tomkins's worries about the worsening political situation, he will have been equally concerned by the plight of his late half-brother's family. Whilst it is possible that his primary reason for visiting London in late 1639 was to attend the Chapel Royal, it is more likely that he had travelled to the capital specifically to collect his young nephews John, Sylvanus and Thomas, whose mother, Margaret, may already have died. She was certainly dead by 1649, when, in a paper addressed to the Committee for Compounding, Nathaniel Tomkins refers to the three children as orphans.[13]

John junior, Sylvanus and Thomas were brought up and educated by their relations in Worcester. John and Sylvanus became King's scholars and gained places in the cathedral choir, leaving traces of their studies at Tomkins's side by scribbling their signatures in one of his autograph manuscripts.[14]

The Worcester Cathedral Treasurer's Book for 1643–4 includes the following list of choristers for that year:

Choristarum Stipendia
Term 3

		li	s	d
Jo Browne	Mr T Tomk	0	16	8
Richd Davyes	Mr N Tomk	0	16	8
Jo Tinker	Mr T T	0	16	8
Richd Tayler	Mr T T	0	16	8
Wm Linton	Mr T T	0	16	8
Nath Browne	Mr T Tomk	0	16	8
Hum Davies	Eliz Barrett	0	16	8
Wm Awbury	Mr N T	0	16	8
Sylvanus Tomkins	Mr T Tomk	0	16	8
Jo Tomkins	Mr N T	0	16	8

(the names in the second column appear to indicate the person to whom the payment was given). Inside the back cover of the book is a note concerning payment of King's Scholars of the College School, some of whom were choristers:[15]

---

13 Richard Newsholme, 'Tomkins: Domestic Life'.
14 Bibliothèque Nationale, Conservatoire de Musique, Paris, Rés. 1122.
15 WCL, Treasurer's Accounts (1643–4), A28.

168   *The Lives and Times of Thomas Tomkins and his Family*

Dec 6 1643
25 Scholler paid   } 13 unpaids
besides R Davies and
Jo Tomkins whose pay I delivered to young
Mrs Tomkins

Of the ten choristers listed, John Tinker (the son of the precentor) and Richard Tayler (the son of the school usher) both came from families living close to the cathedral, and Nathaniel Browne is of particular significance and will be mentioned below. Humphrey Davies may well have been boarding with Elizabeth Barrett. She lived in the parish of St Michael in Bedwardine and her brother had also been in the choir. Of the rest a majority may have had to make boarding arrangements, and it is tempting to suppose that they were split between Nathaniel and Thomas Tomkins, whose names appear by the payments. 'Young Mrs Tomkins' was presumably Nathaniel's wife Theodosia, who would have been thirty-five.[16]

In spite of his advancing age, Tomkins remained fully committed to his duties at Worcester, and even played daily for morning prayers held at 6.00 a.m. in the Lady Chapel, for which he received a small additional quarterly fee.[17] During 1639 and 1640 the Gloucester dean and chapter again sought Tomkins's advice about the specifications for a new organ there, paying him two shillings for each of his visits. Twenty-three years had passed since Dean Laud's unsuccessful attempt to raise the necessary funds to purchase a new organ for Gloucester Cathedral. Now Archbishop Laud expected action:

> The [Gloucester] accounts for 1639–40 show that at last something was done. Thomas Cooke was paid 2s. 'for assuring the organ loft and goeing three or four miles to newe timber for it' and 6s. was given to 'a messenger to Worcester twoe severall tymes to Mr Tomkins about the agreemt with Dallam for the new organ'. Cooke was also paid 10s.9d. for taking down the old organ, and 6s.8d. was paid to 'Coward Meason, Sadler, for leather and mending the organ bellowes'. Of the new organ itself no description survives, but it was 'approved' by Tomkins in 1641.[18]

Unfortunately, friction between the corporation of Worcester city and the cathedral had continued unabated, and reached such a pitch by 1641 that the civic authorities presented a petition to parliament protesting against the dean and chapter. The situation of the cathedral, in the parish of St Michael in Bedwardine, within the walls but outside the city, had long been a potential source of conflict. None the less, the arrangement had worked reasonably well until the unpopularity of Laudian reforms fuelled open hostility.

---

[16] Newsholme, 'Tomkins: Domestic Life'.
[17] WCL, Treasurer's Accounts (1639), A26, 66.
[18] Frith, *Organs and Organists*, 3.

Distracted Times   169

The dispute was not limited to the provision of seats in the cathedral for the mayor and corporation; the stone altar and altar rails put in place by Dean Mainwaring, the chapter's contribution to the poor and highways, the right to burial in the cathedral churchyard, and school management were all causes of grievance. The petition no longer exists, but a copy of the chapter's response to it indicates that Nathaniel Tomkins, a particular target for civic anger, had been obliged to make a grovelling apology:

> Mr Tomkins knows not wherein he hath offended any of the city in word or deed. His father hath bin very charitable to their poore, and soe hath he. He is sorry that he hath lost their love, and much desires it, and will be most ready and willing to recover it by all offices of love and curtosie hereafter, and will carry himselfe with all submission, respect, and humility, to the Lord Bishop, his Diocesan.[19]

Peace seems to have been restored as the result of a conference between the dean and chapter and the corporation of the city. 'Amongst the terms of the understanding that was reached was "the school to be reduced to the old place". Noake remarks that "complaints were made by the friends of the scholars of the unwholesome smells from the human remains deposited in the vault underneath the chapel, then used as the school".' [20] So Nathaniel's eager endeavour to convert the Capella Carnaria into a school-house, a move both expensive and unpopular, was thrown into reverse; the King's School scholars trooped back to the College Hall.

This small defeat was as nothing in comparison to the troubles of the king. In 1640 Charles finally found himself opposed by the entire political nation. The three elements essential to the smooth running of the state machine: king, parliament and the judiciary, had split apart. A second Bishops' War against the Scots resulted in defeat for Charles, parliament was again recalled in November 1640, and this session, known as the Long Parliament, was not constitutionally dissolved until 1660. From the outset, the first parliamentary priority was religion. Prynne, Burton and Bastwick were released from their imprisonment in Jersey, Guernsey and the Isles of Scilly respectively, and on 16 November the Commons sent Black Rod to the Tower to free Bishop Williams. Cheering crowds lined the streets of London to hail the triumphal return of all four men. A few days earlier the Commons had impeached the earl of Strafford, a prime target for revenge, unforgiven for having advised the king to make war upon his own subjects. Within weeks Archbishop Laud was also impeached, and both men lay prisoners in the Tower, separate and forbidden to meet.

---

[19] WCL, D312.
[20] Alec MacDonald (1936), *A History of the King's School, Worcester*, London, 119, quoting J. Noake (1866), *The Monastery and Cathedral of Worcester*, Worcester, 459.

170   *The Lives and Times of Thomas Tomkins and his Family*

Strafford went on trial for his life on 22 March 1641. The Lords found the evidence against him too flimsy to uphold a conviction, but the Commons pushed through an act of attainder, effectively ordering the execution of that most steadfast of Charles's supporters. The king, under duress, abandoned Strafford to his fate, assenting to his attainder on 10 May 1641, a betrayal for which he never forgave himself.

Two days later, at noon, Laud stood at the window of his room in the Tower as Strafford was led to his death. The doomed earl looked up: 'My Lord, your prayers and blessing,' he asked. The archbishop raised a trembling hand in silent benediction, and then fell back fainting. Later, in his lonely confinement, Laud confided bitterly to his diary that the king whom he and Strafford had served so faithfully had been unworthy of their loyalty – 'he knew not how to be or be made great'.[21]

The future of monarchy itself was now in doubt, and the time when Tomkins might safely pay his personal tribute to the great earl was yet to come. He had admired Strafford and Laud. Both had laboured in the cause of a great vision. Tomkins had striven to play his part in achieving that vision; he had, as E.H. Fellowes wrote of Byrd, 'devoted his best gifts ... to the high purpose of beautifying the spirit of Worship'.[22] Now, Strafford was dead, the head of the Church a captive of the State, and demonstrators were demanding an end to bishops. Tomkins must have sensed that worse was to come, that his entire *raison d'être* was threatened – and then fate conspired to take away his life companion of forty-five years. Tomkins's devoted wife Alice died on 29 January 1642, in her seventy-ninth year.

That closest of family friends, John Toy, gave a heartfelt sermon at Alice's funeral on 2 February. His words, sincere and emotional, give us a valuable insight into her generous nature and modesty. They also reveal much about the constancy and integrity of her husband.

> We are met here to do the last honour to our departed Sister, and in her name I thank this worthy Assembly that come to wait on her deserved Obsequies; would she had a better Orator, this presence, especially this subject deserved it; my happiness is the goodness of the subject will help out my imperfect Oratory. I know by her no infirmities that I should need to hide or colour; I need not rack, or torture my invention to force her a praise; I need not strain or dissemble a syllable; she hath filled my mouth with true and real honour.
>
> This text is true in her, we have our time, and she had hers, God be thanked a time of peace and plenty; our time is short, 'tis true, hers was near fourscore, almost two lustres beyond the age of man, if we reckon the number of days, and innumerable grievances of life; she lived long I must confess, but if we measure her life by the affection of her friends, and neighbours, they will I know confess with me, that hers was too too short, she died much too soon. Our time is appointed, so was hers; she was not cut off by untimely chance, she shortened not

---

[21] Scot and Bliss (eds), *The Works of Laud*, III, 445.

[22] E.H. Fellowes (1941), *English Cathedral Music*, London, 71.

Distracted Times

her days by intemperate diet, she long enjoyed a quiet and entire old age, and like an undisturbed taper burnt out to the last week, yea a good while since with prophetic prediction she points out the time of her departure. We shall have our change, she hath waned some few weeks and now hath hers, from corruptible to incorruption, from mortal life to life immortal, from the light of this world, by which we see a world of misery, to the light of heaven, and Righteousness, which shall never be changed, obscured, nor eclipsed.

This for her we may well presume, for my own part I desire from my soul my last end may be like unto hers, with firm faith, cheerful hope, settled patience, and perpetual preparation, she waited, expected, called, and invited Christ. So far with my Text, but I should wrong her much to say no more, she was an excellent neighbour, I speak it before them that know it, and have most ingeniously confessed it, she was grateful to the best, gracious to the poor, peaceable, officious, and affable to all.

She was an excellent wife, witness the many tears her husband shed, truer tears I dare say never fell at funeral; witness his charge, and charity to bring her home with honour. She like that Emblem of a good Housewife was seldom far from home, at home most neatly industrious, but especially so loving to her husband, that where to pattern such sweet conjugal Society I profess I know not; Let us learn it, (beloved,) believe it, it is a great advantage for heaven to be well skilled in the duty of marriage; this marriage is but for a time, death will divorce it, the second time we should be married to Christ, and will he wed them to himself whom he knew forward and unchaste to a former Spouse? This true good tree hath borne good fruit to the honour and good of this Church, they that have tasted it truly, have praised it for a fragrant and gracious savour, not many Orchards afford the like; she was happy in it to the last.

But which is above all, she was a very good Christian, witness her meekness, one of the truest marks of a Christian, meek she was as appeared by her Matron-like plainness; so meek, that she scorned not to hold discourse with a Child that could scarce speak again to her, an argument of that childish innocency by which we attain heaven.

A good Christian she was, witness that great Example of her devotion, she lived like *Anna* as it were continually in the Temple, twice a day for many decades of years, she attended the worship of God Almighty in this Church, nor would she leave that holy use, for age and weakness, but spite of sickness, as if she meant to sacrifice her life to God, she came still, till the heavy weight of death detained her in her bed.

For her Charity, a main part of the essence of a *Christian*, I must say for that part of Charity that pertains to the tongue, in judging and censuring, she did excel, she loved not to hear, she abhorred to speak evil, of any, she would give fair and candid constructions to all actions, loving and reverent counsel to all that came near her. As for the Charity of her purse, I know not what it was, nor indeed was it her desire that any should know; but this know, she bred up Orphans, sent often meat, and money to her sick neighbours, her servant hath been seen to distribute good pieces of money to many poor families from year to year, from house to house, I am sure if it were known who sent it, it was the servant's fault, for she charged her the contrary; she loved (happy woman) to hide her treasure, and keep the left hand ignorant of what the right had done. I am fain to glean and guess at her Charity, surely if all were known, it would amount to a great sum, and her great glory, she rather desired that God might have the glory, to whom of due it belongs. Go to the Earth blessed Earth, and sleep there sweetly, till the Resurrection, thy other part is ere this safe arrived to the bosom of *Abraham*: Blessed Lord, give us grace so to follow her holy example, that we may

172   *The Lives and Times of Thomas Tomkins and his Family*

at last come to those unspeakable joys, which thou hast prepared for all them that unfeignedly love thee, and expect thy coming. *Even so come Lord Jesus.* AMEN.[23]

Alice was buried in the Lady Chapel of Worcester Cathedral, from where fragments of her gravestone were ultimately removed to the crypt:

Alicia, or
Ales, the wife of Thomas Tomkins,
One of the Gentlemen of His Majesty's
Chapel Royal, a woman full
of faith and good works
died the 29 January, 1641.[24]

At least she had been spared the madness of Civil War.

The king set up his standard at Nottingham on 22 August 1642, marking the beginning of the conflict. Fighting began in Warwickshire the next day, soon spreading to Worcestershire. Royalist troopers plundered the house of William Stephens at Broadway, taking money, silver plate, and setting fire to his hayricks.[25] On 16 September, Sir John Byron and his dragoons took Worcester for the Crown; it was a temporary victory – a Parliamentary army had already set out westward from London *en route* to Worcester. Only four miles from the capital they paused at Acton and broke into the church, 'defaced whatever was decent therein; tore the Bible and Book of Common Prayer; sticking the leaves of them upon the walls with their excrement'.[26] On 24 September, they marched into Worcester and occupied the city.

> And when their whole army, under the command of the Earl of Essex, came to Worcester, the first thing they there did, was the prophanation of the cathedral; destroying the organ; breaking in pieces divers beautiful windows, wherein the foundation of that church was lively historified with painted glass, and barbarously defacing divers fair monuments of the dead. And as if this were not enough, they brought their horses into the body of the church, keeping fires and courts of guard therein, making the quire and side aisles, with the font, the common places, wherein they did their easements of nature. Also, to make their wickedness the more complete, they rifled the library, with the records and evidences of the church; tore in pieces the Bibles and Service-books pertaining to the quire; putting the surplices and other vestments upon their dragooners, who rode about the streets with them.[27]

An army of more than 15,000 men had descended upon a community of less than half that number. Their commander's first act was to arrest the

---

[23] 'A Sermon Preached in the Cathedrall Church of Worcester ... at the funeral of Mris Alice Tomkins wife unto Mr Thomas Tomkins ... By John Toy ...', London, 1642. BL Thomason Tracts, E154. See also Stevens, 54–6.

[24] The date, 1641, is in accordance with the old style of reckoning, i.e. 1641/2.

[25] See Malcolm Atkin (1995), *The Civil War in Worcestershire*, Stroud, 33 ff.

[26] William Dugdale (1681), *A Short View of the Late Troubles in England*, London, 557–8.

[27] Ibid.

Distracted Times 173

mayor, Edward Solley, who was 'made to go down on his knees and beg Essex's pardon for having surrendered the city without a fight to the Royalists'.[28] Solley and Alderman Green were put under arrest and carted off to London. Many of their fellow citizens held distinctly Parliamentarian sympathies, but even they must have been badly shaken by this first intimation of the horrors to come. Nor can the outrageous behaviour of Essex's troops have done anything to win their hearts and minds.

By 1642 Tomkins's superb Dallam organ at Worcester was nearly thirty years old, and in April that year 9*s.* 5*d.* had been spent on 'candles, glue, leather and whipcord', to repair 'the great bellows'.[29] The sight of so much wanton destruction to the cathedral must have been profoundly painful to Tomkins, and one wonders if he was actually present in the building to see crude hands wrenching organ pipes from the beautiful Robert Kettle case and flinging them clattering to the floor. If so, he would also have seen one of the organ's attackers lose his footing, fall from the screen, and break his neck.[30]

It may be that this fatality caused a pause in the mindless wrecking-spree before the organ was completely destroyed. Within weeks, the Parliamentary army evacuated Worcester in unseemly haste, the city was reoccupied by Royalist troops, and in November the king appointed Sir William Russell as governor of the garrison. The damage to the organ seems to have been repaired soon afterwards, but even the Royalists were no angels: they stripped lead for bullet-making from the cathedral roof.

Much worse was to come. On the morning of 29 May 1643, Sir William Waller, commanding a Parliamentary force of around 3000 men and eight cannon, made an unsuccessful attempt to wrest back the city, concentrating his attack upon the south and east sides. 'It started with an artillery barrage and then direct attacks towards Friar's Gate and Diglis – both of which failed.'[31] The Royalists successfully repulsed Waller's men from their position just outside the city walls below Castle Hill, using eleven barrels of gunpowder in the battle to fire two hundred shot. Tomkins's house, lying in the direct line of fire, was smashed by the cannonade.[32]

Outraged by these assaults, Tomkins made his protest in a verse anthem of 198 bars (omitted from *Musica Deo sacra*) *O God, the heathen are come into thine inheritance*, taking his text from the opening of Psalm 79:

> O God, the heathen are come into
> thine inheritance: thy holy temple have they

---

[28] J.W. Willis Bund (ed., 1915), *Diary of Henry Townshend of Elmley Lovett, 1640–1663*, Worcester (WHS), II, 89.

[29] WCL, Treasurer's Accounts (1642) A26, 22/3. Music was also bought at the same time.

[30] Valentine Green (1764), *A Survey of the City of Worcester*, enlarged into *The History and Antiquities of the City and Suburbs of Worcester* (1796), I, 114.

[31] Atkin, *Civil War*, 50–51.

[32] Ibid.

defiled, and made Jerusalem a heap of stones.

The dead bodies of thy servants
have they given to be meat unto the fowls of
the air: and the flesh of thy saints unto the beasts
of the land.

Their blood have they shed like
water on every side of Jerusalem: and there
was no man to bury them.

We are become an open shame and rebuke
to our enemies: a very scorn and derision
unto them that are round about us.

Lord, how long wilt thou be angry:
shall thy jealousy burn like fire for ever?

Pour out thy indignation upon the
heathen which have not known thee: and
upon the kingdoms which have not called
upon thy name.

For they have devoured
Jacob: and laid waste his dwelling place.

O remember not our old sins, but have
mercy upon us, and that soon: for we are
come to great misery.

Help us, O God of our
salvation, for the glory of thy name: O deliver
us, and be merciful unto our sins,
for thy name's sake.

In addition to the emotional trauma inflicted on Tomkins by the savage bombardment of the city, the destruction of his home and household goods, it is possible that irreplaceable music manuscripts might also have been lost. It is also possible that a portrait of Tomkins himself might have perished in the attack. His study had been in a high turret at the top of the house, approached by a staircase leading off from a third-floor garret. It seems that this room, which he probably used for composition, would have suffered maximum damage. Three months were to pass before any attempt was made to render the roof watertight. Cathedral records show that on 13 September 1643, 4s. 4d. was paid 'To the Mason for tiles, lime and work done in reparation of Mr. Organist's house, ruined by cannon shot when Waller attempted the taking of the city, May 29, 1643'.[33] The house would have been uninhabitable for many weeks, forcing Tomkins, his servants and the choristers in his care to seek shelter elsewhere.

Worcester was in turmoil following the Waller siege. Determined that any

---

[33] WCL, Treasurer's Accounts (1643), A28, 66.

Distracted Times 175

future Parliamentary force would be denied cover, a decision was taken to demolish buildings and works outside the walls. To spare the soldiers, this work was undertaken by 400 of 'the ordinary sort of women out of every ward within the city', who joined in companies and set out 'with colours and drums, striking up with spades, shovels and mattocks'.[34] All the buildings were cleared for 600 yards outside the Fore Gate, and work to strengthen the city's defences began immediately.

At about this time, a widow named Martha Browne began to play an important part in Tomkins's life. Martha's husband, Arthur Browne, a lay clerk, had died in October 1641, leaving Martha with two young sons, Nathaniel (aged 8) and Arthur (aged 5). Nathaniel was a cathedral chorister, one of the boys for whose 'teaching, keeping, dieting, apparelling, ordering and lodging' Tomkins was responsible. Perhaps the ghastliness of the times drew the young widow and the elderly widower together. Martha was to become Tomkins's second wife, and she was clearly much younger than his son, Nathaniel. Apart from the obvious need for love and companionship, it is not difficult to appreciate why Tomkins and Martha should choose to marry. Both were alone and responsible for bringing up young children. Sylvanus Tomkins was probably living with Tomkins *père*; his brother John with Nathaniel and Theodosia; and Martha needed security for herself and her two boys.

Martha Browne's marriage to Thomas Tomkins is mentioned in a paper annexed to a petition received by the Committee for Compounding on 30 October 1649. It is headed 'A true particular of the estate real & personal of Nathaniel Tomkins …' and it contains an entry that 'There is to come to him and his heirs, after the death of the compounder's father and his father's now wife, younger than the compounder, certain tenements in the city of Worcester worth per Annum £7.0s.0d.'

> There is nothing in the Worcester parish registers about this marriage, but a Christian name is given in the Parliamentary Survey of the dean and chapter's possessions made in 1649–50:
>
> > Thomas Tomkins in right of Martha his wife assignee of Catherine Feriman, by Indenture of Lease dated 25th day of November in the third year of the late King Charles … Doth hold all that messuage or tenement situate and being in the churchyard of the said cathedral church, near unto a tenement of John Ellis on the south part, and adjoining to A Stone Wall of the late bishop's palace on the west … and consisting of a hall, a parlour, a kitchen, a buttery, 3 chambers over and a top loft, with a little court before the door.
>
> The legal language here signifies that the lease of the building was originally granted by the Dean and Chapter to Catherine Feriman, who later conveyed the property to Martha, and it then became Thomas Tomkins's after their marriage,

---

34 Willis Bund, *Diary of Henry Townshend*, II, 123–4.

176 *The Lives and Times of Thomas Tomkins and his Family*

as a woman's possessions were deemed to belong to her husband. The information is helpful as the tenement can be identified in other cathedral records as the house of Arthur Browne ... Martha may have been Arthur Browne's second wife, as an entry for 1625 in the registers of St Swithun's Church, Worcester, records the burial of 'Joan, wife of Arthur Browne'. He seems to have become a lay clerk in 1626, and he is titled 'Mr' in the parish churchwardens' accounts, and wealthy enough to give alms to the poor at 'the time of the hard frost & great snow' in January 1634/5 [i.e. 1635].

The date of Tomkins's marriage to Martha is not known, but Nathaniel Browne was a chorister by 1642, and a King's scholar at the school by 1644. He is likely to have been taught to play the virginals by his step-father because when, in his twenties, his left hand was injured by a gunshot, he consulted one Thomas Wogan, chirurgeon, and

> ... faithfully promised that if his said hand should be so well cured and healed as that he could play upon the virginal with the same; that then he, the said Nathaniel, would give the said Thomas twenty pounds ...

A few months later, the wound having healed, Browne was heard to play the virginals on several occasions, but he welched on the agreement and the surgeon took legal action to claim the debt.[35]

Interestingly, the cathedral accounts show that a 'Mr Browne' was engaged as instructor of the choristers in 1643. This was probably Richard Browne, a minor canon who went on to become organist of the cathedral in 1662. It is possible that Richard Browne was Martha's brother-in-law, and a lay clerk named John Browne may also have been related to her. In any event, it is not surprising to find that Thomas Tomkins, in his seventy-first year, was content to delegate an important part of his responsibilities to a younger man.

War was now raging throughout the country. Giles Tomkins would have witnessed appalling scenes in Salisbury in December 1644 when the virtually defenceless city suffered attack and counter-attack, and was badly plundered by rampaging troops. Emerging victorious, the Royalist soldiers sought revenge for an earlier defeat, subjecting the citizens to 'three days of sustained terror'.[36] At Thomas Tomkins's childhood home of St David's, the organist was lucky to escape without injury when Parliamentary troops set about the desecration of the cathedral.

> The rebels were consulting in the choir about what other sacrilegious mischiefs they should perform; it was at length agreed to destroy the organ.

---

[35] Newsholme, 'Tomkins: Domestic Life', quoting Particular and Petition of Nathaniel Tomkins: TNA *State Papers* 23/218/342 and 343; lease of tenement near bishop's palace, Parliamentary Survey (WHS), 196; Arthur Browne's house, WCL A125(2), A125(3), A286, fol. 27r, A86 p. 366; WRO, St Michael in Bedwardine parish registers; the Cathedral Installations Register (WCL A65) records a Nathaniel Browne admitted as lay clerk on 23 June 1626, but this may have been a mistake for Arthur Browne as a Nathaniel does not appear elsewhere as a lay clerk: WRO, St Michael in Bedwardine Churchwardens' accounts fols 203r, 211r, 247r.

[36] See John Wroughton (1999), *An Unhappy Civil War*, Bath, 134.

Distracted Times   177

The organist, who had secreted himself within the organ-loft, heard the same; knowing that if they perpetrated their intended mischief, he should lose his bread, he threw a large stone into the choir; which falling on the head of one of Cromwell's aides-de-camp, killed him: dreading the consequence of his being discovered and taken by the rebels, he fled; they perceived and pursued him: when he had taken the presence of mind to get into one of the bells, which hung low, and there supported himself by the clapper, until they had given up the search.[37]

On 10 January 1645 a large and noisy crowd packed around the scaffold on Tower Hill to witness the beheading of William Laud, and on 24 September that year, William Lawes lost his life, serving the king at the siege of Chester, 'one of the bloodiest slaughters of the war'.[38] Thomas Fuller described what followed:

In these distracted times his [Lawes's] loyalty engaged him in the War for his Lord and Master, and though he was by General Gerrard made a Commissary on design to secure him (such officers being commonly shot-free by their place, as not exposed to danger), yet such the activity of his spirit, he disclaimed the covert of his office, and betrayed thereunto by his own adventurousness was casually shot at the Siege of Chester, the same time when the Lord Bernard Stuart lost his life.

Nor was the king's soul so engrossed with grief for the death of so near a kinsman, and noble a lord, but that hearing of the death of his dear servant William Lawes, he had a particular mourning for him when dead, whom he loved when living, and commonly called the Father of Music.[39]

Then, in May 1646, a Parliamentary army again attacked Worcester. Cannon bombardment began on 11 June; the city was put under siege, and many of its poor, terrified inhabitants were soon facing near-starvation. Anticipating the probable outcome of the conflict, the Dallam organ in the cathedral was dismantled on 20 July and hidden safely away, possibly in Tomkins's house:

The organs were this day taken down out of the cathedral church. Some parliamenters hearing the music of the church at service, walking in the aisle, fell a-skipping about and dancing as it were in derision. Others, seeing the workmen taking them down said: 'You might have spared that labour; we would have done it for you'. 'No,' said a merry lad (about ten years old) 'for when the Earl of Essex was here the first man of yours that plucked down and spoiled the organs broke his neck here, and they will not prevent the like misfortune.'[40]

Three days later 'at 6 of the clock prayers, many Gentlemen went to make their last farewell and meeting at the College at Common prayers of the Church, and to receive the Bishop's blessing, saying "The Grace of our Lord" &c.'[41] They then left the cathedral, marched out to Rainbow Hill, and

---

[37] Geraint Bowen (2001), *The Organs of St Davids Cathedral*, Haverfordwest, 4.
[38] See Murray Lefkowitz (1960), *William Lawes*, London, 21.
[39] Thomas Fuller (1662), *The Histories of the Worthies of England*, London, 157.
[40] Willis Bund, *Diary of Henry Townshend*, I, 191.
[41] Ibid., 192.

178   *The Lives and Times of Thomas Tomkins and his Family*

surrendered. At about 5.00 p.m., Colonel Thomas Rainsborough marched into Worcester with several regiments of foot and occupied the city.

Property in all parts of Worcester had been destroyed in the two sieges, including all the houses in the suburb of St Oswald's, where, under Humphrey Withy's stewardship, construction of the hospital had continued until 1642. Not even the suburb of St Clement's across the Severn, where Tomkins held a lease on land, was spared.

The final decade of the sixteenth century and the first quarter of the seventeenth, the years of Elizabeth and James, had been periods of relative stability, peace and harmony. For all his shortcomings, James I maintained a firm grip on kingly power and managed to hold together the brittle fault lines of religious difference. Under Charles, inept and vainglorious, all this had been swept away. Tomkins's world had been shattered, and he would have been all too sadly aware that he was one of the last representatives of an artistic golden age. He looked out upon a bleak, occupied cityscape, the cathedral silent and locked, his life's work seemingly as much in ruins as the city around him. But if he could no longer provide music for the Church, music itself could provide consolation. He turned once again to composing in the more intimate forms that had served to lift his spirits at various times throughout his life: music for keyboard and for consort.

It was a deeply reflective Tomkins who, in late September 1647, finished the composition of a belated tribute to the tragic Thomas Wentworth, the short version of the *Pavan & Galliard: Earl Strafford*. A few days later he completed an extended version of this work, and in that same year he composed a tribute to William Laud, the *Pavan: Lord Canterbury*.

> These two touching tombeaux seem to have started the 75-year-old composer on a new and yet reminiscent phase of musical activity. Works couched in forms and styles that were current in the early part of Elizabeth's reign began to fill the pages of his music-book: the youthful emotions recollected there in the tranquillity of old age lent a feeling of controlled brilliance at once sober and lively.[42]

These pieces, in common with others from the final decade of his life, are written in a more conservative style than that of his earlier keyboard music; very different from the chromatic, richly ornamented style of his well-known setting of the popular sixteenth-century ballad tune *Barafostus' Dreame*,[43] written some thirty years earlier. By the time Tomkins returned to the composition of music for the keyboard, his style was already long out of date:

---

[42] Stevens, 59.

[43] *Barafostus' Dreame*, a popular tune that also went by the name of 'The Shepherd's Joy', was set by several composers and became popular in seventeenth-century Dutch songbooks. It appears with various spellings, including 'Bar'ra Faustus'. Another 'Faustus', Christopher Marlowe's *Dr Faustus*, written around 1589, was first published in 1604, and may have been familiar to Tomkins.

Distracted Times 179

of the late sixteenth rather than the mid-seventeenth century. But in old age he chose naturally to cling to the forms and style he had learned as a youth from Byrd, the forms that enabled him to return mentally to a happier and less revolutionary time.

The bulk of Tomkins's keyboard works are contained in an autograph manuscript held at the Bibliothèque Nationale in Paris,[44] and this same volume contains notes that hint at Tomkins's domestic and financial difficulties during these years. Henry Townshend described the plight of the starving poor in Worcester during the siege of 1646. There were, he wrote, 'at least 1,500 poor of all sorts in the city that have not bread but from hand to mouth'.[45] Within this context, it is easy to understand why Tomkins should have thought it necessary to stockpile wheat and corn, noting down the quantities and prices in his autograph book of keyboard music: 'October 1647. Received of Mr. Wood three bushels of wheat 25s.6d. Then paid John Bullock for all reckonings and for two bushels of mooncorn 15s.'[46]

On the morning of Tuesday, 30 January 1649, Charles I walked from St James's to Whitehall, his ill-starred journey from throne to scaffold at an end. William Juxon, who had been with the king throughout his trial, remained by his side in these final hours. 'There is but one stage more', he said, as the king faced the block, 'this stage is turbulent and troublesome. It is a short one. But you may consider it will soon carry you a very great way – it will carry you from Earth to Heaven, and there you shall find a great deal of cordial joy and comfort.' It was Juxon who helped to choose the grave of the king in St George's Chapel and, with other friends, bore the coffin through driving snow. Tomkins's final tribute to his king, the sombre, moving and faultless *Sad Pavan: for these distracted times*, was completed a few days later, on 14 February 1649.

Following his marriage, Tomkins would have been able to move back into the restored house in College Green with Martha, her sons, and his nephew Sylvanus, albeit that he was obliged to pay a fine to the Parliamentary Committee for the privilege of remaining in his own home. An inventory written by Tomkins into his autograph book of keyboard music shows that his household goods, removed, presumably for safekeeping, had been returned without loss. The list may also hold a clue to the location of his refuge during the time when his house had been uninhabitable:

> God keep all honest men in thy fear and service.
> Tho: Tomkins received from Shellsley

---

[44] Rés. 1122.
[45] Willis Bund, *Diary of Henry Townshend*, I, 130.
[46] Bibliothèque nationale, Rés. 1122, 192.

4 beds and 4 bolsters/4 pillows/5 blankets/3 rugs – 2 red and one green/one green coverlet/4 red curtains of stuff with valance/with fringed lace belonging to the same/one pair of green fringed valance hangings of striped stuff which hanged in the dining room/3 carpets of Turkey work – one long two short:/6 Turkey work cushions/6 arras cushions/one old defaced chair/3 black velvet cushions bottomed with taffeta/one yellow cushion with 2[?] gold laces/2 pieces of old dornix/2 red cloth cushions stools/5 red leather chairs/one old fire shovel and 2 pairs of tongs/2 pair of small hand irons/one bar of iron of Mr Westfoleing not brought.[47]

By 'Shellsley' Tomkins was referring to Shelsley Beauchamp, or possibly Shelsley Walsh, villages between Worcester and Tenbury. An additional clue is given in the name 'Westfoleing' (Westphaling or Westfaling): in the 1643 Worcester Cathedral Treasurer's Book a Mr Westphaling receives the supply of firewood due to Canon Stephen Boughton.[48] Although no first name is given, the surname is sufficiently unusual to imply that there was only one Mr Westphaling in Worcester at the time and that he was subletting Stephen Boughton's prebendal house.

Unfortunately, even on Tomkins's return to College Green, there were difficulties with his next-door neighbour, Thomas Chiles, or Giles, the College brewer, an undertenant of Tomkins. When the Parliament surveyed the possessions of the dean and chapter in June 1649 they mentioned a dispute between the two neighbours:

Thomas Tomkins by Indenture of Lease bearing the date the 17th day of November in the 16th year of the late King Charles from Christopher Potter late dean of the Cathedral Church of Christ and Mary the Virgin of Worcester and the Chapter of the same church Holdeth to him and his assignees All those 2 messuages and tenements newly built lying and being within the precincts of the said Cathedral Church consisting of about 4 bays and a half of building together with the soil and ground thereunto adjoining and a little stable situate between the Songschool and the late stable of Doctor Thornton and Doctor Wight containing in length north and south 9 foot and 6 inches and in breadth east and west 8 foot and 7 inches. All which said 2 houses newly built and all the ground and soil whereupon the old houses and buildings did stand containing in length westward from the wall of the old brewhouse in the occupation of Thomas Chiles 27 yards or thereabouts from the east end thereof unto a room or bay parcel of the same building now in the tenure of Richard Hall gentleman situate and being eastward and westward between the said brewhouse and the house of the said Richard Hall and having on the south part thereof the Castle of Worcester and on the north the common ground of the said church To have and to hold all the said premises from the ensealing of the Lease for and during the term of 40 years next ensuing at the yearly rent of 5s. payable the 24th July only. One of which messuages aforesaid being now in the tenure and possession of the said Thomas Tomkins containing in breadth 18 foot and in length 34 foot.

And the same consisteth of a hall, a kitchen, a buttery five chambers above stairs and a garret over them the staircase leading to a high turret or study. Also a

---

[47] Bibliothèque Nationale, Rés. 1122, 188.
[48] I am grateful to Dr Richard Newsholme for this information.

Distracted Times 181

garden in breadth 34 foot and in length 42 foot with a pump of water therein likewise a woodhouse or coalhouse.

All which said messuage in possession of him the said Thomas Tomkins before rented is worth per annum above the said rent of 5s., £5 00s. 00d. The other messuage or tenement is now in the tenure of Thomas Chiles and was built by him the said Thomas Chiles upon the soil and ground before mentioned and we are credibly informed that the said Thomas Tomkins was trusted by the said Thomas Chiles to purchase the same for him, the said Thomas Chiles, but contrary to that trust the said Mr. Tomkins did take it in his own name after such time as the said Thomas Chiles had built thereon, to his great cost and charges; and therefore humbly craves he may be admitted to purchase the inheritance thereof.

The site of which last recite messuage or tenement containing in breadth 18 foot and in length 33 foot having the castle on the south a gatehouse there on the north Mr. Tomkins on the west and the brewhouse of the said Thomas Chiles on the east. And the same house of Thomas Chiles aforesaid consisteth of a kitchen a parlour and 3 chambers with a garret over them which said tenement is worth by the year to be let £3 00s. 00d.[49]

Tomkins mentions Thomas Giles in a list of creditors recorded in his autograph keyboard manuscript, and this is almost certainly the same man as the 'Thomas Chiles' who lived next-door to him in College Green. Giles appears to have been unsuccessful in his appeal in 1649, but even after Tomkins's death, Giles's widow continued to press her right to a lease on the house.

As known Royalist sympathizers, both Thomas and Nathaniel Tomkins found themselves victims of Parliament's sequestration policy, under which Royalists lost possession of their estates and were unable to receive their rents. They were, however, allowed to compound for their estates – to pay a sum equal to the value of their lands. We have seen how, coincidentally, Nathaniel's responses to the Committee for Compounding of Delinquents in 1649 provided evidence of his father's marriage to Martha Browne. Nathaniel also advised the Committee of £300 left to John and Sylvanus Tomkins by their father, claiming that he had invested the money in the name of the two orphans. 'Nathaniel also alleges that a further £450 has been lent out in trust for them, making a small fortune in all, although he may well have been using this as a ploy to avoid confiscation of his own funds.'[50]

Nathaniel's financial problems also affected his father, who shared property and interests with him at Dodderhill, Droitwich:

Since Nathaniel was a minor canon, and therefore liable to be dispossessed of his property, Thomas was understandably anxious that his own part of the estate should remain in the possession of the family. Even the Bishop of Worcester, John

---

[49] WRO, *Parliamentary Survey of the Lands of the Dean and Chapter of Worcester* (WHS, 1924). See also Newsholme, 'Tomkins: Some Reflections on his Personality'. A bay is the space between the principal vertical posts in a timber-framed building.

[50] Ibid., quoting TNA State Papers 23/218/343.

182   *The Lives and Times of Thomas Tomkins and his Family*

Prideaux, had suffered hardship and deprivation as a result of the new Parliamentary laws, and he died in 1650 almost penniless. Nathaniel Tomkins tried to appeal against the sequestration, but did not succeed, as the following summary of the case shows:

> 30th October 1649. Nathaniel Tomkins being unable to prosecute his appeal against sequestration, now before the Barons of the Exchequer, begs to compound for his estate. Is sequestered on pretence of delinquency. 20 March 1650. Fine at 1/6, £208 16s. 8d.
>
> 9th April 1650. The Committee for Compounding being informed of an undervalue, require a certificate thereof.
>
> 9th July 1650. Thomas Tomkins complaining that demesne lands and tithes in Dodderhill are sequestered as the estate of his son, Nathaniel, who has no interest therein, the County Committee are to certify.
>
> 23rd July 1650. Begs that the profits of his sequestered lands may be secured in the tenant's hands undisposed of, till the hearing of his case.
>
> 30th July 1650. County Committee to show proofs why they consider the estate in question to belong to Nathaniel Tomkins.
>
> 26th September 1650. The County Committee to discharge the sequestration, with arrears from 24th December last, if they do not forthwith show cause to the contrary.[51]

Nathaniel Tomkins's wife, Theodosia, died at about this time, and the searching investigation of the State into every last farthing of his and his father's assets must have been both distressing and demeaning. Nathaniel, who had been a controversial figure in Worcester, was unable to prevent sequestration of his lands. He was deprived of his house in College Green, moved to Elmbridge, a small village between Droitwich and Bromsgrove, and in 1649 complained that he had 'for these four years lost the benefit of his estate which is almost the utter ruin of him'. His father, on the other hand, had never been in dispute with the Worcester city fathers. He had been commended by them for his generosity to the poor, and in a certificate dated 17 June 1650 the mayor and aldermen of Worcester made it quite plain to Parliament that Thomas Tomkins, although formerly a servant of the late king, was no enemy of the State:

> To all whom it may concern: We, the Mayor and Aldermen of the city of Worcester do by these presents certify that Thomas Tomkins (late one of the Gentlemen of the late King's chapel) being of the age of 78 years, has lived here very near 60 years. Always reputed an honest quiet peaceable man, conformable to all orders and ordinances of Parliament, and ever since the troubles began has had his constant abiding with us.

---

[51] Stevens, 62–3, quoting TNA, *Calendar of State Papers* (Committee for Compounding), 1643–60, III, 2132: 'Thomas Tomkins, late King's Chaplain [sic] and Nathaniel Tomkins, Elmridge, Co. Worcs., his Son'.

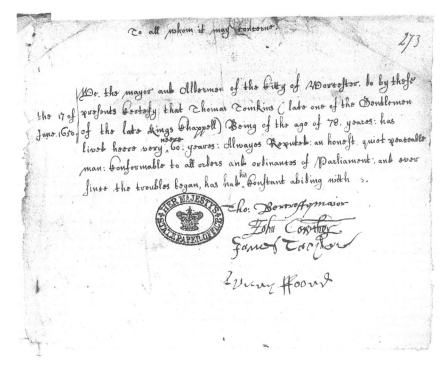

Fig. 12.2   Certificate of the Mayor and Aldermen of Worcester, dated 17 June 1650, showing that Thomas Tomkins was 78 years of age in that year.

                         THOMAS BERCROFT, Mayor.
                         JOHN COWTHER
                         JAMES TAYLOR
                         HENRY FOORD[52]

    The Committee for Compounding had also pursued Thomas's half-brother Peregrine, who was a wealthy man as a result of his marriage to the daughter of Sir Henry Hastings. It was revealed that he had travelled to the court at Oxford, and was said to be 'in arms against the Parliament' and 'a servant in attendance on the king'.[53]

> He was then described as being 'of London, and Dronfield, co. Derby', and the fine was £90. Three years later Peregrine begged that his delinquency might be taken off, or his fine reduced so that he might be able to pay it without ruin. The remark about his having been in arms against the Parliament, interlined in the former certificate, was objected to as contrary to his consent. There is a further

---

52 TNA, SP23/124/273.
53 TNA, SP Committee for Compounding, II, 1378 (G184, 172).

184   *The Lives and Times of Thomas Tomkins and his Family*

> plea stating that the £600 secured from the farms at Humberston was his wife's dowry and that he was under oath not to touch the money. On 8th January the fine was reduced to £10.[54]

Richard Dowdeswell of Pull Court was another who had displayed loyalty to the king and suffered sorely for it. When Sir William Russell came from Strensham in February 1642 to take possession of Tewkesbury, Dowdeswell rode with him at the head of his men. Constantly in trouble with the Parliamentary faction, Dowdeswell was ordered to London in 1644, imprisoned, his estates sequestrated, and his goods and cattle taken to the value of £525. The time was long gone when Tomkins might have composed a light-hearted 'Toy' at Pull Court.

By 1650, Thomas Tomkins was living quietly in the shadow of the cathedral, content in the composition of pavans, verses, a *Clarifica me pater,* and settings of *Miserere* and *In Nomine.* But the city was not to be quiet for much longer. Although monarchy had been abolished in England after the execution of Charles I, Scotland remained loyal to the Crown. In June 1650 Charles II landed in Scotland, accepted the Covenant, and so signalled the start of the Third Civil War. In January 1651 he was crowned at Scone in Scotland, raised an army of approximately 11,000 Scots, and on 6 August crossed the border into England, hoping that large numbers of English troops would join him on his rapid progress south. When only a little more than 2000 Englishmen answered his call, Charles decided against marching on the capital. The town of Shrewsbury refused to comply with his order to surrender, and so he and his exhausted army headed towards the 'Loyal City' – Worcester.

The Parliamentarian garrison commander, unable to put up any opposition, even against this footsore body, capitulated without a fight. The royal standard was once again raised in Worcester on 22 August. Charles took up his quarters at a house in New Street and the weary troops went into billets in and around the city; the deanery seems to have served as an officers' mess. But Cromwell and his roundheads were hard on Charles's heels, and many of the king's demoralized generals believed, correctly, that the Royalist cause was hopeless. Five days later, Cromwell's army gathered at Evesham.

Cromwell commanded a force of between 25,000 and 30,000 men. On 28 August he established a bridge of boats across the River Severn, near its junction with the Teme, and the next day his troops surrounded Worcester. By 3 September he was ready to wage the final, bloody battle of the war, a decisive defeat for the Royalists.

Charles watched the fighting from the top of the cathedral tower until, having seen that defeat was inevitable, he managed to flee from the chaos and

---

[54] Stevens, 21.

Distracted Times

carnage of Worcester, eventually escaping to France. Of the Scots, 3000 had been killed, thousands more were taken prisoner and driven into the cathedral, and many who escaped the city were slaughtered in ambushes. Worcester, its streets strewn with the dead, many of its buildings ablaze, had suffered more plunder and destruction in two weeks than during the whole of the first Civil War. 'The losses caused by the "Burning of the suburbs, hospitals, &c &c" were valued at £100,000 … It is possible that as many as 400 houses, one-fifth of the city's total, were destroyed'.[55]

Deprived of his living, Tomkins was in serious financial difficulties and forced to endure greatly reduced circumstances. His autograph book of keyboard music[56] contains a list of his creditors in 1651:

My debts are these the 24th May

To Mr Bron [Bronell?] — 50	To Mr Kent	17s.
To Mr W Allyes ———30	To the tailor	8s.6d.
To Ed. Pennell ——— 3	To the smith	11s. the carpenter— 5s.
To Tho. Giles ——— 4	To the poor	10s. mason — 6s.
	The shoemaker — 2s.	
To Marjorie Taylor ——— 7	To goodman Abrah. 9d.	
To Mris Boughton —— 40	To the mercer Mr Will Gough 13s.	
To Mr Ashe ——————— 4		

And at midsummer for interest to Mr Bronell 4s

Beside: what for law charges

£	s	d
5	7	8

in all—

The left-hand column probably represents money borrowed from friends. The right-hand column is reserved for smaller sums owed to tradesmen, and it is a mark of Tomkins's generous nature that even in these hard times he would set aside ten shillings for the poor of Worcester. It is clear that he had also borrowed 50s. from William Brommall ('Mr Bronell'), the Royalist owner of the Talbot Inn in the parish, and was still paying off the interest at 8 per cent. Brommall was also steward to Lord Coventry of Croome, and in 1651 held £1000 of his money in a chest at the Talbot, allegedly destined to support Charles II, but possibly to secure it in case Croome Court was seized

---

55 Stephen Porter (1994), *Destruction in the English Civil Wars*, Stroud, 205, quoting John Nash (1782), *Collections for the History of Worcestershire*, II, app., cvi.

56 Bibliothèque Nationale, Rés. 1122, 185.

186 *The Lives and Times of Thomas Tomkins and his Family*

and looted by either side. Richard Dowdeswell of Pull Court was also involved with this covert banker; the Committee for Compounding accused him of persuading Brommall and his wife to perjure themselves on his behalf.

Then, as now, the cost of litigation was high, and the fees owing to his lawyer, probably incurred in the appeal against the sequestration of his property, were substantial. Having listed his debts it appears that Tomkins had either run out of energy or enthusiasm: he failed to add up the total.

Thomas Giles was, as we have seen, Tomkins's next-door neighbour. '[Edward]Pennell was one of the few commissioners who performed his duties in a satisfactory way, if we are to believe Henry Townshend, and it may have been for this reason that he still held office in 1660, at the first quarter-sessions of Charles II. Perhaps the Marjorie Taylor and Mrs Boughton named in the list were related to Canon Taylor and Canon Boughton.'[57]

Many another of his countrymen shared Tomkins's understandable despair. John Aubrey recalled how the engraver Wenceslas Hollar (1607–77) left England when the Civil Wars broke out. 'He went into the Low Countries where he stayed till about 1649. I remember he told me that when he first came into England (which was a serene time of peace) that the people, both poor and rich, did look cheerfully, but at his return, he found the countenances of the people all changed, melancholy, spiteful, as if bewitched.'[58]

Cromwell pronounced himself lord protector in 1653, a year in which Tomkins composed nothing. It is unlikely, however, that his silence resulted from a sadness no deeper than that caused by the appalling political situation or his loss of worldly fortune. Martha, his wife of little more than ten years, seems to have died at about this time, inevitably leaving him desolate and dispirited.

It was Tomkins's son Nathaniel, an adept survivor, who found the perfect answer to both his own problems and those of his father. He was 55 years old, an eligible widower at a time when many good men had been killed in the wars. Isabella Folliot was the twice-married daughter of Guthlake Folliot, a former chapter clerk at the cathedral, whose family had lived in Worcestershire since the reign of Henry I. The Folliots' first estate had been at Morton-Folliott in the parish of Longdon, a district later to be called Castlemorton. This was the area where Nathaniel's maternal ancestors had farmed for centuries, and close to where John Tomkins the clothier and his successors had settled.

Nathaniel and Isabella married in January 1654. She 'had inherited the manor of Merton or Martin and the patronage of Martin Hussingtree Church from her first husband, John Haselock. It was this wealthy and amiable widow

---

[57] Stevens, 64.
[58] Aubrey, *Brief Lives*, 163.

Distracted Times 187

who provided shelter for Nathaniel and his father, and though Habington calls it a "meane Manor" he may have been referring to its size rather than its character or aspect.'[59] Thomas Tomkins paid his hostess the compliment of composing a keyboard piece in her honour: *Galliard, The Lady Folliot's*, and gratefully set out for his new rural surroundings.

One can only imagine Tomkins's thoughts as he made his way northwards out of Worcester for the last time, much of the city in ruin; beyond the Fore Gate lay a scene of devastation. Martin Hussingtree lies four miles north-east of Worcester Cathedral, just off the old Roman road to Droitwich, and Tomkins arranged to transport his property to Nathaniel's home there, leaving behind one bedstead in College Green, where it became the property of Henry Townshend.[60]

Martin Hussingtree remains essentially unaltered in character from the delightful village that Thomas Tomkins knew, and in which he spent his last years. The manor house, its barn (now converted), the simple church and its churchyard gather together beside a little pond into which a willow trails delicate fingers. It is a peaceful place; a place for undisturbed contemplation; the perfect place in which to find the last fruits of a creative life.

On 30 June 1654 the 82-year-old composer began work on an *Ut re mi fa sol la* variation, but left only a fragment. And then, on 4 July, in spite of physical frailty and a shaking hand, he completed a set of keyboard variations on a popular gallows song of the time, the humour of which attracted not only Tomkins, but also Byrd, Sweelinck and many other composers. This was *Fortune My Foe*, a piece that in Tomkins's realization has rightly been described as 'a model of keyboard and variation art'.[61]

In his later years, Tomkins, his thoughts turning increasingly to posterity, set out his 'Lessons of Worth' in the precious volume of keyboard music that was never far from his hand. Then, with great modesty, added:[62]

> I could wish that the great book which was my brother John's should be fair and carefully pricked with so judicious a hand and eye that the player may venture upon them with comfort, which he may easily do: if the notes be distinctly valued with the semibreve or minim, and not too closely huddled up together.
>
> My son's judgement may give better directions than these weak expressions: but this by the way.
>
> These especially, & none but lessons of worth, to be pricked.

---

[59] Stevens, 64, quoting Habington, *Survey*, I, 349.

[60] See *Inventories of Worcestershire Landed Gentry: 1537–1786*, Worcester (WHS) (1998), 192.

[61] Bernhard Klapprott (1994), notes to *Thomas Tomkins – Keyboard Music*, vol. I of the recordings of *Complete Keyboard Music of Thomas Tomkins* (Dabringhaus und Grimm: MDG 607 0563-2).

[62] Bibliothèque Nationale, Rés. 1122, 186.

Fig. 12.3 Martin Hussingtree Church, Worcestershire.

Mr Tallis his offertory.
All Dr Bull's offertories
and Innomines, the choice
of them. And all especial good
lessons in that key of A are
To be placed together.

Mr Carleton's (Fading)
comes not short in value
or worth with most of the
best. So does Dr Bull's
Walsingham.

If it please him some of mine in their place, if worthy to come in place.
So Mr Byrd's likewise. His Ut. Re. My. Fa. Sol. La, & Ut. My. Re
& his Walsingham & old ground
& his old Fancy
with Dr Bull's Ut. Re. My. Fa. Sol. La
They being in the key of gamut [G] to be suited and sorted together.

And whatever Fancies or selected voluntaries of worth, to be placed in their own native keys, not mingling or mangling them together with other of contrary keys, but put in their right places.

Whether or not it pleased Nathaniel to have John Tomkins's great book carefully pricked is unknown, but Thomas Tomkins valued the opinion of his son above all others. He knew his own worth and was concerned that something of his life's work should survive, albeit that in 1654 there was no use whatever in dreaming of a future for church music. He survived until 1656, a year of appalling weather. Henry Townshend wrote in his diary that he had never remembered a spring of 'such strong winds, storm, snow, sleet

Distracted Times 189

and slobbery weather – to so great hindrance of the countryman's sowing'.[63] May and June brought great heat and drought, so much so that hay was fetching £40 per ton and the grass was 'mostly burnt up'. In July, Townshend wrote that 'this hot, dry year has caused great sickness, especially the small pox and measles, whereof many have died in all places'.[64]

The end came for Thomas Tomkins in the midst of this great heat. He was buried in the churchyard at Martin Hussingtree, where many of his relatives were to find their rest in the years to come, the church registers recording that 'Mr Thomas Tomkins organist of the King's Chapel and of the Cathedral Church of Worcester was buried the 9th day of June 1656'.

Charles II returned to England on 29 May 1660 and was proclaimed king. Services in Worcester Cathedral were restarted on 31 August, and by Easter 1661 a choir had been formed and was ready to sing choral services. In August 1661, Giles Tomkins (1633–1725), the second son of Thomas Tomkins's brother Giles, of Salisbury, was appointed organist. The new dean, John Oliver, died within the year and was succeeded by Thomas Warmestry, a former scholar of the Worcester King's School. Giles Thornborough, the sub-dean, who had been at Salisbury with Giles Tomkins, installed Warmestry on 27 November 1661. Both Warmestry and the new bishop, George Morley, were given an enthusiastic welcome at the first revival of the Anglican service in the cathedral, Henry Townshend recording the general elation that accompanied Morley's enthronement:

> Dr George Morley, Bishop of Worcester, was solemnly brought into Worcester by my Lord Windsor, Lord Lieutenant of the County, and most of the gentry and all the clergy, their being ten trumpets then attending, and some volunteer militia, horse, the trained bands of the city, and clergy – band of foot in arms giving divers volleys of shot. As soon as he had vested, within half-an-hour the Bishop, with all the prebends and the quire meeting him at the college steps in their formalities, sang to the Quire, where he was enthroned, performing the ceremonies. Then Quire service. So to his palace, where was noble treatment prepared.[65]

Richard Dowdeswell of Pull Court, released from imprisonment, returned to Tewkesbury as one of the members of the new parliament. He was on the committee for the trial of the regicides and for the rebuilding of London after the Great Fire. His brother, William Dowdeswell, was made a canon of Worcester Cathedral in 1661, preached the first sermon in the cathedral after the Restoration, and represented the chapter in the Convocation of 1662, which introduced the new prayer book.

---

[63] Willis Bund, *Diary of Henry Townshend*, I, 32.
[64] Ibid.
[65] Ibid., cvii.

190   *The Lives and Times of Thomas Tomkins and his Family*

Old Giles Tomkins remained at Salisbury at the Restoration. He had 'managed to remain in occupation of his hard-won house during the whole period of the Commonwealth. What he had to live on is a mystery … In 1667, nearly forty years after his original appointment, the cathedral register records that:

> The progress of the choristers in the art of music is to be required of Mr Tomkins, instructor of the said boys in which office greater diligence is expected of him in the future.

Ill health was probably the cause of his inattention to duty, for five months later, on 4 April 1668, he died',[66] and his place was taken by John Blow. Giles's son, Giles junior, was not a success at Worcester, absenting himself from duty on many occasions:

> Eventually the Dean had to declare the appointment terminated, naming Richard Browne as his successor. His musical career at an end, Giles followed the example of his grandfather: he entered the Church, was presented to the living of Martin Hussingtree, married, and had six children. His span of life even exceeded that of his uncle, for he was 93 at the time of his death in 1725. His death and burial are recorded in the parish registers of Martin Hussingtree, whose church he had served as rector for more than half a century.[67]

Tomkins's three brothers, Robert, Nicholas and Peregrine, all died before the Restoration. Nicholas, of Savoy Parish, Middlesex, died on 8 December 1656[68] and left his possessions to Peregrine, whose own will was proved in 1659,[69] the year in which Henry Purcell was born. Robert, of St Paul's, Covent Garden, Middlesex, died in the following year and his will was proved on 9 February 1660.[70]

Nathaniel Tomkins returned to take an active part in the restoration of Worcester Cathedral, where, in a Chapter Act dated 6 April 1661, he was described as 'our Receiver for the time being'. The cost of making good the 'damages by the late powers' was estimated at the huge sum of £16,345, and Nathaniel was presumably much involved in helping to raise the necessary funds. He had always taken a deep, personal interest in the maintenance and preservation of the building, and Thomas Habington recalled something of his diligence:

> I saw under an arch of the quire the anatomy of a dead man wasted to bones, his robe a shroud, and under his head a mitre. This is somewhat defaced, yet was worser abused when it was turned from a monument to a mantel tree, but was worthily restored by Mr Nathaniel Tomkins, who doubtful where it first stood, placed it here [in the Lady Chapel].[71]

---

[66] Robertson, *Sarum Close*, 195 and 200.
[67] Stevens, 20.
[68] TNA, PCC PROB 11/260.
[69] TNA, PCC Pell, fol. 437.
[70] TNA, PCC PROB 11/303.
[71] Habington, *Survey*, II, 447.

Distracted Times 191

Nathaniel continued to behave in a controversial manner and it was not very long before he had crossed Dean Warmestry, who found him 'scandalously and intolerably contumacious'. Plans were made to replace the organ in the cathedral, and Thomas Harris came to Worcester from London in 1662 'to treat about making a new organ'. In the following year William Hathaway was paid £5 'towards his journey and the new organ',[72] and in November 1663 was paid £30 'towards the new organ'. But having fixed the chair organ, Hathaway was prevented from building the great organ. Bishop Robert Skinner, Morley's successor, wrote to the archbishop of Canterbury:

> He [Hathaway] complained to the bishop about the dean, Thomas Warmestry, of whom the bishop said, he 'had no more skill in an organ than a beast that hath no understanding'. But the bishop points out that Hathaway had waited for above a whole year, during which time he made no approach to the dean and chapter. Apparently Thomas Harris had said something against Hathaway or his work. 'An artist maligns his brother artist,' but the bishop, speaking of Nathaniel Tomkins, son of Thomas Tomkins, says, 'I rely very much upon Mr Tomkins's skill, bred in his cradle, and all his life among organs ... His letter will show what his judgement was before this difference was started. Little reason have I had to interpose in the least in Mr Dean's case, but I cannot forbear to stand up for Innocency though joined with much folly.'[73]

Harris was awarded the contract, and the specification of the resulting instrument 'is so much like the Dallam 1613 organ, that one might be forgiven for thinking that the Harris organ was a rebuild of Dallam with a few additions'.[74] If the 1613 organ had indeed been hidden away in 1646 in Thomas Tomkins's house, it might have been there still when the house and other possessions were inherited by his nephew John. Worcester Cathedral records[75] seem to show that John Tomkins sold an organ to the dean and chapter following the Restoration, and this could well have been the Dallam instrument:

1661-2

Paid Mr John Tomkins for the organs in the choir £40. 0. 0

(the other 40 marks being given by Mr N T)

1662 Mr Tomkins in pap exceptiones 4.12. 6

This abovesaid sum and £2 more

being allowed him for the charge

of damage in removing the organ

---

72 WCL, Treasurer's Accounts, A26.
73 Butcher, *The Organs*, 11.
74 Ibid., 13.
75 WCL, A 125(3) Receiver General's Book for 1661–62; D 508.

He is to allow for it £38	
Organ being in order	40. 0. 0
Mr Tomkins to refollow £3 bad money	1. 0. 0

Young John Tomkins married Elizabeth Baynham of Hereford, and the family flourished in Herefordshire and Worcestershire for many generations. John Tomkins was granted probate to administer his Uncle Thomas's will, and he was also the main beneficiary of Nathaniel Tomkins's will. His youngest brother, Thomas, a gifted academic, owed much to Nathaniel Tomkins, by whom he was brought up and educated at Worcester. He never married, attended Balliol College, Oxford, was elected a Fellow of All Souls, gained the degree of DD, and subsequently became chancellor of Exeter Cathedral and chaplain to the archbishop of Canterbury. In this latter capacity Thomas acted as a censor of books submitted for licensing by the government. One such volume, John Milton's *Paradise Lost*, received by Thomas in 1667, prompted him to make some slightly critical comments, on political grounds, to the following lines in Book I:

> ... as when the sun new risen
> Looks through the horizontal misty air
> Shorn of his beams, or from behind the moon
> In dim eclipse disastrous twilight sheds
> On half the nations, and with fear of change
> Perplexes monarchs.

Thomas knew well of Milton's loyal service to the Commonwealth, but he did not persist in his objections; a licence was granted, as too were licences for *Paradise Regained* and *Samson Agonistes*, both published in 1671. Thomas Tomkins died in 1675.

The seventeenth century was not an age of biography. No chronicler of the time would have contemplated writing a book about even the most esteemed of musicians; and Nathaniel Tomkins did not consider it necessary to provide a short life of his father in a biographical preface to *Musica Deo sacra*. In all probability it never even crossed his mind. He was a strong-willed, obstinate and manipulative man, but British music will remain forever in his debt for bringing *Musica Deo sacra* to publication in 1668. Without it, almost half of Thomas Tomkins's known output would remain totally unknown to us.

When Charles II was proclaimed king, his accession was formally back-dated to 1649, as though to deny that the interregnum had existed. William Child was appointed 'Composer to the King', but the fracture in the continuity of Anglican church music could not be glossed over so effortlessly. From fourteen to eighteen years had passed since chant or anthem had risen to the cathedral vaults, and scarcely any choir books remained. The music of Thomas Tomkins, like so much else, could all too easily have crumbled to dust.

Distracted Times 193

Thomas Tomkins hoped to be remembered by posterity, and by great good fortune that aspiration has been realized. His music, both exceptional and at times forward-looking, served to ennoble and enrich British cultural life in an age of political turmoil. But he also sowed the seeds of future greatness, handing on the baton of creative genius to composers he could not know and at whose achievement he could perhaps only guess.

> The final section of *Almighty God, the fountain of all wisdom*, with its partial use of the whole-tone scale, is a remarkable conception. Although it retains a polyphonic idiom, its daring comes from the underlying harmonic language, which foreshadows the compositional method of Henry Purcell (1659–1695). If it had not been for the Commonwealth period in English history, which lasted from 1649 to 1660 and led to the suppression of the Anglican Church and all the musicians employed by it, I believe Tomkins would now be seen as 'Father' to a generation of composers who would have bridged the stylistic gap between himself and the post-Restoration school of Purcell and others.[76]

---

[76] Peter Phillips (1991), extract from sleeve-note to The Tallis Scholars' CD recording: *Thomas Tomkins, The Great Service* (Gimell Records Ltd, CDGIM 024). See also Peter Phillips (1991), *English Sacred Music 1549–1649*, Oxford, chapters 4 and 8.

PART TWO

THE MUSIC OF THOMAS TOMKINS

Denis Stevens

Chapter 13

Musica Deo sacra

> And I think he hath not a mind well tempered, whose zeal is not inflamed by a heavenly anthem.
>
> (Owen Feltham, *Resolves* (1628))

It is highly probable that Tomkins regarded his church music as the most important single branch of his widely varied musical activities. Unlike his secular music, which may be assigned to definite phases in his career, or else affords its own evidence of sporadic, even occasional interest, the church music appears as an almost lifelong task, pervading all times and places, and still remaining in the foreground of his thoughts even when circumstances brought about by political and military manoeuvres denied him the *raison d'être* for its continued composition. The lines engraved beneath the frontispiece of Lawes's *Treasury of Musick*, published in 1669, aptly sum up a situation which Tomkins had known and suffered from 1642 until the end of his days:

> Although the cannon, and the churlish drum
> Have struck the choir mute, and the organs dumb,
> Yet music's art, with air and string and voice,
> Makes glad the sad, and sorrow to rejoice.

He began writing music for the Anglican Church in his early twenties, when he was first appointed organist at Worcester, and for the next forty-five years the stream of anthems and services flowed on steadily, increasing in quality though not necessarily in complexity, with the result that his son Nathaniel was able to assemble sufficient material for the posthumous publication known to us as *Musica Deo sacra*.

The idea of such a publication must long have haunted the composer's mind. In 1622 he had so far modified the conventional contents of a madrigal book as to include four anthems, one of which was later reprinted in *Musica Deo sacra*, but after that date he saw nothing of his own through the press. The times were unpropitious for the publication of church music, and in spite of Barnard's excellent anthology of services and anthems published in 1641,

---

Revised extracts from Denis Stevens (1957), *Thomas Tomkins: 1572–1656*, London, repr. with additional preface, New York, 1967.

public interest was at a low ebb. Barnard had transcribed enough material to enable him to plan for a further publication, which would have included works by composers then living, among them Thomas Tomkins, but this ambitious project never matured. Meticulously copied volumes, still in existence,[1] testify to the industry of Barnard and the apathy of his clientèle, besides indirectly confirming the all-powerful influence of the manual copyist, whose work was undoubtedly cheaper and occasionally even more accurate than that of the printer.

The appearance of Barnard's collection, which was apparently not acquired by Worcester Cathedral until twenty years after the date of publication,[2] may, however, have raised Tomkins's hopes to a certain extent, while at the same time acting as a deterrent. It must have been obvious that a large-scale collection of music by one composer could not follow too closely upon an anthology of the magnitude of John Barnard's *Selected Church Music*. As his keyboard music shows, Tomkins was a conscientious compiler of his own music, and there is no reason to believe that he was less conscientious when it came to the preservation and classification of anthems and services. Like many of his fellow organists, he compiled an organ book containing accompaniments for use both in choir practice and at service time, the folio marked 'E' in his private collection of manuscript books[3] being a very likely candidate. Nathaniel Tomkins would naturally have used this book as the basic text for the Pars Organica of *Musica Deo sacra*, unique in being the only printed organ book in seventeenth-century England, although manuscript organ books are quite common.[4]

There can be no doubt that the hope of publication receded from Thomas's mind as the long and empty years of the Commonwealth wore on. From the time of the second siege of Worcester, last of the Royalist cities to hold out against the Parliamentarian troops, he had turned more and more towards the composition of keyboard music, almost to the extent of turning a deaf ear to the entreaties and encouragements of his son. The desire to publish, once strong in the father, passed naturally to the son; and as the father became more absorbed in his clavichord and his chamber organ, so the son lost his youthful enthusiasm for keyboard instruments and directed his thoughts to the collection and collation of that vastly impressive corpus of church music which was probably a family heirloom. The death of Thomas in 1656 brought matters to a climax: from then onwards Nathaniel knew that his bounden

---

[1] Royal College of Music (RCM), MSS 1045–51.

[2] Atkins, *Early Occupants*, 63.

[3] See p. 239.

[4] Durham Cathedral MS A 1–5; Bodleian Library, Tenbury MS 791 (Adrian Batten); Christ Church Library, Oxford, MS 1001; Ely Cathedral MS 1 (John Ferrabosco and James Hawkins); General Library of the University of California at Berkeley, M2 C645 Case B (? Thomas Cappell of Chichester).

Musica Deo sacra 199

duty was to create an imperishable musical memorial to his father's skill and piety. At that time Nathaniel was the only person who could adequately perform such a task, for he had inherited most, if not all, of his father's manuscripts, and had lived with him long enough to understand and carry out his wishes. It has sometimes been suggested that Thomas Tomkins (1638–75), chancellor of Exeter Cathedral, was responsible for editing *Musica Deo sacra* and seeing it through the press,[5] but there is no proof that this eminent and learned divine had any great knowledge of music or deep interest in it.

Documentary evidence also favours Nathaniel's claim as editor, for he wrote on the verso of a long letter to John Sayer of the Chapel Royal, in May 1665, a message for William Godbid, the music printer of Aldersgate Street:

> Sir, I pray you speak to Mr. Godbid to send me one sheet of the bass of I.i. or fol.121.122.123.124 of the mean of Q.q. or fol.147.148.149.150.[6]

John Milsom has shown that those very sheets are now in the copy of *Musica Deo sacra* at Christ Church, Oxford, and that they are dated 1 June 1665 (Mus. 706: Bassus, sig. Ii) and 2 February 1666 (Mus. 703: Medius, sig. Qq). 'The hand that wrote the letter to Sayer corresponds exactly with the hand in the Christ Church books.'[7] It was William Godbid who printed *Musica Deo sacra* in 1668, and Nathaniel was clearly reading the bassus and medius parts in proof up to three years before the date of publication. That he performed this difficult and tiring task extremely well, if a little mechanically, is proved by the relatively small number of corrections ('Notes which may be added by the pen') which appear at the end of each partbook, as well as by the consolidated judgement of the editors of *Tudor Church Music*, who found the printing of the notes singularly accurate in all four vocal partbooks.[8]

The same editors are, with some justification, less pleased with Nathaniel's care in seeing to the correct underlay of text to music. It is highly unlikely that he had a score of the anthems and services before him, although he did have an organ score, and so was able to check vocal and organ parts, which (apart from very few exceptions) correspond satisfactorily. In order to secure a really musical and singable underlay, Nathaniel would have had to sing through, not once but several times, every voice part of every work in *Musica Deo sacra*, and amend the printer's copy accordingly. Nathaniel, in spite of his genuine devotion to his task, might understandably have baulked at such a proposition, for he was a fine organist but not an especially good singer. He was, according to Bishop Skinner, 'bred in his cradle, and all his life among

---

5   *DNB*, article on Thomas Tomkins.
6   Bodleian Library, MS Add. C 304a fol. 141v.
7   John Milsom (2001), 'Tracking Tomkins' *Musical Times* (Summer), 55.
8   *Tudor Church Music*, VIII, xiv.

The Music of Thomas Tomkins

organs ... an excellent organist, and hath ever maintained an organ in his house'.[9]

He evidently placed his trust, not unwisely, in the ability of singers to adapt the text in a convincing and artistic manner to the varying lengths of the musical phrases. They were not all like the common singing men of whom John Earle, in the genial vituperation of his *Microcosmographie*, said:

> they are so religiously addicted that they serve God oftest when they are drunk ... the old Hebrew names are little beholding to them, for they miscall them worse than one another. Though they never expound the scripture, they handle it much and pollute the gospel with two things, their conversation and their thumbs.

This from a bishop of Worcester and Salisbury might well be accounted the unprejudiced evidence of an eye- and ear-witness, if it were not for the fact that the *Microcosmographie* of 1629 contains other and equally amusing exaggerations of the same kind.

Musica Deo sacra has, in its way, been just as much maligned and misunderstood as the singing men who first made its symbols live in sound. Fétis, misled by the reference to Charles I on the title-page, stated that the work appeared in 1623, which was probably a typographical error for the year of Charles's accession. Burney, a little nearer the mark, dated one of the Christ Church copies 1664[10] and threw much subsequent scholarship into a state of confusion. The greatest confusion of all, however, is brought about by the correct date (1668) and a short title reference; for without the knowledge that Charles I is mentioned on the title-page, the music is apt to be judged by post-Restoration standards, and accounted well-nigh anachronistic. Nathaniel Tomkins probably realized that rapidly changing musical fashions would limit the potential audience for his father's music, and he lost no time in placing an advertisement in the London *Gazette*, the original draft of which reads:

> Lately printed, Musica Deo sacra et ecclesia Anglicanae; or music dedicated to the honour and service of God and to the use of cathedral and other churches of England, by Thomas Tomkins sometime Gentleman of His Majesty's Chapel Royal and Organist of Worcester: in ten books whereof one is the organ part. They are to be had at the Chanter's House of Westminster.[11]

Why this set of four voice parts and one organ book should be sold as a set of ten is somewhat mysterious, even when due allowance has been made for the typically generous exaggerations of advertising terminology. A working maximum would be nine, to include two copies each of medius, contratenor, tenor and bassus, and one copy of Pars Organica. Since the decani and cantoris parts are printed opposite one another in each book, at least two

---

9 Bodleian Library, MS Tanner 45, fol. 19.
10 Charles Burney (1776–89), *A General History of Music*, ed. Mercer (London, 1935), II, 291.
11 TNA, SP 29-187-209.

Musica Deo sacra 201

copies of each would be needed by the lay clerks for anthems of normal dimensions, and more if they were to sing the eight-, ten- and twelve-part anthems in reasonable comfort. Extra copies of the medius part, for the boys, would naturally be copied by hand, since no establishment would want to include the entire contents of *Musica Deo sacra* in its repertoire, and it was therefore easier to duplicate medius parts of whatever works were chosen. Occasionally the printed text was used as a basis of complete sets of parts, again perhaps for reasons of economy, and this explains why certain of the later seventeenth-century manuscript sources (especially the Durham ones mentioned by the editors of *Tudor Church Music*, VIII) contain the same errors as the original publication.

The account books of Worcester Cathedral indicate that the usual method was to acquire a set of printed books, decide upon which anthems and services to use, and then arrange for one of the lay clerks to copy out extra medius parts for the boys. In 1661 the following entry may be seen:

Books bought to furnish the Church.

For a set of printed song-books for the choir,

Box and carriage £12.15s.6d[12]

John Brown, one of the four lay clerks who returned to the choir at the Restoration, was soon set busily copying:

Joanni Brown laico p[ro] canticis variis depin gendis £2. 0s. 0d.[13]

Twenty-two years later, the books were still in use, though an inventory of 'plate and other utensils' submitted to the treasurer makes it quite clear that they were showing their age:

Eight new service books, twelve old ones, besides those the singing men have in their boxes.[14]

The 1661 inventory could only refer, of course, to Barnard's *Selected Church Music*, and similarly the 'eight new books' mentioned in the later document must have been *Musica Deo sacra*. The number eight rather than nine is given because the Pars Organica was undoubtedly up in the organ loft when the list was in process of compilation. Seven partbooks are still to be seen in the cathedral library, as well as four of the Barnard set.

One particular set of the *Musica Deo sacra* partbooks is of more than usual interest: it is the copy that was formerly at St Michael's College, Tenbury, and is now in the Bodleian Library. The Pars Organica, besides possessing the usual three pages of corrections (bound in this instance between the Index and

---

12 WCL, Treasurer's Accounts (1661), A 73, p. 53.
13 Ibid. (1662) A 29, p. 18.
14 J. Noake (1866), *The Monastery and Cathedral of Worcester*, 547.

202 *The Music of Thomas Tomkins*

page 1) has yet another page bound into the volume immediately following the last page. The lower third of this leaf presents two items of information concerning the speed and pitch of music. A solitary semibreve, printed on a clefless stave, is thus described:

> Sit mensura duorum humani corporis pulsuum, vel globuli penduli, longitudine duorum pedum a centro motus.

The semibreve then appears once more, on the F line of a bass stave, with the following remark:

> Sit tonus fistulae apertae longitudine duorum pedum et semissis: sive 30 digitorum Geomet.

Nathaniel clearly added these instructions as an afterthought: he wished to make it understood that absolute values for tempo and pitch could be given; and that his father's music, if it were to be correctly performed, should proceed at thirty-six semibreves to the minute (one semibreve equalling two heartbeats) and at a pitch whose tenor F should correspond to the sound produced by an organ pipe two and a half feet long.

The loss of traditional tempi due to the silencing of choirs, and the undoubtedly vague attitude towards pitch resulting from sub-standard workmanship (in many cases all that was available) in the impoverished organ-building profession, may well have moved Nathaniel to add these instructions as a kind of postscript. Strangely enough, Nathaniel did not dedicate the publication to a private patron, nor did he state explicitly that it was a memorial to his father. There is no preface, and no indication of the author's identity. Thus the unique instructions in the Tenbury copy are all that remain of Nathaniel's self-effacing personality.

Musica Deo sacra contains five services, five psalm tunes, the Preces and two proper psalms, and ninety-four anthems.[15] Among the items not included in this publication are two Evening Services, two psalm tunes, two settings of the Litany and one of the Responses, and eighteen anthems (see Chapter 18). The First and Second Services are usually classed as 'short services' or relatively simple and straightforward compositions, but in fact the Second Service looks forward to the more complex type ('great service') in its *Te Deum*, where there are verses for SSATB.

The First Service is notable for its bold use of a head-motif, a full bar which appears at the beginning of *Te Deum, Benedictus* and *Nunc Dimittis*. Tomkins uses thematic links in all of his services, and may have been consciously

---

15 *Tudor Church Music*, VIII, xvii, gives the number as ninety-three, since the Burial Service is counted separately. As many anthems proper to other special services are contained in *Musica Deo sacra*, it has been thought best to include the music for the Burial Service among the main body of texts, as the original index does. Cavanaugh mentions ninety-five anthems: he counts *Behold I bring you glad tidings* and its chorus 'Glory be to God' as two separate works.

following in the footsteps of Tallis and Farrant, both of whom used this technique during the reign of Elizabeth I. Little use, however, is made of contrasts in colour between groups of upper and lower voices. It is not until the *Creed* that the three lower voices have a phrase to themselves ('who for us men') and a little later there is a brief expansion to five-part harmony at 'I acknowledge one Baptism'. The main contrast comes from the alternation of the two sides of the choir, and is thus spatial rather than dynamic or tonal. Usually Tomkins begins and ends the canticles with full choir, using alternation for the body of the texts with the exception of certain phrases which require more dignified and sonorous treatment. 'Thou art the King of Glory' (*Te Deum*), 'To perform the oath' (*Benedictus*), 'Very God of Very God' (*Creed*), and 'He hath filled the hungry' (*Magnificat*) are a few of the phrases singled out for performance by both sides of the choir. Similarly those phrases which imply alternation are generally set in that manner: 'To Thee all angels' and 'To Thee Cherubim', as well as 'The glorious company' and 'The goodly fellowship' (*Te Deum*). In neither instance is there any attempt to relate the phrases musically, though at certain points in the *Venite* there are matching, though not mechanically exact, musical phrases. Occasionally madrigalian methods creep in at such obvious places in the *Benedictus* as 'and hath raised up', 'the prophet of the highest', 'the day-spring from on high', all of which are set to ascending scale-passages. Conversely, 'came down from heaven' (*Creed*) bears a descending phrase. There is a particularly graphic illustration of 'he hath put down' in the Magnificat, employing subdivision of voices and contrast of timbre as well as spacial contrast (Ex. 13.1).

Although similar to the First Service in matters of general style, the Second Service has particular differences which set it apart. There is no organ in *Venite* and *Kyrie*, and the intonation of *Te Deum* is set. This time there is a double example of the use of head-motifs: the opening of *Te Deum* occurs again in *Magnificat*, and that of *Jubilate* at *Nunc Dimittis*. *Jubilate* is set in place of *Benedictus*, but otherwise the number of separate canticles or texts is

Ex. 13.1

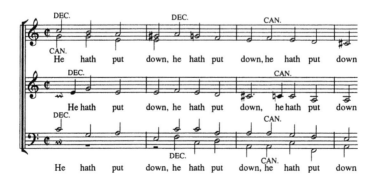

the same for both services. A comparison of the two settings of *Te Deum* is instructive in that it shows Tomkins to be quite free in his choice of a scheme of alternation and use of full choir. In the Second Service, there is a wider range of contrasting textures, especially noticeable at the two sections which obtain an effect of gymel by subdividing the trebles at 'When Thou tookest upon Thee to deliver man' and the counter-tenors at 'Thou sittest at the right hand of God'. These are in effect verse sections,[16] though it is not until the *Jubilate* that the use of this technique becomes decisive ('O go your way'). At many places in the *Creed* all-pervading homophony is relieved by an active and interesting tenor part, and there is an effective instance of cumulative fervency in the use of a rhythmic half-drop (to borrow a term from the visual arts) at 'And He shall come again' (Ex. 13.2).

Ex. 13.2

The customary ascent is heard at the word 'ascended' and there is a novel touch at the word 'together [is worshipped and glorified]' where the two sides of the choir start singing together in the middle of a phrase. A similar example of illustration verging on misplaced ingenuity may be seen at 'throughout all generations' in the tenor part of the *Magnificat*. Most successful of all perhaps is the *Nunc Dimittis*, with its beautifully balanced sequence at 'For mine eyes have seen'; and its impressive use of full choir, yet suggestive of antiphony (even of canon), from 'To be a light' to the end.

The Third Service, although one of Tomkins's more complex works, is not quite as overpowering as it appears from the twelve-stave pages in *Tudor Church Music*, VIII. His organ part, present throughout, is not indispensable, but it should be used in any performance which lays claim to historical accuracy. The ten voice parts often combine to form five, and in fact extended passages of even six-part writing are relatively uncommon. There is, however, a noticeable increase in the overlapping of antiphonal phrases, which creates a tightly woven musical texture and a smoother transmission between decani and cantoris. Doubtless more antiphony was used than is actually marked in *Musica Deo sacra* and its published transcription, and consequently more verse

---

[16] The second is not so designated in *Tudor Church Music*, VIII, 59.

sections. It is too frequently forgotten that the restoration of such features to church music of this period is as essential aesthetically as the restoration of lacunae caused by missing partbooks is essential musically. *Jubilate*, with its joyful waves of sound at the opening, and *Magnificat* and *Nunc Dimittis* (with hinted head-motif) are among Tomkins's loftiest achievements. The quietly reverent way in which each of the latter two canticles begins is an illustration of the fine use to which verse technique can be put; and the skilful deploying of melodic sequences and passages of close imitation come as yet further proof of Tomkins's unerring instinct for choral sonority. Not least remarkable is the frequent use of false relations as a harmonic ingredient rather than a means of expression (Ex. 13.3).

Ex. 13.3

The organ part in the Fourth and Fifth Services is an integral part of the texture, and even though Tomkins gave no more than a sketch of what he would have played, it is clear that he favoured a greater degree of elaboration than was common among his contemporaries, chief of whom in the realm of verse service were Gibbons and Byrd. The head-motif that is common to both the *Magnificat* and *Nunc Dimittis* of the Fourth Service is indeed taken over from a similar point in Byrd's Second Service, by way of tribute from pupil to teacher. It is no more a 'curious example of plagiarism'[17] than the parallel quotation of Dowland's *Lachrymae* in *O let me live for true love* in the *Songs* of 1622. The very beginning of *Te Deum* is of special significance owing to the paraphrase of the well-known intonation that was taken over by the Anglicans from the Sarum liturgy. A link with the First and Third Services may be seen in the octave skip at 'heaven and earth', where the organ part assumes considerable importance.

Madrigalian quirks are present at 'the sharpness of death', where (in common with the *Te Deum* settings of all the other four services) chords containing one or more sharps appear. To the same category belongs the verse for two basses in the *Magnificat*: 'He hath put down the mighty'.

---

[17] Fellowes, *English Cathedral Music*, 90.

Bass verses are a remarkable feature of the Fifth Service, which may well have been composed with some particular singer in mind. Even in the chorus parts there is far more declamation than in the other services, postulating a more intimate *milieu* of performance such as a private chapel. The *Jubilate*, with its short but florid 'Amen', affords one more instance of the composer's fondness for reminiscence: the phrase at '[O] be joyful in the Lord' echoes that of the *Jubilate* in the Third Service (Ex. 13.4).

Ex. 13.4

But the unique thematic link occurs between the 'Glory be to the Father' of *Magnificat* and *Nunc Dimittis*. The music is almost note for note the same, but the key in the latter canticle is B flat as against G minor in the former. Thus the emotional differences inherent in the two canticles are brought out in a subtle but telling manner.

The five-part Preces and Psalmi Festivales compare favourably with the best of Jacobean settings, and even though the Preces cannot be used in their entirety owing to slight changes in the liturgy since Tomkins's day, they are a valuable adornment to any service. Psalm 47 (Whitsun) and Psalm 15 (Ascension) are dignified, largely homophonic settings that have, in the past, met with little but deliberate misuse. Fragments from them have been transposed, altered, and underlaid with verses from *Magnificat* and *Nunc Dimittis*; these verses, termed 'fauxbourdon' for no apparent reason, have then been made to alternate with plainchant verses, a procedure with which Tomkins certainly never became acquainted.[18] In their pristine form, they are

---

[18] Editions by Burgess and Shore (Novello's Parish Choir Book, Nos 889 and 1037).

Musica Deo sacra 207

splendid examples of artistically contrived psalm settings, *O clap your hands* being especially noteworthy for its paired verses and alternating use of similar and dissimilar musical material.

The logical division of Tomkins's anthems is into two main categories, full and verse, and the latter of these he chose to call 'songs to the organ'. He learned from his master Byrd the basic technique of verse anthem composition, which (contrary to general supposition) was not something new and revolutionary. Byrd, who was a Catholic, and therefore not unfamiliar with the great achievements of the pre-Reformation masters, knew well that the contrasting of large and small groups of singers was a commonplace occurrence even though it was rarely marked in any special way. In the Eton Choirbook verbal texts are written in red and black in order to differentiate between the two kinds of sonority, the solo group and the ensemble. A generation later, two-, three- and four-part sections call for soloists through the very difficulty of their execution: witness the second *Agnus Dei*, with its complex proportional notation, in Taverner's *Missa O Michael*. Henrician composers could not, of course, reduce their texture to anything smaller than a duo, but the 'verse anthem' principle was there, and it only needed the organ (which in pre-Reformation times alternated with, rather than accompanied the choir) to usher in the last refinement of all, the verse for solo voice.

There are other divisions, separate from stylistic ones yet not influenced by them, which deserve consideration. Just as the word 'motet' can be made to hide a wide variety of highly individual liturgical forms, so the word 'anthem' covers many different forms and styles. There are, in *Musica Deo sacra*, at least twenty-one works written for special occasions, including eleven settings of Collects,[19] music for the Burial Service, music for the Communion Service (*Gloria, Sanctus*, and Offertory *He that hath pity*), a Coronation anthem for Charles I (*O Lord grant the King a long life*), another – possibly for James I – *Be strong and of good courage*, and four special anthems for St George, St Stephen, Christmas, and Easter.

About two-thirds of the total number of anthems in *Musica Deo sacra* make use of texts from the psalms. Usually the selection of verses is regular and consecutive, but once in a while Tomkins makes up his own sequence of verses (*Arise O Lord God lift up thine hand*) or draws upon one of the favourites in Sternhold and Hopkins (*My shepherd is the living Lord*). Besides this latter, there are three other poetical texts, two of which, *Above the stars my saviour dwells*,[20] described as 'An Hymn', and *Leave, O my soul, this baser world below*[21] share a similarity in style and are probably by Joseph Hall during his time as dean of Worcester; the third is *Not in the merits of what I have done*.

---

[19] *Turn thou us* (for the Commination) is set twice.
[20] Also set by Robert Parsons.
[21] Sometimes listed as *Stripped of my merits* and *Hear O my soul*, respectively.

208 *The Music of Thomas Tomkins*

One prose text appears to be freely composed: *O Lord do away as the night even so my sins.* It is found among the three-part anthems for men's voices, as are two further texts of more than usual interest. One is a setting of the Preces, employing the same text as the five-part version, but including also the intonations. The responsorial character of the Preces is thus obliterated, yet the music would serve quite satisfactorily as an anthem with text from various psalms, like *Arise O Lord God.* In *Glory be to the Father,* there is a coda of unusual interest built upon a florid *Alleluia,* suggesting that the composer had an Easter performance in mind. *Alleluia* is also interpolated into the Sanctus previously mentioned, but it is unlikely that the two works are closely connected since the setting of *Holy holy holy* is for five voices. Three anthems have double texts, and were probably underlaid in this way when Nathaniel came upon them. He did not apparently stop to unravel the peculiarities of *Blessed is he that considereth the poor,* for these words appear in two of the voice parts, while *O Lord graciously accept* appears in three others. The bassus has both texts, but it is clear that the second fits badly, and is unlikely ever to have been sanctioned by Thomas Tomkins. Two five-part anthems have Latin texts as well as English,[22] the former being possibly intended for use in the Chapel Royal or in a collegiate chapel where Latin was permitted.

The texture of the full anthems varies from the richly scored *O praise the Lord all ye heathen* (*a* 12) to the three-part anthems for men's voices, all of these latter being without an organ part. *O praise the Lord,* besides being a *tour de force,* offers lively proof of the Englishman's immunity from the dispersed choirs of the Italian manner. No regrouping is needed in order to perform the work in its most striking and effective manner: Tomkins has divided into three each section of a four-part choir, and the resulting cohesion is as strongly felt in the smooth and dignified counterpoint of the opening bars as it is in the quasi-echo effects of 'for His merciful kindness'.

This work may well have been written for some great occasion of state, or possibly for Tomkins's degree exercise in 1607. There is some indication that the anthems for more than six voices were all early works. Certainly *O God the proud are risen* (*a* 8) and *O sing unto the Lord* (*a* 7) may be dated before 1617, for they are both found in the tenor partbook copied by Jarvis Jones of Oxford in that year.[23] The one other full anthem *a* 7 is *Be strong and of good courage,* already mentioned as appearing in the list of anthems used at the coronation of James I in 1603.

Typical of the six-part anthems is *Who shall ascend the hill of God,* with its varied interplay of three, four and five voices before the full choir is heard at 'from the God of his salvation'. The inevitable ascent of the first phrase

---

[22] *Why art thou so full of heaviness/Domine tu eruisti animam; Lord enter not into judgement/Non nobis Domine.*

[23] Bodleian Library, Tenbury MS 1382.

contrasts admirably with the almost static homophony supporting 'and stand before His holy seat', whilst later the solidity of salvation is brought home by a long dominant pedal. The coda is repeated, with slight changes in verbal text, after the fashion of the English anthems published by John Day early in the reign of Elizabeth.

The fifteen anthems *a* 5 are among the finest in *Musica Deo sacra*. Tomkins displays his reverence for the mood of the text and his delight in the opportunities offered by salient words and phrases: both the breadth of design and the finesse of detail are dear to him. Besides the well-known *When David heard* there is another, even more expressively dramatic setting of a verse from the Second Book of Samuel – *Then David mourned*. Seldom in English church music has there been so successful a working of the pathetic vein as this (see Ex. 13.5).

Ex. 13.5

Both moving and pathetic in a different way are the ululatory motives at the beginning of *Why art thou so full of heaviness*, an anthem that is almost entirely lacking in homophony, perhaps to illustrate the word 'heaviness' with its relentlessly unfolding counterpoint. Usually Tomkins introduces passages of homophony at just the right point, so relieving the ear and throwing the text into relief. The impression is one of solemnity at 'Thou and the ark of Thy strength' in *Arise O Lord into Thy resting-place*, of prayerful humility at the opening of *Have mercy upon me O God*; of supplication at a similar point in *O Lord I have loved the habitation of Thine house*.

Occasionally these chordal sections are prefigured by the uppermost voice; a venerable device to be sure, but also a remarkably effective one, especially at 'for in Thy sight' (*Lord enter not into judgement*) and at 'O Lord, let it be Thy pleasure to deliver me' (*Withdraw not Thou Thy mercy*) (see Ex. 13.6).

This latter anthem assigns a double role to the middle of five voices – as bass of one trio and treble of another – at the phrase 'for innumerable troubles', and a similar example may be found in *Great and marvellous*, where 'Who shall not fear Thee O Lord' is passed from a trio of high voices to one of low voices. *Almighty God the fountain of all wisdom* is a beautiful setting of the Fifth Collect at the end of the Communion, and is noteworthy for its particularly fine and extended 'Amen'. Both *Arise O Lord God* and *He that hath pity* (an Offertory Sentence from the Communion Service) are prayers

Ex. 13.6

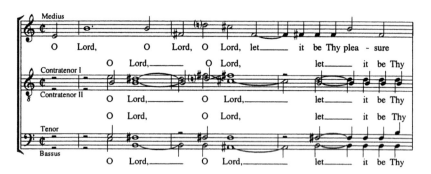

for the poor and needy, whose plight was keenly felt and often remedied by Tomkins and his first wife Alice.

Among the four-part anthems are several examples of Tomkins's finest workmanship. *Turn thou us* (the Last Collect of the Communion) is an ingenious canon four in one, yet its musical worth far surpasses the brilliance of its construction, and as Burney said it is 'well worthy the disciple of the admirable Byrd'.[24] The music for the Burial Service includes moving and dignified settings of the three texts at the beginning of the ceremony, and of the text to be said or sung after the interment.[25] Liturgically linked with *Turn thou us* is the Collect for Ash Wednesday, which offers two or three instances of Tomkins's fondness for repeating a phrase one note higher for emphasis. *The heavens declare the glory* brings in a touch of madrigalian technique when contrary motion is used to illustrate 'the ends of the world', but it is skilfully written and deserves to be better known. The same might well be said for *O how amiable*, which compares favourably with the excellent setting by Weelkes.

Most of the three-part anthems are based on psalm texts, and their especial use is confined to smaller, but not necessarily men's choirs. The combinations of voices for these nineteen works without organ vary considerably. Outstanding among their number are the Seven Penitential Psalms, all without exception good examples of the expressive and original effects that may be drawn out of a relatively unpromising medium of only three voices. Tomkins avoids mechanism in his imitative writing by delaying the third entry somewhat, but for the rest he does what is expected of him: an augmented triad for 'heavy displeasure' (*Put me not to rebuke*), a sudden veering to D major at 'Thy great goodness' (*Have mercy upon me*), and a deep bass voice at the beginning of *Out of the deep*.

In the verse anthems, or 'Songs to the Organ', Tomkins has left a solid and impressive monument to the taste of the times, a taste that he, as a virtuoso organist, shared to a large degree. Only in the verse anthem was it possible for the instrument to become a vital, creative part of the texture: it stood on a par with the voices, supporting them in the choruses as well as it did in the full anthems, but besides this it gave life and meaning to the solos, duets, and smaller ensembles that are so important a feature of the Jacobean verse anthem.

If one of the advantages of the verse anthem is to be found in the scope it gives the organist, one of its disadvantages is the standard of singing required of the soloists. Unless the solo and ensemble passages, as opposed to the choruses, are sung with exceptional poise and accuracy, the entire effect of the music is lost. Given first-rate soloists, and an organist with a discreet flair for

---

24 Burney, *General History*, II, 114.
25 This latter, 'I heard a voice from heaven', was edited separately by Atkins.

212 *The Music of Thomas Tomkins*

pre-Restoration style, the verse anthem becomes a vehicle for the best kind of individual musical appeal. Yet it does not attempt to supplant polyphony by an overdose of monody, as some of its continental contemporaries did; nor does it oust the chorus in order to bathe the soloist in garish illumination. The verse anthem enfolds within its wide compass many of the most outstanding features of the music current during the previous century, but there is no secret in the fact that its most successful advocates were three men who by their position in the Chapel Royal were able to achieve performances very near to perfection – Byrd, Gibbons and Tomkins.

It seems that of these three masters, Tomkins was decidedly the most prolific, with forty-one verse anthems, and also the most determined in seeing to it that the greater feast-days should be celebrated by music in this style. The Collects in particular contain much of his finest music. His setting of the Collect for Christmas makes apt use of rising melodic sequences and the overlapping and exchange of phrases between solo voices; brilliant too is the brief use of a double choir effect in the chorus passages. All Saints has several similar passages, and is rounded off by a splendid eight-part 'Amen'. A flowing and impressive bass solo tells of St Mark, though one of the longest verses must be the five-part opening of the Collect for the Holy Innocents. The five voices are hardly ever used together, thus proving one of the main structural features of the verse anthem: it was fundamentally a display of contrasts in register and timbre. In this same anthem Tomkins demonstrates his skill in building up the listener's interest (see Ex. 13.7).

Several of Gibbons's verse anthems are intended to be accompanied by a consort of viols, and there are two by Tomkins (*Above the stars* and *Thou art my king O God*) for which string parts survive intact.[26] They were almost certainly written for the Chapel Royal, where such extra musical resources could be found from amongst the players at court. *Behold I bring you glad tidings*, a Christmas anthem of considerable stature, may also qualify for a London rather than a Worcester origin, for its single solo verse is followed by a ten-part chorus that would severely tax the powers of all but a large and entirely professional choir.

Not all of the chorus sections are of such power and complexity. The main function of the shorter choruses is to repeat and confirm the words uttered by the soloist, music as well as text being repeated in some instances: *Above the stars*; *O Lord let me know mine end*; *Praise the Lord O ye servants*. Less usually the very first phrase is repeated immediately after the soloist has stated it, as in *Hear my prayer* (Ex. 13.8).

---

[26] See also David Pinto and Ross Duffin (1994), *Thomas Tomkins: Five Consort Anthems*, Fretwork, for editions of these two anthems by Tomkins, and others that survive with ensemble accompaniment restored.

Ex. 13.7

My shepherd is the living Lord, described as 'Psalm 23 of the ordinary metre',[27] employs two different techniques in its two short choruses. The first does not repeat the words of the soloist, but instead goes on with the psalm text, leading into the next verse section. The final chorus, however, does restate both text and musical motives of the preceding duet.

One particular verse anthem is sometimes indexed under the incipit 'My help cometh from the Lord', these being the first words sung by the solo counter-tenor. The entire anthem is to be introduced by the intoning of verse 1 of Psalm 121, *I will lift up mine eyes*. There is a typical example here of the subjugation of phrase by word, when a solo bass voice in its deepest and darkest register sings 'The Lord shall preserve thee from evil'. Similarly striking is the bass solo that begins *Leave O my soul* (Ex. 13.9).

Irregular treatment of verse and chorus relationship is found from time to time, and suggests that Tomkins was unwilling to follow any hard-and-fast plan, other than the understood method of beginning with a verse and ending

---

[27] A reference to the then still popular psalter of Sternhold and Hopkins.

Ex. 13.8

with a chorus. In *O pray for the peace of Jerusalem* the first chorus echoes the verse in the accepted manner, then a bass verse repeats the text once more before new material is reached. This rhetorical repetition is not of the kind that irritates critics: their strictures apparently refer to the repetition of a phrase, or part of a phrase, at the end of a section.[28] It is perfectly true that Tomkins frequently does this, but he is in excellent company because Byrd, Gibbons and Weelkes also provide plentiful examples of the same alleged fault.

Several of the verse anthems are intended for feast-days but are not based on Collects. The Easter anthem, *Christ rising again from the dead*, is one of the most successful of these, and arrests the attention by its unusual opening phrase, its florid organ part, and the delightful tripla for the second section, 'Christ is risen' (Ex. 13.10).

The text of the anthem for St Stephen's Day is taken from the First Lesson, the contrast between narrative and speech being heightened by contrast of

---

[28] Fellowes, *English Cathedral Music*, 91.

Ex. 13.9

chorus and verse. No less than six verse soloists are heard, in varied, almost kaleidoscopic combinations of register. St George's day demanded no special text, composers being left to choose their own collaboration with their ecclesiastical superiors. Tomkins chose *Who is this that cometh out of the wilderness* (The Song of Solomon 3: 6) and clearly enjoyed setting this unusual text to music.

The wide variety of procedures and musical ideas in these anthems, together with the high degree of skill apparent in the very best of them should be more than sufficient a recommendation to those who have the means to perform them. As Tudway once said, they are indeed 'very elaborate and artful pieces, and most deserving to be recorded and had in everlasting remembrance'.[29] Even more significant than Tudway's judgement, although endorsing it, is the view expressed by Peter Phillips in his excellent book, *English Sacred Music 1549–1649*. Phillips acknowledges that many of Tomkins's full anthems are of the highest quality. 'His achievement there', he writes, 'is perhaps paralleled in the work of Gibbons and Weelkes; but he explored the possibilities of the verse anthem as no one else did.' And another contemporary testimonial to the greatness of Tomkins's music comes from the pen of Sir David Willcocks, a world-renowned musician and father-figure of choral music, who was formerly one of Tomkins's successors in the office of organist and master of the choristers at Worcester Cathedral:

---

[29] BL Harley MS 7339, fol. 66.

Ex. 13.10

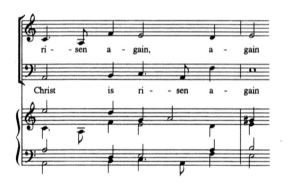

Wherein lies the greatness of Tomkins's art? To some extent it resides in the shape and beauty of his melodic lines, and in his contrapuntal ingenuity. But more especially his genius is to be found in the unusually bold and rich harmonic progressions, achieved by free use of Passing and anticipatory notes, chromatic intervals, and frequent false relations. Such works as *A Sad Pavan: for these distracted times* and *When David heard that Absalom was slain* are unsurpassed for poignancy of musical expression.

Chapter 14

Songs of 3, 4, 5 and 6 Parts

In his songs there is melody and accent, as well as pure harmony and ingenious contrivance.

(Charles Burney, *General History of Music* (1776))

Although Thomas Tomkins began his professional career in music when the composing and singing of madrigals was nearly at the height of its popularity, he did not venture into the field of publication until 1622, when much of the enthusiasm for this kind of musical entertainment had given place to an extensive cultivation of the lute-song repertoire. He never wrote lute songs or lute solos, but he admired the skill of Dowland and Danyel, dedicating to them two of the songs in his late but outstanding collection. If he had admiration for the new trends in Jacobean music, he was content to show it without attempting to copy those trends or to break faith with his own deep-seated reverence for the traditions he had learned from his master, William Byrd. Thus his published book of *Songs* (as he called them, in common with Vautor, who also avoided the term 'madrigal') appears as a late example of the madrigalian idiom, whether viewed by his contemporaries or by critics of the present century.

Burney scored the first one of the set[1] but did not apparently persevere to the extent that Vincent Novello did. In 1844, Novello scored twenty-three of the total number of twenty-eight,[2] though nothing was made available to the public until Barclay Squire edited two of the *Songs*[3] and Fellowes issued the entire set, together with the one madrigal in *The Triumphs of Oriana*, in 1922, just three centuries after the original publication. Late though they came in the stream of madrigal books published during the latter part of Elizabeth's reign and the reign of James I, these *Songs* enjoyed a success that was immediate enough to warrant further printing. It is doubtful, however, that the second printing was made in the same year, as Fellowes and others assumed.

Of the two editions known, one is dated 1622 while the other replaces this

---

[1] BL Add. MS 11587; there are also five keyboard reductions, probably by Tomkins himself, in Add. MS 29996 (*O let me live for true love; O let me die for true love; Oyez! Has any found a lad?; Weep no more, thou sorry boy; Yet again, as soon revived*) and one incomplete keyboard version – not by Tomkins – in Paris, Bibliothèque Nationale, Rés. 1186.

[2] RCM, MS 616.

[3] *Ausgewählte Madrigale.*

217

date with a rule and the words *Cum privilegio*. The undated edition cannot have been printed before 1622 since it was not until May of that year that William Heather, referred to as Dr Heather in the dedication of *Music Divine*, actually took his degree of Doctor of Music at Oxford. It could have been printed later than 1622, since the type was frequently stored in case of need, and the inference of the term *Cum privilegio* points to a desire for prestige as well as restocking. The privilege to print music came, of course, from royal sources; and the renewal of privilege when a new king came to the throne may well have been the occasion for rejoicing. It is certainly not unlikely that such a renewal would prompt Mathew Lownes, John Browne, and Thomas Snodham to reissue some of their earlier publications with the two words *Cum privilegio*, so much sought after, in place of the date. In the case of Tomkins's *Songs*, there would be an added reason for a reissue of this kind, for the death of Orlando Gibbons in 1625 had brought Tomkins to the forefront of musical life in London, and his music for the funeral of James I and the coronation of Charles I added very considerably to this reputation. It is therefore quite possible that the undated edition was printed in the first year of the reign of Charles I, both as a tribute to Tomkins, and by way of a discreet celebration of the renewal of privilege to print music.

Unfortunately for Tomkins, the historical importance of his *Songs* has often been stressed to the detriment of their purely musical appeal, which (as any madrigal group can confirm) is very considerable. Even a rapid reading of the entire book is more than enough to convince singers and listeners of the high standard of the *Songs*, the best of them reaching a summit of musical beauty that can only be matched by the finest creations of Weelkes, Gibbons, and Wilbye. One of the first to recognize this high quality was E.H. Fellowes, who refers to the *Songs* as

> The last volume of first-rate importance in the great series of English madrigals … It is consequently very remarkable that Tomkins's music should have experienced such complete neglect, as has been the case, ever since the popularity of madrigal-singing declined in his own lifetime. Except for one or two recent reprints, none of the work of this very notable English musician is known to his own countrymen, and it is not improbable that a large number of musicians of the present day have never even heard of his name.[4]

Neglect of Tomkins's *Songs* is now, mercifully, a thing of the past, for they have found dedicated advocacy in the expert hands of vocal ensembles such as I Fagiolini, whose director, Robert Hollingworth, has described the 1622 collection as 'Unique for a book of (mostly) English madrigals in its unremitting quality and breadth of invention. Not only is every piece very fine, but many are outright masterworks.'[5]

---

[4] E.H. Fellowes (1921), *The English Madrigal Composers*, Oxford, 293.
[5] Sleeve-note to the I Fagiolini recording of Tomkins's *Songs of 3, 4, 5, and 6 parts* (Chandos, *Music Divine*, CHAN 0680 (2002)).

Even in the madrigal that Tomkins contributed to *The Triumphs of Oriana* there is mastery of an unusual strength for a young composer not yet 30. He accepts graciously and wittily the pictorial conventions of the time, investing *The fauns and satyrs* with a rustic freshness and simplicity that he never quite recaptured in his later works.[6] The quasi-canonic chordal passage babbles 'of fresh cool brooks' with as much persuasiveness as the finely contrasted section following tells of 'those of woods and mountains', three lower voices being echoed by three upper ones in traditional though touching fashion. The altus has the pleasure of singing the highest part of the three lower voices, and the lowest part of the ready-made trio aloft. When the demi-gods are mentioned, there is a subtle reminder of their half-way status in the half-tone step heard in all three voices (see Ex. 14.1).

Ex. 14.1

Although there is nothing at all out of the ordinary in Tomkins's harmonic palette, key-colour and cadential contrast are obviously part of a careful plan. The envoi is allowed to begin in the darker region of the subdominant, so that gradually it can move towards the brightness of the home key. As the music travels pointedly, though without rigidity, from C to G its texture undergoes a corresponding change from epigrammatic homophony to the long, flowing lines of the final cadence, where fair Oriana, supported by a plinth-like dominant pedal, makes her gracious bow of acknowledgement.

It was a creditable beginning for a young man, but since he was a modest man and saw himself surrounded by madrigalists of tremendous gifts, he produced no further examples in this style until his friend Thomas Myriell invited contributions to *Tristitiae Remedium*, an anthology compiled during the years immediately preceding 1616, when it was apparently completed. Tomkins wrote six compositions for Myriell, and three of these appeared later in the *Songs*. Assuming that his B.Mus. degree, his work at Worcester, and his conferences with Dallam about the new organ together accounted for the greater part of his leisure during the years 1602–13, it is likely that these six works were written between 1613 and 1616. The idea of Myriell's collection, a *mélange* of serious anthems, delightful madrigals, and novelties such as the *London Cries* of Orlando Gibbons, may have inspired Tomkins to compile his own anthology as well as to plan it with variety in mind. Thus there are four

---

[6] This madrigal was formerly thought to be the work of Thomas Tomkins the elder.

220   *The Music of Thomas Tomkins*

sacred songs among the total of twenty-eight, calling to mind the principle followed by so many editors and publishers of the Renaissance: let there be secular music by all means, provided that a motet, grace, or anthem round off the collection and serve to sanctify the contents. Tomkins was a little anxious about this, for he mentions in his dedication to the earl of Pembroke 'the lightness of some of the words ... an old (but ill) custom, which I wish were abrogated'.

As with the madrigal books of Byrd, Weelkes, Wilbye, and Ward, that of Tomkins includes music for any number of voices from three to six. Because of its sonority as well as its variety, five-part harmony still remained the prime favourite of composers during the early part of the seventeenth century, and Tomkins sets the largest group of his *Songs* for five voices. Together with these ten, there are six each of three-part, four-part, and six-part *Songs*, making a well-balanced group with adequate contrast in style and type.

The *Songs* set out for cantus, altus, and bassus show considerable ingenuity as well as remarkable contrapuntal resource: the individuality of treatment is scarcely less notable a feature of their design, and (unlike some of Ward's three-part madrigals) they can hold their own against the more elaborate texture of the other groups. The text of *Our hasty life* is particularly apt for Thomas Tomkins the elder, who was then in his late seventies. It will be noticed that the dedication of the first song to his father is nicely matched by the dedication of the last one to his son. For Thomas, family life embraced all things, even a book of musical compositions. The harmonic scheme of this first madrigal of the set is simple but effective, especially in the middle section where the imitative passage – 'before we know what we have lost' – becomes a genuine sequence and touches upon A minor and G major on its way to the cadence. Although Tomkins never plays off two voices against two, using a similar technique to the three-versus-three trick in five-part texture, he does vary the sound by using two voices to echo one. At 'hours into days' the structure of the opening point is mirrored by the rhythmically identical 'years make a life', while at the end of the peroration ('when we are waxed old') there is a similar device, more taut than before, as a final cadence deserves.

No more will I thy love importune shares with two of the following three-part songs an imitative scheme at the very beginning that sets off a held note against two canonically mobile voices.[7] The phrase set to 'importune' sets up a graphic chain of treading upon heels, but Tomkins shows that he is more than a *glossateur* in his deft harmonic scheme for 'or pity use' (see Ex. 14.2).

The latter third of the song is entirely devoted, as is so often the case, to an extended setting of the last line of the six-line lyric. It is the last line that gives the twist to the lyric, and it is therefore understandable that more time and

---

[7] Cf. Nos 4 and 5 of the set.

Ex. 14.2

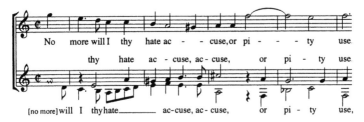

effort should be expended upon it. 'Since I can never hope, I never may desire' grows smoothly, though inexorably, from an initial point handled in a manner that is typical of the later madrigalists in general and of Tomkins in particular: the first imitation is immediate, the second delayed and slightly altered. This feeling for asymmetrical patterns betrays a Baroque attitude that may not always be allied to a Baroque style. Coming from Tomkins, a traditional composer by design, and a transitional one by accident, this is not surprising. Other traits belonging to the same common cause will be noticed as time goes on.

Sure there is no god of love, for Humphrey Withy, is more than usually interesting from a metrical point of view. Although the standard time-signature ¢ is employed in all three voices, the true metre is triple, with frequent hemiolas. Beginning with the first note of the bassus, it would be possible to bar the song in 3/2 6/4 time, thus preserving the natural rhythmic aspects of many of the individual phrases. The alternation between chordal and contrapuntal manner coincides, remarkable enough, with the progress of the lyric from one line to the next. The form of the verse itself, but not its rhyme scheme, is therefore brought out and enhanced by the texture of the music.

Nicholas Tomkins, who died a bachelor, was the recipient of the fourth song:

> Fond men, that do so highly prize
> A woman's forehead, lips and eyes,
> And look not to the better part
> What virtues dwelleth in the heart;
> Such kind of loving showeth plain,
> You please the sense and not the brain.

The words 'that do so highly prize' are consistently set to an ascending phrase, whilst 'the better part' emerges as a busy and complex piece of polyphony. Once again the last line of the poem receives the lion's share of the music, a final envoi descanting gaily and unrepentantly above a discreet dominant pedal.

How great delight paraphrases a text by Guarini,[8] which was set by

---

[8] G.B. Guarini (1737), *Delle opere del Cavalier Battista Guarini*I, Madrigali, lxx. Monteverdi's setting of this text appears in Malipiero's edition of the *Complete Works*, VII, 137.

222

The Music of Thomas Tomkins

Monteverdi in his seventh book of madrigals, first published in 1619. As *Con che soavità*, the madrigal is well known as a particularly fine example of concertato style: a solitary voice is richly and elaborately accompanied by three interdependent instrumental groups. In view of the appearance of Monteverdi's book some three years before the *Songs* of 1622, it is possible that Tomkins knew *Con che soavità* and admired its pioneering mastery without wishing to emulate it; he made use, however, of a translation of part of its text and set the words for three solo voices unaccompanied, rather than for one solo voice accompanied by three groups of instruments. Tomkins permits homophony to underline the text now and then, varying the texture slightly for the sake of a sensuous little gruppetto on 'feel (them kiss)', and extending the sonority of a simple cadence at 'wonders'. The gruppetto first heard in connection with the word 'feel' recurs at 'kisses', but only in the two upper voices. In the bassus, there is a slowly moving line which acts fairly consistently as the bass part of the triads implied, except at the final cadence, where imitation occurs.[9]

The last of the three-part songs, *Love, cease tormenting*, like the previous one, is dedicated to a colleague of Tomkins in the Chapel Royal. William Cross and Thomas Day may well have been pleased with these short but charming compositions. There are poignant suspensions for the word 'tormenting', but nothing extraordinary happens at the first statement of 'cruel'. A change of mood and movement accompanies a repeat of the phrase 'pitiless and cruel', and this is the signal for expressive clashes involving the interval of the diminished fourth. Considered as a group, these six songs are pleasantly varied in text and texture, and they tend to show in a small way certain of the most important characteristics of Tomkins's style. His grasp of harmonic resource and his mastery of contrapuntal writing are apparent throughout these half-dozen madrigalistic miniatures, for in spite of the modest designation of 'song' they manifest all that is most highly prized in the technique of madrigal composition.

The first two of the group of four-part *Songs* are linked together by their texts, their style, and their dedicatees. There is something touching about the way in which Tomkins quotes the well-known opening phrase of Dowland's *Lachrymae* in the uppermost voice of *O let me live for true love*. Countering this genial plagiarism with congenial persiflage, he brings to an abrupt end this tearful exclamation and introduces a flippant *fa-la*. This pattern is repeated, and gives way to a homophonic section in which the phrase 'yet let me live no longer' takes on an air of urgency from the breath of a tripla figure. The last and most extended of the *fa-la* sections makes considerable use of

---

[9] The text, as given in *The English Madrigal School*, XVIII, 23, seems to be corrupt: 'or grant her speaking words' (lowest voice) should read 'and grant her kissing words'. Similarly, on p. 22, the last four words of this voice part should read 'and grant her kissing'.

Songs of 3, 4, 5 and 6 Parts

triple metre, which adds to the contrast between these light-hearted passages and the mock-serious, heavy rhythm of the *Lachrymae* borrowings. Unlike Barley, Byrd, Farnaby, and Morley, who all borrowed Dowland's theme and used it in their works, Tomkins found in it material for gentle satire as well as genuine tribute.

If Dowland was the greatest of the English lutenists, John Danyel was a worthy runner-up and a striking and original composer in his own right. The song dedicated to Danyel has for its text the second part of the lyric used in the song dedicated to Dowland: *O let me die for true love*. The opening phrase is also derived from a melodic fragment in the previous piece, but the *Lachrymae* theme does not appear until the words *O let me die for true love*, immediately after the first *fa-la*. The persiflage persists, and a tripla figure, matching that of the previous song, occurs at the phrase 'let not hope or old time come to end my woe'. This time the final *fa-la* has a more four-square feeling about it, so that the two songs, performed in succession, demonstrate artistic cohesion and contrast to a high degree.

Oyez! has any found a lad? makes use of the then popular device of basing a text upon the jargon of the town crier, who appears in the *Cries of London* by Dering and Gibbons as a kind of stock character, hearty to the extent of being somewhat coarse. Tomkins sublimates his town crier in a text whose Marinistic conceits of Cupid would have greatly pleased the Italianate Coperario, to whom the song is inscribed. The harmony becomes momentarily purple when this colour is cited as an attribute of Cupid's wings, and a little later it is removed altogether for a short space whilst bare monophony stresses 'in naked beauty', which uses exactly the same melodic figure as 'with bare gifts' in *The Fauns and Satyrs*. Word-painting is found when the words 'lieth' and 'flieth' occur, the latter giving rise to melismatic parabolas, vivid in expression and plausible in contour.

The second half of the four-part group follows the same pattern as the first half: there are two paired songs, followed by an isolated one. The paired ones, dedicated to his brothers Peregrine and Robert, are based on two verses that constitute a single lyric. *Weep no more thou sorry boy* adds to the pathos of its opening phrase by avoiding too firm a tonality, and Tomkins's acquaintance with the practice of Italian madrigalists is shown by his portrayal of 'sighs' as crotchet rests (*sospiri*),[10] which create a hocketing effect between the upper voice and the three lower ones. The fickleness of love is nicely depicted by Gesualdo-like chordal juxtapositions at 'laughs and weeps' (see Ex. 14.3).

Similarly, 'dancing' gives rise to a fleeting tripla; 'angry eye' a harmonic jolt which far transcends the bounds of Augenmusik, and brings with it a false relation or two for good measure. The lover, thus rebuked, sits down in a

---

[10] Cf. G.F. Malipiero (ed. 1926–42), *Monteverdi: Complete Works*, Vienna, VIII, 287: 'un gran sospir dal cor'. Germaine Bontoux (1936), in *La Chanson en Angleterre au temps d'Élisabeth*, p. 644, comments on the delicacy of expression in Tomkins's song.

Ex. 14.3

recurring and unmistakable octave drop, and true to certain traditions takes an unconscionable time a-dying.

Yet again, as soon revived is an admirable sequel, and (like its prototype) begins with a statement of the opening line or title by the three upper voices, repeating it when the bassus joins in. Joy and grief, aptly portrayed, lead to the phrase 'change there is of joy', at which the metre obediently changes to triple time, returning as suddenly at the word 'sadness', long held on a soulful chord of A flat. There is a bold and expressive touch when a cadence on 'gladness', purposely deprived of its third, leads to a broad hint of E minor at the words 'then weep no more, thou sorry boy', recalling the opening line of the first verse. With weeping joy, sighing and dying, dancing and singing, the song moves towards its close, evoking shades of Monteverdi's *Zefiro torna*,[11] with its contrasting music for 'hor piango, hor canto'. But Tomkins's masterstroke is left to the very end, when crocodile tears are suggested by ululating downward sequences and an optimistic ending in D major.

The group is rounded out by another song dedicated to one of Thomas's brothers, this time Giles. *Was ever wretch tormented* is a conventional enough love lyric, yet rich in contrasting words that call up powerful musical images. Not without very good reason did Tomkins choose a relatively low tessitura for the voices: their dark colours prove to be effective and compelling in the middle section of the song. At the outset, the three lower voices reach out tortuously and expressively for a cadence on 'tormented' (see Ex. 14.4).

Ex. 14.4

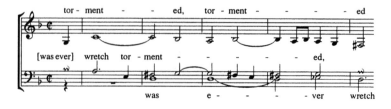

---

[11] Monteverdi: *Complete Works*, IX, 9.

Songs of 3, 4, 5 and 6 Parts

Significantly, three out of the four voices sing their highest note at the mention of 'heaven', and later there is a deep and fiendish ostinato for 'hellish firing'. There is still a strong proclivity for word-painting in its most individual form, as opposed to a consistent emotional mood, for the sake of relief and change: the ascending runs on 'flames' and the infectious gaiety of 'delighted' are the only rays of light in this sad and solemn portrayal of 'pinish grief and anguish'.

Seven of the ten songs for five voices are written in the style of the ballett, yet this group is far from being wholly light and bucolic. The first of the sacred songs, *When David heard*, appears here amidst the richness and variety of five-part vocal colour, and it is the only one of the group to depart from the otherwise standard practice of having the two uppermost voices of equal and even tessitura. *To the shady woods* (possibly a pun on the name of Robert Chetwode, its dedicatee) is a short but charming song in which Tomkins begins at once to make use of the possibilities of voice-exchange afforded by the cantus and quintus. The two *fa-las*, one in duple and the other in triple metre, offer rhythmical as well as thematic contrast, and do much to dispel the notion that these simple refrains were no more than mechanically composed codettas of little importance. The tripla section at the end is introduced, in the original partbooks, by no less than four different mensuration signs: against the probability that the printer was feeling whimsical may be set the more likely explanation that such signs were no longer called for at the time when the *Songs* were published. It is true that one or two archaic time-signatures continued until the end of the seventeenth century, but there is no evidence to show that printers were keen to keep them in stock.

Too much I once lamented is a finely contrived song, and one that surely made Byrd (to whom it is inscribed) proud of his pupil. The expected suspensions and harmonic twists accompany the opening line and its successor, 'while love my heart tormented', but the gloom is dispelled by a fascinating *fa-la* that rises in two-bar sequences, changing the texture as it goes. There is much expressive and unusual melodic beauty in the lines that carry 'alas and ay me', but once again the sorrowful mood is done away with by neat homophony and a vivacious *fa-la* whose essence lies in its pairing of voices.

Nathaniel Giles, whose exercise in proportional notation was reprinted by Hawkins,[12] could hardly fail to be amused by the song dedicated to him: *Come shepherds sing with me*. The verse form is treated in cavalier fashion so that the second line, which begins with the word 'thrice' can change to a tripla, while three voices remain singing as far as the *fa-la*. The falseness of love is suggested

---

[12] Burney, *General History*, III, 462.

by shifting syncopations, beneath which the bassus firmly resolves 'to love false love no more' in a series of long, held notes. The last *fa-la* is one of the longest Tomkins wrote, yet it is splendidly organized, with texture changing from groups of three and four voices until the final chorus from all five, and well-balanced modulation leading through G minor and B flat back to the home key of F.

Cloris, whenas I woo (for Orlando Gibbons) uses deft and effervescent counterpoint to suggest the maid's refusal, the 'no no no' corresponding to a *fa-la* refrain, and occupying the same place in both lyric and music. The second refrain is especially interesting for its use of ascending sequential phrases over a chromatic altus, which reiterates 'no' until all join in and the scheme is repeated, this time with the bass ascending in diatonic but none the less forceful negatives.

See, see the shepherd's queen was dedicated to John Stevens, one of the composer's colleagues in the Chapel Royal. Its text is that of an extended ballett, with three couplets each followed by a *fa-la* refrain. This time, even Tomkins's ingenuity is severely taxed to find adequate variety in the refrain sections, which occupy about two-thirds of the total time of performance. He emerges from this artistic ordeal with flags flying: the first *fa-la* is deliberately conventional, so that when the second is heard, with its vivacious solo roulades, interest and excitement grow apace. The third and longest refrain returns to the epigrammatic, paired phrases of the first, but with certain differences: a long and slowly descending bass line seems to bind together the more quickly moving upper parts, while the final cadence is reached by way of an upward surging sequence of insistent *fa-las*, leading back to the key of G major. The couplets themselves, especially 'then dance we on a row', have characteristically subtle rhythmic schemes, and make up for their shortness by their full and sonorous texture.[13]

There is a possible link between the lyric of *Phyllis, now cease to move me* (for Henry Moule of Worcester) and the previous one beginning *Come, shepherds, sing with me*, which ends

> From hence we all have swore
> To love false Love no more.

The second, and last couplet of *Phyllis* seems to echo these lines, though to be sure the oath is singular rather than plural:

> Content thee! I have swore
> To love false Love no more.

Four upper voices administer the dissuasive understatement with which the song begins, and their declamation is consistent in its natural and easy flow;

---

[13] The music is used also for the *Sanctus* in *Musica Deo sacra*.

there is something of speech rhythm here, and the exaggeration (if it is present at all) is just that of a testy rebuke (see Ex. 14.5).

Ex. 14.5

The first *fa-la* is of the sequential type, where rising repetition gains momentum from the overlapping of the two equal upper voices. True to the accepted scheme of the ballett (of which this is the last of a continuous group of six) the second couplet is regaled with lilting homophony, and as soon thrust aside for a refrain compounded of bold melodic figures and subtle rhythms. On its first and second appearance, the *fa-la* phrase well exceeds the octave; paired, it keeps within bounds but is doubly exciting. So too is the tenor part, with its delightful symmetry and syncopation (see Ex. 14.6).

Ex. 14.6

However moving or beautiful the settings of David's lament by East and Weelkes, there is one English composition on this wonderful theme that can hold its own, in sheer poetry and dramatic effect, against the settings of Josquin des Prez, Jacob Handl, and Heinrich Schütz. It is Thomas Tomkins, whose 'exquisite invention, wit, and art' (to quote from Charles Butler) endowed this lament with such feeling and expression. His mastery of madrigalian idiom stands him in good stead when these same principles are applied, in a reserved and reverent way, to the well-known text from 2 Samuel 18, 33. Thomas Myriell, to whom the work was dedicated, and who included it in his musical anthology *Tristitiae Remedium*, must have been an especially good friend of Thomas Tomkins to deserve so fine a gift.

The work falls roughly into two halves: the narration and the lament. *When David heard that Absalom was slain* begins as if it were a four-part composition for cantus, quintus, altus, and tenor, and the voices rarely exceed the total compass of a twelfth as they sing, with hushed expectancy, of David's grief. Even when the tenor rises to an octave G at 'he went up to his chamber' there is no impression of a lack of restraint in word-painting: if such a phrase occurred in a song, it would be set to some gay scalic ascent. Here, the clean but audible change of octave does all that is required of it. The near-sequential lines of the upper voices ('and wept') achieve their effect too, without an extravagant display of chromatic emotion, and the quasi-apostrophic half-close at the end of the section prepares the way eloquently for the high, ringing, and solitary tenor note on which the lament begins.

From this point onwards the polyphony unfurls its sad beauty with a mastery that defies description. To the ever-shifting contrasts of vocal colour Tomkins adds contrasting motives to the same word, the key-word of the lament (see Ex. 14.7).

Ex. 14.7

There is a shift, this time of harmonic emphasis, on the phrase 'would God I had died for thee', which seems to express the ever-changing, ever-renewing aspects of David's sorrow. Perhaps the most wonderful touch of all is the way in which Tomkins seems to bring in a note of quiet resignation as the descending, cambiata-like point for 'Absalom, my son' gives place to an ascending figure, set to the same words, and enclosed as it were in the comforting embrace of a dominant pedal and an inverted tonic pedal. As devices in the successful building up of a musical peroration, these are simple, even commonplace: used with the skill and judgement that Tomkins lavishes upon them, they take on a character that is nothing if not ethereal.

The title of *Phyllis, yet see him dying* clearly recalled *Phyllis, now cease to move me*, for both songs begin with exactly similar rhythm and initial change of chord. Beyond this, there is nothing in common, for the verse forms differ, and there is no *fa-la* refrain in this charming song inscribed to Nicholas Carlton, Tomkins's fellow madrigalist and near neighbour. The texture, accentuation, and spirit of the music are apt to change (as in certain of the previous songs) as soon as a new line of the lyric is reached, but if there is a touch of the mechanical here it is effectively dispelled by certain irregularities that cannot fail to strike the ear. The first really noticeable one is the augmented triad, on a strong beat, where the word 'dying' occurs for the second time. Although this chord was not unknown to Elizabethan and Jacobean writers, it was sufficiently rare to produce that *nouveau frisson* which Tomkins clearly intended. A further irregularity is heard at the last mention of the word 'hateful', when the cantus declines to allow its seventh (G) to resolve downwards in normal fashion, moving up instead to a B flat which creates a sharp momentary dissonance with the A of the quintus. Perhaps the boldest stroke in the entire song is the reappearance of the augmented triad, followed briskly by a false relation, at 'thine eyes have slain' (see Ex. 14.8).

Ex. 14.8

As in many other songs of this type, there is an extended and optimistic codetta, rich in word-painting and the crossing and pairing of voices.

The last of the five-part balletts is dedicated to Phineas Fletcher, the poet and divine who had been such a good friend to John Tomkins during their Cambridge days. *Fusca, in thy starry eyes*, begins conventionally enough with altus alone calling out the lady's name; but soon there is a tripla, set to the words 'Love in black still mourning dies'. There is, of course, no reason at all for Love to die in a lilting triple metre. Had there been allusion to 'change' or 'dance' as in *Yet again, as soon revived*, the new time and tempo would be easy to understand: here the operative word is the innocent-looking epithet 'black'. In the original edition, in fact, the phrase is set to black notation, which was still occasionally used by Elizabethan composers for *proportio sesquialtera*, or three notes in the time of two. Almost equally remarkable at this point is the harmonic progression of three, then four voices: practically every chord is in its root position, and the effect is quite as odd as the *Augenmusik* itself. In the second couplet, the mock pathos of 'so many slain' leads quickly and naturally to the capricious rhythms of 'thou hast loved none again' and the coquettish syncopations of the final *fa-la*.

Adieu, ye city-prisoning towers, for William White of Durham, is a delightful eulogy of country life, with a brilliant portrayal of budding trees, musically related birds singing upon hedges, and a hocket-like passage to illustrate their chirping. Cantus and quintus overlap enthusiastically at 'delay not', and although there is delaying, even dallying, at the cadence which follows, the coaxing, cajoling tripla for 'come, come, sweet love' is as gracious an invitation as any since the time of 'veni, dilecti me' in Dunstable's *Quam pulchra es*.[14]

The addition of a sixth voice (sextus) in the last six songs does not give rise to a texture that is noticeably more dense or more rich, though it certainly becomes more varied. Tomkins uses real six-part writing very rarely in *When I observe those beauty's wonderments*, written for his Chapel Royal colleague Thomas Warwick. There is a brief example of full sonority at the last repetition of 'how do you mourn' and a slightly longer one when the tenor sings, for the last time, 'open her deaf ears or close mine eyes'. For the rest, Tomkins is content to play with his vocal colours in kaleidoscopic fashion, blending and changing them as the spirit moves him, and less attentive than usual to the demands of the text. The pairing or otherwise associating of two equal middle voices (altus and quintus) as well as two equal upper voices (cantus and sextus) tempts many a fruitful point of imitation: homophony is here subservient to the inventive flexibility of Tomkins's superlative counterpoint.

In *Music Divine*, perhaps a compliment to Dr Heather on the receipt of his degree from Oxford, there is more six-part writing than in the previous song. Indeed, it is called for in such phrases as 'where tuneful concords sweetly do agree', and in the righteous indignation of the final line 'to call that love which is indeed but lust'. What must have pleased the good doctor even more than these, even more than the joyful octave leaps on the last word of 'proceeding from above', were the daring cambiata chains set to the word 'harmony'. Now alone, now in pairs, the voices attempt these festoons of minute and scintillating discords with genuine verve, here and there anticipating a chord by adhering firmly to the descending melodic sequence: B flat below a chord of F, C minor below G major.

Oft did I marle, dedicated to John Ward, whose book of madrigals had preceded Tomkins's *Songs* by some nine years, is one of the compositions included in Myriell's anthology,[15] and may be dated before 1616. The title is announced by one voice, then by three, and by four, alternating in pairs. Apt roulades suggesting 'water and fire' disappear at the words 'did well together', when the harmonious ensemble of the elements is expressed through the medium of all six voices in chordal style. The succeeding phrase, 'seeing 'tis known in contraries' invites the contrast of texture that Tomkins deftly supplies, with a heightening of effect brought about by the contrary rhythm of hemiola.

A corresponding example of word-painting in vivid perspective is heard immediately after this, when three or more voices sing 'each seeks the hurt and

---

[14] Cf. *Musica Britannica*, VIII, 112.

[15] The error in the printed partbooks mentioned by Fellowes (1922), *The English Madrigal School*, XVIII, 166, is confirmed by the manuscript copy in *Tristitiae Remedium*.

spoil of either' in actively overlapping downward scales, whilst a slowly moving motif in semibreves gradually creeps upwards. Tomkins, obviously enamoured of the sound, repeats the idea three times before moving on to the next line of the lyric, which (as harbinger of the final couplet) takes up a sizeable portion of the composition as a whole, in the same way as in the four-part and five-part songs (see Ex. 14.9).

Ex. 14.9

The three sacred songs, according to Fellowes, 'do not quite reach the same standard as the rest of the volume',[16] an opinion which is echoed, rather forcefully in the case of *It is my well-beloved's voice*, by Stainton de B. Taylor, who finds it 'one of the least satisfactory of the set'.[17] Taylor shows a more generous appreciation of *Woe is me*, whose texture he likens to that of a six-part fancy for viols. In view of Charles Butler's account of the performance of *When David heard*, it is not difficult to concede that a similar manner of performance would be apt for the other sacred songs. The collections by Leighton, Amner, and Tailour[18] encouraged instrumental participation, and this may well have been the rule rather than the exception, even though title-pages tend to be uncommunicative.

Woe is me, based on a verse from Psalm 120, was written for John Tomkins, who had been appointed organist of St Paul's Cathedral only a year or so before the publication of the *Songs*. The text was a strange one to choose for a younger brother, unless it may be taken as an expression of regret at being domiciled far away in Worcester:

> Woe is me! That I am constrained to dwell with Mesech; and to have my habitation among the tents of Kedar.

---

[16] E.H. Fellowes (1921), *The English Madrigal Composers*, Oxford, 295.
[17] Stainton B. Taylor [1933?], *Thomas Tomkins: A Short Account of his Life and Works*, London, 6.
[18] Leighton (1614), *The teares or lamentacions of a sorrowfull soule*; Amner (1625), *Sacred hymnes of 3.4.5. and 6 parts*; Tailour (1615), *Sacred hymnes*.

232   *The Music of Thomas Tomkins*

In 1620, the year after John's appointment, Thomas was made a gentleman of the Chapel Royal, and the two brothers were thereafter able to keep a little more closely in touch. If the text does contain a shade of personal feeling, then it is likely that the date of composition was 1619. Most notable among the sombre features of this work, where the tessitura of all voices is low and dark, are the discords of the opening section, as altus and cantus sing the word 'woe'. The individual parts show little disposition to be active until after the short, tripla-like passage 'and to have my habitation': when this portion of the text is repeated, there is more animation and variety of rhythm. The coda is given up to the tents of Kedar, at first sparsely pitched, and then slowly more and more crowded, as the texture expands from three to six voices.

Dedicated very suitably to a learned Doctor of Divinity, Theophylus Aylmer, *It is my well-beloved's voice* draws for its text upon the Song of Solomon 2: 8. The version of the text is a metrical paraphrase of the psalm verse, and affords many opportunities for brilliant word-painting. Aptly enough, the voice of the well-beloved is first heard in the upper register, as if from a distance. As he approaches, the lower frequencies become more and more audible, and the pulsating heartbeat is characterized by a subtle, though ever-present hemiola. Lively rhythmic figures help to animate the final section, which sings of hopping and skipping, of hills and mountains, making uninhibited use of every known pictorial device in the musical vocabulary. Yet, conventional as this setting may be, it has a key-scheme that is almost modern in its approach to the question of tonal balance. After the dominant is reached, and its own dominant avoided by an interrupted cadence, there is a momentary return to the tonic; then the same pattern unfolds, but this time there is no interrupted cadence to ward off the brightness and sparkle of A major. The tables are quickly turned, however, and the darker tones of the subdominant emerge to balance the former brightness, leading the way to a well-prepared and satisfying cadence on G.

Turn unto the Lord, for Nathaniel, son of Thomas, takes its text from Joel 2: 13, and Psalm 100: 4. Nearly half of the composition is given up to a descriptive interweaving of the phrase 'from generation to generation'; this type of polyphony pervades the opening portion also, giving the impression of a Latin motet texture rather than that of an English anthem. The general sentiment of the text is honoured here, and only occasionally are there found slight hints of musical imagery, as when the word 'turn' gives rise to contrary motion, or 'everlasting' has the effect of avoiding clear-cut cadences. It is a noble ending to a book of songs whose excellence cannot be over-rated.

Chapter 15

Music for Keyboard Instruments

> If he be musical, and can bear a part in a consort, though never so meanly,
> they will prefer him before Tomkins the organist and Dowland the lutenist.
>
> (Thomas Nash, *Quaternio* (1633))

Dowland is John without a doubt, for his son Robert never achieved great eminence as a performer; but Tomkins is not quite certainly Thomas. John and Giles, his half-brothers, were both highly respected for their talents and extremely well known in the musical profession, the former by reason of his fame as organist of St Paul's, and the latter by reason of his notoriety achieved during the *affaire* Holmes at Salisbury. In the very same year that Nash published his *Quaternio*, both John and Giles were appointed joint organists 'to wait on His Majesty in his Scottish journey',[1] and thus managed to come before the eyes of more than one public.

Thomas nevertheless has a reasonable claim of his own, as the rightful subject of Nash's forward-looking though backhanded compliment. Nash, like Thomas Tomkins, was both an Oxford graduate and a staunch Royalist; moreover, he owned property in Worcestershire, at Mildenham Mills, near Claines,[2] where Thomas's renown as cathedral organist for thirty-six years was at its height. Nash would have known him in London as well as in Worcester, for the appointment as organist of the Chapel Royal dated from 1621. When it is a question of organ music, rather than organ playing, Thomas takes pride of place over his brothers through the sheer bulk of his writing for the instrument. Some fifteen solo pieces are known,[3] apart from the often elaborately worked out organ accompaniments to the forty-one verse anthems in *Musica Deo sacra*. Without doubt he penned far more than this during his sixty-year tenure of the office of organist at Worcester Cathedral, since every service at which the organ played would require two or more voluntaries or 'still verses' as they were sometimes called.[4] Much of this material was as

---

[1] Lafontaine, 'The King's Musick', 84.

[2] Nash is not to be confused with his more illustrious namesake, the dramatist and poet.

[3] See *Musica Britannica*, V, xvi, for a note on the instruments. The pieces with Latin titles do not, of course, necessarily imply the use of an organ; e.g. *Clarifica me pater*.

[4] There are several mentions of a still verse (a quiet organ voluntary) in the Bishop of Durham's form for the consecration of the chapel at Auckland Castle on St Peter's Day, 29 June

234 *The Music of Thomas Tomkins*

improvisatory in character as it is in our own day, yet it is certain that the methodical Thomas would have wished to preserve the best of it for his immediate successors' use in particular, if not for posterity in general.

Besides the organ music, there are more than fifty pieces apparently written for the virginals, harpsichord or clavichord. It is not known which of these instruments Thomas owned, for there are no references to them during his lifetime, and no trace of them after his death. The possibility of their being named in his will is ruled out by the fact that no will was ever made: instead an administration was granted to his nephew John in 1659, and this document gives no specific details of personal property.[5] Generations of Tudor choirboys had learned their elementary keyboard technique on the clavichord, and Thomas (whose duties included the teaching of choirboys) must have owned a clavichord if only for that purpose. His comfortable though by no means affluent financial circumstances may well have permitted him the luxury of a pair of virginals, or even a small harpsichord, for it is these two instruments whose characteristics are suggested by the greater part of his extant keyboard music.

His acquaintance with English keyboard music was both profound and practical, for he was the fortunate possessor of a large volume of organ music whose earliest compositions date from the middle years of Henry VIII's reign.[6] The composers named are sometimes well-known figures like John Redford and Philip ap Rhys of St Paul's, John Thorne of York and Thomas Preston of Windsor; men of lesser musical stature, such as Kyrton, Strowger and Wynslade, help to fill out the contents of these early pages, and Thomas has seen fit to annotate them from time to time in generous and commendatory fashion. Of an anonymous setting of *Salvum fac* (fol. 24v) he writes 'an excellent verse', possibly to show his approval of the neatly turned passage in 3.1 proportion. An anonymous set of verses for *Magnificat* (fol. 26) brings forth such comments as 'a good verse ... 3 to the semibreve', whilst the margin offers him room to recopy a short musical passage which was poorly written out by the original scribe. 'Note this', writes Thomas of an oddly juxtaposed pair of parts, in black and white notation respectively, on fol. 34v.

Even more frequent and voluble are his remarks in the section of the manuscript containing an incomplete cycle of alternatim hymns for the church year. He appears to have found these splendidly written but unfortunately anonymous works particularly congenial, recognizing at once that they are mostly based not upon the hymn melody itself, but 'upon the

---

1655. (Lambeth, Archbishop's Library, Gibson MS 929, No. 85. Printed in J. Wickham Legg, (1911), *English Orders for Consecrating Churches*, London, 224 (Henry Bradshaw Society, xli).

[5] TNA, PCC A.A. 1659, fol. 54.

[6] BL Add. MS 29996. See also John Caldwell (1964–5), 'British Museum Additional MS 29996: transcription and commentary', Ph.D. thesis, University of Oxford.

faburden of these plainsongs'. The faburden, as he knew from his lessons with William Byrd, was formed by adding a freely decorative part a sixth (or sometimes an octave) below the hymn melody. Although there are no examples of the use of this technique in those of his keyboard works based on a liturgical cantus firmus, he was clearly able to see and appreciate its use in the music of others. Sometimes his remarks reveal the wary eye of a musician much practised in dealing with corrupt and badly copied manuscripts: 'the cliff changes' (fol. 158v); 'tripla to the semibreve' (fol. 159v); 'a crotchet rest' (fol. 177v). Most often, however, he is content simply to write 'good', or an occasional superlative like 'a good old indeed, very good' (fol. 165) or 'a dainty fine verse' (fol. 176v). He loves to light upon canons in middle voice parts, writing regularly on these occasions 'two parts in one in the fourth' and is only very rarely mystified by a strange proportional sign, such as the ƆC on fol. 177: 'note this mark receives 3 to the minim and six quavers but I know not the reason for it'.

All this is evidence of an enquiring mind and a well-exercised critical faculty, and it also shows Thomas as a great respecter of tradition, in spite of the fact that fundamental changes in liturgy divided his world of organ music from that of his early Tudor predecessors. Nevertheless, certain of the plainsongs used liturgically by Redford and his contemporaries survived the Reformation by becoming secular, notably the short antiphon *Miserere mihi Domine* and the long offertory *Felix namque*. Neither too long nor too short (like Cherubini's definition of the ideal fugue subject) was *In Nomine*, otherwise known as *Gloria tibi Trinitas*, but this was never set by the early organists since its origin was not strictly liturgical, but rather a short section from a polyphonic setting of the Ordinary of the Mass by John Taverner.[7] Tallis, Byrd, Bull and Thomas Tomkins all set one or more of these plainsongs more than once, the usual motives being sheer virtuosity and rhythmic inventiveness.

The later sections of Thomas's organ book consist of music by his own contemporaries – Byrd, Nicholas Carlton, Gibbons, Ferrabosco, Farmer and Morley – in his own hand. There is even a piece by his brother, John, suitably enough a set of variations on *John, come kiss me now*. By no means all the music in this section qualifies as solo keyboard music, for there are a number of straightforward keyboard scores of madrigals and balletts, including some of his own from the *Songs* of 1622. Important as this holograph is, it cannot match the fascinating and fundamental importance of the manuscript in the Bibliothèque Nationale, Paris.[8]

---

[7] See John Caldwell (1965), 'Keyboard Plainsong Settings in England 1500–1660', *Musica Disciplina*, 19, supplemented by Addenda and Corrigenda in vol. 34 (1980); see also John Irving (1989), *The Instrumental Music of Thomas Tomkins 1572–1656*, New York and London, chapter 3.

[8] Bibliothèque nationale, Paris, Rés. MS 1122.

Once the eighth of a set of manuscript music books in Thomas's own library at Worcester, this volume reached Paris by way of Oxford and London only after some two hundred years had elapsed. It belongs to the most mature period of its composer and compiler, who (although he included works by Byrd and Bull) devoted the greater part of the available space to his own works. Many of the pieces are accurately dated, the earliest being the *Fancy* (9 September 1646) and the latest *The Perpetual Round* (7–8 September 1654). If we are to accept the general view that these dates refer to composition and not to copying – and there are historical facts to show that this view is correct – this late flowering of Thomas's genius provides a steady coverage for the period stretching from the second siege of Worcester to the removal of Thomas and his newly married son Nathaniel into the manor of Martin Hussingtree. Some of the undated works included in this volume, however, are probably copies of earlier compositions. It is unlikely, for instance, that the *Toy: made at Poole Court* could have been written after 1644, by which time the owner of that property, Richard Dowdeswell, was dispossessed and imprisoned.

There is every indication that Thomas intended his last collection of music to be a fair copy rather than a sketchbook; yet as the pages are turned, it becomes increasingly clear that the aged composer gave up his early resolve, supplanting it with a desire to create and re-create, to polish and repolish,

Fig. 15.1   Thomas Tomkins's List of Books.

Music for Keyboard Instruments

however bewildered the reader becomes, and however bleary his eye. The book is thus a human document as well as a musical one, for it displays the agile and resourceful workings of Thomas's mind, his considerably less agile penmanship, and his determination to say in forthright musical terms what he thought and believed to be the best in works of that kind. It is a matchless musical testament.

The history of the manuscript is remarkable in itself, embracing the names of famous collectors of early music both in France and in England. Strangely enough, its first short journey from Worcester to Oxford has so far proved most difficult to trace, because Nathaniel is generally assumed to have taken charge of Thomas's property. The discovery of the administration naming John, Thomas's nephew and the son of John Tomkins of St Paul's, has clarified matters considerably. It was through this nephew, born in 1631, that the male line of the Tomkins family was continued until the late eighteenth century, when the name was changed to Berkeley. The last of the family to bear the name Tomkins was a great-grandson of nephew John: the Reverend Richard Tomkins, who went up to New College, Oxford, in 1742, when he was 21 years old, and took his BA degree four years later. During his residence at Oxford, a young man named Thomas Bever, of Stratfield Mortimer in Berkshire, arrived as a gentleman scholar of Oriel College. It is not impossible that the manuscript changed hands between 1744 and 1746, for Bever began to collect rare and valuable books at an early stage in his subsequently illustrious career. He became a DCL, a fellow of All Souls, judge of the Cinque Ports and chancellor of Lincoln and Bangor, and by the time of his death in 1791 he had assembled a fine and valuable library, including many rare musical items.

Bever left the greater part of his library to a lay vicar of Westminster Abbey named John Hindle, but Hindle died within five years of this bequest and the library was put up for sale in 1798. According to a contemporary report,[9] the library

> contained among many other curious articles, the complete works of Luca Marenzio, Orlando di Lasso, Morley, Weelkes, Wilbye, Bennet, Purcell and other eminent composers of the late 16th and 17th centuries ... the whole in fine preservation obtained and purchased with great judgement and indefatigable pains, at considerable expense during a long course of years by Dr Bever. The several articles fetched very high prices.

Annotations in the manuscript by known and unknown hands of the early nineteenth century indicate that the volume changed hands more than once before making its final journey. There is reason to believe that a certain J. Finley Foster was one of the owners, and that later on it became part of the library of Edward Jones, some of whose manuscripts were sold by Sotheby in 1825. Item 441 of the Jones sale catalogue reads as follows:

---

[9] *The Gentleman's Magazine and Historical Chronicle*, 68 (1798), 715.

> Virginal books: containing the Compositions Gibbons, Dr Blow, Farinelli, W. Byrd, Dr Bull, Tallis and others, on six-line staves. 6 vol. 1635–95.

The composers named here almost match those of another virginal book now in the Bibliothèque Nationale, Paris,[10] with the sole exception of Byrd. This indicates that the rough catalogue description does not refer to any one of the six books, but was made by somebody who thumbed quickly through the volumes and picked out composers' names at random. Music by Byrd and Bull appears in the Thomas Tomkins autograph, as we have seen, and these two names may well have been taken from this very volume. The six manuscripts were bought by a bookseller named Thomas Thorpe, and it was he who ultimately sold four of them to M. and Mme Farrenc of Paris.

Farrenc's references to these treasures in his introductions to volumes 1 and 6 of *Le Trésor des pianistes* are well known. He tells of his acquisition of two virginal books, and later of several very valuable ones bought in London. But no music from the Tomkins volume is printed, nor is any specific mention made of it. The fact that it was among those valuable manuscripts is conclusively proved by the article on Thomas Tomkins in the famous dictionary of Fétis,[11] published in 1864: 'M. Farrenc possesses an original manuscript of pieces by Thomas Tomkins for harpsichord and organ; the last of these pieces bears the date 1654.' When Mme Farrenc died in 1875, the manuscripts were presented to the library of the Paris Conservatoire, and they remained there unobserved until the first decade of the next century.

They were duly examined and mentioned by their accession numbers – but not studied in detail – by Charles van den Borren, who was then in course of writing a valuable and pioneering book on English keyboard music.[12] Thanks to the interest shown by van den Borren, the librarian of the Conservatoire was able to send a brief description of them, together with some tracings of signatures and scribbles, to Sir Ivor Atkins, whose indispensable account of Worcester organists was being prepared for the Worcestershire Historical Society.[13] In acknowledging the help of Mlle Pereyra, the librarian, Sir Ivor called attention to the fact that a complete description was not then possible, as the Tomkins autograph, together with other valuable items, had been removed to a place far from the destructive hazards of war.

By 1926 a very thorough series of articles by Mlle Pereyra began to appear in

---

[10] Rés. 1186 bis.
[11] F.J. Fétis (1860–65), *Biographie universelle des musiciens*.
[12] C. Van den Borren (1913), *The Sources of Keyboard Music in England*, London.
[13] Atkins, *Early Occupants*, 37–78.

Music for Keyboard Instruments

the *Revue de Musicologie*,[14] and they dealt with three of the Paris manuscripts of virginal music, but not with the Tomkins autograph. At about the same time Margaret Glyn was assembling materials for her book on virginal music,[15] and E.H. Fellowes was similarly engaged in his work on William Byrd. Both of these authors had either seen the manuscript itself, or photostats of it, but it was not until Stephen Tuttle of Harvard came to study it in detail that the true worth of both music and annotations came to be known. Thus, almost three centuries after the death of the composer, Stephen Tuttle's edition of the keyboard works (most of which are found in the Paris manuscript) came before the general public.

The letter H appears not only outside but also inside the front cover of the volume, and the significance of this letter is explained by a list of books on page i. Beneath a note dated October 1647 by Thomas Tomkins, in which he records the purchase of wheat and mooncorn, the following list can be seen in the handwriting of Nathaniel Tomkins (see Fig. 15.1):

Mr Thomas Tomkins His Booke

composed

A	4to	• Thomas Farington•	1600
B	4to	russet lether	1620
C	4to	Jo. Tomk. wth ye K. arms	1630
D	folio	J T T T	1645
E	folio	Thomas Tomkins autograph on to June • 9 •	1656 X
F.	fol:	Rich. Brown and N.T. hand	
G	a lesser fol. Rich Brownes hand		
H	T		1646

Against the last date, which coincides with that of the *Fancy* already mentioned, some comparatively recent annotator has written 'to 19 July 1654', although there are three items dated slightly later than this. A brief biographical note on Tomkins has been added to the bottom-left of the page by the same annotator. The reason for some of the other dates in this list, which seems to have been drawn up by Nathaniel Tomkins after his father's death, is not always clear. The first four seem arbitrarily chosen (unless the word 'composed' written just to the left of, and above '1600' is taken at its face value) and the fifth corresponds exactly with the date of Thomas's burial. They may have been added to show that the volumes stood in chronological as well as alphabetical order.

---

[14]   1926, p. 204; 1927, pp. 36, 205; 1928, p. 235; 1929, p. 32; 1931, p. 22; 1932, p. 86; 1933, p. 24.

[15]   M.H. Glyn (1924; 2/1934), *About Elizabethan Virginal Music and its Composers*, London.

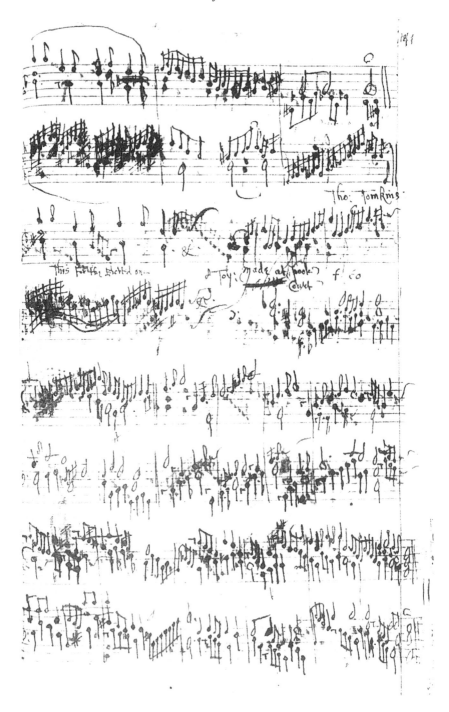

Fig. 15.2 Thomas Tomkins: 'A Toy made at Poole Court'.

Music for Keyboard Instruments

The page has been scribbled over by less mature hands, including that of Sylvanus Tomkins, and has been adorned, both horizontally and vertically, with doodles, attempts at lettering, simulated signatures and prayer fragments. The entry for volume A, 'Thomas Farington', has been overwritten with the name 'Thomas Tomkins' in a more florid, sloping hand than that of Nathaniel Tomkins. Because the word 'Tomkins' follows 'Farington', assumptions have been made that the full name of Thomas Tomkins's father was Thomas Farington Tomkins, and that volume A had originally been in his possession. However, it was very rare for an individual to have more than one Christian name at this period; the name Farington appears more likely to have been a surname than a Christian name; and it is not to be found in any other manuscript concerning Tomkins *père*. Furthermore, Nathaniel has enclosed the name 'Thomas Farington' between two distinct dots. It can safely be concluded therefore that volume A, the first in Tomkins's collection, had belonged to one Thomas Farington.[16]

Nothing is known of Farington, but the name is not especially common. The gentleman in question may have been Thomas Farrington, who was born in London in 1539, married Alice Heald in Chorley, Lancashire, on 13 August 1559, and died sometime after 1601. The couple had four children, one of whom, also named Thomas, was born in 1561.

Sadly enough, no volumes bearing on their cover the letters A to G have ever been found, and it must therefore be assumed that the greater part of this fine collection of early manuscripts is lost beyond recall. It does seem likely, however, that Add. MS 29996, with its extensive annotations by Thomas, and so many of his compositions, remains a strong candidate for inclusion in this gamut of music books. There is no sign of a letter on its cover now, although an earlier binding or loose cover may have afforded the necessary evidence. It also has a good claim to be the 'Thomas Farington' volume – especially so as Tomkins apparently owned Add. MS 29996 from around 1600, the year shown against volume A in Nathaniel's list, and which could well have been the year of acquisition. But the possibility remains that the volume referred to by Thomas elsewhere in the autograph as the 'redish clasped book' could be Add. MS 29996, since one of the pieces said to be found there, and confirmed by a written-out theme,[17] the *Ground* dedicated to Arthur Philips, does in fact appear in it.

Thomas refers to an '(Old) Black Clasped Book' and to a 'Red Old Book'; but there is no possibility of proving their identity, because no list of pieces occurring in these two books corresponds with any known keyboard manuscript now extant. The 'Lessons of worth' on page ii of the autograph

---

[16] I am grateful to Dr Richard Newsholme for bringing this interpretation of the Farington name to Anthony Boden's attention and to Mr Boden for passing it on to me.

[17] Bibliothèque Nationale, Rés. 1122, ii.

242   *The Music of Thomas Tomkins*

volume gives many titles that are now unknown or uncertain,[18] but the list is of great value not only for giving us an insight into Thomas's musical taste (he mentions only Bull, Byrd, Carlton, Gibbons, Tallis and brother John) but also because at least one item – *Robin Hood* – is named there as a work of Thomas, whereas the only piece of music with this title appears anonymously in Will Forster's Virginal Book. It has thus been assumed that this unclaimed *Robin Hood* is indeed by Thomas, and is included as such in the complete edition of keyboard music.[19]

The autograph volume in Paris is remarkable for the amount and frequency of letter–figure combinations written usually at the beginning of the music. The *Pavan of 3 parts* has for example 'F.169 Ib.57 / E.252 f.57'. *Fortune my foe* bears the legend 'Ib.214 c.21 F 243'. These references appear to have been placed in a conspicuous position in order to show the player where another version may be found, and it is quite possible that the letters refer to the volumes marked A–G, and the numbers to pages in the volumes. Tomkins uses the letters B–G in these letter–figure combinations, and even overshoots the gamut on two occasions with a mention of K, suggesting that his son Nathaniel failed to complete the list on page i. If the numbers do refer to pages, it is clear that some of the volumes must have been very extensive collections, for the numbers go as high as 385 in one instance and 472 in another. All the more reason, therefore, to bewail the loss of the other volumes in the set.

The orderly way in which Thomas would set about a task is concisely shown on page 186 of the autograph, in which he refers to the third volume in the collection, marked 'C 4to Jo. Tomk. wth ye K. arms'. He writes: 'I could wish that the great book which was my brother John's should be fair and carefully pricked', etc. [Anthony Boden has quoted the full text in Chapter 12 above.] These instructions remain as a vivid memento of the aged organist's mind and character, just as a random remark on page ii of the same autograph gives us an insight into his critical opinions. Two compositions of Bull (the *Quadran pavan in gamut* and the *Ut re mi fa sol la*) are described respectively as 'Excellent for the hand' and 'For the hand', whereas Byrd's *Quadran pavan and galliard* is 'Excellent for the matter'. In a further note the rival claims of technique and expression are joined by a third quality, for Thomas recommends two of Byrd's works 'for substance', which they undoubtedly possessed, if the *Ut re mi* on the very first page of the Paris manuscript is a typical example.

In the following discussion of the keyboard music, the grouping and

---

[18] Details of these are given in *Musica Britannica*, V, 157 and 158.
[19] But see Irving, *Instrumental Music*, 106.

Music for Keyboard Instruments 243

Fig. 15.3 Thomas Tomkins: 'Fortune my foe' (4 July 1654).

244   *The Music of Thomas Tomkins*

numbering is that of Professor Stephen D. Tuttle's monumental edition, *Thomas Tomkins: Keyboard Music* (*Musica Britannica* V (2nd, rev. edn, London, 1964). The reader is also referred to John Irving's authoritative study of Tomkins's keyboard and consort music, *The Instrumental Music of Thomas Tomkins 1572–1656.*

Although the two Preludes are not markedly different from numerous examples of this style in *Parthenia* and in contemporary manuscript collections, their grandiose and heavily ornamented proportions stamp them as the work of a man who could, on occasion, say very little in an imposing and often brilliant manner. The function of a Prelude was twofold: to allow the player time and opportunity to warm up to his task, and to set the prevailing key of the music to follow. In this respect, Tomkins had the same attitude of mind as Couperin and Bach, even if his figuration and his fingering were both unlike theirs. In its first form, Prelude (1) could serve as an introduction to *Robin Hood* (63); whilst its alternative ending (to which we are referred by the composer himself in a note *vide 146* – the page concerned in the Paris autograph) leads to a close in D, and a suitable link with, for example, *Barafostus' Dream* (62). A cadence on a major chord, and a fresh start with the same chord in its minor form, was a typical feature of much Renaissance music, and it works well not only in the combination just cited (1+ 2, 62) but also in the juxtaposition of the Prelude (3) with *Fortune my foe* (61) or *What if a day* (64). The eight settings of *In nomine* (six really, if we exclude alternative versions of two pieces) would of course be equally suitable, since the cantus firmus is always used a fifth above its normal pitch, beginning and ending on A. No Prelude, therefore, is a disembodied and meaningless object if it is employed in a practical, companionable manner, and this manner is surely near to the intention of the composer, even though he may not have expressly associated other works with his Preludes. There is evidence, nevertheless, that Tomkins aimed at a higher degree of internal cohesion in the *Prelude in A* (3), for a motive heard soon after the preliminary flourish occurs again before the final cadential cascade, recognizably, and doubtless intentionally.

Clarifica me pater[20] is an example of a little-known secularized plainsong being used well over a century past the time when it ceased to have any liturgical significance. Why Tomkins used it is a small mystery, for he did not even know its correct title, and can hardly have had access to an Antiphoner containing the original chant. He calls it *Glorifica me*, copying an earlier source of keyboard music that was either corrupt already or not clearly written. There are three pieces by Tallis, in the *Mulliner Book*,[21] based on this

---

   [20] According to the Use of Sarum, this antiphon was sung on the sixth Sunday in Lent and the Vigil of the Ascension. See *Antiphonale Sarisburiense*, plates 201, 266.

   [21] *Musica Britannica*, I (1951), 99, 101, 104; *Commentary* (1952), 38.

plainsong; but all three are untitled. Byrd has two settings in the *Fitzwilliam Virginal Book*,[22] and although these have a title – *Miserere* – it is not the correct one. Scribes who interchanged with impunity *In nomine* and *Gloria tibi Trinitas* probably thought that the same could be done with *Clarifica me pater* and *Miserere*. But Tomkins, a pupil of Byrd, may well have seen the originals when studying with him, mis-spelling the title through unfamiliarity with the Catholic liturgy. Since this setting (dated September 1650) is non-liturgical, it was doubtless intended for virginals or harpsichord just as much as the *In nomine* pieces were. Like these, *Clarifica me pater* shows the composer's preference for the transposed form of a Dorian cantus firmus.

The *In nomine* pieces were all written between 1647 and 1652, and thus represent a late phase of an already latter-day aspect of the composer's art. He apparently found it difficult at first to return to this admirable but archaic style of composition, although he had made some previous essays in the same form for a consort of three viols. The first keyboard setting (5) begins boldly enough with a strong dactylic figure entirely typical of Tomkins, and proceeds by way of a lyrical, two-notes-against-three section to a display of uninhibited virtuosity. No less than six alternative endings were provided, though the first of these has been cancelled by the composer himself. The third ending, which forms the principal text of (6), gives this item its longest form, whereby the cantus firmus is used for only two-thirds of the composition, the remaining one-third acting as an enormously extended coda. It is true that the other settings of *In nomine* own a more than usually generous residuum after the point at which the plainsong comes to a cadence on A; but this third ending of (6) outstrips them all in length and complexity.

A new departure may be seen in the very first bars of (7) which present a foretaste of the first three notes (A C A) of the cantus firmus, in an ornate and flowing triple time. The fourth entry of the point is the cantus firmus itself, in the bass, duly decorated in accordance with the preceding voices: so that we here have an example of an infectious and interesting rhythmic scheme successfully disturbing the solemn progress of the cantus firmus for some little time. The points and figurations are varied in expert fashion, much use being made of repeated notes of identical pitch (Ex. 15.1).

Ex. 15.1

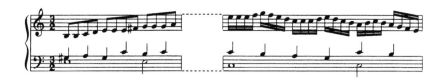

---

[22] Vol. II, 230, 232, of the edition by Fuller Maitland and Barclay Squire (Leipzig, 1899; repr. New York, 1963). Also Byrd, *Complete Works*, ed. Fellowes, XX, 137, 140.

The rhythmic contours, basic time, and opening style of (8) recall those of (7) written during the previous month, but now there is a stronger contrapuntal feeling, and an increasing reliance on tightly woven imitation. All this gives rise to an impression of elegant intellectual brilliance, as if Tomkins had already begun to master the subtleties of this kind of keyboard writing. The coda is distinguished by a display of figuration in thirds and sixths, ultimately relaxing into an expressive cadence on a tonic pedal.

The cantus firmus suggests the first point of imitation in (9), others of independent origin following in smooth succession. A short yet effective setting, it makes good use of sequential material in its closing bars, and preserves a good sense of balance between the elements of ingenuity and display. Much longer, and much more difficult for the player is (10) and its variant (11), both being remarkable for a last-minute pull in tonality towards D, and an opening point that covers two octaves in a rolling, sweeping descent (Ex. 15.2).

Ex. 15.2

At certain points in the body of the piece, the figuration is not greatly different from the kind of thing one finds in music written a century previously; Thomas Preston's *Felix namque*[23] is a typical specimen of what could be done by an earlier generation of keyboard virtuosi. As Tomkins once owned the manuscript containing this piece, it is possible that he had played it through and found its configuration worth developing.

The last *In nomine* (12) has its imitative figures in a relatively high tessitura, for the cantus firmus remains in the bass and supports the counterpoint, now staid, now decorative, in the upper parts. Just before the plainsong theme reaches its close, an imitative duet almost reaches the status of a fully-fledged canon at the octave, but it is soon deflected into a brilliant cadential flourish. The settings of *In nomine*, taken as a group, certainly present music that is at the same time academic in its insistence on strong contrapuntal interest and virtuosic in its demands upon the player. It is in striking a balance between the two elements that Tomkins succeeds as a writer of keyboard pieces in this genre.

Technically speaking, the eight *Miserere* settings are very similar to the *In nomine* pieces. They are shorter, because the cantus firmus itself is shorter than

---

[23] Printed in *Altenglische Orgelmusik* (1954), Bärenreiter-Ausgabe 385, Kassel.

Music for Keyboard Instruments 247

that of *In nomine*, but the prevailing texture is generally of three parts, excepting for certain final sections (14, 18, 20) and the position of the cantus firmus is varied between treble, alto and bass. The first four settings (13–16) use an opening point based on the descending motive C B A G or a variant or transposition. The slight significance of these melodic similarities is, however, quite overshadowed by certain other factors of form. *Miserere* (18) repeats the plainsong twice, first in the treble, then the tenor; while *Miserere* (16) presents it three times, in tenor, treble and tenor respectively. The appearance of a liturgical tenor in double or triple cursus was an accepted feature of motets and Masses of the *ars nova* and the Renaissance, and it is by no means entirely unknown in the field of keyboard music. The Exeter organist John Lugge composed an *In nomine* with double cursus[24] and there are earlier examples by Bull in one of the Paris manuscripts of virginal music.[25] Tomkins is thus in good company, even if he cannot be dubbed an innovator.

His really new contribution to the *Miserere* situation was, oddly enough, a resuscitation of an old principle. From his perusal of Add. MS 29996, he knew that settings of *Miserere* were grouped together by the early Tudor organist in suites of three or four, and this principle he endeavoured to follow when compiling his own anthology. At various points in the manuscript he has written the figures 1, 2, 3 and 4 among the *Miserere* settings, and if they are grouped in this fashion the first of these suites consists of (17), (13), and (18). Since the last of these is a double cursus piece, there is formed a group of four *Miserere* settings after the pattern of those on the very first pages of Add. MS 29996. There, the purpose was a liturgical one, for according to the Sarum rite either three or four psalms were sung at Compline, and the organist had to be prepared to play a short keyboard version of the antiphon after each psalm. It may perhaps be not too far-fetched to consider others among the Tomkins *Miserere* pieces as likely to form a group: those on pages 162–3 of the original manuscript (14), (19), and (20), and the tripartite setting which is in itself a suite (16).

The influence of the liturgical element, however distant in point of time, must always be seriously considered in the keyboard music of Tomkins. The *Offertory* (21), misread by some earlier scholars as *Affection*, recalls in its scope the tremendously long and involved pieces that Tomkins knew from the volume containing *Miserere* settings. These long settings of plainchants for the offertory were usually based on *Felix namque*, although other chants were used from time to time before the Reformation. Tallis wrote his two settings of *Felix namque* during the reign of Elizabeth, and it was largely due to him that the form became secularized whilst still retaining its former title, even though this might be corrupted into *Felix nunquam* and the like.

---

[24] Christ Church Library, Oxford, MS 49.
[25] Bibliothèque Nationale, Rés. 1185, 134, 156.

The Henrician organists almost invariably set that part of the chant beginning at the word *namque*, in order to allow the celebrant to intone the word *Felix*. Tallis, however, set this intonation, and even suggested by repeat marks that it should be played through twice. But this is not all: the final stage in this liturgical *reductio ad absurdam* was to come from Tomkins, who ignores the entire body of the chant but sets instead the intonation, using it as a ground throughout the piece. A comparison of Tomkins's theme and the original plainchant for *Felix* demonstrates the close relationship between the two (Ex. 15.3).

Ex. 15.3

This composition is thus an elaborate set of variations on a ground that freely paraphrases the Sarum plainsong for the word *Felix*. The ground is not simply a bass; it moves freely throughout the texture without any prearranged plan or system of tonality. There are some fifty-five appearances of the ground, in treble, tenor and bass, and all these appearances except one begin and end on A. A momentary transposition to D takes place at bar 277, but the principal tonality is quickly restored.

At certain cadences of the *Offertory* pauses have been placed, and their exact function has from time to time been questioned. Although dated 1637, it is certain that the work was composed in short sections over a considerable period of time, and the date given by the Bodleian manuscript may refer to the year in which the entire set of variations was completed. Once this is assumed to be correct, the pauses can be regarded as indications of the progress of the work at different times: again and again Tomkins returned to his task, adding new sections and fresh pauses as the music proceeded. Purely practical considerations suggest a somewhat different, though not entirely opposed viewpoint; and that is to accept the *Offertory* as an effective and useful accompaniment to the collection of alms after the offertory sentences at Matins or Communion. The use of the organ at this point in the service is borne out by the description of *The Princely Coming of Her Majesty to the Holy Communion at Easter*, in 1593, as transcribed at the end of Chapter 5 above.

The internal pauses written over certain cadences might then serve to regulate the length of the composition, which had of course to depend upon the amount of time available to the organist at that point in the service.

Of the twelve examples of *Fancy, Voluntary and Verse* (22–33) the title, character and style of the Fancies point to secular use, just as the *Voluntaries*

Music for Keyboard Instruments 249

and *Verses* suggest a close link with the organ music used for the Anglican liturgy. Some of the earliest examples of the *Fancy* and the *Voluntary* occur in the *Mulliner Book*, a compilation of keyboard music which was completed shortly before Tomkins was born. As he grew up, he heard these comparatively new and free forms in mansions and cathedrals, and later composed them himself.

The texture of four of the *Fancies* (22, 23, 25 and 29) often recalls the clarity of string writing, though there is enough freedom in the contrapuntal element – usually in four parts – to give the keyboard player a feeling of ease and the right idiom. Sometimes the point is maintained for only half the total length of the piece (22, 25), rarely for the whole (23); whilst an even slighter degree of thematic insistence is found in the A minor *Fancy* (29) with its opening phrase so reminiscent of the French chanson type.

In writing his *Fancy: for two to play* (32) Tomkins was probably less concerned with writing eight-part, or even six-part harmony, than with exploring the sonorities of the virginals.[26] Even in some of the polyphonic duet sections there are often no more than four real parts, yet the sound is so vastly different from that produced by only one player because of the extended tessitura. Antiphonal effects between upper and lower registers are common, yet in some cases a theme is shared between the left hand of the treble player and the right hand of the bass player. A similar duet, perhaps the source of Tomkins's inspiration, was written by his friend Nicholas Carlton, and this is found in the same manuscript.[27]

The *Fancy: for five viols* (33) is a keyboard paraphrase of a string piece no longer extant. Much of the detail has inevitably been lost in the process of paraphrase, though as written out by Tomkins the piece is well accommodated to its new medium. It would be an interesting but difficult task to attempt a reconstruction of the original from the keyboard version, though the result, if successful, would fill a gap in the catalogue of Tomkins's music for strings, for there are no fantasias for five viols among his otherwise representative output. His keyboard version (56) of the *Pavan in A minor* shows a far more satisfactory presentation of idiomatic and effective writing.

Of the three *Voluntaries*, only one (24) bears a date, 10 August 1647, which places the work in the year following the second siege of Worcester, when the cathedral organs were dismantled and services were suspended. Tomkins may have written down this richly contrapuntal *Voluntary* for use when the services were resumed, but that day he never lived to see. It is certainly the most mature of the three, and shows much inventive skill besides a fine sense of structural feeling. The *Voluntary* in A minor (28), although equally long and

---

[26] See H.M. Miller (1943), 'The Earliest Keyboard Duets', *Musical Quarterly*, 29: 439.
[27] See F. Dawes (1951), 'Nicholas Carlton and the Earliest Keyboard Duet', *Musical Times*, 92: 542.

rich in dexterous keyboard counterpoint, relies a little too much on the opening point, new material being brought in only during the last third of the composition. Once again, however, the modulatory scheme is well planned and there is adequate contrast of key colour. The third *Voluntary* (30) is much shorter than the others, and maintains the point throughout, with deft play on the false relation inherent in the opening phrase (Ex. 15.4).

Ex. 15.4

With the *Verses*, we have yet another triptych of which only one aspect is dated. Again the date in question (12 August 1650) stands within the period when cathedral services had ceased, so that it may be more expedient to classify this *Verse of 3 parts* (26) as a *Fancy*, under which heading it is entered in the original index to the Paris autograph. There are two main sections and two main points, one grave, the other gay. The *Short Verse* (27) tends on the other hand towards monothematicism, and a unity that is achieved by a clever touch of diminution towards the end (Ex. 15.5).

Ex. 15.5

In his *Substantial Verse: maintaining the point* (31) Tomkins demonstrates his resource in the matter of faithful yet varied presentation of a single theme. True to its title, this *Verse* keeps the point on active service right until the final statement of the last two bars, where it is discreetly hidden in the tenor. Yet there is careful avoidance of epigrammatic and short-winded statements; the contrapuntal flow is regular and possesses more than adequate momentum.

Byrd, Bull and Tomkins all loved to exercise their musical and technical ingenuity on hexachord variations, a genre of composition that had a comparatively short though brilliant career. There is a set marked expressly *for a beginner* (34) and a lengthy set which might well be marked *for a virtuoso of remarkable stamina* (35). Musically they have nothing at all in common except this six-note figure, ascending then descending, and carrying with it the most

Music for Keyboard Instruments 251

extraordinary displays of keyboard virtuosity. Like the *Offertory*, there is ample evidence that the gigantic *Ut re mi* (35) was composed piecemeal, and that Tomkins never succeeded in joining together all the sketches and fragments scattered throughout his manuscript volume. Two of them (36 and 37) may well have been intended as parts or variants of the main setting, the former being an example of the use of triple time in the hexachord itself, rather than in its accompanying counterpoints. Nothing is dated except a fragmentary *Ut re mi* (71) whose conclusion is almost illegible due to the composer's weakening hand. By 30 June 1654, he was in his eighty-second year.

Tomkins liked to transpose his themes to the upper fifth, possibly for greater brilliance, or else in order to suit the compass of his instruments. Just as the *In nomine* pieces are in transposed Dorian, so the *Ut re mi* variations (with the exception of 71) begin and end on G, a fifth above the normal compass of the hard hexachord. Within the vast and varied structure of (35) other hexachords are used: C–A and D–B, and these occur between statements of the main G–E hexachord rather in the manner of episodes in a rondo. In one work (38) Tomkins employs the hexachord in broken thirds, so that the title is *Ut re mi*. After a somewhat mechanical beginning, there flow in one after the other a tremendous variety of figures, many of them apparently designed to exercise inflexible wrists. As transcendental studies of the late Renaissance, these hexachord settings have perhaps more technical than musical value, or as Tomkins would say, excellent for the hand rather than for substance.

Both the pieces called *Ground* are based on seven-note figures. The monotony inherent in a figure such as that heard at the outset of (39) is to some extent avoided by alternate statements in treble and bass, while the care shown by Tomkins in avoiding too frequent cadences can hardly be accidental. The theme of the *Ground* is very similar to that of Farnaby's *Up tails all*, which is found in the same source,[28] but there is no proof of anything more than melodic kinship, since the two composers do not seem to have been particularly close friends. Tomkins's variations are notable for their technical demands, especially at the point where rapid runs in thirds occur, and later on where intervals in the theme are filled in and the texture thickens. The other *Ground* (40), headed by the name of Arthur Philips (1606–95),[29] is hardly less brilliant, and may very well be an occasional or dedicatory composition. Tomkins was fond of dedicating his music to friends and colleagues, and this is borne out not only by the *Songs* published in 1622 but also by the string pieces he wrote for his friend Withy and the keyboard pieces inscribed to Archdeacon Thornborough, as discussed in the next chapter. Perhaps this *Ground* was a kind of musical gift for Philips.

---

28 *Fitzwilliam Virginal Book*, II, 360.
29 Organist of Bristol Cathedral in 1638 and in the following year was appointed Professor of Music at Oxford; B.Mus. 1640.

252   *The Music of Thomas Tomkins*

Some of the very finest of Tomkins's keyboard music is found in the *Pavans* and *Galliards*, of which there are four paired sets (41–50), the first being available in two versions; seven apparently separate *Pavans* (51–7); and three *Galliards* that also seem to be independent works (58–60). It is in this extended group of pieces that Tomkins makes the greatest use of his very considerable harmonic resource, his instinctive grasp of formal elements, and his power to move his hearers by sheer and sincere musicianship. This is not to underestimate the difficulty of execution which many of these pieces present, nor their wealth of ornament and richness of polyphony. These are available in ample measure, yet their very brightness is made to seem dim by the expressive and emotional qualities of the music itself.

It is not coincidental that three of these pieces belong to the category of music sometimes known as *tombeau*: that is, in memory of a friend or of some dignitary worthy of musical tribute. Earl Strafford was a loyalist whose warrant for execution Charles I signed under duress. It is not surprising to find Tomkins commemorating the earl's death in the form of a Pavan and Galliard. The short versions (41 and 42) differ from the long ones (43 and 44) in one major respect: the repeats in the long versions are written out in full and ornamented in noble and fiery fashion. Although written in 1647, some six years after Strafford's execution, this memorial piece is not lacking in solemn and meaningful passion. Archbishop Laud was put to death in 1645, and the city of Worcester was besieged for the second time in the following year: by 1647 Tomkins was ready to pen these touching memorials to Strafford and Laud, little knowing that worse was to come in 1649, when the king himself suffered the extreme penalty.

The *Pavan: Lord Canterbury* (William Laud, archbishop of Canterbury) is available in only one source, from which the removal of a folio has deprived us of the third strain of this remarkable and moving composition (57). As in the long versions of the *Pavan: Earl Strafford*, the repeats are highly decorative and elegantly contrived. Yet there is a serious beauty in the unadorned first and second strains, the first with its three-note sigh, repeated again and again in notes of higher pitch; the second with its chromatic cry of indignation, rising too, in four distinct statements, just as the first strain did.

The *Sad Pavan: for these distracted times* (53) is dated 14 February 1649, only a few days after the execution of Charles I. Again, there is much tense emotion packed into a little space; and the unornamented repeats together with remarkable symmetry in the melodic structure give an overall impression of conciseness and unity. A skilful use of suspensions and unessential notes brings out the pathos of the first strain, which nevertheless exhibits a symmetry of design by no means unusual in this group of compositions. Treating the first chord as an anacrusis gives the pattern shown in Ex. 15.6, in which note-values are reduced by half.

Ex. 15.6

Of the remaining Pavan and Galliard pairs, only the 1654 group (almost the last works Tomkins wrote) has common thematic material (47 and 48). The subtle rhythm of the Pavan is built on a characteristic hemiola pattern (Ex. 15.7).

Ex. 15.7

The Galliard is one of the liveliest that Tomkins wrote, and owes much of its appeal to the lilting dotted rhythm of the first strain, the rapid imitation of the second, and the well-placed melodic climax of the third. Written four years previously, the long Pavan and Galliard (45 and 46) with their varied strains and effective ornamentation prove that Tomkins enjoyed considerable facility at the keyboard in spite of his advanced age. The Pavan and Galliard (49 and 50) both 'of three parts' may be thought of as an exercise in a more transparent contrapuntal style. There is no feeling that the composer is hampered by his own restrictive practices, however, and the impression given by this well-balanced pair is one of clarity and elegance.

Of the separate Pavans not discussed so far there are three of the short variety, and two with fully-fledged repeats. One of these longer Pavans (55) is called 'short' by Tomkins, and short it is by comparison with the great A minor Pavan from the *Fitzwilliam Virginal Book* (56). In the two (51 and 52) written within a few days of each other in the month of September 1647, Tomkins uses one of his favourite scalic configurations, involving rapid upward runs within the compass of a seventh. Pavans 54 and 55 are notable for their symmetry of design, especially in the first strains, as well as for their economy of material.

The most famous of the Pavans is undoubtedly the one that has been longest known, by reason of its publication many years ago in the *Fitzwilliam Virginal Book*. It was well known, however, even in Tomkins's day, for besides another copy of the keyboard version there are several manuscripts containing string versions, and one printed book[30] which brought it to the notice of continental musicians. The power of the piece lies in its finely contrasted

---

[30] T. Simpson (1610), *Opusculum neuer Pavanen, Galliarden, Couranten und Volten.*

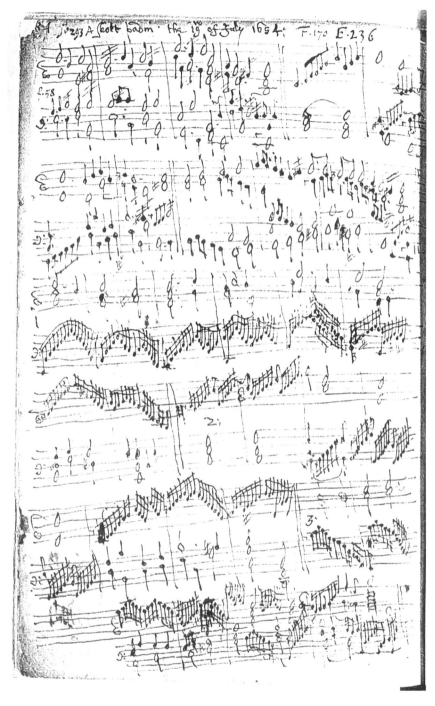

Fig. 15.4 Thomas Tomkins: 'A Short Pavan' (19 July 1654).

Music for Keyboard Instruments 255

harmonic aspects: the first strain establishes the home key, the second reaches the dominant by traditional though colourful methods, and the third returns to A by way of descending chromatic digressions in the best Italian manner. It is not unusual to find exceptional brilliance (which some have censured[31]) in a work written early in the composer's career, when he was – as it were – fresh from school and anxious to show his skill.

The *Hunting Galliard* (58), if not definitely descriptive, at least portrays some of the excitement and movement of the chase. In the intensity and vigour of its figuration it is not unlike the music of Bull, for it certainly demands the kind of virtuoso performance that would be out of place in the other two galliards. The one named after *Lady Folliott* (59) is a short but charming composition, designed perhaps as a tribute to Isabella, daughter of Guthlake Folliott, a chapter clerk of the cathedral. In 1654 Tomkins's son Nathaniel married Isabella, and the three retired to Martin Hussingtree, whose manor house, together with the patronage of the church, Isabella had inherited from her first husband John Haselock. The variations of the three strains in the last Galliard (60) vary between the harmonic and melodic types: there is a constant shift of interest, which lends the music a subtle and distinctive quality.

The four sets of variations on popular songs of the sixteenth century are found in four different sources, and they may well belong to different periods of Tomkins's life. The *Fitzwilliam* set, based on *Barafostus' Dream* (62), must be fairly early, and seems to belong stylistically to the first decade of the seventeenth century. The tune, sometimes known as *The Shepherd's Joy*, is mentioned in a poetical anthology called *The Golden Garland of Princely Delights*, published in 1622; but it was certainly current at a much earlier date. There is an anonymous set of variations on this tune in the same manuscript[32] besides a consort piece in Rosseter's publication of 1609. Tomkins wrote his variations in a brilliant and dashing style, with the accent on melodic rather than harmonic interest.

At the other end of the scale lies the very expressive (though by no means easy) set based on *Fortune my foe* (61), which was composed in the summer of 1654 at Martin Hussingtree. Late as they are, these variations compare favourably with the settings by Byrd, Sweelinck and Scheidt and they display many characteristic features of Tomkins's decorative style, especially his liking for repeated notes, dactylic figures and formations of broken sixths.

Robin Hood (63) uses the major version of the tune that appears in a Cambridge lute manuscript[33] and Ravenscroft's *Pammelia* in the minor key.

---

[31] Van den Borren, *Sources of Keyboard Music*, 283, mentions the 'too prominent character of its figuration'.

[32] *Fitzwilliam Virginal Book*, I, 72. Compare also *Jacobean Consort Music*, No. 95.

[33] Cambridge University Library, Dd ix, 33.

256 *The Music of Thomas Tomkins*

There are ten variations, of which the sixth is noteworthy for a delightfully syncopated cadence, the seventh and eighth for flowing tripla tunes, and the tenth for its canonic flavour. Much shorter is the set based on *What if a day* (64), a poem by Thomas Campion that was set to music by Alison in *An Hour's Recreation in Music*, published in 1606. The tune used by Tomkins is not the same as that used by Alison, but it does correspond with the tune that is found in a setting for keyboard by Richard Creighton, and dated 27 October 1636.[34] It is possible that the variations by Tomkins are much earlier than this, for they are reminiscent of Bull's most brilliant writing, and appear to belong to the same period as *Barafostus' Dream*. The structure is taut and effective, with each of the three strains varied immediately after its initial appearance, and then a repeat of this pattern involving all the resources of the keyboard virtuoso.

In *Worcester Brawls* (65) the composer pays gracious tribute to the city which sheltered him for more than sixty years. The term 'brawl' now implies something less elegant than the *bransle simple* from which the English dance was originally derived: Morley, in his *Plain and Easy Introduction*, comparing it to the alman, says that it 'goeth somewhat rounder in time ... otherwise the measure is all one'. *The Perpetual Round* (66) is probably Tomkins's last composition, for it is dated 7–8 September 1654. The theme of the round rises gently to the fourth above the opening note; it is then repeated at the new pitch until the note c' is reached. A third repetition then follows, and here the pattern perforce comes to an end. If it were to be continued, the theme would eventually arrive back at its starting point; hence it is in a sense perpetual. The new material which follows the opening point has similar characteristics, this time descending, and its accompanying counterpoint – also sequential – eventually moves to the treble and continues the *moto perpetuo* impression. A division, or variation on this material, makes considerable use of conventional figuration in scale-passages and broken thirds.

The *Toy: made at Poole Court* (67) is interesting since it is the only one of Tomkins's pieces, barring the *Worcester Brawls*, to mention a place-name. In Chapter 6, Anthony Boden has revealed the correct location of Poole Court in Worcestershire, thus dispelling the long-held belief that it was the home of the Trelawney family at Menheniot in Cornwall. It now seems almost certain that Tomkins never visited the county of his ancestors. When he stayed at Poole Court, however, the cheerful atmosphere was at least pleasant enough to inspire this 'light, frivolous, or lively tune', which was the meaning of the word *Toy* in those days.

The mysterious piece (68) from a Christ Church manuscript appears to be founded on a plainsong, but the theme does not possess plainsong

---

[34] Bibliothèque Nationale, Rés. 1186, fol. 15.

Music for Keyboard Instruments 257

characteristics. The initial descent of a major sixth, stepwise, is atypical of any plainsong form; and whilst it is possible that the opening of the melody as given by Tomkins is not the real opening, it is more likely that the melody was simply invented for the piece. The three-part texture, of gradually increasing complexity and innovation, is reminiscent of certain *In nomine* and *Miserere* settings.

One of the most interesting of the pieces printed in the appendix to the keyboard works is the *Toy* (69), inscribed to 'Mr Curch' in one of the New York Public Library manuscripts.[35] Nothing is known of this dedicatee, nor is it certain that the music is by Tomkins. Under the title of *Almain*, it is associated with the name of Tomkins in a Christ Church source,[36] but the *Fitzwilliam Virginal Book* has the attribution 'Giles Farnaby'. Stylistically, the music resembles that of Farnaby rather than Tomkins, and as far as is known the mysterious Mr Curch was not among Tomkins's circle of friends.

Edward Thornborough, archdeacon of Worcester, was among that circle, however, and there are three pieces in a Bodleian manuscript[37] that seem to have been expressly written for him. Edward, to whom the first two pieces are inscribed, was collated archdeacon on 3 August 1629, and died in 1645.[38] The third piece carries a more formal inscription: 'For Mr. Arch[deacon] Thornborough' and is, unlike that on the other two, undoubtedly in Tomkins's handwriting. All three pieces have the character of short *Fancies*, and although they are slight in musical importance and are not signed by Tomkins (which is perhaps the reason why they are not included in the collected edition of keyboard music) the internal evidence of the handwriting and dedications is sufficient to enable them to qualify as genuine works of Tomkins.

Fétis, in his short article on Tomkins, found room for a rather surprising critical remark that compares the work of Tomkins with that of a contemporary German master: 'The pieces for organ and harpsichord in M. Farrenc's manuscript are exact imitations of the style of Samuel Scheidt's *Tabulatura Nova* published in 1624.'[39] If Tomkins imitated anyone, it was William Byrd; but in modelling his style upon that of his master he brought certain new characteristics of harmony and figuration which are often more than enough to prove the power of his musical personality. The fact that he chose to write the bulk of his keyboard music towards the end of his life, and

---

[35] New York Public Library, Drexel MS 5612.
[36] Christ Church Library, Oxford, MS 1112.
[37] Bodleian Library, Oxford, [MS] Mus. Sch. C 93, fols 80, 81v.
[38] J. Le Neve (ed. T. Duffus Hardy, 1854), *Fasti Ecclesiae Anglicanae*, III, 75.
[39] Fétis, *Biographie universelle*.

cannot therefore be placed in a neat historical pigeon-hole, may be looked upon as a sign of weakness by certain critics. But there is no real reason why a retiring, or indeed retired, organist of the Chapel Royal should not compose in a highly traditional manner for his own pleasure and amusement. Even at 60, he had ample technique besides a very wide experience of music, and that is the main reason why so much of his keyboard writing is fresh, idiomatic, and rewarding to the player. In his introduction to the keyboard works of Tomkins, Stephen Tuttle has summed up the position in the following words:

> The music of his later years is written in a more conservative style, which resembles that of his teacher William Byrd. Here in the years of the mid-century the circle has closed. Tomkins, the last of the school, returns at the end of his life to the style of his master, the first, and perhaps the greatest, of the virginalists.[40]

---

[40] *Musica Britannica*, V, xiii.

Chapter 16

Consort Music

You need not seek outlandish authors, especially for instrumental music;
no nation (in my opinion) being equal to the English in that way; as well for
their excellent, as their various and numerous consorts, of 3, 4, 5 and 6 parts.

(Christopher Simpson, *A Compendium of Practical Music* (1667))

Although the surviving consort music by Thomas Tomkins exceeds thirty individual items, and although this music was composed over a period of more than thirty years,[1] he was never acknowledged by his contemporaries as an outstanding consort writer. There was an uneasy tremor in the late nineteenth century, though its effects cannot, in the nature of things, have made a very vigorous or widespread impression:

His biographers all do justice to Thomas Tomkins ... but I nowhere find any mention by them of his instrumental compositions. Rimbault does not name him among viol writers, in his notes to Gibbons' 'Fantasies'; and neither Burney, nor Hawkins, nor the writer for Grove's Dictionary, adds any instrumental writing to the list of his known works, whether printed or in manuscript.[2]

Neither Mace nor Simpson mentions Tomkins in his list of consort composers, and later scholar-musicians like Anthony Wood and Roger North are equally silent, in spite of their love for consort music. This silence was duly copied by Burney, Hawkins and Rimbault, who were content to leave the situation as they found it: a complete and utter blank.

Whether or not the article in the *Quarterly Musical Review* for 1888 ever came to the notice of Arnold Dolmetsch is a matter for conjecture; but one thing is certain, and that is the appearance of a Tomkins fantasia in the first of the annual Dolmetsch Festivals, held in the year 1925. Inspired either by the almost shocked tone of the *Quarterly Musical Review*, or by his own researches into consort music of the Elizabethan and Stuart eras, this energetic champion of early music and early instruments transcribed works by Tomkins, Locke, Jenkins and Lawes and had them played in public, possibly for the first time in centuries. The healthy reactions of one critic are altogether noteworthy:

---

[1] A pavan *a* 5 appeared in Simpson's *Opusculum neuer Pavanen, Galliarden, Coranten und Volten* of 1610; another (no. 43 in Bodley MS Mus. Sch. E 415–18) bears the date 1641.

[2] M.L. Armitt (1888), 'Old English Viol Music' *Quarterly Musical Review*, 4: 186.

> Already at this half-way stage of the Festival many musicians have come to realise
> the extreme importance of the period (roughly from 1550 to 1650), when the
> English fantasy was cultivated. As a result it may reasonably be hoped that the
> sphere of pure chamber music will be widened to include the concerted music for
> viols. A fund of wealth, beauty and invention will be discovered there, and we
> shall regard the complexities of modern music from a new and enlightened
> standpoint.
>
> We cannot hope to produce contemporary composers of the same calibre as
> Thomas Tomkins, Matthew Lock, John Jenkins, and William Lawes, but we can
> fall back on their amplitude and immense calm for a while, and begin the battle
> afresh with something of their courage and, above all, something of their clarity.[3]

Critical opinion has been gradually revised during the course of the last half-century, and the long neglect of Tomkins's consort music is now, happily, at an end. The works have been published in *Musica Britannica*, vol. LIX (1992), many have been recorded, and public performances are now not at all uncommon. One of the greatest authorities on English Baroque music expressed a view that the consort music of Tomkins was rather uneven in quality, but affirmed that it is 'Real viol music, and not (as for example the excellent Ward) merely good counterpoint conceived really in the vocal mood'.[4]

This was a splendid tribute to Tomkins, for his main interest was in the music of the Church, and he had constantly before him the ideals and methods of the great Elizabethan composers of vocal music. The first music for instrumental consorts in the second half of sixteenth century stemmed from vocal sources, either sacred (the *In nomine* derived from a four-part section in the *Benedictus* of Taverner's *Missa Gloria tibi Trinitas*) or secular:

> But thus far is material, the earlier consorts were composed for 3, 4, and more
> parts, for songs in Italian or Latin out of the Psalms, of which I have seen divers,
> and mostly in print, with the names of the *patroni* inscribed. And in England
> when composers were scarce, these songs were copied off, without the words, and
> for variety used as instrumental consorts, with the first words of the song for a
> title.[5]

In addition to the songs in Italian, North might well have mentioned the numerous French chansons that were used as consort music, confirming a general practice which still had its adherents in the reign of James I. Tomkins was not one of those adherents: he embraced the new art of fantasia with its indomitably instrumental personality, its rhythmical freedom apt for the subtleties of the bow, and its wide variety of melodic leaps, safe and sure upon 'so many equal and truly-sized viols; and so exactly strung, tuned, and played upon, as no one part was any impediment to the other'.[6]

---

[3] *Daily Telegraph*, 31August 1925.
[4] Communication to the author from the late Mr Robert Donington.
[5] R. North (1846), *Memoirs of Music*, ed. E.F. Rimbault, 73.
[6] Thomas Mace (1676), *Musick's Monument*, 234.

Consort Music 261

Dance forms held an almost equal fascination for him, and it is not without significance that his most famous work is a Pavan, printed in 1610 by Thomas Simpson, and still available in six manuscript sources, four for viols and two for keyboard instruments.

Tomkins's strong preference for genuine viol music can hardly be doubted, for a mere five of his sixty or more verse anthems were provided with an alternative accompaniment for viols, either intact or restorable. Where vocal music was concerned, his chosen instrument was the organ, and he may even have felt that stringed instruments were out of place in service time. At home, however, the chest of viols was distinctly welcome. His brother Robert was a professional player in the king's service, and his neighbours Humphrey and John Withy (whose names are inscribed in an unfortunately incomplete set of partbooks at Oxford[7]) were assiduous collectors and players of consort music. Their partbooks are dated 1642, when trouble was already brewing in and about the city of Worcester, thanks to the attentions of Essex's unruly troops. Then, perhaps more than ever, North's *bon mot* on the subject of violence versus viols held good:

> And amongst other arts, music flourished, and exceedingly improved, for the king being a virtuous prince loved an entertainment so commendable as that was; and the fantasia manner held through his reign and during the troubles and when most other good arts languished music held up her head, not at court nor (in the cant of those times) profane theatres, but in private society, for many chose rather to fiddle at home, than to go out and be knocked on the head abroad; and the entertainment was very much courted and made use of not only in the country but in city families, in which many of the ladies were good consortiers, and in this state was music daily improving more or less till the time of (in all other respects but music) the happy restoration.[8]

The viol players may sometimes have been joined in consort by the chamber organ of Nathaniel Tomkins, this manner of performance being then current and very much in fashion, as Mace and North affirmed many years later.[9] But the role of the organ, when its part was not expressly composed, remained a minor one, strongly under the influence of the *basso seguente* tradition and yet not strong enough to assert itself beyond that role.

Tomkins certainly learnt much from the consort music of his contemporaries, who had been busily occupied with the exploitation of genuine instrumental texture evolving, paradoxically enough, from the cantus firmus type of consort rather than copies of vocal models, however sprightly and decorative the latter might be. He can hold his own in the exacting and

---

[7] Bodleian Library, MS Mus. Sch. E 415–18. At the end of 417 is written 'Mr. Tho: Tomkins /Mr. Humphrey Withy 1642'; 418 (fols 17 and 25v) mentions J. Withy.

[8] R. North (1925), *The Musical Grammarian*, ed. H. Andrews, 18–19.

[9] Mace, *Music's Monument*, 234; North, *The Musical Grammarian*, 28, and *Memoirs of Music*, 105.

translucent style of the three-part fantasia, matching the best of Lupo, Mico, Ward and Coperario, and even surpassing on occasion the music of his friend and colleague Orlando Gibbons. Similarly, his two *In nomine* pieces display a keen sense of instrumental aptitude and technical skill although they are of slighter stature than the keyboard settings of this particular melody. In the dances for five and six viols, Tomkins is often more sedate and serious than his fellows, rarely indulging in the flights of brilliant virtuosity that can be found in the dances by Ferrabosco, Weelkes, Dering and Philips. His four six-part fantasias are worthy to stand by the finest of the consorts of his friends Coperario, Ward and White, with whom he probably exchanged music whenever the opportunity presented itself. It is pleasant to think of a friendly rivalry between composers of similar stature and interests, and even if Tomkins surpassed them in age and ability he would (from what we know of his character and personality) have refrained from being either patronizing or aloof.

His consort works consist of a group of fifteen three-part Fantasias; a single five-part Fantasia that survives only in a keyboard version; four six-part Fantasias; two settings of *In nomine a* 3; three four-part works: an *Ut re mi*, a Pavan and an Alman; nine five-part Pavans; and a Pavan and *Galliard a* 6. The three-part Fantasias are far from being stereotyped; indeed some of them go out of their way to appear downright unusual. A favourite example of the fantastic element is his modulating Fantasia, No. 10,[10] which is a canon three in one at the fifth below.

Each repetition of the theme in each voice occurs one tone lower, so that the sixth statement leads back to the original key of C sharp minor. There are no jolts in this smooth descent by whole tones, since each part retains something of its own key colour whilst contributing in a thoroughly convincing manner to the whole (see Ex. 16.1).

Kaleidoscopic but logical, the scheme must have appealed to Tomkins, for he allows the canon to perpetuate itself as far as three further statements, when a free codetta leads towards A minor, a new point, and a perfectly normal second half. Thus Tomkins achieves a nice artistic balance between a mechanical and modulatory introduction, and a freely composed continuation and ending. From a formal point of view, this is rare enough both in the music of Tomkins's contemporaries and in wider historical vistas. There is nevertheless a certain parallel to be drawn between Tomkins's three-part canon and Bach's two-part canon (with an independent but also repetitive part) in *Das musikalische Opfer*.[11] Both Tomkins and Bach separate their thematic statements by whole-tone steps, Tomkins choosing the downward path and Bach the upward. But whereas Bach, by using canon at

---

[10] See catalogue of Consort Music in the List of Works.
[11] Canon *a* 2 per tonos (No. VI in Hans T. David's edition, published by G. Schirmer).

Ex. 16.1

the octave, confirms and consolidates his temporary tonality, Tomkins seeks the other extreme by having the successive voice parts enter a fifth below the previous statement of the theme, thus destroying on purpose any feeling of rigid tonality and building in its place a powerful and intriguing chromatic edifice.

There are, too, other remarkable fantasias among this group. Both 3 and 4 are to be noted for the broad sweep of their opening points, the former being maintained almost until the tripla section, and the latter encompassing a wide range in the first treble part, spanning well over two octaves. An unusual feature about 12 is the way in which it begins: quite atypical of the accepted fantasia style, the second bass states the theme, but remains silent while the theme is restated by the first bass beneath a counter-subject played by the treble viol.

Some of the passage-work is outstanding by reason of its brilliance and complexity: 1 and 2 contain extended passages in broken fourths, while 1 and 8 share a penchant for smoothly flowing broken thirds. Often one finds cascades of scales, crossing and intertwining in their headlong progress, and reaching a high pitch of excitement in 5, 11, 12 and 13. Academic devices, on the other hand, are rarely used, although diminution of the first point occurs in 5, and both 3 and 7 are enlivened by a short tripla section. The actual themes themselves may be lyrical or epigrammatic in quality, flowing or concise, yet invariably well balanced and adaptable. An opening paragraph of exceptional length and strength is found in 8 (Ex. 16.2).

A completely different outlook is apparent from the very first notes of 11,

Ex. 16.2

where short and succinct phrases abound, with much variety of rhythm and movement (Ex. 16.3).

Ex. 16.3

Fantasias 6 and 9 also exude radiant lyricism; 7 and 10, on the other hand, agree more with the temper of 11. In general, the structural scheme seems to be one of gradually increasing busyness, the longer note-values appearing near the beginning of the piece, and the shorter ones at the end. The middle section, often replete with a point of its own, acts as a transition from stately polyphony to scintillating peroration, though very occasionally (as in 14) there is a quieter atmosphere and a sense of elegant repose.

The two *In nomine* settings were certainly written as a pair, for they are contrasting and to a large extent complementary. The first has the cantus firmus in the middle voice, and the time is duple apart from a short passage in sextupla proportion about two-thirds of the way through the piece. First treble and bass are kept fairly well apart by the cantus firmus (in the alto range), although they both touch extremes of compass from time to time and range widely over their respective tessituras. The left hand of the organist sometimes looms large in the bass viol part, more especially perhaps at the very end (see Ex. 16.4).

The second *In nomine* has its theme in the bass, in a solemn trochaic rhythm. Above the quasi-ostinato, only twice broken into figural patterns, the two trebles display variety and agility in their neatly contrasted sections, now thematic, now decorative. With a keyboard continuo, the texture would be not unlike that of a trio sonata, admittedly of a very special kind. The main

Ex. 16.4

Consort Music 265

feature, however, is the ease with which Tomkins invents new melodic and rhythmical ideas, gently persuading the two parts to interchange their roles, following one another in lively imitation, then combining in chains of thirds until the next theme is reached. Even North, who had little enthusiasm for the *In nomine* in spite of his sociological explanation of its vogue, may have approved of this one:

> But in the In nomines I never could see a cadence complete, but proffers and baulks innumerable. That which was properly termed Air was an entire stranger to this sort of harmony, and the audience might sit with all the tranquillity in the world, and hear continual shiftings of tones, with numberless syncopes and varieties, such as they were, and not be in the least moved, if pleased it was enough. And on the other side, if we consider that times were peaceable, and men were not so much drawn from home to follow the court, or city, or to travel as hath been since, but enjoyed their fortunes plentifully at home, where anything to entertain the time was welcome; and then such music, being loud and variegated, pleased and never offended.[12]

No settings of *In nomine* for larger consorts of four, five or six viols by Thomas Tomkins are known to exist. For these more sonorous consorts he chose the fantasia.

The *Ut re mi* fantasia for four viols has, of course, certain affinities with the *In nomine*, as North noticed in his discussion of descant upon a plainsong: 'The plain-song was an order of plain notes of considerable length, perhaps a large or two breves;[13] very often the gamut notes ascending or descending, which were sung to the syllables of In nomine domini [*sic*].'[14] It is not as extensive or as elaborate as the keyboard version preserved in Paris and Oxford,[15] and in method and structure it is far more straightforward than the *Ut re mi* pavan. The hexachord, ascending and descending, is presented by the various instruments in turn, amid surrounding counterpoint of a somewhat solid though amiable nature. The keyboard version, in spite of its length, is nevertheless the more successful of the two, for there is more opportunity for decoration and disguise of the theme than in the consort, with its more limited technical resources.

With the five-part fantasia, exactly the opposite is true. But unfortunately its original form, as a consort, has not come down to us; all that remains is a reduction of the five parts for keyboard, and consequently (as so often happens in these cases) a good deal is left to the imagination. The keyboard version is nevertheless useful enough to demonstrate the lost excellences of this unique five-part consort.

The four great six-part fantasias represent a noble achievement among

---

12 North, *The Musical Grammarian*, 9.
13 Here he writes a *longa*.
14 North, *The Musical Grammarian*, 7.
15 See previous chapter.

Tomkins's consort music; indeed they rank along with the best of the five-part pavans as music of outstanding dignity and character. In spite of the fact that the first three are firmly anchored to a G tonality (the fourth is in F) there is more than enough contrast of melody and style to set each work apart as a highly individual contribution to consort literature. Tomkins's near-symphonic outlook upon the development and integration of his themes can be seen at its clearest in the first of the group. The main subject (Ex. 16.5) has an invertible (and adjustable) counter-subject built on a *cambiata* figure (Ex. 16.6) and these are grafted on to an independent bicinium played by the two middle parts. Fragments of all these are used in close imitation to lead up to the first important cadence on a chord of G major. The E flat chord which follows introduces, together with its new colour, an ostensibly new point. But this has in fact evolved, by a process of augmentation and centonization, from the opening point and its counterpoint, in reverse order (Ex. 16.7).

Ex. 16.5

Ex. 16.6

Ex. 16.7

The tail of Ex. 16.7 is then used as a point in its own right, over a long pedal D; but after the next cadence on G there is a short section in free style, in the nature of transition. The first treble rises, then falls, with a touch of chromaticism, and a new point appears, some four bars in length, and remains active for some time with the aid of judiciously spaced rests, which lighten the texture to three or four voices for the most part. A common cadential suspension provides the idea and impetus for the next point, which is doubled either in sixths or thirds and has a distinctive counterpoint. From these three parts there is a gradual building up until the full consort is heard, with the unerringly logical suspension motive serving once again, and for the last time, as a fortification of the cadence. Throughout the fantasia Tomkins shows an instinctive feeling for musical equilibrium, the balance between texture and structure, and the appeal of melody and polyphony. Rarely at a loss for melodic ideas, he is not simply inventive and fertile because these things come naturally to him; he creates new material out of the old, binding together disparate elements and contrasting those that seem at first to be most alike.

The three other fantasias for six-part consort have similar though by no means identical virtues. A chromatic, curling descent characterizes the second fantasia, perhaps the best known of the four because of its early availability in print.[16] The middle section abounds in lively dotted rhythms and syncopation, and at the end all is aglow with scale-motifs which pile up on each other until a final climax is reached.

The third fantasia has an initial point that pervades all six parts. The succeeding point, with its surge through an ascending fourth, tends towards key transition, but shorter motifs soon follow and their progress is mainly diatonic. Further points lean towards the harmonic and virtuosic elements respectively, and scales both ascending and descending cross and convolute until the final cadence.

Like its fellows, the fourth fantasia is firmly constructed with motives strong in themselves yet lyrical enough (as in the opening theme especially) to command attention and remembrance. The individual parts are of wide range and there is considerable and effective crossing of parts, making for a smooth and even texture. Much use is made of sequential motives within a theme, especially in the middle section, which is more animated in style. Contrary to custom, there is no display in the coda, although syncopations and offbeat patterns play a large part in the last few bars. In general, however, the fantasias of Tomkins are not far removed from the classical type described by North:

> The method of the old fancies was to begin with a solemn fugue, and all the parts entered with it one after another, and often in different keys, which is the best garniture of fugues, and then followed divers repeats, retorts, and reverts, of which art the audience was little sensible, and being but labour in vain must be passed upon account of industry and striving to do well; but with all that, if the music was not so airy, it was sound and good, and after the fugue spent nothing could be more full than the harmony was. And then entered another fugue, intended to be more airy, and performed much quicker, not unlike our Allegros, and when that was spent, a tripla perhaps, or some yet freer air, but the tripla for the most part is of the graver sort, and concluded after with a l'envoye as they called it, and not with a jig as now the mode is, but rather an adagio with this stately semiclose.[17] And of these fancies whole volumes are left, scarce ever to be made use of but either in the air for kites or in the fire for singeing pullets.[18]

---

[16] Edited by E.H. Fellowes (1931) (Stainer & Bell).
[17] Here North makes a fair guess at a decorated $^6_4\,^5_3$ close *a* 4.
[18] North, *The Musical Grammarian*, 12–13.

268 *The Music of Thomas Tomkins*

Many of the dances must, alas, have gone the same way. There is only one example of a four-part dance by Tomkins, and of nine pavans *a* 5 three are so fragmentary that reconstruction is an impossibility. A fine pavan and galliard *a* 6 has survived, however, and although they are not thematically related, and thus agree with the usual English custom in this respect, they are paired in the manuscript partbooks at Oxford and Dublin. It may well be that none of these was intended for dancing, for they have a more learned air than the instrumental dances of Holborne, Philips, Tregian and Brade. In spite of the popularity of dancing at court, and the constant call for a lighter kind of music for masques and pageants, it seems that Tomkins was never called upon to provide music of this type. The Reformation had brought with it a strange new kind of decorum, eventually banishing the choirboy plays and relieving the master of the choristers of his former versatility, whereby he not only provided plays and lyrics but also songs and dances. By the time Tomkins began to compose his dances for viols, many of the forms had been sublimated to the extent that their rhythmical interest was a secondary consideration.

The *Alman a* 4[19] is sufficiently regular in the extent of its three strains to qualify for genuine dance music, but even so the texture is eminently polyphonic and much use is made of short motives apt for development. It probably belongs to the same period as the later five-part pavans, which date from 1640 onwards. These too make some use of imitation, together with occasional harmonic sequences, and they consist of the usual three strains, the middle one ending normally on the dominant or subdominant. The fourth pavan of the Bodleian set is based on the hexachord, but there is no attempt at chromatic treatment in the manner of the two versions of Ferrabosco's hexachord fantasia.[20] Tomkins uses principally the notes G and E in ascending and descending forms, although the third strain has C to A as a cantus firmus in two of the parts, now rhythmicized, now in regular and even notes. John Withy is the dedicatee of this musical merger of dance and cantus firmus, as the inscription on fol. 25v of the bassus partbook proves.

The fifth pavan is of especial interest in view of the date, 9 October 1641, in three of the partbooks. This date, together with the signatures of Thomas Tomkins and Humphrey Withy (1642) on the endpaper of the tenor book, helps to place the majority of these compositions in the later period of Tomkins's life. The length of the pavan, and the economy with which the thematic material is deployed, affords ample evidence of the composer's lively mind, and of his desire to remain active in spite of his wife's illness and the impending threat of the siege. He even found time to revise his early pavan, which had appeared in Thomas Simpson's *Opusculum neuer Pavanen, Galliarden, Coranten und Volten*, published in Frankfurt in 1610. In this

---

[19] *Musica Britannica*, IX, 33.
[20] Ibid., 23 and 29.

Consort Music

269

revision, there is considerable alteration of the individual parts as well as a transposition up a minor third, which makes for greater brilliance within the emotional framework of the minor key. This same work had served as the basis of a keyboard pavan, where, of course, the opportunity to decorate and ornament the repeats of each strain had been grasped and exploited to the full.

Although the six-part pavan[21] shows us Tomkins at his most dignified, the hint of a dactyl, reminiscent of countless chansons, lends a certain air of lightness to the opening point, whose rhythm is echoed at the beginning of the second strain. Its melodic shape, now in a new rhythmic pattern, is called to mind in the third strain, where (as in the previous two) the texture becomes progressively more dense as the cadence is approached. In the galliard, there is gracious exchange of phrases at the same pitch between the two treble parts, and similarly between the two bass parts, so that what Tomkins achieves is an elegant conversation between two quartets – the interchange of personalities rather than timbres – within the essentially six-part texture.

The prospect of a venerable church musician providing dances for a consort of viols was not unusual in Jacobean and Caroline society. Gibbons, Dering, Philips and Weelkes had all contributed noteworthy pieces for the fast-growing repertoire, and there is no sign that they were in any way ashamed of their contribution. If anything, the fault is an excess of learning rather than an excess of frivolity, for this dance music with a difference had, as we have seen, passed from the realm of the court masque and the ballroom to the quiet and intimacy of the home, and there it served as a leavening for the more serious fantasias and *In nomine* settings. English consort music had reached a high pitch of variety and excellence by the middle of the seventeenth century, and the situation is boldly summed up by Matthew Locke, in the very year of Tomkins's death, in the preface to his *Little Consort of Three Parts*:

> And for those mountebanks of wit, who think it necessary to disparage all they meet with of their own countrymen's, because there have been and are some excellent things done by strangers, I shall make bold to tell them (and I hope my own experience in this science will enforce them to confess me a competent judge) that I never yet saw any foreign instrumental composition (a few French corants excepted) worthy an Englishman's transcribing.

---

[21] *Musica Britannica*, IX, 92 and 93.

PART THREE
FURTHER COMMENTARIES

Chapter 17

Thomas Tomkins: An Appreciation

Bernard Rose

Thomas Tomkins must have been a man of great energy, for as well as his duties as organist at Worcester and his journeyings between there and London, his output of compositions was considerable. All his secular choral works were published in the *Songs* of 1622. These are of three different types – madrigals, madrigals with *fa-las*, and biblical songs. Both the quality of these pieces and their wide range of expression places them with the best examples of the English Madrigal School. The lateness of this publication compared with the majority of the Elizabethan sets of madrigals no doubt accounts for some of the more remarkable passages which it contains, but this does not detract from their boldness and originality. In *Come shepherds, sing with me* a most striking effect is obtained by superimposing triple rhythm upon the basic duple rhythm over a distance of some twenty-four bars.

The awakened interest in the writing for instruments amongst Tomkins's predecessors, particularly Byrd, had a considerable influence upon vocal style. Such figuration as demonstrated in Ex. 17.1 from Byrd's motet *In resurrectione tua* has an obvious instrumental origin (all examples are written at their original pitch) and Gibbons clinched the matter by his subtle use of the figure in his three-part fantasia, which opens with it. Tomkins was no exception to this influence, and there are many examples in the *Songs*, particularly in *It is my well-beloved's voice* and *Oyez! has any found a lad*.

Ex. 17.1

He seldom allowed himself to be *outré* for the sake of being original, but was very sensitive to the meaning of his text. He followed the well-worn custom in the setting of such words as 'heaven', 'hell', 'ascend' and 'descend', but also used far more subtle methods by which to express a particular mood,

---

The edited text of a lecture given to the Royal Musical Assocation on 15 May 1956, and reproduced by kind permission of the RMA and Gregory Rose.

274 *Further Commentaries*

or to give more meaning to a point in the text. In the madrigal *Was ever wretch tormented* there is an original effect as the result of a *pes* in the bass part at the words 'in midst of hellish firing'.

He knew well how to make effective use of vocal 'scoring', as in the opening passage of his setting of part of Psalm 120, *Woe is me*. The entry of the alto and first soprano on the dissonant minor second adds to the dolefulness of the scene. This passage shows another quality in Tomkins – his breadth of style, and this is shown to perfection in what is perhaps his finest choral work, *When David heard*, which occurs in the *Songs* and in his sacred collection, *Musica Deo sacra*. This holds its place amongst the masterpieces of the English school mainly by the way in which he sustains this breadth of style throughout its entirety. The poignancy of the text is wonderfully portrayed by the music by means of the judicious repetition of phrases, by tonal sequences, slow harmonic movement, and by the very effective use of the *nota cambiata* figure towards the end. The similarity between the last twelve bars and a passage in *Alleluia. I heard a voice* by Weelkes is of some interest. Another example of his breadth of style combined with a sense of sheer beauty is the closing passage of *When I observe*. The most original works from the *Songs* are the two madrigals which form a pair and which are inscribed to his brothers Peregrine and Robert – *Weep no more thou sorry boy* and *Yet again as soon revived*. True it is that he makes play with individual words at the expense of the real sentiment of a poetic line, but the variety which results from it and the fact that the total effect is a well-balanced whole justifies the means. The text of *Weep no more* contains the antitheses 'laughs and weeps', and 'sighs and sings', and Tomkins most effectively follows a 'flat' chord by a very 'sharp' one in each case. The setting of the latter phrase might be described as musical onomatopœia. The last dozen bars, based upon the tonic and dominant arpeggios create an atmosphere of complete serenity.

With the publication of vol. V of *Musica Britannica*, all Tomkins's known keyboard works came under one cover, and were collected and edited by the late Professor Stephen D. Tuttle. Most of the pieces are in the forms which were general at that time – voluntaries, fancies, *In nomines*, pavans and galliards, pieces on the notes of the hexachord and so forth – with the interesting exception of the *Fancy: for two to play*, which together with Nicholas Carlton's *In nomine* is probably the first English piece for two at one keyboard. There are two pieces of exceptional length, *Offertory: 1637* and *Ut, re, mi, fa, sol, la*. Both are *ostinati*, for although the *Offertory* is in the nature of a fancy for the first fifteen bars, the remaining 289 bars present the original 'point' in equal note-values fifty-four times. It would have been better placed with the ostinati rather than with the fancies in this volume. The *Ut, re, mi* has thirty-eight variations. The composition of these two works was not quite the marathon that it would appear to have been, for, as pointed out by

Professor Tuttle, it is obvious from the MSS that they were both written over a period of time, as inspiration came to him. A remark in Tomkins's hand on the MS of the *Ut, re, mi* might also apply to the other piece, 'Use as many or as Few as you will of these many wayes upon this playnesong'. The amount of variety of rhythm and figuration which exists in these long pieces is considerable.

As well as the rapid scale-passages which were a feature of contemporary and earlier keyboard figuration, Tomkins writes rapid broken sixths and rapid repeated notes. The two examples (Ex. 17.2a and b) might well be taken for excerpts from a book of Loeschhorn pianoforte studies (with the addition of an accidental or two). The fingering in the left-hand part of Ex. 17.2(b) is Tomkins's own, and this is a feature of his. It should be mentioned that the thumb and little finger are frequently indicated. One of the five pieces from the Fitzwilliam Virginal Book, *Ground*, tempts one to assume that he was acquainted with 'Boys and girls come out to play', and that the pause on the seventh note is snook-cocking (Ex. 17.3).

Ex. 17.2a and b

Ex. 17.3

A Sad Pavan for these distracted times obviously refers to the execution of Charles I, for it is dated 14 February 1649. It is a heartfelt piece and one of the loveliest of all. Half of these keyboard works were written during the last ten years of his life. This is significant, for the second siege of Worcester occurred in 1646, when the organ was pulled down – the Dallam organ for whose construction he had been mainly responsible: '... and written about the

Organ, By the meditation and mediation of Thomas Tomkins, Organist heare unto the Righte reverend Bishop and venerable Deane, who gave these munificent guiftes and invited their fryndes by the industry of the said Thomas Tomkins'. It is not surprising that he should have devoted so much of his remaining life to writing for the domestic keyboard instrument rather than for the Church.

Tomkins's most obvious claim to fame is his *Musica Deo sacra*, which was published in 1668 and printed by William Godbid. This great collection contains five settings of various parts of the English service, the Psalmody,[1] and ninety-four anthems of which fifty-three are full anthems and forty-one are verse anthems; nineteen are in three parts for mixed voices, and six are in four parts for men only. The preponderance of verse anthems shows Tomkins following Gibbons in the new style, and the anthems for men only may be the result of the poor quality of the treble voices at certain times at Worcester, for in 1619 cornets were engaged to double the treble parts.[2] The Second Service contains a progression either at the beginning of each movement or soon afterwards, which occurs so often in Tomkins's music that one tends to associate it with him. It merely involves the sharpening of a previously flattened third of a triad either in the same or in another voice with the dominant chord in between (Ex. 17.4).

Ex. 17.4

Examples of this progression in works already mentioned occur at the opening of *When David heard*, and *A Sad Pavan*. The richness of Tomkins's harmonic vocabulary will be discussed in more detail later, but the passage at the words 'He hath shewed strength with his arm' from the *Magnificat* of the Second Service shows a most strikingly original effect, which is obtained by the simple use of passing notes.

His three 'great' services are in the tradition of Byrd, Weelkes and Gibbons, and certainly stand up to comparison with any previous settings. The Fourth and Fifth Services both contain much writing for solo voices, and in both the

---

[1] These settings and the Psalmody comprise vol. VIII of *Tudor Church Music* (*TCM*) (Oxford, 1928).

[2] Atkins, *Early Occupants*, 47.

organ accompaniment to the solo sections is very florid, more so than in any cases by other composers of this time. The ghost of his 'reverenced master' could not have been far from him when he composed the opening phrase of the *Magnificat* and *Nunc Dimittis* of the Fourth Service, as a comparison with Byrd's Second Service will show! The unusual passage in the organ part which accompanies the bass solo 'Vouchsafe, O Lord', in the *Te Deum* of the Fifth Service seems somewhat unjustifiable in the context, but the fine sweeping bass part to the 'Amen' of the *Jubilate* in the same Service is in the English tradition of Tallis and Byrd, though more Baroque in style (Ex. 17.5).

Ex. 17.5

The Elizabethan composers took much pleasure in dealing with those undemocratic characters in the *Magnificat* – the proud, the mighty and the rich – and Byrd appears to have been the first person to use the descriptive rhythm for 'scatter-ed the proud', in combination with the leaping intervals, in his 'Great' Service and Second Service. Tomkins follows the precedent in all five of his settings in *Musica Deo sacra*.

In the preface to the Tomkins volume of *Tudor Church Music*[3] the editor says 'His full anthems are almost all of real musical value and interest, and in those of the later style his touch becomes sure, if never quite inspired ... The tentative experiments of Gibbons in this kind reach fuller maturity in Tomkins, but in neither case do they make much appeal to modern taste; and the space occupied in *Musica Deo sacra* by 'Songs to the Organ' tends to obscure the composer's worth and to impair his fame. Only by a knowledge of the whole of his work, old style and new, can he be fairly judged ...' etc. The last sentence is a truism, and the remainder of the quotation is an indication of the considerable change that has taken place in musical taste since this was written in 1928, when cathedral choirs were still singing music of this period at its written pitch, as the present writer knows from experience; and the opinion of this editor is perhaps equally out of date, for the majority of people today would not share it. The full anthems, fine as some of them are, are very much in the old contrapuntal style of his predecessors and older contemporaries while in the main lacking the intimate eloquence of many of them. The large-scale full anthems are an exception, particularly the great twelve-part *O praise the Lord all ye heathen*,[4] and *O sing unto the Lord a new*

---

[3] *TCM*, VIII, xvii *et seq.*
[4] *TCM*, 8vo edition.

song, which is in seven parts. Both of these contain finely wrought imitative music of a jubilant character, the latter having a splendid ringing 'Alleluia'. Of quite a different nature is the five-part prayer *Arise, O Lord God, lift up thine hand* – a lovely setting in which the changes of mood in the text are movingly portrayed. The most original music in this set of twenty-eight full anthems is the setting of the 'Amen' in the five-part *Almighty God, the fountain of all wisdom*, the opening of which must be quoted (see Ex. 17.6).

Ex. 17.6

On stylistic grounds the seven three-part anthems for men and the nineteen four-part anthems for mixed voices appear to be earlier than the rest of the anthems. Their value as anthems is somewhat limited, but they do contain points of harmonic interest. The text underlay in some of *Musica Deo sacra* is notoriously bad, and at its worst in the three-part anthems, witness the two examples from *Thou healest the broken in heart* shown in Ex. 17.7.

The editor of the Tomkins volume of *Tudor Church Music* says quite rightly that the underlay in the services is occasionally 'so strange and uncouth' that neither Tomkins nor his son Nathaniel (the compiler and editor) could have been responsible for it, and assumes that it was the printer's interpretation of the MSS. This theory may be possible in the case of the services, but if we accept the fact that the actual notes of the three-part anthems are as Tomkins

Ex. 17.7

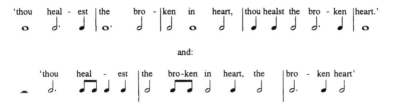

wrote them, this theory is hardly tenable in their case. If we refer to two examples from *Thou healest* (and these are two among many in this piece) an unmusical printer might well produce such gibberish, but it would require more than genius to fit the given words to the given notes in either case in point, and at the same time produce something sensible, unless the word 'healest' is reduced to 'healst' each time, which is unlikely and most undesirable. We shall attempt to prove that some at least of these three-part pieces were not in fact intended as anthems by the composer. We understand that pitch in sacred music at this time – indeed on Tomkins's own evidence – was about a minor third higher than ours today. The version of *When David heard* in *Musica Deo sacra* is written a fourth lower than it is in the *Songs* – and yet the treble parts in five of the nineteen three-part anthems go up to top G or A, some 'leads' begin on top A, and it is in these anthems in particular that text and music fail to combine satisfactorily. In complete contrast are the settings of the Seven Penitential Psalms, in which there is only one top G, and in which the compass of each voice part seldom exceeds a tenth, and the lines are much more vocal than in the other pieces. The present writer contends that these factors suggest that some of these pieces, rather than being composed as anthems, had originally either secular texts – were in fact three-part madrigals, for that is their style – or no text at all, being in the nature of counterpoint exercises; and that some person unknown (the printer?) added the texts which they now have. Perhaps these extracts and a comparison of the opening of *The hills stand about Jerusalem* with one of his fantasies, shown in Ex. 17.8, will help to substantiate this view.

Admittedly this does not account for the 'strange or uncouth' underlay in the remainder of *Musica Deo sacra*, but nowhere is it as absurd as it is in these three-part pieces. Another point of interest is that there is no organ part for any of the three-part anthems, and the pitch of these lies higher than in any of the services and other anthems. The five particular 'anthems' mentioned above have the treble G clef in the partbooks, and these are the only cases of its use throughout the collection. In fact it would appear on practical grounds that they must be performed at their written pitch, i.e. the so-called 'secular' pitch. A further conclusion from this is that the expression 'church music

Ex. 17.8

(a)
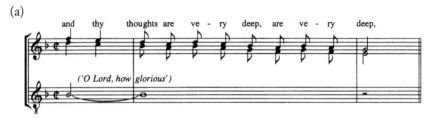

(b)

(c)
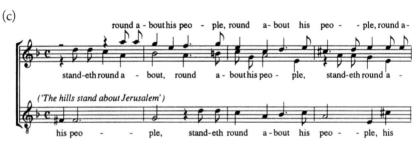

Ex. 17.8 concluded

(d)

pitch' should be qualified by the words 'with' or 'without organ accompaniment'.

The forty-one *Songs to the Organ* contain some of Tomkins's most original and finest music. The few writers who have made reference to them always cite the first, *Behold, I bring you*, as an example of the quality of the collection, but this anthem is by no means the best. His setting of *My beloved spake* is most beautiful, and is a good example of how he could react to a colourful text, without a suspicion of cheapness or vulgarity. The antiphonal treatment (in the treble parts) of the final words 'and come away' is most apt. In contrast with this is *Sing unto God*, with its fine robust solo for the bass. *Out of the deep* is again picturesque without being exaggerated.

In this he pays the perfect compliment to Gibbons by quoting almost note for note the final phrase of *The Silver Swan!* The organ part in several of these anthems is very florid, particularly so in *Above the stars*; *My shepherd is the living Lord*; *O Lord, let me know mine end*; and *The Lord, even the most mighty God*. It is interesting, in comparing them with his keyboard works, to see the large number of similar phrases he uses in both. He frequently uses the flourish of semiquavers covering the octave, and also uses them to produce a measured trill (Ex. 17.9).

Ex. 17.9

The organ assists in description in *Above the stars*, where its florid movement at 'ravish my soul' is most effective. Some of these anthems are long, and in some there is considerable repetition of text. These factors may to some extent account for the fact that they are neither available nor performed.[5] That they possess musical value of a high order seems indisputable.

There are at least thirty string pieces by Tomkins in partbooks, mainly in Dublin, the British Library, and the Bodleian [published in *Musica Britannica*, vol. LIX (1992)]. They range from three to six parts and consist of fantasias, *In nomines*, pavans and galliards. The two most interesting works are the Fantasia *a* 3 in A, the opening of which is quoted by Ernst Meyer,[6] and the Fantasia *a* 6 (2). Both are very chromatic, but whereas the six-part one avoids modulation, the three-part example modulates clearly to as remote a key as A flat minor, and it is built to a very systematic canonic design. It is a very extended composition, being ninety bars long. The design is similar to that used by Ferrabosco II in his fantasias on the hexachord, where the first note of the hexachord is a semitone lower at each statement; Bach adopted the same plan in one of the canons in *The Musical Offering*. The chromaticism in the six-part fantasia already mentioned persists for less than half of the composition, and the third 'point' has a dance-like quality which is also a feature of some of the fantasias of his teacher, Byrd, and of Orlando Gibbons. One must admit that Tomkins's pieces do not possess the poise and serenity of those of Byrd nor the essential melodiousness and homeliness of those of Gibbons in four parts. And nowhere does Tomkins approach the rhythmic complications and subtleties of Byrd's *Browning*.

It is to Professor Tuttle and the Revd A. Ramsbotham that we are indebted for the bulk of Tomkins's music. Only one who had a strong love for Tomkins (and time at his disposal) would have 'scored' the whole of *Musica Deo sacra*

---

[5] All of Tomkins's full and verse anthems included in *Musica Deo sacra*, ed. Bernard Rose, have subsequently been published in the Early English Church Music series (Stainer & Bell, 1965–92, in six volumes).

[6] E. Meyer (1946), *English Chamber Music*, London, 170.

from the partbooks as Ramsbotham in fact did. His manuscripts cover 425 closely written pages, excluding the five services, and one cannot refrain from expressing regret that his great work and industry has not borne fruit in publication.

It is not surprising that Tomkins's music shows a wide range of differing musical styles when one realizes that he lived and worked during the reigns of Elizabeth I, James I and Charles I; that he was born about thirteen years before Tallis died, and died only two years before Purcell was born.

We have remarked upon the old contrapuntal style of the full anthem and the modern florid style of the *Songs to the Organ*, and reference has been made to specific, interesting features of his work such as the chromatic three-part fantasia. Amongst the large number of examples of his original harmonic touches which could be given, there is space for only a few. One would expect the more adventurous cases to occur in the madrigals, and this is the case. In addition to those mentioned earlier, one of his most original and certainly one of his loveliest pieces is *O let me die for true love*, where the simultaneous use of passing-notes and changing-notes during the first *fa-la-las* is as essentially logical as it is effective, and the same can be said of the fine drawn-out cadence at the end of the first section.

One of Tomkins's most endearing qualities is his ability to write a good tune, and the *Songs to the Organ* offer many instances, such as the opening 'verse' of *Above the stars* (Ex. 17.10), (each phrase is preceded by an organ passage),

Ex. 17.10

A further weapon in defence of the theory that some of the cases of bad text underlay were nothing to do with Tomkins is the fact that on numerous occasions he goes out of his way to ensure 'just accent' in his setting of words which have a Trochaic ending, by doing precisely that which we associate with Purcell when the latter writes:

284 *Further Commentaries*

and follows it by a rest. And it is this kind of behaviour which makes even stronger the contention that the so-called three-part anthems were not written as such by Tomkins.

It would show a lack of perspective and discernment to claim that Tomkins was a great genius; he lived in an age of great men, but in spite of the fact that his work does not maintain the consistently high level of that of Byrd, the result of research during the past thirty years puts him into the same category as Byrd with regard to output and versatility. There were few composers of his time who could claim a large volume of keyboard works, some excellent string works, a book of madrigals, seven services and over 100 anthems, of which nothing falls to an embarrassingly low level and much maintains its place amongst the best in an age of great achievement.

Chapter 18

Sacred Music omitted from *Musica Deo sacra*

Peter James

Musica Deo sacra (1668) comprises fifty-three full anthems (including nineteen three-part works), forty-one verse anthems and five services together with various other liturgical pieces: a set of Preces, two festal psalms and five metrical psalm tunes. But for its publication, much of Tomkins's sacred music would have been lost or have survived only in fragmentary form. Of the forty-one verse anthems, for example, only fifteen remain in anything like a complete state, an indication of how much music of the period has been lost.

The importance of *Musica Deo sacra* has tended to overshadow Tomkins's surviving sacred music omitted from the collection which provides a further valuable insight into the composer's output: eight full anthems, thirteen verse anthems and two verse services as well as a set of Preces and Responses, two metrical psalm tunes and two litanies.

The extent of this neglected area of Tomkins's work is demonstrated by the following list [the List of Works includes details of sources]:

Full anthems [* = probably intended for extra-liturgical use]

1   *Almighty and everlasting God we humbly beseech Thee* (Inc.– text only)
2* *Dear Lord of life* (C)
3* *From deepest horror of sad penitence* (C)
4   *Grant us, gracious Lord, so to eat* (Inc. – text only)
5   *O Lord, wipe away my sins* (Inc. – tenor only)
6* *Turn unto the Lord* (C – 'Songs' [1622])
7* *Woe is me* (C – 'Songs' [1622])
8   *Zadok, the priest* (Inc. – text only)

A revised version of the writer's 'Thomas Tomkins: Sacred Music omitted from *Musica Deo sacra*', published in *Soundings* II (1971).

286 *Further Commentaries*

Verse anthems[1] [† = anonymous but almost certainly by Tomkins]

9   *Death is swallowed up* (R)
10† *Have mercy upon me, O God* (R – tenor, bass and organ)
11   *Jesus came when the doors were shut* (C – except countertenor verse)
12   *Know you not* (C, essentially)
13   *My dwelling is above* (Inc. – organ and text)
14† *O God, the heathen are come into thine inheritance* (R – tenor, bass and organ)
15† *O Lord, let my mouth* [be filled with praise] (Inc. – organ only)
16   *O think upon Thy servant* (Inc. – organ and text)
17   *Rejoice, rejoice* (C, essentially)
18   *Sweet Saviour* (Inc.– organ only)
19   *The Lord bless us* (R – tenor, bass and organ)
20   *Withdraw not Thou Thy mercy* (Inc. – text only)
21   *Ye people all* (Inc. – bass only)

Services

22   *'Sixth' Service* [Magnificat and Nunc Dimittis] (C – except sop. 2 [verses] and alto 1 [all])
23   *'Seventh' Service* [Magnificat and Nunc Dimittis] (Inc./R – organ only)

Varia

24   *Preces and Responses* (C – except alto 2)
25   Metrical psalm tunes – *Dunfermline and Worcester* (C – both in *The CL Psalms of David* [1615] and Ravenscroft's *The Whole Book of Psalms* [1620])
26   *'First' Litany* (C)
27   *'Second' Litany* (C)

C: complete; R: reconstruction possible; Inc.: incomplete.

Two pieces not by Tomkins, but sometimes attributed to him, should also be mentioned. In 1970, the writer discovered that an anonymous full anthem, *Set up thyself, O God*, in a Worcester Cathedral manuscript, and in the hand

---

[1] All of Tomkins's verse compositions omitted from *Musica Deo sacra* [except numbers 10, 14 and 15 above] are included in the writer's doctoral dissertation (1968), 'A study of the Verse Anthem from Byrd to Tomkins', II, University of Wales, Cardiff.

Sacred Music omitted from Musica Deo sacra

of Nathaniel Tomkins – hence its previous attribution to Tomkins[2] – is in fact Byrd's festive *Exalt thyself, O God*. The restored work affords a deeper appreciation of Byrd's full anthems.[3] Set out in score by Nathaniel, quite probably at his father's prompting, it is a further reminder of Tomkins's indebtedness to his 'ancient and much reverenced master'. The verse anthem *Everlasting God, which hast ordained* is by Nathaniel Giles.[4] Although attributed to Tomkins in the 'Dunnington-Jefferson' bass partbook at York Minster, it is ascribed to Giles in all its remaining sources. Coincidentally, Giles was born and bred in Worcester and was a predecessor of Tomkins as organist at the cathedral there before taking up a similar post at St George's Chapel, Windsor.

Denis Stevens refers to a verse anthem by Tomkins for St Thomas, *Almighty and everlasting God*, which, he says, appears in the 'Batten' Organ Book.[5] This is, in fact, *Jesus came when the doors were shut* (listed above), the error being explained as follows: *Jesus came* begins in the middle of a page, the top part of which contains the concluding bars of *Almighty and everlasting God, we humbly beseech Thy majesty*, a verse anthem for the Purification. The page is headed 'Almighty and everlasting God', a description mistakenly thought to refer to *Jesus came*, which is simply entitled 'Anthem for St. Thomas Day T.T.'.

Full anthems

The texts and surviving sources of four of Tomkins's eight 'full' sacred works indicate that they were intended for liturgical use. Unfortunately, none can be reconstructed. Two so-called 'sacred madrigals' – *Dear Lord of life* and *From deepest horror of sad penitence* – are extra-liturgical works, as are two of the three *Songs* of 1622 – *Woe is me* and *It is my well-beloved's voice* (the latter being a secular work despite its biblical text). However, the remaining one, *Turn unto the Lord*, was copied into liturgical partbooks at Peterhouse, Cambridge.

No music exists for *Almighty and everlasting God, we humbly beseech Thee*. This setting of the Collect for the Purification is listed among the full anthems in two books of anthem texts assembled in the 1630s. The books also include a verse anthem (included in *Musica Deo sacra*) set to the same text, although its title has 'Thy majesty' for 'Thee'.

---

[2] Atkins, *Early Occupants*.

[3] See the writer's article (1998), 'Exalt thyself, O God: the rediscovery of Byrd's festive anthem', *Annual Byrd Newsletter* (4), June. The article also describes how *Exalt thyself, O God* served as a model for Orlando Gibbons's *Hosanna to the Son of David*.

[4] Ed. J. Bunker Clark (1979), Early English Church Music, 23, Stainer & Bell.

[5] Stevens, repr. 1967 with additional Preface, New York, p. xiii of this Preface.

288 *Further Commentaries*

Dear Lord of life appears in a set of partbooks (Christ Church MSS 61–6) mainly compiled and edited by Thomas Myriell.[6] The set also includes single parts of *It is my well-beloved's voice* and *Know you not*, while the compiler's best-known collection, *Tristitiae Remedium* of 1616 (BL Add. MSS 29372–7), includes six pieces by Tomkins: two secular and two sacred madrigals[7] as well as two verse anthems.[8] Evidence of Myriell's editing is to be found in *Dear Lord of life*, where he pasted over different clefs apparently to make the piece suitable for secular use. The original clefs are discernible as baritone (F3) with treble (G2), Myriell's amendments being F4 (bass) and C1 (soprano). Allowing for the clef code and 'church pitch',[9] the earlier (and presumably original) reading would therefore have sounded in the 'key' of B flat minor, the nearest pitch approximation which could be achieved by the mere substitution of clefs. The work displays a number of madrigalian devices, notably abrupt modulations and changes of texture, and each phrase of the text is set so that the music alternates between drawn-out and highly rhythmic sections, and between moods of poignancy and restlessness. The shifting tonalities give rise to several remarkable passages, notably at the words 'which dries his tears' and 'these bleeding drops of love' (Ex. 18.1). In terms of sheer expressiveness, *Dear Lord of life* ranks as one of Tomkins's most striking compositions.

The sacred madrigal *From deepest horror of sad penitence* is set to an evocative early seventeenth-century text. It, too, appears in Myriell's *Tristitiae Remedium*. Like *Dear Lord of life* it demonstrates madrigalian features but its level of inspiration is less well sustained. It does, however, include a number of distinctive passages, notably the opening (Ex. 18.2), where the lower voices, deployed in their bottom registers for some nine bars, portray the text in a suitably lugubrious manner which would no doubt have appealed to Tomkins's contemporaries. The contrasting moods and rhythms from one section to the next also recall *Dear Lord of life*. Unusually, the final section, 'Shew mercy, Lord, that mercy has in store, on him that is resolved to sin no more', is directed to be repeated (recalling this practice in sixteenth-century anthems) as if to emphasize the moral pointed out by this couplet.

Only the text of *Grant us, gracious Lord so to eat* survives. It is derived from the so-called Prayer of Humble Access from Anglican Holy Communion Service.

---

[6] P.J. Willetts (1968), 'Musical Connections of Thomas Myriell', *Music and Letters*, 49: 37.

[7] *Oft did I marle* (dedicated to John Ward, who copied several pieces into Christ Church MSS 61–6), also *From deepest horror of sad penitence*, *It is my well-beloved's voice* and *When David heard* (dedicated in the *Songs* of 1622 to Myriell himself).

[8] *Sing unto God* and *Thou art my King, O God*.

[9] See D. Wulstan (1967), 'The Problem of Pitch in sixteenth-century English Vocal Polyphony', *Proceedings of the Royal Musical Association*, 93: 97–111.

Ex. 18.1

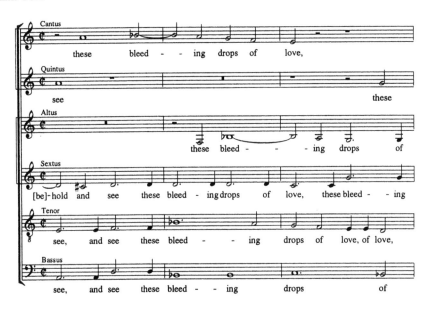

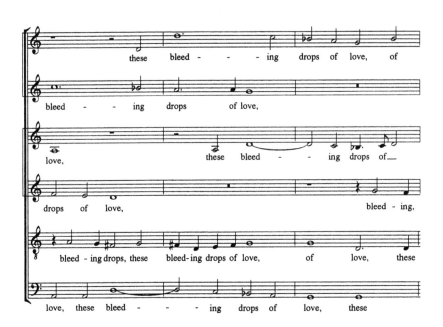

Ex. 18.1   concluded

The tenor part of *O Lord, wipe away my sins* is found in a partbook dated 1617 and originally belonging to Southwell Minster. This fruitful source of Tomkins's music includes six full and nine verse anthems. Each 'point' of the text – 'O Lord, wipe away my sins that my soul may be saved in the day of judgement' – is developed at some length, the anthem being forty-nine bars long.

Turn unto the Lord was the concluding work in the composer's *Songs* of 1622, where it was dedicated to his son, Nathaniel. It was copied into several sets of early seventeenth-century secular partbooks, but its appearance in the liturgical sources, dating from *c*.1635, at Peterhouse, Cambridge, indicates that it was also performed liturgically as an anthem. It is a setting of great breadth, the counterpoint interweaving and unfolding on a broad canvas with almost all its motifs based on slow-moving ascending or descending scale figures so reminiscent of Gibbons. Apart from necessary changes in its first seven bars and a four-bar 'coda', its forty-two bars follow exactly the composer's setting of the same text in the *Jubilate Deo* of his Third Service, a work of 'great service' proportions. Tomkins evidently held the Service in high regard, so it is not surprising that he dedicated *Turn unto the Lord* to his son.

The remaining sacred madrigal, *Woe is me*, a setting of Psalm 120: 4, was dedicated in the Songs to John Tomkins, the composer's half-brother, who deserves to be remembered on his own account (see pp. 159 and 160). It is. The desolation of the opening words is portrayed by drawn-out phrases and

Ex. 18.2

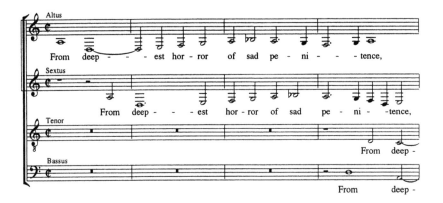

suspensions. At 'and to have my habitation', the pace quickens into a hemiola rhythm but the sombre mood returns at 'the tents of Kedar', the deliberately static tonality creating a mood of utter misery. The unusual final cadence also occurs in Tomkins's keyboard duet, *Fancy: for two to play*.[10]

As chief organist at the Chapel Royal following Orlando Gibbons's death in June 1625, Tomkins had prime responsibility for providing music for the Coronation of Charles I in February 1626 (see pp. 126 and 127). The familiar coronation text, *Zadok the Priest*, was set by Tomkins for the occasion, but only the text survives.[11]

---

[10] In S.D. Tuttle (ed., 1955), *Musica Britannica*, V, London.

[11] *Cheque Book*, 157. The list of works sung includes several others which may have been among Tomkins's 'many songs': (i) *Glory be to God on high (Gloria in excelsis)* – about which Archbishop Laud wrily noted in his copy, 'Here the choir should have sung Glory be to God on high, but because they could not take Arch Bp's voice so far off, it was read' (quoted in A. Hughes, 'Music of the Coronation over a Thousand Years', *Proceedings of the Royal Musical*

292 *Further Commentaries*

Verse anthems

All thirteen of Tomkins's verse anthems omitted from *Musica Deo sacra* were written with liturgical performance in mind; even the distinctive *Rejoice, rejoice* survives in a bass partbook at Gloucester Cathedral. Unlike the verse anthems of Byrd and Gibbons, whose structures conform to several clearly defined categories, Tomkins's verse anthems do not follow any particular structural patterns. Indeed, the most striking feature is the diversity of their scoring and layout, none of the fifty-four verse anthems comparing exactly in the scoring of their verse sections and in the relationship between their verse and chorus sections. The verse anthems omitted from *Musica Deo sacra* demonstrate the full range of the composer's verse technique, from a verse for one soloist, with the chorus commenting on this material (*Jesus came when the doors were shut*) to complex layouts such as *Know you not*.

Death is swallowed up is a distinctive work of high quality, its text being drawn from the Burial Service (1 Cor.: 54–7). A relatively late date of composition is indicated by its 'madrigalian' rhythmic figures (notably at the words 'O grave, where is thy victory?') and its abrupt 'key' changes associated with quite original and unexpected false relations. One of its two music sources, an organ book originally in use at King's College, Cambridge, mainly comprises occasional pieces, such as Tomkins's *Know you not*. It is quite possible, therefore, that *Death is swallowed up*, with its funeral associations, was written upon the death of a significant person – perhaps James I in 1625, or even the composer's father two years later.

It is surprising that *Jesus came when the doors were shut*, an anthem for St Thomas's Day, was not printed in *Musica Deo sacra*, since its surviving manuscript sources indicate that it enjoyed wide popularity in the seventeenth century. The work takes the form of a narrative (countertenor) and, later, a dialogue between Thomas (countertenor) and Jesus (bass) with the chorus taking up the final motifs of each verse section and developing them afresh as if commenting and reflecting on the words of the soloist.

Three verse anthems were recently identified as being almost certainly by Tomkins.[12] Several sets of *Musica Deo sacra* include bound-in manuscript-paper sheets to allow for the inclusion of further works. In the set in the Library of Christ Church, Oxford, annotated and added to by Nathaniel Tomkins himself, three anonymous verse anthems follow Tomkins's *Know you not* (see below). The texts of all three may well be seen as relating to the

---

Association, 79: 93. (ii) *Behold, O God, our Defender* (the second part of the verse anthem *O Lord of Hosts*). Although *O Lord, grant the King a long life* is headed 'The Coronation Anthem' in *Musica Deo sacra*, no anthem with this title appears in the inventory of pieces, so it was probably written for the general coronation festivities.

12 Milsom, 'Tracking Tomkins'.

Sacred Music omitted from Musica Deo sacra 293

difficult days at Worcester in the early 1640s, so their special nature (like *Know you not*) made them less suitable for inclusion in *Musica Deo sacra*. *Have mercy upon me, O God*, a setting of verses from the penitential Psalm 51, is subtitled 'for a base & contratenor'; three parts survive. *O Lord, let my mouth* [be filled with praise], a setting of verses from Psalm 71, is the most fragmentary of the three with just an organ part surviving. *O God, the heathen are come into thine inheritance* is one of the longer verse anthems of the period, extending (in modern terms) to 198 bars. Like William Child's setting of verses from the same Psalm, and dating from 1644,[13] Tomkins's work is, in effect, a 'protest' anthem reflecting the sad state of affairs in Worcester at the time. It reworks material from Byrd's motet *Deus venerunt gentes*, which sets verses from the same Psalm and which, too, is apparently a 'protest' work. Three parts survive: tenor, bass and organ.

Know you not was written on the occasion of the death, in 1612, of James I's highly regarded and musical son, Henry, prince of Wales.[14] It was almost certainly one of the 'several anthems to the organs and other wind instruments' performed at his funeral in the Chapel Royal.[15] Tomkins may have been prompted by motives of personal ambition to write this ambitious anthem with unseemly haste. It is an unusual, even remarkable work on which, despite its hasty composition, he obviously lavished much care and attention, suggesting that he had special cause to impress those connected with the music of the Chapel Royal. Perhaps he had just become a gentleman of the Chapel Royal, but it is more likely that he hoped that a favourable reception of this anthem would soon lead to such an appointment; although he was first mentioned as a gentleman as late as 1620, he probably took up such a post some years earlier. Despite the anthem's omission from *Musica Deo sacra*, Nathaniel Tomkins evidently thought it worthy of preservation (albeit not entirely complete) by adding it by hand to his set of the 1668 edition. Its high degree of chromatic writing (Ex. 18.3) sets it apart as a virtually unique contribution to the late-Renaissance verse anthem. The surviving parts, with one exception, indicate that the work was conceived with instrumental (as distinct from solo organ) accompaniment. Even its early organ part, dating

---

13 *O Lord God, the heathen are come into thine inheritance*: a note in one source states that the anthem 'was composed in the year 1644, on the occasion of the abolishing The Common Prayer and overthrowing the constitution both in Church and State'.

14 Alfonso Ferrabosco II was his music instructor while Thomas Ford and Robert Johnson were lutenists in his service. Robert Jones dedicated his only published set of madrigals of 1607 to him as well as his *Third Book of Ayres* (*Ultimum Vale*) (1608). After his death, John Coperario published his *Songs of mourning for the death of Henry, Prince of Wales* (1613), and Robert Ramsay composed his *Dialogues of sorrow upon the death of the late Prince Henry* (mentioned in E. Thompson (1963) 'Robert Ramsay', *Musical Quarterly*, 49: 211), a collection which has not survived.

15 See Stevens, 32.

from c.1630, appears to be a reduction from instrumental parts. As well as its chromatic writing, *Know you not* is characterized by abrupt changes of key and varied and imaginative scoring. An unusual feature is the isolated appearance of a high G, a note reserved for the high treble voice, near the end of the final chorus.

Ex. 18.3

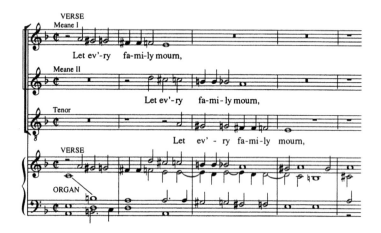

All that survives of *My dwelling is above* and *O think upon Thy servant* are their texts and organ parts. *My dwelling is above* is not an especially notable work. *O think upon Thy servant* is more interesting with an imaginative tonal scheme, its bold chorus writing contrasting strikingly with the florid organ part.

Rejoice, rejoice is an unusual work in many respects. It has been suggested[16] that it is not by Tomkins since it does not represent the composer at his best or most characteristic. However, it is attributed to Tomkins in three partbooks of its principal source (it is anonymous in the remaining two), while valuable confirmation of Tomkins's authorship is provided by its attribution to him in a bass partbook at Gloucester Cathedral. This source contains several pieces by Tomkins which did not enjoy wide circulation and which, in all probability, were copied from holograph parts from nearby Worcester.[17] *Rejoice, rejoice* was written 'for the Annunciation' – as it is subtitled in one partbook. It is one of just five of the composer's verse anthems for which instrumental parts survive, although the organ writing in several others also implies an instrumental texture. Most unusually it begins with a chorus, and

---

[16] Le Huray, *Music and the Reformation*, 282–3.
[17] See Stevens, 7 and 52.

Sacred Music omitted from Musica Deo sacra

not a verse, one of just a few such examples. Others include an anthem by Henry Loosemore and the evening canticles of Weelkes's 'Second' (the *Nunc Dimittis* only) and 'Third' Services. With its distinctly angular instrumental writing, it is a competent if not especially remarkable portrayal of the vivid text. The choruses are in six parts with a concluding eight-part one.

An organ part is all that remains of *Sweet Saviour*, whose text is almost certainly of early seventeenth-century origin. The direction 'for 2 meanes and a bass' indicates the likely vocal scoring of its verse sections. The work is characterized by liberal use of sequence and florid organ writing. Its final verse and chorus sections, mainly in triple time, abound in hemiolas.

Although only tenor, bass and organ parts of *The Lord bless us* survive, the anthem can be reconstructed convincingly. The index of the tenor partbook states that the verses are for Cantus (meane), Altus (counter-tenor) and Tenor, and these voices apparently share most of the solo material. The anthem is a reflective setting of a familiar sixteenth-century prayer found in the Ash Wednesday Commination. As with a number of the composer's verse anthems, it includes abrupt and unexpected key changes (as distinct from modulations) at the beginning of new sections, usually to the flattened sub-mediant 'key' (Ex. 18.4). The close resemblance, in the fourth chorus and fifth verse section, to music by Byrd – the opening of both evening canticles of his 'Great' Service and part of the motet *Exurge Domine* – illustrates further Tomkins's regard for his 'much reverenced master'.

Musica Deo sacra includes a full anthem entitled *Withdraw not Thou Thy mercy*, a setting of verses from Psalm 40, but the 'verse' and 'chorus' directions in two contemporary books of texts indicate that Tomkins also set it as a verse anthem, despite its location among the full anthems – an error repeated in the indexes. The work comprises three verses each of which is followed by a chorus which repeats the latter part of each section of text.

All that survives of *Ye people all*, a setting of the Sternhold and Hopkins metrical version of Psalm 47, is a bass part. With its four strophic choruses, the anthem is a unique instance of a work by Tomkins based on such a design. It is not a festal psalm, since such pieces were always set to the Prayer Book prose version of the Psalms, rather than a metrical text.

Services

The 'Sixth' Service (Denis Stevens's numbering) survives very nearly complete. Although the material lacks the second meane in the verse sections and the first counter-tenor in its entirety, these are largely supplied by the earlier of two distinctly different versions of the organ part. In this earlier (Durham) reading, the top line of the organ part in the verse sections doubles the top-

Ex. 18.4

sounding meane but adds a counterpoint above the counter-tenor where this is the highest-sounding part. However, in the later version (in the 'Batten' Organ Book) a counterpoint is added above the solo vocal parts in all circumstances. The verses are for one or two meanes and counter-tenors, so recalling the allocation of verses to these voices in almost all early verse anthems and services (the tenor verse at 'He hath put down' in Byrd's Second Service is a later alternative to the original counter-tenor). The Service's low-lying chorus tenor part and its Elizabethan-type cadential formulae are reminiscent of Byrd, and even Tallis. All these features indicate that the 'Sixth' Service is an early work written under the influence of Tomkins's mentor, Byrd. The earlier organ part therefore represents the work's original version while its reworking reveals the composer's maturer further thoughts. Although probably written in the 1590s, when the composer was in his early twenties, the setting displays sound craftsmanship and sturdy solo and choral writing. The first chorus beginning 'For he hath regarded' brings to mind the same section in Morley's Short Service, while the strict canon between the two solo voices in the section 'He hath shewed strength with his arm' recalls this device in Byrd's Third Service.

The organ part of the 'Seventh' Service is sufficiently detailed to convey a convincing idea of its scoring, and it can be seen to provide a stylistic bridge between the early 'Sixth' Service and the mature Fourth Service (entitled 'Third' in the early sources). The more ambitious scoring of its verses, apparently including tenor and bass soloists, a post-Elizabethan approach to tonality and harmony, and a strong and characterful sense of rhetoric, even evoking Tomkins the madrigalist, all indicate a date of composition a decade or so after 1600. The scoring of three of the verse sections for four upper voices, a texture employed in all four of his verse services, recalls Byrd's Second Service (at 'To be a light'). The virtually identical settings of 'Amen' in the *Nunc Dimittis* and the composer's verse anthem *The Lord bless us* exemplify a sharing of material between canticle and anthem settings which was by no means uncommon at the time.[18]

The chronology of Tomkins's four verse services provides a fascinating insight into the development of the composer's verse-service technique. For reasons already set out, the 'Sixth' Service was almost certainly written in the 1590s, while the 'Seventh' Service, with its stylistic advances, was probably composed *c*.1610. The Fourth Service displays a mature and assured approach, particularly in the distinctiveness of its musical ideas and the imaginative scoring of its verse sections; a date of composition *c*.1620 is realistic. On the other hand, the Fifth Service, with its distinct *stile nuovo* elements, was probably written a decade or so later. This projected order of composition is borne out by the titles of the Services in the seventeenth-century manuscripts (the two Services included in *Musica Deo sacra* are numbered Fourth and Fifth simply because they follow the three full Services). The 'Batten' Organ Book numbers them First ('Sixth' Service), Second ('Seventh' Service) and Third (Fourth Service); the Fifth survives only in *Musica Deo sacra*. Crucially, the index of the Bass Cantoris book of John Barnard's set assembled *c*.1625 (Royal College of Music, London, MSS 1045–51) lists a number of works not in the collection but presumably intended for inclusion. The list includes Tomkins's 'first', 'second' and 'third'

---

[18] The setting of 'Amen' in Tomkins's verse anthem *Behold, the hour cometh* is another reworking of the same music. Other such examples include (i) Adrian Batten's Short Service, paired with three of his full anthems, and (ii) Thomas Weelkes's 'Sixth' Service, paired with his verse anthem *Why art thou so sad?*.

298 *Further Commentaries*

verse services, so confirming their descriptions in the 'Batten' Organ Book and their order of composition.

A comparison of the layout of the four sets of evening canticles demonstrates that Tomkins adopted a consistent approach, as Table 18.1 shows. The settings are listed chronologically. The Fifth deviates most from the scheme and must surely have been composed some years after the other three Services. It features solo writing for a bass, quite probably with a specific singer in mind.

Table 18.1

MAGNIFICAT

Service	v. 1	vv. 2-3	v. 4	v. 5	v. 6	v. 7	v. 8	v. 9(a)	v. 9(b)	Glory be	As it was
'Sixth'	M+A	Ch	M+ MMA	Ch	MA	Ch	Ch	A+M AA	MM	A+M	Ch
'Seventh'	A+M A	Ch+A +Ch	SSAT	Ch	A+ MM	Ch	Ch	A	SSA A	Ch; 2x(V+ Ch)	Ch
Fourth	M+A	Ch	MT	Ch	MA AT	BB	Ch	MMT	MM TT	Ch	Ch
Fifth	B	Ch	MMA A	Ch	B	M AB	Ch	B	MM	Ch	Ch

NUNC DIMITTIS

Service	v. 1	v. 2	v. 3	v.4(a)	v. 4(b)	Glory be	As it was
'Sixth'	A	Ch	Ch	M	MMA+Ch	M+M	Ch
'Seventh'	M+MMA	Ch	V	Ch	V+Ch	2x(V+Ch) +V	Ch+2x(V+ Ch)
Fourth	M+MTBB	MMA T	A + MATB	Ch	MMAT+ Ch	A + Ch; V+Ch+V	Ch+A+Ch +V+Ch
Fifth	B+MAB	Ch	Ch	AA	MAAB	Ch	Ch

M: meane; A: counter-tenor; T: tenor; B: bass; V: verse (voice unknown); Ch: chorus

Sacred Music omitted from Musica Deo sacra

The allocation of solo material in the first three Services is strikingly similar, despite the Fourth being laid out on more elaborate lines. The increasingly dramatic role of the chorus, culminating in the Fifth Service, is an important feature. Tomkins's later penchant for melodic development by sequence is hardly evident in the two earlier Services but is an integral part of the Fifth. The composer's extensive use of head and tail motifs both within canticles and between the movements of his services – as with Weelkes[19] – is a technical device which performs an important integrating role.

Varia

Musica Deo sacra includes a set of Preces – but not Responses – which reworks a similar version found in manuscript sources. Both sets merit a place in the cathedral repertoire.

Seven metrical psalm tunes by Tomkins survive, of which five are included in *Musica Deo sacra*. Two others – *Dunfermline and Worcester* – appeared in early seventeenth-century published collections. In both, the melody is in the tenor, rather than the top part, reflecting this earlier practice. Tomkins probably composed the *Worcester* tune but it is likely that he provided only the harmonization of *Dunfermline*. The latter, associated with the Sternhold and Hopkins translations of Psalms 35 and 89, retains a certain currency.[20] *Worcester*, in triple time, was set for Psalms 13, 47 and 97. Tomkins's metrical psalm tunes may well have been written for the Sunday afternoon nave services, such as those held at Worcester Cathedral in the early seventeenth century.

The two Litany settings survive in the partbooks at Peterhouse, Cambridge. The first, for four voices (SATB), is based on the traditional 'plainsong' in the tenor, while, in the second (for SSATB), a less orthodox priest's 'singing part' gives rise to a more interesting setting.

The titles of several keyboard works by Tomkins[21] ('Offertory', 'Voluntary', etc.) indicate that they were written for the organ in a liturgical setting. Performers should be prepared to give due consideration to the transposition of such pieces. The pre-Restoration church organ was a transposing instrument, the music sounding a fifth lower than written, while account should also be taken of organ/church pitch in the early seventeenth century.[22]

---

[19] D. Brown (1969), *Thomas Weelkes*, London, 185.

[20] The melody (originally in the tenor part) is printed in *Hymns Ancient and Modern Revised* as Hymn 209.

[21] (i) Tuttle, *Musica Britannica*, V, and (ii) D. Stevens (ed. 1959), *Thomas Tomkins: Three hitherto unpublished Voluntaries (Fancies, Verses)*, Hinrichsen.

[22] Wulstan, 'The Problem of Pitch'. Although this matter is regarded by some as contentious, the writer considers that Wulstan's thesis regarding church pitch is strongly supported by well-established evidence about the pitch of church organs in Tomkins's day.

The character and texture of a work can be seriously distorted if it is performed at an inappropriate pitch.

The occasional nature of works such as *Dear Lord of life, Death is swallowed up* and *Know you not* probably accounts for their not being included in *Musica Deo sacra*. On the other hand, the omission of works such as *Jesus came when the doors were shut*, which was widely circulated in Tomkins's day, is less easy to explain. It can probably be assumed that its source material was quite simply not available when the task of assembling the 1668 collection was in hand. Much of this work must have taken place at Martin Hussingtree in the final decade of Tomkins's life, when he and his son, Nathaniel, would no doubt have discussed its format and content in detail. In the 1660s Nathaniel Tomkins's responsibilities as a canon of Worcester Cathedral would doubtless have left him little time or opportunity to amend or add to the scheme.

While *Musica Deo sacra* provides ample material for a study of Tomkins's sacred music, the works omitted from it have received less attention. *Dear Lord of life* and *Know you not* rank amongst his finest pieces, while the two unpublished early Verse Services help to provide a fascinating insight into the development of his verse-service technique. Such works bear further testimony to the stature of Tomkins's music, which occupies a distinguished place in an age of great musical achievement.

Chapter 19

Thomas Tomkins: Borrowings, Self-borrowings and Homage

David R.A. Evans

Thomas Tomkins, the most gifted member of a family of musicians, prospered under the patronage of the Anglican Church and the early Stuart kings. He was by inclination a royalist and it seems that he was clearly much in sympathy with the High Church policies of William Laud. Tomkins spent all his working life in the service of the Church, first at Worcester Cathedral and later at the Chapel Royal. For fifty years he was able to develop and refine his compositional style whilst writing the liturgical music expected of him by his employers. However, the onset of the Civil War brought the good times to an end and the cessation of choral services in the cathedrals after 1645 forced Tomkins into retirement.

He was fortunate to live through a period that has become generally known as the 'golden age of English music'. Religious reforms during the sixteenth century had obliged English composers to develop a new style of writing suitable for the Anglican liturgy. The majestic prose of the Book of Common Prayer and the Elizabethan Bible provided a great stimulus to a succession of gifted composers whose music for the new English services often matched the standard of their European contemporaries. Tallis and Byrd produced sacred and secular compositions in English while still maintaining their allegiance to the writing of music for the Catholic Church. The next generation of composers, led by Gibbons, Weelkes and Tomkins, were equally versatile, writing daring madrigals which sometimes showed the influence of the Italian style, and composing religious music using primarily English texts. Tomkins outlived his two major contemporaries by just over thirty years and therefore had every opportunity, had he wished, to develop his musical style in new directions.

The Baroque innovations of late sixteenth- and early seventeenth-century Italian music quickly became known in England, yet native composers were slow to incorporate elements of continental style into their works. The long-

---

My thanks are due to Dr Peter James, who read my typescript and made a number of valuable observations.

302 *Further Commentaries*

acknowledged English tendency to compromise led composers in Britain to accept some of the new Italian ideas and integrate them successfully with native elements of style.[1] Tomkins's music shows all these characteristics, and he was as comfortable writing under the influence of Italian chromaticism in *Know you not* or *Weep no more thou sorry boy* as he was in using the antique form of the *In nomine*. A study of his music reveals that the balance between the intellectual and the purely musical aspects of his style is finely poised; in this respect his music is similar to that of J.S. Bach. Despite writing some works which could be described as abstract, the great German master always remained fully aware of contemporary musical developments and incorporated some of these new elements into his style, whilst maintaining the best of the old. Tomkins did likewise during his middle years but regularly turned his attention to more cerebral forms of composition during the last period of his life, as did Bach when writing such masterworks as the *Musical Offering* and *The Art of Fugue*.

Tomkins's music, more than that of many other English composers of his day, displays the direct and indirect influences of his contemporaries. There are significant numbers of melodic fragments, harmonic progressions and rhythms found in Tomkins's compositions that seem to echo the works of others. In many cases it is impossible to say who imitated whom but it is clear that his teacher, William Byrd, must have had a powerful effect on Tomkins's musical thought at a vital stage of his development. Denis Stevens, writing almost fifty years ago, was one of the first to recognize the musical connection between the two: 'If Tomkins imitated anyone, it was William Byrd; but in modelling his style upon that of his master he brought certain new characteristics of harmony and figuration which are often more than enough to prove the power of his musical personality.'[2]

It has long been acknowledged that William Byrd had a formative influence on many of his younger English contemporaries. His music often provided a model for some, a touchstone for others, and his skill as a teacher directly affected the output of his most illustrious pupils Thomas Morley, Peter Philips, John Bull and above all Thomas Tomkins. The dedication attached to his madrigal *Too much I once lamented* (*Songs* of 1622) reads 'to my ancient and much reverenced master William Byrd'. This tantalizing piece of evidence provides proof of the nature of their relationship but little else. Anthony Boden has investigated Tomkins's apprenticeship with Byrd[3] and has constructed strong arguments to amplify the composer's statement. In the

---

[1] The tendency, and the musical hiatus which occurred during the Commonwealth period, held back the full development of the English Baroque until the restoration of the monarchy in 1660.

[2] Stevens, 154, and Chapter 15 above.

[3] See Chapter 4 above.

Borrowings, Self-borrowings, Homage 303

eighteenth century, knowledge of Byrd's activities as a teacher was still circulating; Sir John Hawkins informs us that 'Thomas Tomkins, Chanter of the choir at Gloucester, who discovered in his son a propensity for music, put him under the care of Byrd, by whose instructions he so profited'.[4]

The similarities of musical style of the two composers had been briefly noted by Fellowes in 1941 but a deeper investigation of the likeness was only undertaken by English musicologists later in the twentieth century, in particular Richard Turbet, Lionel Pike and John Irving. Editions of Tomkins's services and anthems which survive only in manuscript sources first appeared in Peter James's doctoral thesis and these have also greatly increased our knowledge of some of his earlier works, presumably written under the influence of Byrd.[5]

Opinion varies upon the degree of influence Byrd's music had on the compositional methods of Tomkins. It is clear that he returned to Byrd's works again and again to provide the starting point for new inspiration but in an age when emulation was common this was not surprising.[6] Perhaps the overpowering musical genius of the older composer had such a lasting effect upon his pupil that he was almost incapable of shaking it off.[7] The degree of correspondence of some of Tomkins's music with compositions by Byrd and others has raised some doubts concerning the consistency of Tomkins's inspiration. Comments regarding this issue range from those who favour the term 'homage' to accusations of plagiarism. The answer probably lies somewhere between the two and it should not be forgotten that it is easy to mistake the use of the musical *lingua franca* of the period for a form of cribbing.

Services

Edmund Fellowes's pioneering editions of English sixteenth- and early seventeenth-century music brought many of the treasures of the period to public attention during the first part of the twentieth century. In his

---

4 Sir John Hawkins (1776), *A General History of the Science and Practice of Music*, London, II, 507.

5 Peter H. James (1968), 'A Study of the Verse Anthem from Byrd to Tomkins', unpublished Ph.D. thesis, Cardiff University.

6 Craig Monson (1992), 'Throughout all generations: intimations of influence in the Short Service styles of Tallis, Byrd and Morley', *Byrd Studies*, ed. Alan W. Brown and Richard Turbet, Cambridge, 83–111.

7 Further evidence of Tomkins's admiration of Byrd's music is provided by the copy of the elder composer's *Exalt thyself, O God*, in Nathaniel Tomkins's handwriting, to be found in Worcester Cathedral Library. Peter James is of the opinion that it could have been written out in score form at his father's behest. See Chapter 18 and also the Preface to his edition of Byrd's anthem published by Cathedral Press.

important study *English Cathedral Music*, Fellowes's comments on Tomkins's music make it clear that he regarded the verse compositions as slightly inferior to those written in the older polyphonic style, a view refuted by more recent scholars. Nevertheless, his opinions were based on a sound knowledge of the composer's church music, and he seems to have been the first to draw attention to the likenesses in the service music of Byrd and his most illustrious pupil (see Exx. 19.1a and b).

> The opening phrase of the *Magnificat* (of the *Fourth Service*) is identical with that of Byrd's *Second Service*, and like Byrd, he assigned it to a solo voice …Tomkins's accompaniment of the phrase … compares unfavourably with that of Byrd; it is too florid to be satisfactory, for it becomes unduly important.[8]

This is probably the best known of Tomkins's quotations from Byrd's service music. Fellowes's statement is not strictly true, for the two phrases are not identical; in using a slightly modified version of Byrd's solo line, Tomkins was obviously paying a direct tribute to his 'much reverenced master'. He was, however, not alone in honouring the older composer in this way. Richard Turbet has identified links to the opening bars of the *Magnificat* and *Nunc Dimittis* of Byrd's Second Service in evening service settings by Morley,

Ex. 19.1a

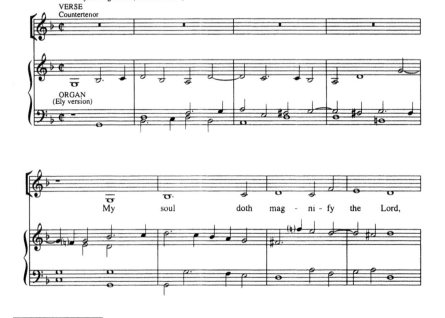

---

[8] Edmund H. Fellowes (1941), *English Cathedral Music*, London, 90.

Ex. 19.1b

Gibbons, Weelkes, Giles and Ward.[9] He also points out a number of connections with Tomkins's Fifth Service, in particular the use of the opening four notes of Byrd's melody as the motif which begins the *Magnificat*. This figure is also found, slightly modified, in the opening bars of the *Te Deum*, *Jubilate Deo* and *Nunc Dimittis* (see Ex. 19.2).

Tomkins's first two services are full settings in the 'short service' manner; his fourth, fifth, sixth and seventh services are compositions in the verse style. The Third Service however falls into the category of 'Great Service', although the work is not given this title in *Musica Deo sacra*.[10] The *Te Deum*, the first of the canticles set by Tomkins, begins with a modified restatement of the opening bars of Byrd's *Magnificat* from his 'Great' Service (Exx. 19.3a and b).[11]

---

[9] Richard Turbet (1988),'Homage to Byrd in Tudor Verse Services', *Musical Times* (September), 129 (1747): 485–90. For further comment regarding this issue, see Peter James (2001), 'The significance of Byrd's verse compositions: a re-appraisal', *Byrd Newsletter*, 4.

[10] Richard Turbet (1990), 'The Great Service: Byrd, Tomkins and their contemporaries, and the meaning of Great', *Musical Times* (May), 131 (1767): 275–7. See also Richard Turbet (1992), 'The Great Service: a postscript', *Musical Times* (April), 133 (1790): 206; and Lionel Pike (1992), 'The Great Service: Some observations on Byrd and Tomkins', *Musical Times* (August), 134 (1794): 421–2.

[11] Tomkins used the opening bars of Byrd's *Magnificat*, or variants of it, in a number of his anthems. Good examples can be found in *The Lord bless us*, and *O pray for the peace of Jerusalem* (verse version).

Ex. 19.2

Ex. 19.3a

Ex. 19.3b

In other places in the Third Service Tomkins uses bass lines derived from Byrd's 'Great' Service as starting points for new contrapuntal development. The most dramatic of these is Tomkins's reworking of 'he hath scattered the proud' from the *Magnificat* (Ex. 19.4b). Byrd's setting of these words (Ex. 19.4a) is an imitative treatment of a vigorous theme which vividly illustrates the text (theme x). Tomkins, using Byrd's motif, produces an equally impressive display of technical skill; the leaping theme is sung antiphonally between the two basses, whilst above, a complex web of thematically linked but looser counterpoint is heard.

Not all the correspondences are at points where the texts are the same in both works. The escape-note use of the dominant seventh at the concluding bars of 'Abraham and his seed for ever' in Byrd's *Magnificat* is mirrored by Tomkins's employment of the same feature in the final cadence of his setting of the words 'hath holpen his servant Israel'. Scalic movement found in the 'Gloria' of Byrd's *Nunc Dimittis* at the words 'world without end' is present in a modified form at 'as it was in the beginning' in Tomkins's version of the same canticle.

Byrd's 'Great' Service seems to have had a profound effect on his pupil, and the Third Service is surely Tomkins's attempt to emulate the achievements of his teacher. References to Byrd's masterwork can be found scattered throughout Tomkins's anthems but only occasionally does he allude to it in his other services. Perhaps the most obvious example is the connection between the opening section of the *Te Deum* of the Fourth Service and 'of thy people Israel' from the *Nunc Dimittis* of Byrd's service (Ex. 19.5a and b).

The *Nunc Dimittis* of the Fifth Service also shows Byrd's influence. The rising harmonic progression at the words 'for mine eyes have seen thy salvation' is surely a variant of the opening measures of the *Magnificat* of the 'Great' Service (Ex. 19.6).

Ex. 19.4a

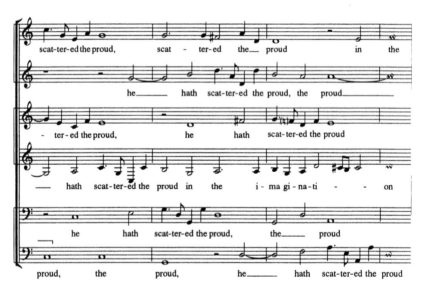

Ex. 19.4b

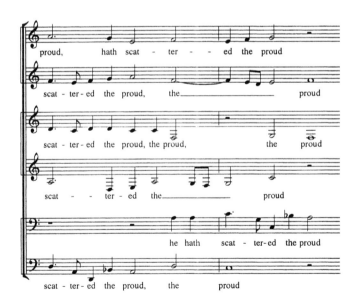

Ex. 19.5a and b

(a)

(b)

Ex. 19.5b concluded

Ex. 19.6

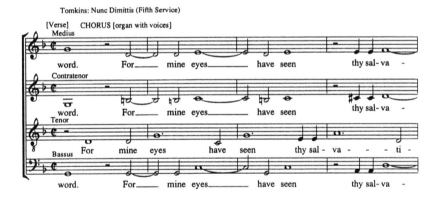

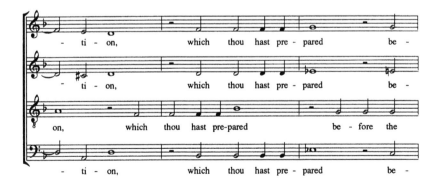

Ex. 19.6 concluded

Anthems

In common with most church composers of his generation Tomkins wrote full and verse anthems, and in both forms his debt to Byrd is once again apparent. Richard Turbet has pointed out the close correspondence between surviving full settings by both composers of words from Psalm 86, 'O God the proud are risen against me'.[12] The similarity between the opening contrapuntal points is striking and other passages of close comparison between the two works make it clear that Tomkins used Byrd's setting as his direct model. The splitting of the opening theme by the use of a rest was a device Tomkins also used to good effect at the beginning of another of his full anthems, *O God, wonderful art thou* (Ex. 19.7a and b).

Tomkins's consummate skill as a contrapuntalist is clearly displayed in *O God the proud are risen against me*. Even though he wrote many more verse than full anthems, some of his greatest achievements were composed in the older style. The emotional range of Tomkins's full anthems is wide, from deepest lamentation, in such works as *When David heard*, to the joyful exuberance of *O sing unto the Lord*. This wonderfully effective seven-part anthem shows Tomkins at the height of his powers, and yet it has many striking similarities to Weelkes's equally fine *O Lord arise into thy resting place*. Both works are scored for SSAATB, a vocal combination associated with compositions intended for the Chapel Royal. There are many musical parallels; the opening imitational point and its working-out are similar in both, and each composer sets the word 'alleluia' to harmonies which admit the clashing of major and minor thirds of chords in a characteristically English fashion. Weelkes's treatment of 'and thy saints sing with joyfulness' and

---

[12] Richard Turbet (1993), 'My Ancient and Much Reverenced Master', *Musical Times* (November), I (1): 15–17.

Ex. 19.7a and b

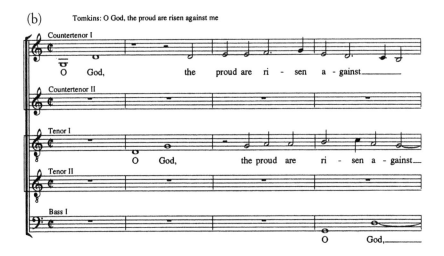

Ex. 19.7b concluded

Tomkins's of 'rejoice in him that made him' use closely matched dotted-note figures and the harmonic relationship of both passages is also immediately apparent when the two works are placed side by side (Ex. 19.8a and b).[13]

Sometimes the similarities between the full anthems of Tomkins and his contemporaries are more deeply hidden, yet detectable. The opening phrase of Tomkins's full anthem *O Praise the Lord* (*a* 5) echoes the harmony of Adrian Batten's first setting of the same words. *Have mercy upon me O God* uses two balanced homophonic phrases at the outset which are reminiscent of *Hear the prayers, O our God*, one of the service anthems for Batten's Full Service. The cumulative effect of the final section of *O God, wonderful art Thou* is achieved by the intensity of Tomkins's lengthy contrapuntal unfolding of the phrase 'he will give strength and power unto his people', and this passage could well have been modelled on the extended development of 'whosoever believeth in him' in Edmund Hooper's evocative anthem *Behold it is Christ*.[14] This work was one of the most popular anthems of the period and no doubt Tomkins knew it well. Similarly Richard Nicholson's effective setting of *O pray for the peace of Jerusalem* was clearly familiar to Tomkins and provided the impetus for his two settings of the text. The four-part full setting is curiously scored for SSTB and there is some internal evidence to suggest that the anthem once existed in a version for a larger number of voices. The unusually early restatement of the

---

[13] David Brown (1969), *Thomas Weelkes*, London, 155–6.

[14] The extended passage exploiting clashing major and minor thirds to be found at the words 'of thy Son Jesus Christ our Lord' in Tomkins's five-part full anthem *Almighty god the fountain of all wisdom* could also have been in emulation of the closing passage of Hooper's anthem, which makes considerable use of such false relationships.

Ex. 19.8a and b

opening theme in the fifth bar of the second medius part may indicate a possible reduction of parts from a version for five or more voices (Ex. 19.9a and b).

Tomkins's output includes fifty-four verse anthems, most of which owe their survival to the publication of *Musica Deo sacra*. He explored many avenues in this genre, developing to its limits the verse form he had inherited from Byrd, and showing great imagination in the setting of words. His choral scorings in the verse anthems are richly varied, and in his more dramatic solo writing he anticipated some of the declamatory gestures of the Restoration period. The verse anthems also betray Tomkins's wide knowledge of the music of his contemporaries, and there are a number of correspondences with their music, both sacred and secular. *Out of the deep*, an atmospheric setting of Psalm 130, contains a direct quotation from the concluding bars of Gibbons's madrigal, *The Silver Swan* (Ex. 19.10a and b).

Dowland's oft-quoted *Lachrymae Pavan* is briefly referred to in *Hear my prayer, O Lord* at the words 'Hold not thy peace at my tears' and the passage 'O spare me a little' has a number of similarities to the treatment of a distinctive sequential theme found in both Gibbons's *Behold thou hast made my days* and Batten's *Out of the deep*.

Hooper's fine full anthem *Behold it is Christ* clearly capivated Tomkins, and echoes of it appear in a significant number of his works, including his own verse setting of the same text. One of the themes, at the words 'whosoever believeth in him', is a thinly disguised version of Hooper's melody (Ex. 19.11a and b).

There are occasions where Tomkins's debt to earlier models relates not only to themes but to structure. His setting of *Christ rising again* follows Byrd's version in nearly every detail; the division of the text into solo and chorus sections is the same in both, and a careful comparison of the two anthems shows that Tomkins must have used his teacher's work as a template. Minor details in both pieces show similarities of approach; compare for example the setting of the words 'Death from henceforth' and 'So by Christ', where both

316   *Further Commentaries*

Ex. 19.9a and b

(a)
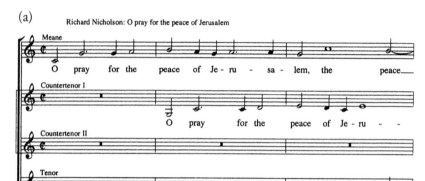

(b)

Ex. 19.9b   concluded

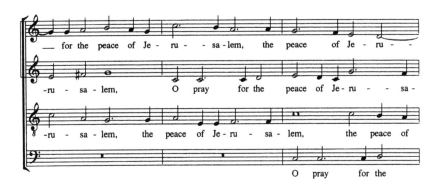

Ex. 19.10a and b

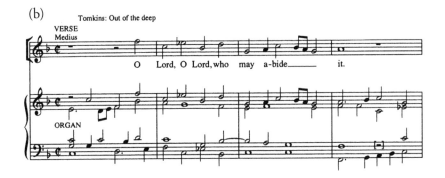

Ex. 19.11a and b

composers use distinctive declamatory phrases divided by rests. In the concluding chorus Tomkins copies Byrd's use of a syncopated rhythm at the words 'restored to life'.[15]

Self-borrowings

The most notable of Tomkins's self-borrowings are associated with his *Songs* of 1622. Whole pieces from his madrigal publication appear in *Musica Deo sacra* with alternative texts, but the success of these adaptations in some cases is questionable. The final piece in his collection of madrigals, *Turn unto the Lord*, dedicated to his son Nathaniel, is based on a text which for the most part draws upon the fourth verse of Psalm 100. Coincidentally, this psalm is also used as the text of the Anglican canticle for morning service entitled *Jubilate Deo*. Tomkins's intense sacred madrigal is of such quality that it is no great surprise to find its musical material employed to great effect in another of his major compositions. All but the concluding bars of his sacred madrigal, with minor rhythmic alterations, also appear in the *Jubilate Deo* of the Third Service, beginning at the words 'for the Lord is gracious', and this passage, containing some of Tomkins's most well-wrought counterpoint, provides a serious note in an otherwise lively setting of the canticle (Ex. 19.12a and b).[16]

It is not clear which of the two works came first but the deployment of the shared material in both was entirely successful. However, two other adaptations found in *Musica Deo sacra* proved to be less effective. The music of his five-part madrigal *See, see the shepherd's queen* appears transformed into a strange version of the Anglican *Sanctus* from the communion service. *Holy,*

---

[15] Byrd's anthem also provided the inspiration for settings of *Christ rising again* by Weelkes and Batten.

[16] Such lengthy borrowing of material is comparatively rare in English music of the period. Another example of this practice can be found in Thomas Weelkes's Service 'for trebles', where the composer incorporates large sections of music directly derived from his five-part full anthem *Alleluia, I heard a voice*.

Ex. 19.12a and b

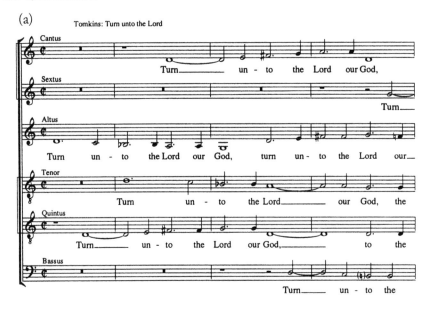

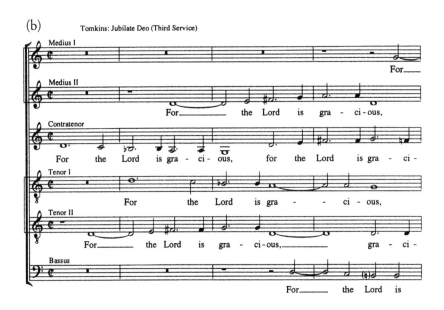

holy, holy is a clumsy adaptation; the tripartite text of the *Sanctus* partially matches all three sections of the madrigal but the original *fa-las* are sung to an interpolated 'Alleluia', which do not form any part of the original liturgical text. It is clear however that *Holy, holy, holy* was never intended as a movement for use in the communion, for it is given a place alongside the anthems in *Musica Deo sacra*. Surprisingly the madrigalian notation of the original is retained, whereas the majority of the compositions in Tomkins's collection are written out in the longer note-values usually reserved for church music. Its appearance in this form, as well as the awkwardness of the word-setting, raises some doubts as to whether the composer was responsible for the adaptation. Perhaps Nathaniel Tomkins hurriedly transformed the madrigal when *Musica Deo sacra* was being prepared for publication, including it to provide an additional jubilant full anthem for a collection where settings of more reflective texts predominate. The appearance of the madrigal adaptations at the end of each partbook in *Musica Deo Sacra* seems to add weight to this suggestion.

When I observe, one of the six-part madrigals included in the *Songs*, also appears as a contrafactum in *Musica Deo sacra*. Its transformation into *Who shall ascend the hill of God* is quite literal. There are very few notational differences from the madrigal, but the fitting of the new text to the music is most awkward in places. This adaptation is even less successful than *Holy, holy, holy* and it may well be that its inclusion in the posthumous collection of Tomkins's church music was not sanctioned by him.

A small number of Tomkins's other compositions also show evidence of adaptation. His only Latin motet, *Domine, tu eruisti animam* is provided with an alternative English text, *Why art thou so full of heaviness, O my soul*. The quality of the word underlay of the English version in *Musica Deo sacra* is poor whereas the Latin text fits the music perfectly. Consequently it can be assumed that the Latin version is the original and that the English text may well have been added later, perhaps by Nathaniel, for inclusion in the publication of his father's works.[17] Peter Le Huray has suggested that two of Tomkins's three-part anthems, *O Lord, how glorious are thy works*, and *The hills stand about Jerusalem*, have many features which indicate that they both may be contrafacta of madrigals now lost.[18]

One of the most poignant phrases in the whole of Tomkins's music is that which opens his madrigal *Too much I once lamented*. This clever use of a semitonal phrase and its inversion, combined with a rare appearance of the chord of the diminished seventh, possibly derives from the first bars of Weelkes's masterpiece, *O care, thou wilt despatch me*. Even if this arresting passage did not

---

[17] David Wulstan (ed., 1971), *An Anthology of English Church Music*, London, 106–15 and 155–6.
[18] Le Huray and Irving, 'Thomas Tomkins', *Grove 7* (2001), xxv, 571.

originally come from Tomkins's pen, he made it very much his own, and it recurs regularly throughout his music, generally in places where the text calls for the most personal response from the composer. The earliest appearance of one of its forms is found in his madrigal *The fauns and satyrs tripping*,[19] and two of Tomkins's most striking uses of it occur in his tribute to Prince Henry, *Know you not*,[20] and also in the opening bars of his supreme essay in lamentation, *When David heard that Absalom was slain*. The phrase had so much resonance for the composer that he found it impossible not to include it in his tombeau for Charles I, *A sad pavan for these distracted times* (Ex. 19.13a and b).[21]

Ex. 19.13a and b

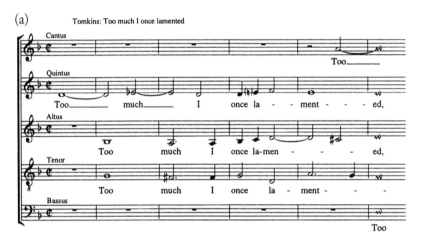

---

[19] Stevens, 98.
[20] Found at the words 'Sigh and say, sob and sing'.
[21] An appearance of this phrase, with its attendant harmonies can be found in the *Nunc Dimittis* of William Deane's Short Service. This and other compositional features in the work show the direct influence of Tomkins's style.

322 *Further Commentaries*

Homage in his madrigals

Although Tomkins could be regarded as a late entrant into the field of madrigal publication his contribution to the genre was surely one of the most distinguished. His *Songs*, which appeared in 1622, are almost the swansong of the short but brilliant period of English madrigal composition, which included printed collections of the highest quality from Wilbye, Weelkes and Gibbons. The madrigals found in his *Songs* represent almost his entire output. Only three others survive: an early work, *The fauns and satyrs tripping*, his single contribution to Thomas Morley's *The Triumphs of Oriana* (1601?) and two sacred madrigals, *Dear Lord of life* and *From deepest horror of sad penitence* which were copied by Thomas Myriell.[22]

Tomkins's madrigal collection reveals much about the composer's life and times. All those who were closest to him were remembered therein, for he dedicated each of the twenty-eight madrigals to a friend, relative or colleague. Tomkins took this opportunity to pay direct homage to three of his illustrious dedicatees, the composers Dowland, Daniel and Ward, by making reference to their best-known works.

Dowland's *Lachrymae Pavan*, which the composer recast as a lute song to the words *Flow my Tears*, was probably the most widely known English song of the early seventeenth century. Its melancholy vocal lines and evocative harmonies, which set off the dark nature of the text, caught the imagination of the time, and echoes of it appear in the music of many of Dowland's contemporaries. Tomkins and Gibbons both included references to it in their church music, and the opening of Bennet's well-known madrigal *Weep O mine eyes* is deeply indebted to Dowland's song.

In Tomkins's collection, two of his madrigals have close connections to it. *O let me live for true love* is dedicated to 'Doctor Douland', and in its sustained opening bars Tomkins makes use of the melody of *Flow my Tears*, clothed round with a subtle reharmonization, equalling the original in its level of pathos. Tomkins's madrigal is a tragic ballett, cast in three distinct sections, where lines of the poetic text alternate with *fa-las*. Tomkins makes reference to the *Lachrymae* theme on three separate occasions in the madrigal, the third entry beginning most effectively in the sub-mediant major.

The madrigal which follows it, *O let me die for true love*, is dedicated to another fine composer of lute songs, John Daniel, and is clearly marked 'the second part'. Peter Warlock was of the opinion that the pair of madrigals had been dedicated to Dowland and Daniel 'as though he (Tomkins) would name them together as the two greatest living masters of accompanied song among his fellow countrymen'.[23] In view of the references to Dowland's song in *O let*

---

[22] See James, p. 288 above.
[23] Peter Warlock (1926), *The English Ayre*, London, 52.

me live for true love, quotations from Daniel's music might have been expected in its companion piece. None are immediately apparent, but three appearances of Dowland's *Lachrymae* theme are easily discernible. However, there is a hidden link, for Daniel's fine song *Eyes, look no more* is closely modelled on the tripartite structure of *Flow my Tears*, and he weaves a number of references to it into his music. By using Dowland's theme, Tomkins is therefore able to honour Daniel without upsetting the overall thematic unity which binds the two madrigals together.

Oft did I marle is dedicated to his contemporary John Ward, whose only collection of madrigals appeared in 1613. The quality of Ward's six-part compositions in his *First Set of Madrigals* has long been recognized, and in them he displays an idiosyncratic use of suspensions and also a tendency to write passages based on cantus firmus-like melodic lines. In recognition of this tendency, Tomkins, himself an accomplished writer in the cantus firmus style, models a passage of his madrigal ('Each seeks the hurt and spoil of either') on a section from Ward's *Out from the vale*, where the music to the words 'Which Daphne's cruelty hath lost' is developed over an ascending bass line written in long values.

Tomkins's knowledge of the repertoire of the music of his own day must have been considerable. His annotations on the Paris Conservatoire MS Réserve 1122, for example, show the level of his knowledge of the keyboard music of his contemporaries.[24] Some evidence remains concerning the size of his personal collection of music, and a few of these manuscripts have survived.[25] It is also possible that one major manuscript of church music, the so-called 'Batten' organ book, also circulated within the family.[26] His work at the Chapel Royal and Worcester gave him daily contact with a large body of sacred music, much of which was contemporary. It is therefore not surprising that some of this music became part of his musical language, but not all of Tomkins's borrowings can be explained away as aspects of the general style of the period. There are too many close parallels to specific pieces by other composers to be mere coincidence. Edmund Fellowes, commenting on Tomkins's use of a melody from Byrd's *Second Service*, stated that 'this is a curious plagiarism whether committed consciously or not'.[27] Could it have

---

[24] Stephen Tuttle (ed., 1964), 'Thomas Tomkins: Keyboard Music' *Musica Britannica*, V, 157–8.

[25] The manuscripts concerned are; Paris Conservatoire MS Rés.1122; BL Add. MS 29996; Bodleian Library, Oxford MS Mus.Sch.C.93; Magdalen College, Oxford, annotations to Tomkins's own copy of Morley's *A Plain and Easy introduction to Practical Music*.

[26] David Evans (1987/8), 'John Tomkins and the Batten Organ Book', *Welsh Music/Cerddoriaeth Cymru*, 8 (7): 13–22.

[27] Fellowes, *English Cathedral Music*.

324 *Further Commentaries*

been that Tomkins sometimes had problems with the invention of original material but no difficulty with reworking and generally improving ideas derived, to a greater or lesser extent, from others? If so, he showed the same tendencies as Handel, who borrowed heavily from lesser composers, always greatly enhancing the originals as a result of his considerable technical skills. Also, in common with Handel, Tomkins indulged in some self-borrowing, although doubt has been raised as to whether he was the instigator of some of the surviving contrafacta. Those 'borrowings' to be found in the *Songs* are however outright examples of direct homage, and the dedication of an entire set of pieces to friends and colleagues, although unusual in his own day, has been paralleled in the twentieth century by Herbert Howells in his collections *Lambert's Clavichord* and *Howells' Clavichord.*

Tomkins's compositional abilities were undoubtedly of the first order, yet despite the discernible tendencies towards Baroque style which can be observed in some of his verse anthems, his sphere of musical influence during his own lifetime seems to have been limited. It is not known if he took composition pupils, and few composers seem to have drawn on aspects of his style for their inspiration. Some features of Tomkins's methods have been observed in the music of William Child but this is not surprising in view of the possible links between the Child family and the composer.[28] In fact the musically gifted sons of Thomas Tomkins the elder – Thomas, John, Giles and Robert – all rose to prominent positions in musical circles, yet what influence they had seems to have died with them. Thomas's longevity placed him in a position to sum up the achievement of a glittering generation. His late keyboard works, some of which hark back to the strict contrapuntal forms of his youth, bring the late flowering of the English Renaissance to a close. It is however not without justification that he was described in his own day as a 'golden' musician.[29]

---

[28] See Chapter 6 above.

[29] Charles Butler (1636), *The Principles of Music,* quoted in M.C. Boyd (1962), *Elizabethan music and musical criticism,* Philadelphia, 88.

List of Works and their Sources

The List of Works starts on p. 331. For the abbreviations in column 2 ('MS sources') refer to the list of MS sources below; for the abbreviations in the third column ('Printed editions') refer to the list of publications on pp. 327–330.

Sources

MS Sources: Manuscripts Containing Music by Thomas Tomkins

Reference Number	Manuscript reference	Place
1	MS 1, Ely Cathedral Library	Ely
5	MS 5, Ely Cathedral Library	Ely
6	Mus. MS 6, Christ Church Library	Oxford
20	MS f.20–24, Bodleian Library	Oxford
23	MS 23 H 13, Fitzwilliam Museum	Cambridge
23Rw	MS Rawl. poet.23 (texts), Bodleian Library	Oxford
24	RM 24 d 3, British Library (Will Foster's Virginal Book)	London
28	MS 28, Ely Cathedral Library	Ely
30	MS 30 G 10, Fitzwilliam Museum	Cambridge
32	MS 32 G 29, Fitzwilliam Museum (Fitzwilliam Virginal Book)	Cambridge
61	Mus. MS 61–6, Christ Church Library	Oxford
64	MS Mus. Sch. C 64–9, Bodleian Library	Oxford
88	Mus. MS 88, Christ Church Library	Oxford
93	MS Mus. Sch. C 93, Bodleian Library	Oxford
180	MS 180, St John's College Library	Oxford
181	MS 181, St John's College Library	Oxford
212	MS Mus. Sch. D 212–16, Bodleian Library	Oxford
245	MS Mus. Sch. D 245–7, Bodleian Library	Oxford
341	MS Z.3.4. (1–6), Marsh's Library	Dublin
347	MS Z.3.4. (7–12), Marsh's Library	Dublin

326　　　　　　　　　　*List of Works and their Sources*

Reference Number	Manuscript reference	Place
437	Mus. MS 437, Christ Church Library	Oxford
530	G.5.30, Peterhouse Library	Cambridge
616	RCM MS 616, Royal College of Music	London
645	M2 C 645 Case B, The General Library, University of California	Berkeley
698	Mus. MSS 698–707, Christ Church Library	Oxford
764	MS 764, Lambeth Palace	London
791	Tenbury MS 791, Bodleian Library	Oxford
1001	Mus. MS 1001, Christ Church Library	Oxford
1002	Mus. MS 1002, Christ Church Library	Oxford
1004	Tenbury MS 1004, Bodleian Library	Oxford
1018	Mus. MS 1018–20, Christ Church Library	Oxford
1021	Tenbury MS 1021, Bodleian Library	Oxford
1045	RCM MSS 1045–51, Royal College of Music	London
1113	Mus. MS 1113, Christ Church Library	Oxford
1122	Réserve 1122, Bibliothèque Nationale	Paris
1220	Mus. MS 1220–24, Christ Church Library	Oxford
1227	Mus. MS 1227, Christ Church Library	Oxford
1303	Tenbury MS 1303, Bodleian Library	Oxford
1382	Tenbury MS 1382, Bodleian Library	Oxford
2039	RCM MS 2039, Royal College of Music	London
3665	Egerton MS 3665, British Library	London
4076	RCM MS 4076, Royal College of Music	London
4078	RCM MS 4078, Royal College of Music	London
4080	RCM MS 4080, Royal College of Music	London
4081	RCM MS 4081, Royal College of Music	London
4087	RCM MS 4087, Royal College of Music	London
4142	Harley MS 4142, British Library	London
4180	Drexel MSS 4180–85, Public Library	New York
5469	Drexel MS 5469, Public Library	New York
5611	Drexel MS 5611, Public Library	New York
5612	Drexel MS 5612, Public Library	New York
6346	Harley MS 6346, British Library	London
7337	Harley MS 7337, British Library	London
7339	Harley MS 7339, British Library	London
11587	Add MS 11587, British Library	London
17784	Add MS 17784, British Library	London
17786	Add MS 17786–91, British Library	London
17792	Add MS 17792–6, British Library	London

29289	Add MS 29289, British Library	London
29366	Add MS 29366, British Library	London
29372	Add MS 29372–7, British Library	London
29427	Add MS 29427, British Library	London
29996	Add MS 29996, British Library	London
30478	Add MS 30478–9, British Library	London
30826	Add MS 30826–8, British Library	London
31421	Add MS 31421, British Library	London
31443	Add MS 31443, British Library	London
R	'Jo: Wythie his Booke', Sibley Music Library, Eastman School of Music, Rochester	New York State
N	MS Mus. Res. MN2 (Chirk), Public Library	New York

SEVENTEENTH-CENTURY partbooks or scores in college, cathedral or chapel libraries, other than those included above, are shown by the following sigla:

d	Durham Cathedral	pt	Peterhouse Library, Cambridge
g	Gloucester Cathedral	wi	St George's Chapel, Windsor
h	Hereford Cathedral	w	Worcester Cathedral
l	Lichfield Cathedral	y	York Minster
pl	St Paul's Cathedral, London	pe	Pembroke College Library, Cambridge

Unpublished transcriptions:

c   R.W. Cavanaugh, *The Anthems in Musica Deo sacra by Thomas Tomkins*. University Microfilms, Doctoral Dissertation Series, No. 5649. (1953).

r   A. Ramsbotham, *Musica Deo sacra*, scored for projected second series of *Tudor Church Music*. (London University Music Library).

Early Printed Books Containing Music by Thomas Tomkins

1601   *The Triumphs of Oriana* (Thomas Morley, editor), London: Cambridge University Library; British Library, London; Royal College of Music, London; Bodleian Library, Oxford (3 copies); Christ Church Library, Oxford.

1610   *Opusculum neuer Pavanen, Galliarden, Couranten und Volten. Auf allerhand musikalischen Instrumenten sonderlich auf Violen zu gebrach* (Thomas Simpson, editor), Frankfurt: Öffentliche

328   *List of Works and their Sources*

Wissenschaftliche Bibliothek, Berlin; Staats- und Univesitäts-
Bibliothek, Hamburg; Bibliothek des germanischen Museums,
Nuremberg.

1622   *Songs of 3.4.5. and 6. Parts*, London: British Library, London;
Royal College of Music, London; Bodleian Library, Oxford (2
copies); Christ Church Library, Oxford; Huntington Library, San
Marino, California.

1668   *Musica Deo sacra et ecclesiae Anglicanae: or Music dedicated to the
Honour and service of God, and to the Use of Cathedral and other
Churches of England, especially of the Chapel Royal of King Charles
the First*, London: Bodleian Library, Oxford; British Library,
London; Cambridge University Library; Christ Church Library,
Oxford (2 copies); Gloucester Cathedral; Huntington Library, San
Marino, California; Royal College of Music, London; Henry
Watson Library, Manchester; St David's Cathedral; St John's
College, Oxford; St Paul's Cathedral, London; Worcester
Cathedral.

In addition, the texts of many anthems by Tomkins were published in James
Clifford, *The Divine Services and Anthems usually sung in the Cathedrals and
Collegiate Choirs of the Church of England* (1663; 2/1664). See also sigla D
and Ra in the following section.

Key to List of Printed Editions of Music by Thomas Tomkins

CHURCH MUSIC

Sacred works by Tomkins are to be found in the following editions, the list of
which is not exhaustive:

A   Sir Ivor Atkins (Novello; Oxford University Press)
AM   *Anthems for Men's Voices* (OUP), ed. Peter Le Huray, Nicholas
        Temperley, Peter Trenchell and David Willcocks (1965)
B   William Boyce, *Cathedral Music*, revised and augmented by Joseph
        Warren (1849)
Br   Broude Brothers (New York), ed. R. Hickok (1954)
C   *Recent Researches in the Music of the Renaissance*, vol. 4, ed. R.
        Cavanaugh (1968)
Ch   J. and W. Chester, ed. Peter James (1971)

CM	The Church Music Society (distributor: OUP)
D	*The CL Psalms of David* (1615)
E	*The English Madrigal School*, revised as *The English Madrigalists*, vol. 18 (Stainer & Bell) ed. E.H. Fellowes (1922), rev. T. Dart (1960)
F	*Five Consort Anthems* (Fretwork Editions), ed. D. Pinto and R.W. Duffin (1994)
H	*Historical Anthology of Music* (Harvard Univ. Press, Cambridge, Mass.), vol. 1, ed. A.T. Davison and W. Apel (1947)
J	*The Choral Responses and Litanies of the United Church of England and Ireland*, ed. J. Jebb (1847)
Ja	Cathedral Press, ed. Peter James
M	*Musica Deo sacra* (1668)
Nov	*Novello Early English Music*, General Editor: Watkins Shaw (1970)
O	F.A.G. Ousley, *Cathedral Services* (1873)
OA	Oxford Anthems Series (OUP)
OU	Oxford University Press, ed. Bernard Rose (1959)
P	Parish Choir Book (Novello)
Ra	T. Ravenscroft, *The Whole Book of Psalms* (1621)
Rg	Rongwen Music (New York), ed. K. Stone
Ro	Early English Church Music, vols. 5, 9, 14, 27, 37 and 39, contain all the anthems of Thomas Tomkins included in *Musica Deo sacra* ed. Bernard Rose (Stainer & Bell)
S	*Songs of 3.4.5. and 6. Parts* (1622)
Sch	Schott and Co. (London)
Schi	G. Schirmer (New York), ed. C.F. Simkins
St	Denis Stevens (ed.), Anthems from *Musica Deo sacra* (Hinrichsen; Concordia Publishing House; or C.F. Peters (New York))
T	*Tudor Church Music* (Oxford University Press), ed. A. Ramsbotham (1928) and others subsequently
T8	*Tudor Church Music*, Octavo edition (Oxford University Press)
Tr	*The Treasury of English Music* (Blandford Press), vol. 2, ed. Peter Le Huray (1965)

SECULAR VOCAL MUSIC

E	E.H. Fellowes (ed.), rev. T. Dart, *The English Madrigal School*, revised as *The English Madrigalists*, vol. 18 (Stainer & Bell, 1922, 2/1960)
EU	Euterpe Series (Oxford University Press)
GW	W.S. Gwynn Williams (Gwynn Publishing Company)
OR	Oriana Series (Novello)

330 *List of Works and their Sources*

S   *Songs of 3.4.5. and 6. Parts* (1622)
TO   *The Triumphs of Oriana* (1601), also as edited by E.H. Fellowes (Stainer & Bell)
SWB   W. Barclay Squire, *Ausgewählte Madrigale* (Breitkopf)

KEYBOARD MUSIC

M5   *Musica Britannica*, vol. V (1955, 2/1964) is devoted to the keyboard music of Thomas Tomkins ed. Stephen D. Tuttle (Stainer & Bell). Individual works are also to be found in the following editions, the list of which is not exhaustive:

AP   André Pirro, *L'Art des organistes*, in Lavingnac's *Encyclopédie de la musique*, ii, 2
FB   *Fitzwilliam Virginal Book*, ed. Maitland and Squire (Breitkopf)
FD   Frank Dawes, *Two Elizabethan Keyboard Duets*, Early Keyboard Music, Book 4 (Schott)
HM   Hugh M. Miller, *The Earliest Keyboard Duets*, in *Musical Quarterly*, 29 (1943), 439
MG   Margaret Glyn, *Thirty Virginal Pieces* (Stainer & Bell)

CONSORT MUSIC

M59   *Musica Britannica*, vol. LIX (1992) is devoted to the consort music of Thomas Tomkins ed. John Irving (Stainer & Bell). Individual works are also to be found in the following editions, the list of which is not exhaustive:

M9   *Musica Britannica*, vol. IX (1955, 2/1962), ed. Thurston Dart and William Coates (Stainer & Bell)
EHF   E.H. Fellowes (Stainer & Bell)
H   Hinrichsen Edition (London)
He   Heinrichshofen, Consortium Edition
Mo   H. Moeck Verlag series *Zeitschrift fur Spielmusik*
IP   *Cambridge Consorts* (Corda Music), edited by Ian Payne
Sch   Schott and Co. (London)
TS   Thomas Simpson, *Opusculum neuer Pavanen* ... (1610)
VGS   Viola da Gamba Society Publications

List of Works

SERVICES

Title (Verse services *italicized*)	MS sources	Printed editions	Remarks
First (Venite, Te Deum, Benedictus, Kyrie, Creed, Magnificat, Nunc Dimittis)	d p y 28 88 180 437 1220 29289	B M O P T Nov	p has an extra copy of *Kyrie* (K); Nov and P contain (M N) only
Second (Venite, Te Deum, Jubilate, Kyrie, Creed, Magnificat, Nunc Dimittis)	y 181 1002	A M T CM	A contains (T J M N) only; CM contains (M N) only, edited by Watkins Shaw; y lacks (V)
Third (T J M N)	791	M T T8	Called 'Mr. Tomkins's Great Service' in 791, which has (T J) only
Fourth (T M N)	791 g	M T Ja Tr	Tr contains (N) only, edited by J. Morehen; Ja contains (M N) only
Fifth (T J M N)		M T OU	OU contains (M N) only
Sixth * (M N)	d 791	Ja	incomplete; Ja reconstructed

332 *List of Works and their Sources*

Title	MS sources	Printed editions	Remarks
Seventh * (M N)	791	Ja	incomplete; Ja reconstructed

* Denis Stevens's numbering.

PRECES AND PSALMODY

Title	MS sources	Printed editions	Remarks
Preces	p 180	J M T CM	Two versions of Preces: (a) in 180, J, M, and T; (b) in p
Responses	p	J CM	
First Litany	p	J	
Second Litany ('Common Litany')	p	J	
Ps. 47: O clap your hands	180 764	M T	Whitsunday
Ps. 15: Lord who shall dwell	180 764	M T	Ascension
Psalm tunes:			
Dunfermline	31421	D Ra C	
Martyrs	r	M C	
Old 113th	r	M C	
St David's	r	M C	
Windsor	r	M C	
Worcester	31421	D Ra C	
York	r	M C	

List of Works and their Sources 333

ANTHEMS

Title (Verse anthems *italicized*)	MS sources	Printed editions	Remarks
Above the stars my saviour dwells	d g pe r wi y 180 212 328 764 791 1220 4142 6346 17784 30478	M Ro T F St	212 includes string parts T edited by John Milsom
Almighty and everlasting God we humbly beseech Thy majesty	d r 23Rw 180 791 1220 6346 30478	M Ro	Purification; listed as a full anthem in 6346*
Almighty and everlasting God which hatest nothing that Thou hast made	c r 181 1045 6346	M B St Ro	Ash Wednesday
Almighty God the fountain of all wisdom	r d g y pl 20 23Rw 181 645 764 1004 1382 4142 4180	M Ro Sch	'A collect after the Offertory' (6346); Sch edited by B. Still

Title	MS sources	Printed editions	Remarks
	5469		
	6346		
	7337		
	17792		
	30478		
	31443		
Almighty God which [who] hast instructed	r 181 791 6346 30478	M Ro	St Mark
Almighty God which hast knit together	d p r 23Rw 181 30478	M Ro	All Saints
Almighty God who hast given	r 180	M Ro	Christmas
Almighty God whose praise this day	r 181	M Ro	Holy Innocents
Arise O Lord and have mercy	r 6346	M Ro	
Arise O Lord God lift up thy hand	c r	M Ro	
Arise O Lord into thy resting place	r 23Rw 6346	M Ro Tr	
Awake up my glory	r	M Ro	
Be strong and of good courage	r	M	Coronation of James I

List of Works and their Sources

335

Title	MS sources	Printed editions	Remarks
Behold I bring you glad tidings; Glory to be God in the highest	c r 5 791	M Ro C	Christmas; 5 contains second part only
Behold it is Christ	r	M Ro	
Behold the hour cometh	p r	M Ro Sch	Sch edited by Bernard Rose
Blessed be the Lord God of Israel	d p r 23Rw 180 791 1220 4142 6346 30478	M Ro	Listed as a full anthem in 6346; anon. in 328
Blessed is he that considereth [O Lord graciously accept]	r	M	
Blessed is he whose unrighteousness	c r	M Ro C AM	Penitential Psalm 2
Christ rising again from the dead	r 181 791	M Ro	Easter
Come let us go up	r	M Ro	
Deal with me O Lord	r	M Ro	

336 *List of Works and their Sources*

Title	MS sources	Printed editions	Remarks
Dear lord of life	r 61		r gives parts only, no score
Death is swallowed up	1382 5469	Ja	incomplete; Ja reconstructed
Deliver me from mine enemies	r 30478	M Ro	
From deepest horror of sad penitence	29372		
Give ear unto my words; My voice shalt thou hear	r	M AM Ro	for men's voices AM contains (Part II) only
Give sentence with me O God	d p r 180 791 6346 30478	M Ro	
Glory be to God on high	c r 791 1382	M Ro	*Gloria in excelsis Deo*
Glory be to the Father	r	M Ro	
God who as at this time	p r 181 791	M Ro St	Whitsunday
Grant us, gracious Lord,	6346		text only; 'For the Communion'
Great and marvellous are thy works	r	M P T8 Ro T	T edited by J. Scott

List of Works and their Sources

337

Title	MS sources	Printed editions	Remarks
Have mercy	r 1382	M Ro	
Have mercy upon me O God	c r	M C OA AM	Penitential Psalm 4
Have mercy upon me O God	698		incomplete ‡
He that hath pity on the poor	r	M P Ro	
Hear me when I call	r	M Ro	
Hear my prayer O good Lord	r 791	M Ro	Verses for 2 countertenors
Hear my prayer, O Lord	r 23Rw 791 6346	M Ro	Verses for medius and bass
Hear my prayer O Lord	c r	M C Ro AM	Penitential Psalm 5
Hear my prayer O Lord	c r	M C Ro	Penitential Psalm 7
Holy holy holy Lord God	r 1382	M Ro	*Sanctus*, with *Alleluias*
I am the resurrection; I heard a voice from heaven	r	A M Ro	For the Burial Service; A contains (Part II) only
I have gone astray	r	M Ro	
I will lift up mine eyes	r 791 6346	M Ro	(=*My help cometh*)

List of Works and their Sources

Title	MS sources	Printed editions	Remarks
It is my well-beloved's voice	62 616 4080 29372 29427	E S	Dedicated to Theolphilus Aylmer. A sacred text but not intended for liturgical use.
Jesus came when the doors were shut	d p r y 181 23Rw 791 6346 30478	Ja	St Thomas. r gives parts only, no score
Know you not	r 61 698 1382 5469	Ch	r gives cantus only, from 61. Funeral anthem for Prince Henry
Leave O my soul	r 791	M Ro	
Lord enter not into Judgement	r 1382 17792	M Ro	
Merciful Lord we beseech thee	r 182	M Ro	St John
My beloved spake	p r y 23Rw 791 6346	M Ro Sch	Sch edited by Bernard Rose
My dwelling is above	23Rw 791 6346		incomplete

List of Works and their Sources 339

Title	MS sources	Printed editions	Remarks
My shepherd is the living Lord	r 4142 17784 30478	M Ro St	'Psalm 23 of the ordinary metre' (M)
Not in the merits of what I have done	r 791	M Ro	791 has *Stripped of my merits*
O be favourable unto Zion	r	M Ro	
O give thanks unto the Lord	r	M T8 Ro	for men's voices
O God the heathen are come into thine inheritance	698		incomplete ‡
O God the proud are risen against me	c r 5 23Rw 181 645 1382 6346 7339	M	645 contains two different settings
O God wonderful art thou	c r	M T T8 Ro	
O how amiable are thy dwellings	r	M Ro CM	for men's voices
O Israel if thou return	r	M	
O Lord do away as the night	r	M Ro	
O Lord God of hosts	r	M Ro	

Title	MS sources	Printed editions	Remarks
O Lord God of hosts	r	M Ro	
O Lord grant the King a long life	r 791	M Ro	Coronation of Charles I
O Lord how glorious	r	M Ro	
O Lord how manifold	c r	M C Ro	for men's voices
O Lord I have loved	p r y 1 23 23Rw 30 180 6346	M P Ro St	
O Lord let me know mine end	r d y 23Rw 180 791 1045 1220 1382 6346 29366 29427 30478	M Ro F	
O Lord let my mouth be filled with thy praise	698		incomplete ‡
O Lord open thou our lips	r	M Ro	
O Lord rebuke me not	c r	M Ro C	Penitential Psalm 1
O Lord thou hast dealt	r 791	M Ro	

List of Works and their Sources 341

Title	MS sources	Printed editions	Remarks
O Lord wipe away my sins	1382		incomplete
O praise the Lord all ye heathen	r	M Ro	*a* 5
O praise the Lord all ye heathen	c r 5 7339	M T T8 C	*a* 12
O pray for the peace of Jerusalem	d p r 1 23Rw 28 180 791 1045 1220 6346 30478	M Ro	
O pray for the peace of Jerusalem	r 181 4142	M Br B T T8 Ro	
O sing unto the Lord a new song	d r 180 1382 6346 17786 29366 30478	M Ro Sch	Sch edited by Bernard Rose
O that the salvation	r	M Ro	
O think upon thy servant	791 6346		incomplete
Out of the deep	d r 181 791 30478	M Ro Ja	The chorus in M are *a* 4, those in the MSS are *a* 5, as is Ja

342 *List of Works and their Sources*

Title	MS sources	Printed editions	Remarks
Out of the deep have I called	c r	M AM C Ro	Penitential Psalm 6
Praise the Lord O my soul	r 23Rw 791 1045 6346	M Ro Nov	Nov edited by John Morehen
Praise the Lord O my soul	r 181	M T T8 Ro	T edited by John Morehen
Praise the Lord O ye servants	r	M Ro	
Put me not to rebuke	c r	M C Ro	Penitential Psalm 3
Rejoice, rejoice	g 17792	F	
Remember me O Lord	r	M Ro AM	for men's voices
Sing unto God	p r 791 29372	M Ro F	
Stephen being full of the Holy Ghost	d r 6346 30478	M Ro	St Stephen
Sweet Saviour	791		incomplete
The heavens declare the glory	r	M Ro St	for men's voices

List of Works and their Sources

Title	MS sources	Printed editions	Remarks
The hills stand about Jerusalem	r	M Ro	
The Lord bless us	g 791 1382	Ja	
The Lord even the most mighty	r 791 1382	M Ro	
Then David mourned	r	M Ro Sch St	Sch edited by Bernard Rose
Thou art my King, O God	c d h l p r wi y 1 6 23Rw 28 180 791 1001 1045 1176 1220 1382 4142 6346 17784 29372 30478 N	M Ro C F	29372 includes string parts. Arranged by Edmund Hooper for 2 bass soloists rather than one: thus in 791, 1045, and partbooks at Durham and Windsor
Thou healest the broken	r	M Ro	
Turn thou us	c r	M Ro	canon four in one

List of Works and their Sources

Title	MS sources	Printed editions	Remarks
Turn thou us O good lord	r 5 791 1382 30478	M Ro	
Turn unto the Lord	p r 4078 17792	E S Ja	Dedicated to Nathaniel Tomkins
When David heard	r 29372	E H M S Schi Rg T	Dedicated to Thomas Myriell Rg edited by K. Stone T edited by John Morehen
Who can tell how oft he offendeth	r	M Ro	
Who is this that cometh	r 23Rw 181 6346	M Ro	St George
Who shall ascend the hill of God	c r	M C	
Whom have I in heaven	r	M Ro	
Why art thou so full of heaviness	c r	M C Ro	*Domine tu eruisti animam*
Withdraw not thou thy mercy	r 23Rw 1021 6346	M Ro	Listed among verse anthems in 6346
Woe is me	17792	E S	Dedicated to John Tomkins

List of Works and their Sources 345

Title	MS sources	Printed editions	Remarks
Ye people all	1045		incomplete
Zadok the priest	23Rw 6346		Coronation of Charles I; text only

* 6346 gives different texts for full and verse anthems, thus postulating a lost full anthem for this feast.
‡ Anonymous in source but attributed to Tomkins. In Nathaniel Tomkins's hand.

SECULAR VOCAL MUSIC

Title	MS sources	Printed editions	Dedicatee
Adieu, ye city-prisoning towers	616 4087	E S	William White
Cloris, whenas I woo		E S	Orlando Gibbons
Come, shepherds, sing with me		E S	Nathaniel Giles
Fauns and satyrs tripping, The		E EU OR TO	Lord Charles Howard
Fond men that do so highly prize	616	E S	Nicholas Tomkins
Fusca, in thy starry eyes	616	E S WBS	Phineas Fletcher
How great delight	616	E S	William Cross
Love, cease tormenting	616	E S	Thomas Day
Music Divine	616 4076	E S	Dr Heather
No more will I thy love	616	E S	William Walker
O let me die for true love	616	E S	John Daniel
O let me live for true love	616	E S	John Dowland
Oft did I marle	29372	E S	John Ward
Our hasty life away doth post	616 11587	E S	Thomas Tomkins the elder
Oyez! has any found a lad?	616	E S WBS	John Coperario

346 *List of Works and their Sources*

Title	MS sources	Printed editions	Dedicatee
Phyllis, now cease to move me	616	E S	Henry Molle
Phyllis, yet see him dying	616	E S	Nicholas Carlton
See, see, the shepherd's queen	616	E S WBS	John Stevens
Sure there is no god of love	616	E GW S	Humphrey Withy
To the shady woods	616 4081	E S	Robert Chetwode
Too much I once lamented	616	E S	William Byrd
Was ever wretch tormented	616	E S	Giles Tomkins
Weep no more thou sorry boy	616	E S	Peregrine Tomkins
When I observe	616	E S	Thomas Warwick
Yet again, as soon revived	616	E S	Robert Tomkins

KEYBOARD MUSIC

Title	MS sources	Printed edition	Remarks
Barafostus' Dream	32	FB M5(*62*)	
Bitts or morcells	1122	M5(*73*)	fragments
Clarifica me pater	1122	M5(*4*)	September 1650
Fancy	1122	M5(*22*)	9 September 1650
Fancy	1122	M5(*23*)	8 July 1647
Fancy	1122	M5(*25*)	24 October 1648
Fancy	1113	M5(*29*)	
Fancy: for two to play	29996	M5(*32*) FD HM	
Fancy: for viols	1122	M5(*33*)	
Fortune my foe	1122	M5(*61*)	4 July 1654
Galliard	5612	M5(*60*)	
Galliard, The hunting	32	FB M5(*58*)	
Galliard, The Lady Folliot's	5612	M5(*59*)	
Go from my window	1122	M5(*72*)	fragment
Ground	32	FB M5(*39*)	
Ground	29996	M5(*40*)	
In nomine (version 1)	1122	AP M5(*5*)	20–28 January 1647

List of Works and their Sources

Title	MS sources	Printed edition	Remarks
In nomine (version 2)	1122	M5(6)	20 January 1647–2 August 1650
In nomine	1122	M5(7)	May 1648
In nomine	1122	M5(8)	16 June 1648
In nomine	1122	M5(9)	27 October 1648
In nomine (version 1)	1122	M5(10)	February 1650
In nomine (version 2)	1122	M5(11)	14 February 1650
In nomine	1122	M5(12)	28 June 1652
Miserere	1122	M5(13)	15 September 1648
Miserere	1122	M5(14)	7 October 1648
Miserere	1122	M5(15)	26 May 1651
Miserere	1122	M5(16)	3–4 February 1652
Miserere	1122	M5(17)	
Miserere	1122	M5(18)	
Miserere	1122	M5(19)	
Miserere	1122	M5(20)	
Offertory	93	M5(21)	1637
Pavan	1122	M5(51)	10 September 1647
Pavan	1122	M5(52)	14 September 1647
Pavan, A sad; for these distracted times	1122	M5(53)	14 February 1649
Pavan	1122	M5(54)	20 August 1650
Pavan, Short	1122	M5(55)	19 July 1654
Pavan	32 1113	FB M5(56)	String version in M9(73)
Pavan, Lord Canterbury	29996	FD M5(57)	1647
Pavan & Galliard, Earl Strafford	1122	M5(41–2)	29 September 1647 (short version)
Pavan & Galliard, Earl Strafford	1122	M5(43–4)	2 October 1647 (long version)
Pavan & Galliard	1122	M5(45–6)	April 1650 1 October 1650
Pavan & Galliard	1122	M5(47–8)	4 September 1654 7 September 1654
Pavan & Galliard, of three parts	1122	M5(49–50)	

List of Works and their Sources

Title	MS sources	Printed edition	Remarks
Plainsong, On a	1113	M5(*68*)	
Prelude	1122	M5(*1*)	
Prelude, Piece of a	1122	M5(*2*)	9 July 1647
Prelude	1122	M5(*3*)	
Robin Hood	24	M5(*63*)	
Round, The perpetual	1122	M5(*66*)	7–8 September 1654
Toy: made at Poole Court	1122	MG M5(*67*)	
Toy: Mr Curch	32 1113 5612	FB M5(*69*)	Entitled *Almain* in 1113. Attr. To Farnaby in 32
Ut re mi	93	M5(*38*)	
Ut re mi fa sol la; for a	1122	M5(*34*)	
Ut re mi fa sol la	93 1122	M5(*35*)	For string versions see Consort Music section below
Ut re mi fa sol la	1122	M5(*36*)	
Ut re mi fa sol la	1122	M5(*37*)	
Ut re mi fa sol la	1122	M5(*70*)	fragment
Ut re mi fa sol la	1122	M5(*71*)	fragment 30 June 1654
Verse of three parts	1122	M5(*26*)	12 August 1650
Verse, A short	29996	FD M5(*27*)	
Verse, A substantial; maintaining the point	1122	M5(*31*)	
[A short verse] for Edward	93	M5(*74*)	Dedicated to Archdeacon Thornborough
Another [short verse for Edward Thornborough]	93	M5(*75*)	Dedicated to Archdeacon Thornborough
[Voluntary (or verse)] for Mr Arc [hdeacon] Thornborough	93	M5(*76*)	Dedicated to Archdeacon Thornborough
Voluntary	1122	M5(*24*)	10 August–10 September 1647
Voluntary	5611	M5(*28*)	

List of Works and their Sources 349

Voluntary	5611	M5(*30*)
What if a day	5612	MG M5(*64*)
Worcester Brawls	32	FB MG M5(*65*)

CONSORT MUSIC

Title	MS sources	Printed editions	Remarks
In nomine *a* 3 (1)	245 1018 17792	M59	Numerical order as in 245
In nomine *a* 3 (2)	245 347 1018 17792	M59 H	
Fantasia *a* 3 (3)	245 347 17792	M59 VGS	
Fantasia *a* 3 (4)	245 347 1018 17792	M59 He	
Fantasia *a* 3 (5)	245 347 1018 17792	M59 He	
Fantasia *a* 3 (6)	245 347 1018 17792	M59	
Fantasia *a* 3 (7)	245 347 1018 17792 R	M59	
Fantasia *a* 3 (8)	245 1018 17792	M59 Sch	
Fantasia *a* 3 (9)	245 347	M59	

350 | *List of Works and their Sources*

Title	MS sources	Printed editions	Remarks
	1018		
	17792		
Fantasia *a* 3 (10)	245	M59	
	347	He	
	1018		
	17792		
Fantasia *a* 3 (11)	245	M59	
	347	He	
	1018		
	17792		
Fantasia *a* 3 (12)	245	M59	Subtitle in 245:
	347	He	'3 parts in one'
	1018	Sch	
	17792		
Fantasia *a* 3 (13)	245	M59	
	17792		
Fantasia *a* 3 (14)	245	M59	
	347	VGS	
	17792		
Fantasia *a* 3 (15)	245	M59	
	347		
	17792		
Fantasia *a* 3 (16)	245	M59	
	347	M9(*13*)	
	17792	He VGS	
Fantasia *a* 3 (17)	1018	M59	
Fantasia *a* 5	1122	M5(*33*)	Keyboard version: no string version survives.
Pavan *a* 5 (1)	415	M59	Numerical order as
	17792	Mo	in 415, which lacks one partbook.
Pavan *a* 5 (2)	415	M59	
Pavan *a* 5 (3)	415	M59	
Pavan *a* 5 (4)	415	M59	
Pavan *a* 5 (5)	415	M59	
		VGS	
Pavan *a* 5 (6)	415	TS	For keyboard
	1113	M9(*73*)	versions

List of Works and their Sources 351

Title	MS sources	Printed editions	Remarks
	2039	IP	see previous
	3665	M59	section
	17792	Mo	
	30826		
Pavan *a* 5 (7)	17792	M59	
		Mo	
Pavan *a* 5 (8)	17792	M59	
		Mo	
Pavan *a* 5 (9)	30826	M59	
Ut re mi *a* 4	64	M59	For keyboard
	341		version see
			previous section
Pavan *a* 4	64	M59	See also the 5-part
	341		setting (No. 1)
Alman *a* 4	64	M59	
	341	M9(*33*)	
Fantasia *a* 6 (1)	64	M59	Numerical order as
	341	He	in 64
Fantasia *a* 6 (2)	64	M59	
	341	EHF	
Fantasia *a* 6 (3)	64	M59	
	341		
Fantasia *a* 6 (4)	64	M59	
	341	He	
Pavan *a* 6	64	M59	
	341	M9(*91*)	
Galliard *a* 6	64	M59	
	341	M9(*92*)	

Bibliography

Armitt, M.L. (1888), 'Old English Viol Music', *Quarterly Musical Review*, 4.

Ashbee, Andrew (1967), 'Lowe, Jenkins and Merro', *Music and Letters*, 48.

Ashbee, Andrew, and Harley, John (eds, 2000), *The Cheque Books of the Chapel Royal*, Aldershot.

Atkin, Malcolm (1995), *The Civil War in Worcestershire*, Stroud.

Atkins, Sir Ivor (1918), *The Early Occupants of the Office of Organist and Master of the Choristers of the Cathedral Church of Christ and the Blessed Virgin, Worcester*, Worcester (WHS).

—— (1946), 'The Authorship of the XVIth Century Description of St David's Printed in Browne Willis's "Survey" (1717)', *National Library of Wales Journal*, 4 (3 and 4), Summer.

Aubrey, John, *The Natural History of Wiltshire*, edited by John Britten (1847) and written between 1656 and 1691, London.

—— (1949; 2/1971), *Aubrey's Brief Lives*, ed. Oliver Lawson Dick, London.

Baldwin, David (1990), *The Chapel Royal: Ancient and Modern*, London.

Bent, J.T. (1893), *Early Voyages and Travels in the Levant*.

Birch, Thomas (1760), *The Life of Henry, Prince of Wales, eldest son of King James I*, London.

Bloxam, J.R. (1853–55), *A Register of the Presidents, Fellows, Demies, Instructors in Grammar and in Music, Chaplains, Clerks, Choristers and other members of St Mary Magdalen College in the University of Oxford*, Oxford.

Boas, F.S. (ed., 1909), *Giles and Phineas Fletcher, Poetical Works*, 2 vols, Cambridge.

Bond, Shelagh (1974), *The Chamber Order Book of Worcester 1602–1650*, Worcestershire (WHS).

Bossewell, John (1572), *Workes of Armorie*.

Bowen, Geraint (2001), *The Organs of St Davids Cathedral*, Haverfordwest.

Brice, Katherine (1997), *The Early Stuarts 1603–1640*, London.

Brightman, F.E. (1915), *The English Rite*, I, London.

Brown, D. (1969), *Thomas Weelkes*, London.

Bülow, G. von (1892), *The Diary of Philip Julius, Duke of Stettin-Pomerania*, London: Transactions of the Royal Historical Society, VI.

Burney, Charles (1776–89), *A General History of Music*, London; ed. Frank Mercer (1935), London.

Butcher, Vernon (1981), *The Organs and Music of Worcester Cathedral*, Worcester.

354 *Bibliography*

Butler, Charles (1636), *The Principles of Music*, London; repr. New York (1970) with an introduction by Gilbert Reaney.

Buxton, John (1965), *Elizabethan Taste*, London.

Caldwell, John (1964–65), 'British Museum Additional MS 29996: transcription and commentary', Ph.D. thesis, University of Oxford.

—— (1965), 'Keyboard Plainsong Settings in England 1500–1600', *Musica Disciplina*, 19; supplemented by Addenda and Corrigenda in vol. 34 (1980).

Carlton, Charles (1987), *Archbishop William Laud*, London.

—— (1995), *Charles I, The Personal Monarch*, London.

Chambers, J.(1820), *History of Worcester*, Worcester.

Daniel, Ralph T., and Le Huray, Peter (1972), *The Sources of English Church Music 1549–1660*, Early English Church Music, supp.1, London.

Dawes, F. (1951), 'Nicholas Carlton and the Earliest Keyboard Duet', *Musical Times*, 92 (542).

Defoe, Daniel (1724), *A Tour through Great Britain*, London.

Dekker, Thomas (1606), *The Seven Deadly Sinnes of London*, London.

Dugdale, William (*c*.1680), *Old St Paul's*, London.

—— (1681), *A Short View of the Late Troubles in England*, London.

Dunlop, Ian (1962), *Palaces and Progresses of Elizabeth I*, London.

Ede, W.M.(1925), *The Cathedral Church of Christ and the Blessed Virgin Mary of Worcester*, Worcester.

Evans, David R.A. (1983), 'Thomas Tomkins and the Prince of Wales', *Welsh Music* (Summer) 7 (4).

—— (1987), 'A Cornish Musician in Wales', *Journal of the Institute of Cornish Studies*, 15.

—— (1987–8), 'John Tomkins and the Batten Organ Book', *Welsh Music/Cerddoriaeth Cymru*, 8 (7).

—— (2002), ' "Cerddor euraid": lle John Tomkins ym marddoniaeth Saesneg yr ail ganrif ar bymtheg'. (' "The Golden Pair": John Tomkins: his place in English seventeenth-century verse'), *Taliesin*, 114 (Spring).

Eward, Suzanne (1985), *No Fine but a Glass of Wine: Cathedral Life at Gloucester in Stuart Times*, Norwich.

Fellowes, E.H. (1921), *The English Madrigal Composers*, Oxford.

—— (1936; 2/1948), *William Byrd*, Oxford.

—— (1941), *English Cathedral Music*, London.

—— (1951), *Orlando Gibbons*, Oxford.

Fenton, Richard (1994), *A Historical Tour Through Pembrokeshire* (facsimile by Dyfed County Council).

Fosbrooke, Thomas Dudley (1819), *An Original History of the City of Gloucester*, London; repr. Stroud, 1976.

Foxe, John (1583), *Book of Martyrs*, London.

Bibliography 355

Frith, Brian (1973), *The Organs and Organists of Gloucester Cathedral*, Gloucester.

Fuller, Thomas (1662), *The Histories of the Worthies of England*, London.

Gardiner, S.R.(1893), *History of England, 1603–42*, 7.

Gee, Henry, (1921), *Gloucester Cathedral its Organs and Organists*, London.

Green, Bertram (rev. 1979), *Bishops and Deans of Worcester*, Worcester.

Green, Francis (ed., 1739–70), *Menevia Sacra* by Edward Yardley, Archdeacon of Cardigan.

Green, Valentine (1764), *A Survey of the City of Worcester*, enlarged into *The History and Antiquities of the City and Suburbs of Worcester* (1796), 2 vols.

Grosart, A.B. (ed., 1869), *The Poems of Phineas Fletcher*, 2 vols.

Habington, Thomas (1639), *A Survey of Worcestershire*, Worcester (WHS), 1899.

Hacket, John (1693), *Scrinia Reserata, A Memoriall Offer'd to the Great Deservings of John Williams, D.D., who sometime held the Place pf Lord Keeper of the Great Seal of England, Lord Bishop of Lincoln and Lord Archbishop of York*, London.

Hawkins, Sir John (1776), *A General History of the Science and Practice of Music*, London.

Heylyn, Peter (1668), *Cyprianus Anglicus, or The History of the Life and Death of William Laud*, London.

Hibbert, Christopher (2001), *Charles I*, London.

Howells, B.E. (1972), *Pembrokeshire Life: 1572–1843*, Pembrokeshire Record Society.

Hughes, Patricia (1990), 'Buildings and the Building Trade in Worcester 1540–1650', unpublished D.Phil.thesis, University of Birmingham.

Irving, John (1984), 'Consort Playing in Mid-17th-century Worcester: Thomas Tomkins and the Bodleian Partbooks Mus. Sch. E.415-18', *Early Music*, 12.

—— (1984), 'Oxford, Christ Church MSS 1018-1020: a Valuable Source of Tomkins's Consort Music', *The Consort*, 40.

—— (1985), 'Keyboard Plainsong Settings by Thomas Tomkins', *Soundings*, 13.

—— (1989), *The Instrumental Music of Thomas Tomkins 1572–1656*, New York and London.

—— (1990), 'Thomas Tomkins's Copy of Morley's "A Plain and Easy Introduction to Practical Music"', *Music and Letters*, 71.

—— (1992), 'Byrd and Tomkins: The Instrumental Music', *Byrd Studies* (ed. A. Brown and R. Turbet, Cambridge.

James, Peter H. (1968), 'A Study of the Verse Anthem from Byrd to Tomkins', University of Wales, Cardiff.

Jones, J. Gwynfor (1989), *Wales and the Tudor State*, Cardiff.

356   *Bibliography*

Lafontaine, H.C. de (1910), 'The King's Musick', *Proceedings of the Musical Association*, 36th Session.

Leach, A.F. (1913), *Documents illustrating Early Education in Worcester, 685–1700*, Worcester (WHS).

Lefkowitz, Murray (1960), *William Lawes*, London.

Legg, J.W. (ed., 1902), *The Coronation Order of King James I*, edited from the Lambeth MS.

Le Huray, Peter (1967), *Music and the Reformation in England 1549–1660*, London.

—— and Irving, John (2001), 'Thomas Tomkins', *Grove*, 7.

Leicester, Hubert (1935), *Worcester Remembered*, Worcester.

Lever, Tresham (1967), *The Herberts of Wilton*, London.

MacDonald, Alec (1936), *A History of the King's School Worcester*, London.

—— (1943; 2/1969), *Worcestershire in English History*, London.

Mace, Thomas (1676), *Musick's Monument*, London.

Mattingley, Joanna (1989), 'The Medieval Parish Guilds of Cornwall', *Journal of the Royal Institution of Cornwall*, NS.

Meyer, Ernst (1946), *English Chamber Music*, London.

Middleton, George W. (1977), *The Streets of St Davids*, St David's: St David's Civic Society.

Miller, H.M. (1943), 'The Earliest Keyboard Duets', *Musical Quarterly*, 29.

Milsom, John (2001), 'Tracking Tomkins', *Musical Times* (Summer).

Monson, Craig (1982), *Voices and Viols in England, 1600–1650: The Sources and the Music*, Ann Arbor, Mich.

Morehen, John (1981), 'The Gloucester Cathedral Bassus Partbook MS 93', *Music and Letters*, 62.

Newsholme, Richard (1996), 'Thomas Tomkins: Some Reflections on his Personality' and 'Thomas Tomkins II: Domestic Life at Worcester', *Leading Notes* (Journal of the National Early Music Association), 5 (1 and 2).

Noake, J. (1866), *The Monastery and Cathedral of Worcester*, Worcester.

North, Roger (1846), *Memoirs of Music*, ed. E.F. Rimbault.

—— (1925), *The Musical Grammarian*, ed. H. Andrews.

Owen, George (1603), *The Description of Pembrokeshire* (1603), Cymmrodorion Society (1892), ed. H. Owen (1906).

Payne, I. (1993), *The Provision and Practice of Sacred Music at Cambridge Colleges and Selected Cathedrals c.1547–c.1646*, London.

Phillips, G.A. (1977), 'Crown Musical Patronage from Elizabeth I to Charles I', *Music and Letters*, 58.

Phillips, Peter (1991), *English Sacred Music 1549–1649*, Oxford.

Pike, Lionel (1992), 'The Great Service: Some observations on Byrd and Tomkins', *Musical Times*, August.

Platt, Frederick (1908), 'Arminianism', *Encyclopaedia of Religion and Ethics*, Edinburgh.

Porter, Stephen (1994), *Destruction in the English Civil Wars*, Stroud.

Pounds, N.J.G. (1979), 'The Duchy Palace at Lostwithiel, Cornwall', *Archeological Journal*, 136.

Reynolds, William (2002), 'A Study of Music and Liturgy, Choirs and Organs in Monastic and Secular Foundations in Wales and the Borderlands, 1485–1645', unpublished Ph.D. thesis, University of Wales, Bangor.

Rimbault, Edward F. (ed., 1872), *The Old Cheque Book or Book of Remembrance of the Chapel Royal*, London; repr. New York, 1966.

Robertson, Dora H. (1938), *Sarum Close, A Picture of Domestic Life in a Cathedral Close for 700 years and the History of the Choristers for 900 years*, London; republished Bath, 1969.

Robinson, H. (ed., 1842), *Original Letters Relative to the English Reformation*, 'Zurich Letters', 1, London.

Rowse, A.L. (1969), *Tudor Cornwall*, London.

Rushworth, John (1659–1701), *Historical Collections of Private Passages of State*, 2, London.

Rye, William Brenchley (1865), *England as Seen by Foreigners in the Days of Elizabeth and James I*, London.

Sampson, George (ed., 1945), *The Concise Cambridge History of Literature*, Cambridge.

Scholes, Percy A. (1934), *The Puritans and Music in England and New England*, London.

Scot, W., and Bliss, J. (eds, 1847–60), *The Works of the Most Reverend Father in God, William Laud*, Oxford.

Scott, Sir W. (ed., 1808), *Memoirs of Sir Robert Carey, Written by Himself*, Edinburgh.

Scrope, R., and Monkhouse, T. (eds, 1767–86), *State Papers Collected by Edward, Earl of Clarendon*, 3 vols, Oxford.

Short, F. (1957), *The City of Salisbury*, London; 2/1970, Wakefield.

Smith, I.G. and Onslow, P. (1883), *Diocesan History of Worcester*, London.

Stevens, Denis (1957; 2/1967), *Thomas Tomkins: 1572–1656*, London.

Thompson, M.W. (ed., 1983), *The Journeys of Sir Richard Colt Hoare*, Stroud.

Thompson, Robert (1991), ' "Francis Withie of Oxon" and his Commonplace Book, Christ Church, Oxford, MS 337', *Chelys*, 20.

Trevelyan, G.M. (1949), *Illustrated English Social History*, II, London.

Trevor Roper, H.R. (1965), *Archbishop Laud 1573–1645*, London.

Turbet, Richard (1990), 'The Great Service: Byrd, Tomkins and their contemporaries, and the meaning of Great', *Musical Times*, May.

—— (1992), 'The Great Service: a postscript', *Musical Times*, April.

358 *Bibliography*

—— (1993), 'My Ancient and Much Reverenced Master', *Musical Times*, November.

—— (1998), 'Homage to Byrd in Tudor Verse Services', *Musical Times*, September.

Victoria County History of Worcestershire (1926).

Vining, Paul (1992), 'Nathaniel Tomkins: A Bishop's Pawn', *Musical Times*, October, 538–40.

Warlock, Peter (1926), *The English Ayre*, London.

Watkins Shaw, H. (1991), *The Succession of Organists*, Oxford.

Webb le Bas, Charles (1836), *The Life of Archbishop Laud*, London.

Wedgewood, C.V. (2001), *The King's Peace 1637–1641*, London.

Welander, David (1991), *The History, Art and Architecture of Gloucester Cathedral*, Stroud.

Weldon, Sir Anthony (1640s), *Secret History of the Court of King James I*, II, London.

West, John E. (1899), *Cathedral Organists*.

Willetts, Pamela (1961), 'Music from the Circle of Anthony Wood at Oxford', *British Museum Quarterly*, 24.

—— (1968), 'Musical Connections of Thomas Myriell', *Music and Letters*, 49.

Williams, G. (1967), *Welsh Reformation Essays*, Cardiff.

Willis, Browne (1717), *A Survey of the Cathedral Church of St David's*, London.

Willis Bund, J.W. (1899), 'Religious Life in Worcestershire in the Seventeenth Century, shown by Sessions Records', *Associated Architectural Societies Reports and Papers*, 24 (2).

—— (1913), *The Battle of Worcester*, Worcester.

—— (ed., 1915), *Diary of Henry Townshend of Elmley Lovett, 1640–1663*, Worcester (WHS).

Wood, Anthony à (1792–6), *The History and Antiquities of the University of Oxford*, ed. John Gutch, Oxford.

—— (1813–22), *Athenae Oxoniensis; Fasti Oxoniensis*, ed. P. Bliss, London.

Woodfill, Walter L. (1969), *Musicians in English Society from Elizabeth to Charles I*, Princeton.

Wrightson, Keith (2000), *English Society 1580–1680*, London.

Wroughton, John (1999), *An Unhappy Civil War*, Bath.

Index

Note: TT = Thomas Tomkins; page references in *italics* refer to illustrations or musical examples. Information in brackets for members of the Tomkins family explains the relationship to Thomas Tomkins, unless otherwise indicated.

Abbot, George, archbishop of Canterbury 126, 127, 137
Abergwili: bishop's palace 19
Above the stars my saviour dwells (verse anthem) 112, 163, 207, 212, 281, 282, 283
Act of Uniformity (1559) 150–51
actors, boy 59–60
Adieu, ye city-prisoning towers (madrigal) 229–30
Alison, Richard 256
All Saints' Day 212
Almain: wrongly attributed to TT 257
Alman (consort music) 268
Almighty and everlasting God, we humbly beseech Thee/Thy majesty (verse anthem) 287
Almighty God, the fountain of all wisdom (anthem) 193, 210, 278
Alvechurch, Worcestershire 115
anacrusis 252–3
Anglicanism 105, 189, 301
Anne of Denmark, queen 95, 97
anthems: 3-part 211, 278–81, 283–4; 4-part 211, 278; 5-part 209–11; 6-part 87, 208–9; bad text underlay 278–81, 283–4; Barnard's anthology 197–8; different styles and forms 207; early 87; influence of other composers on 312–18; Latin texts 208; for men only 276; in *Musica Deo sacra* 87, 197, 202, 207–16, 276, 277–82; in Myriell's anthologies 93, 94, 227, 288; not included in *Musica Deo sacra* 285–6, 287–91; scoring 208; in Tenbury MS 1382 67–9; texts 207–8; wrongly attributed to TT 286–7; *see also Musica Deo sacra*; verse anthems; *and individual anthems*
ap Rhys, Philip 234
Arcadelt, Jacob 78
Argas, Richard 37
Arise O Lord God lift up thine hand (anthem) 207, 208, 210–11, 278
Arise O Lord into Thy resting place (anthem) 209
Armada, Spanish 25, 35, 62, 70, 77

Arminianism 105, 157; Charles I and 124–5, 153, 161, 162–3; Juxon and 150; Laud and 105–6, 153–4, 157, 161–4
Arminius, Jacobus 105
art: Charles I and 139; religious 161–2
Ash Wednesday 211, 295
Ashbee, Andrew 49, 56
Atkins, Ivor 23, 27, 28, 35, 61, 238
Aubrey, John: *Brief Lives* 76–7, 107, 150, 186; *The Natural History of Wiltshire* 134, 135
Aylmer, Theophyllus 111, 232

Babbington, Gervase, bishop of Worcester 88–9
Babington conspiracy 62, 71
Bach, Johann Sebastian 244, 262–3, 282, 302
balletts 79, 111, 225, 226, 227, 229, 235, 322
Barafostus' Dream (keyboard music) 178, 244, 255, 256
Barley, William 223
Barlow, William, bishop of St David's 18, 30
Barnard, John 197–8, 201, 297
Barnston, Dr 136, 138
Baroque style 221, 277, 301–2, 324
Barrett, Elizabeth 167, 168
Barton, Matthew 134
Bassano, Anthony 139
Bassano, Henry 139
basso seguente tradition 261
Bastwick, John 164, 169
Batten, Adrian 102, 140n, 297n, 314, 315
'Batten' Organ Book 140, 296, 297, 298, 323
Be strong and of good courage (anthem) 87, 207, 208
Beaumont, Henry 115
Behold I bring you glad tidings (verse anthem) 212, 281
Behold it is Christ (verse anthem) 315, *318*
Behold, O God our Defender see *O Lord God of hosts*
Behold, the hour cometh (anthem) 297n

359

360 *Index*

Benevolence Tax 11–12
Bennet, John 83, 322
Beoley, Worcestershire 120, 121
Berio, Luciano: *The Cries of London* 54
Bever, Thomas 237
Bible: Elizabethan 301; Welsh translation 18–19
Bibliothèque nationale: Réserve 1122
    manuscript 179, 235–42
Bilson, Thomas, bishop of Worcester 73
Bishops' Wars: first 164; second 169
black notation 229
Blackfriars: theatre 59, 60
Blessed is he that considereth (anthem) 208
Blitheman, William 63
Blow, John 57–8, 190
Bodinghurst, William 57
Bodleian Library 67, 89–90, 201–2, 268, 282
Bohemia 125
Bonner, Edmund, bishop of London 46–7
Book of Common Prayer 12, 301; and Scotland
    164; 1662 revision 189; Welsh translation 18
Bossewell, John 41
Boughton, Mrs 185, 186
Boughton, Richard 128
Boughton, Stephen 121, 122, 158, 180
Bowle, John, dean of Salisbury 136, 138
Brade, William 268
brawls 151
Brett, Philip 49
Broad, Theodosia *see* Tomkins, Theodosia
Broadgate, Richard 47–8
Brome, Richard: *The English Moore* 118
Brommall, William 185–6
Browne, Arthur (lay clerk) 175, 176
Browne, Arthur (son of above) 175
Brown(e), John (lay clerk) 176, 201
Browne, John (publisher) 218
Browne, Martha *see* Tomkins, Martha
Browne, Nathaniel 167, 168, 175, 176
Browne, Richard 176, 190
Buckden, Huntingdonshire 148, 149
Buckingham, George Villiers, duke of 107, 115,
    122–3, 125, 131, 132, 148
Bull, John: anthems 68; and Chapel Royal 62, 63;
    hexachord variations 250; included in TT's
    personal anthologies 236, 238; influence on
    TT 63, 255, 256; and James I's coronation 87;
    music praised by TT 188, 242; plainsong
    settings 235; as pupil of Byrd 302; reputation
    as organist 90; use of double cursus 247
Burghley, Lord *see* Cecil, William
Burial Service 207, 211, 292
Burney, Charles 200, 211, 217, 259

Burton, Henry 164, 169
Butler, Charles 94, 159, 227, 231
Byrd, William: anthems 67, 286–7, 312, *313*,
    315, 318; background and life 42–4; on
    benefits of singing 78–9; Catholicism 55, 301;
    and Chapel Royal 42–4, 57; as dedicatee of
    works by TT 110, 225; and Dowland's
    Lachrymae 223; and Elizabeth I 55; *Exalt*
    thyself, O God 286–7; Fellowes and 170, 239;
    Fortune My Foe 187, 255; Gurney on 53;
    hexachord variations 250; *In resurrectione tua*
    (as example of vocal style with instrumental
    origin) 273; included in TT's personal
    anthologies 121, 235, 236, 238; influence on
    TT's music 205, 257, 258, 276, 277, 293,
    295, 296, 297, 302–12, *313*, 315, 318, 323;
    licence to print music 43, 78, 79; madrigal
    books 78–9, 220; music praised by TT 152,
    188, 242; plainsong settings 235, 245; quality
    of TT's music compared to 282, 284; Services
    205, 276, 277, 296, 297, 303–12, 323; TT as
    pupil of 42, 43–4, 58, 60, 61, 87, 207, 217,
    235; verse anthems 207, 212, 214, 292
Byron, John 172

Calvin, John 20, 105
Calvinism 51, 73, 104, 105, 124, 125
cambiata figure 266, 274
Cambridge, University of 61, 94; *see also* King's
    College, Cambridge
Camden, William 34, 55
Campion, Thomas 98, 256
canon 262–3
Canterbury Cathedral 123, 124
canzonets 79
Carey, Henry, Lord Hunsdon 59–60
Carey, Robert 84
Carlton, Nicholas 110, 120–21, 188, 228, 235,
    249, 274
Castlemorton, Worcestershire 76
Catesby, Robert 88
Catholic music 12, 13, 55, 301
Catholics: James I and 88; *see also* recusancy
Cecil, William, Lord Burghley 73
Chamberlain, John 124
Champigny (French ambassador) 54
Chantries Act (1548) 8–9
Chapel Royal 44, 54, 56–64; Byrd and 42–4, 57;
    and Charles I's coronation 126, 127; and
    Charles I's wedding 123; choristers 42, 43–4,
    56, 58–60; clerks of the cheque 56–7; and
    drama 59–60; education 58–9, 60; Elizabeth I
    and 14, 44, 59, 62–3, 83; gentlemen 56, 62;

Index

361

gentlemen extraordinary 62; John Tomkins (TT's half-brother) as organist 47; John Tomkins of Worcester's son as chorister 38; Laud and 107, 128, 132–4; links with Gloucester and Worcester 106; masters of the children 56, 58; members as dedicatees of TT's songs 110–11; *Old Cheque Book* 56–8, 62–3, 121, 123, 127; payments 127; TT as chorister 41, 42, 43–4, 58; TT as gentleman extraordinary 62, 83, 106–7; TT as gentleman in ordinary 58, 62; TT as organist 107, 121; TT's need to impress 293; typical vocal combination 312; and universities 61; and verse anthems 212

Charles I: accession 121, 122; and art 139; becomes heir 98; and Buckingham's death 132; character 131, 132; and Civil War 172–3; coronation and its music 125–8, 207, 218, 291, 291–2n; execution 179, 252, 275; and Laud 124, 126, 127, 148; and Mainwaring 154; marriage 122–3, 124; policies and disputes with parliament 124–5, 132, 153, 166, 169–70; and religion 105, 124–5, 133; Scottish coronation 140–41, 233; Scottish policies 164–6, 169; and Star Chamber 162–3; Tomkins family and 47, 137, 138; TT's appointment as Composer-in-Ordinary revoked by 129–31, 135; Warwick as royal musician to 111

Charles II 184–5, 186, 189, 192
Chetwode, Robert 111, 225
Child, William 59, 77, 192, 293, 324
Childe family 76–7, 120
Chiles, Thomas 180–81, 185, 186
choristers 41; Chapel Royal 42, 43–4, 56, 58–60; St David's 19, 20–21, 36, 37; Worcester Cathedral list 167–8
Christ Church, Dublin 65
Christ Church, Oxford 112, 118, 256, 257, 292
Christ rising again from the dead (verse anthem) 214, *216*, 315, 318
Christian IV, king of Denmark 89
Christmas 207, 212
chromaticism 302
church finances 41–2
Chynowith, Richard 8
Civil War 172–87, 252, 275, 301; role of music 261
Clarendon, Edward Hyde, earl of 107
Clarifica me pater (keyboard music) 184, 244–5
Clark, James 136, 137, 138
clavichord 234
Cloris, whenas I woo (madrigal) 226

clothing trade 38, 145
Cob, John 163
codettas 229
Codner, Dr 23
Coke, Edward 132
Collect for the Holy Innocents 212, *213*
Collects 207, 210, 211, 212, 287
colonies 89, 107
Colt Hoare, Richard 17
Come, shepherds, sing with me (madrigal) 59, 225–6, 273
Committee for Compounding 183, 186
Communion Service 207
Confortare see *Be strong and of good courage*
consort music 259–69, 282; galliards 268, 269; *In nomine* settings 260, 262, 264–5, 269; pavans 261, 262, 265, 266, 268–9; *Ut re mi* 265; *see also* fantasias; *and individual works*
Coperario, John 98, 110, 134, 135, 139, 223, 262, 293n
Cornwall: festivals 11; Muster Roll (1569) 15; *see also* Lostwithiel
Couperin, François 244
Court of the Marches of Wales 88–9
Courtes, Richard 9
Covenanters 164–6, 184
Cranmer, Thomas 12, 13
Creighton, Richard 256
Croce, Giovanni 81
Croft, William 58
Cromwell, Oliver 184, 186
Croome Court, Worcestershire 185–6
Cross, William 110, 127, 222
Curch, Mr 257

Dallam, Thomas 90, 103, 168, 191, 219
dance music 261, 262, 268, 269; *see also* galliards; pavans
dancing 97; country 151
Danyel, John 110, 217, 223, 322–3
Davenant, John, bishop of Salisbury 136, 137, 161–2
David, St: shrine 34
Davies, Humphrey 167, 168
Davies, James 107
Davies, John, of Hereford 110–11
Davies, Richard, bishop of St David's 18–19, 23, 37
Davison, Francis and Walter 107–9
Day, Thomas 110, 222
Day, William 73, 209
Dear Lord of life (sacred madrigal) 287, 288, *289–90*, 300, 322

362 *Index*

Death is swallowed up (verse anthem) 122, 292, 300
'Declaration of Sports' 151
Defoe, Daniel 7–8
Dekker, Thomas 53
De La Broderie (French ambassador) 96
Dering, Richard 134, 223, 262, 269
Dodderhill, Droitwich 181–2
Dolmetsch, Arnold 259
Domine, tu eruisti animam (motet) 320
Domingo, Dr 124
Donne, John 79, 98, 99, 102, 107, 109, 134, 137
Dorian cantus firmus 245, 251
double cursus 247
Dowdeswell, Richard 76, 184, 186, 189, 236
Dowdeswell, Roger 76
Dowdeswell, William 189
Dowghton, Bridget 47–8
Dowland, John 110, 205, 217, 222, 233, 315, 322, 323
Dowland, Robert 233
drama 59–60, 79, 118, 120, 163, 268
Drayton, Michael: *Poly-Olbion* 17, 97
duets 120–21, 274
Dunfermline (psalm tune) 112, 299
Dunstable, John 230
Durham Cathedral 90

Earle, John: *Microcosmographie* 200
East, Michael 227
Easter 62–4, 207, 208, 214
Edinburgh 106, 164, 166
Edney, William 57
Edward VI 8, 12, 13, 30
Edward, the Black Prince 7
Edwards, Richard: *The Paradise of Daynty Devises* 58
Elgar, Edward 76
Eliot, John 153
Eliot, Thomas 19, 20, 22, 23
Elizabeth I 18, 35, 73, 77, 81, 90; and Chapel Royal 14, 44, 59, 62–3, 83; death 83–5; grants printing licence 43; injunction on church music 13–14; lover of music 54–6; and religion 20, 70–71, 84; threats to 62; visit to Worcester 93
Elizabeth of Bohemia 125
Elmbridge, Worcestershire 182
Eltham Palace 54
episteller, office of 56
Erasmus, Desiderius 12
Essex, Robert Devereux, 2nd earl of 55
Essex, Robert Devereux, 3rd earl of 172–3

Eton Choirbook 207
Evans, David 22–3, 100–102, 103
Eveseed, Henry 57
Exeter Cathedral 192, 199

faburden 235
Fagiolini, I 218
fancies (keyboard music) 248–9, 250, 257
Fancy (1646, keyboard music) 236, 239
Fancy: for two to play (keyboard duet) 120–21, 274, 291
fantasias (consort music) 262–4, 265–7, 269; 3-part 262–4, 282; 5-part 265; 6-part 265–7, 282; classical type 267
Farington, Thomas 239, 241
Farmer, John 152, 235
Farnaby, Giles 223, 251
Farrant, John ('the elder') 134, 203
Farrant, John ('the younger') 134
Farrar, Robert, bishop of St David's 18
Farrenc, M. and Mme 238, 257
Fauns and Satyrs tripping, The (madrigal) 83, 219, 223, 321, 322
feast-days, music for 207, 212, 214, 287, 292
Felix namque, settings of 247–8
Fell, Samuel 118
Fellowes, Edmund H. 170, 217, 218, 231, 239, 303–4, 323
Felthan, Owen 197
Felton, John 132
Fenton, Richard 27, 35–6
Feriman, Catherine 175
Ferrabosco, Alfonso, II: dance music 262; death 129, 131; 'Fancies for the vyolls' 152; hexachord fantasias 268, 282; included in TT's personal anthologies 121, 235; as music master to Prince Henry 96, 293n; musical career 129, 134; sons 139; Wiltshire connection 135
Festa, Costanzo 78
Fétis, F.J. 200, 238, 257
Fido (Fideau), John 65–7, 68–9, 154
Fido brothers 69
Finch, John 166
Fitzwilliam Virginal Book 253, 255, 257, 275
Flemish composers 78
Fletcher, Giles 98, 99
Fletcher, John 60
Fletcher, Phineas 99–102, 103, 111; *An Hymn* 99; *Piscatoriae Eclogues* 100–101; poems for John Tompkins 101; *The Purple Island* 99, 100; TT's dedication to 103, 111
Fletcher, Richard, bishop of Worcester 73

Index

Folliot, Isabella *see* Tomkins, Isabella
Folliot family 186
Ford, Thomas 293n
Fortune My Foe (keyboard music) 187, *243*, 244, 255
Foster, J. Finley 237
Frederick, the Elector Palatine 125
Frederick of Württemberg, Count Mümppelgart 54
French chansons 260
From deepest horror of sad penitence (sacred madrigal) 287, 288, *291*, 322
Fuller, Thomas 177
Fusca, in thy starry eyes (madrigal) 103, 111, 229

Galliard: Earl Strafford (keyboard music) 178
Galliard, The Lady Folliot's (keyboard music) 187, 255
galliards: for consort 268, 269; for keyboard 150, 178, 187, 252–5
'Game at chess, The' (poem) 166–7
Gardiner, Stephen 46
Gibbes, John 45
Gibbons, Elizabeth (*née* Patten) 123
Gibbons, Orlando: consort music 262, 269; *Cries of London, The* 53, 219, 223; death 123–4, 127, 218; as dedicatee of works by TT 110, 226; *Do not repine fair sun* (for James I's progress) 106; fantasias 273, 282; full anthems 215, 277; included in TT's anthologies 120, 235; influence on TT's music 281, 290, 315, *317*; inspired by Byrd 305; inspired by Morley 79; and James I's funeral 121, 122; madrigals 218, 301, 322; marriage 123; reputation as organist 90; setting of Fletcher's *An Hymn* 99; services 205, 276; *The Silver Swan* (madrigal) 100, 281, 315, *317*; TT as 'junior' organist to 107; verse anthems 212, 214, 276, 292
Giles, Nathaniel: anthems in Tenbury MS 68; as choirmaster at St George's Chapel 59; as dedicatee of works by TT 59, 110, 225; *Everlasting God, which hast ordained* 287; influenced by Byrd 305; and James I's funeral 122; as master of the children 59, 60, 121; music for royal events 87, 121, 125; positions as organist 54, 59; and proportional notation 225
Giles, Nathaniel (son of above) 110
Giles, Thomas *see* Chiles, Thomas
Giraldus Cambrensis 17, 28
Globe theatre 60
Glorifica me (keyboard music) 244
Glory be to the Father (anthem) 208

Gloucester: Bishop Hooper's execution 13, 45–6; Byrd's connections with 43; consistory court 47; Tomkins family in 36, 39, 41–5, 47–8; Tomkins *père's* church livings 44, 45
Gloucester Cathedral: bassus partbook 67, 69–70, 292, 294; irregularities and neglect (1580) 45; Laud as dean 103–6, 168; links with other establishments 69, 106; Merro and 51; misbehaviour of lay clerks 47–8; need for new organ 103–4, 168; organists and masters of the choristers 45, 51; Parry and 89; Tomkins *père* as minor canon 36, 39, 41–2, 43, 44–5; Tomkins *père* as precentor 47
Glyn, Margaret 239
Godbid, William 199, 276
'golden age' of music 77, 79, 301
Golden Garland of Princely Delights (anthology) 255
Goldsborough, Henry 145
gospeller, office of 56
Grant us, gracious Lord, so to eat (anthem) 288
Great and marvellous are thy works (anthem) 210
Green, Alderman (of Worcester) 173
Green, Francis 27
Greenwich Palace 54
Grenville, Richard 25
Griffith, Lewis, dean of Gloucester 44, 45
Griffiths, Sylvanus, dean of Hereford 140
Grindal, Edmund, archbishop of Canterbury 45
Ground (two keyboard pieces) 241, 251, 275
gruppetto 222
Guarini, G.B. 221–2
guilds 8, 9
Gunpowder Plot 88
Gurney, Ivor 53

Habington, Thomas 90, 190
Hacket, John 147–9, 150
Halciter, John 157
Hall, Joseph, dean of Worcester 106, 112
Halwell, Thomas 9
Hampton Court conference 88
Handel, George Friederic 324
Handl, Jacob 227
Hargest, Anne *see* Tomkins, Anne
Hargest family 37
Harley, John 56
harpsichord 234
Harris, Thomas 191
Haselock, John 186, 255
Hassard family 76
Hastings, Henry 140, 183
Hastings, Jane *see* Tomkins, Jane

364 *Index*

Hathaway, William 191
Have mercy upon me, O God (full anthem) 210, 211
Have mercy upon me, O God (incomplete verse anthem) 112, 293
Hawkins, John 303
He that hath pity on the poor (anthem) 210–11
head and tail motifs 299
Hear my prayer, O Lord (verse anthem) 212, *214*, 315
Heather, William 111, 121, 122, 125, 218, 230
Heavens declare the glory, The (anthem) 211
Hellyer, Thomas 15
hemiola pattern 253, 291
Henrietta Maria, queen 118, 122–3, 124, 126, 139, 163, 164
Henry VII 12, 70
Henry VIII 8, 12, 17–18, 59, 70
Henry, prince of Wales *96*, 96–8, 101, 106, 107, 110, 112, 293
Henry of Navarre 70
Hentzner, Paul 54
Herbert, Philip 107, 131–2, 135
Herbert, William *see* Pembroke, William Herbert, earl of
Hereford Cathedral 63, 65–7, 68, 69
Hertford, Edward Seymour, earl of 135
hexachord variations 250–51, 265, 268, 282
Hills stand about Jerusalem, The (anthem) 279, *280–81*, 320
Hindle, John 237
Hoard, Samuel: *God's Love to Mankind* 51
Holborne, Anthony 268
Hollar, Wenceslas 186
Hollingworth, Robert 218
Holmes, Dulcibella 136, 137, 138
Holmes, John 135–6
Holmes, Thomas 136, 137
Holy, holy, holy (anthem) 208, 318–20
homophony 209, 222, 227
Hooper, Edmund 107, 314, 315, *318*
Hooper, John 12, 13, 45–6, 90
Houghton, Adam, bishop of St David's 27, 35
How great delight (madrigal) 110, 221–2
Howard, Charles *see* Nottingham, Charles Howard, earl of
Howard, Henry *see* Surrey, Henry Howard, earl of
Howard, Thomas 25
Howells, Herbert 324
Huett, Thomas 18–19, 36–7
Huett, William 20–21, 24, 41
Humfrey, Pelham 57–8
Humphrey, Laurence, dean of Gloucester 45

Hunnis, William 58–9
Hunsdon, Lord *see* Carey, Henry, Lord Hunsdon
Hunting Galliard (keyboard music) 150, 255
Hutton, Matthew 49

I will lift up mine eyes (verse anthem) 213
In nomine, settings of: for consort 260, 262, 264–5, 269; for keyboard 184, 244, 245–6, 251, 257
Irving, John 303; *The Instrumental Work of Thomas Tomkins 1572–1656* 244
Isles, William 51
It is my well-beloved's voice (anthem) 94, 111–12, 231, 232, 273, 287, 288
Italian music 301–2; madrigals 78, 79, 110, 301; songs 260

Jackson, Harries 22
James I: accession 87, 89; admirer of Parry 89; anthem for 87, 207, 208; appearance and character 94–5, 97; death and funeral 121–2, 123, 218; 'Declaration of Sports' 151; Ferrabosco and 129; lack of interest in music 87; and Laud 103, 106, 107; provides relative stability 178; and religion 88; royal progress to Scotland 106; and Thirty Years War 125; visit to King's College 111
James, Peter 121–2, 303
Jamestown, Virginia 89
Jenkins, John 259–60
Jesus came when the doors were shut (verse anthem) 287, 292, 300
Johnson, Robert 293n
Jones, Edward 237–8
Jones, Inigo 107
Jones, Jarvis 68, 69, 87, 208
Jones, Robert 293n
Jonson, Ben 60, 79, 99, 109, 129, 135, 139
Josquin des Prez 227
Jubilate Deo 203, 205, 206, 318, *319*
Juxon, William, dean of Worcester 150, 154–5, 179

Kendall family 15
Kettle, Robert 91, 92–3
keyboard music 178–9, 198, 233–58, 274–6, 299–300, 324; Bibliothèque nationale manuscript (Réserve 1122) 179, 235–42; duet 120–21, 274, 291; fancies 236, 239, 248–9, 250, 257; galliards 150, 178, 187, 252–5; *Ground* (two pieces) 241, 251, 275; *In nomine* settings 184, 244, 245–6, 251, 257; influence of liturgical element 247; not known what

Index

instrument TT owned 234; *Offertory 117*, 247, 248, 251, 274–5; pavans 178, 249, 252–5, 269; preludes 244; TT's books and manuscripts 234–5; *Ut re mi* variations 251, 265, 274–5; verses and voluntaries 116, 248–51; *see also* organ music; *and individual works*

Kings, Samuel 145

King's College, Cambridge: Arthur Mann and 81; Dallam's organ 90; Fido's visit 67; Giles Tomkins as organist 134; James I's visit 111; John Tomkins as scholar and organist 47, 94, 100, 101; organ book 292

King's Musick 47, 138, 139

King's School, Worcester 119, 120, 147, 155–7, 167, 169, 176

Kirby, Anthony 128

Know you not (anthem) 98, 101, 112, 288, 292, 293–4, 300, 302, 321

Kyndersley, Robert 139

Kyrton (composer) 234

Lake, Arthur, dean of Worcester 90–91, 98

Lanier, Nicholas 107, 139

Latimer, Hugh 13

Laud, William *162*; and Arminianism 105–6, 153–4, 157, 161–4; and Chapel Royal 107, 128, 132–4; Charles I and 124, 126, 127, 148; as dean of Gloucester 103–6, 168; dislike of lectureships 157, 158–9; enmity with Bishop Williams and recruitment of Nathaniel Tomkins 147–50, 163; execution 177; impeachment 169, 170; and James I's death 121; love of music 163; and Mainwaring 154, 155; nightmare about Thornborough 115–16; promotions (to bishop of London, then archbishop of Canterbury) 153, 154; and Scotland 164, 165; and Star Chamber 161, 162–4; TT's tribute to 178, 252

Lawes, Henry 107, 128, 134, 135, 139, 160

Lawes, William 128, 134, 135, 139, 259–60; death 160, 177; 'Elegy on the death of John Tomkins' 160; *Treasury of Musick* 197

Leave, O my soul (verse anthem) 112, 207, 213, 215

lectureships 157–8

Le Huray, Peter 320

Leighton, Alexander 161

Leighton, Kenneth 99

Leland, John 7

'Lessons of Worth' 187–8, 241–2

letters 151–2

Lewes, Mr, of Llwyn-Derw 34, 36

Lincoln Cathedral 42, 43, 67

litanies 286, 299

literature 79

Locke, Matthew 259–60, 269

Loeschhorn, Albert 275

London 53–4, 94, 101, 118, 172; music inspired by 53–4, 134–5, 219, 223 ; plague 124, 125;

Long Parliament 169

Longdon, Worcestershire 74, 76, 186

Longney, Manor of, Gloucestershire 43

Loosemore, Henry 295

Lord bless us, The (verse anthem) 295, *296*, 297

Lord Chamberlain's Men 60

Lord enter not into judgement (anthem) 210

Lord, even the most mighty God, The (verse anthem) 281

Lords of the Articles 165

Lostwithiel, Cornwall 7–8, 9–12, 14–15; Riding of St George 9, 11

Loudoun, Lord 165, 166

Louis XIII, king of France 122

Love, cease tormenting (madrigal) 222

Lownes, Mathew 218

Lugge, John 247

Lupo, Theophilus 139

Lupo, Thomas 139, 262

lute music 217, 223

Lyly, John 59

madrigals 77–83, 110–12, 217–32, 235, 273–4, 283, 287, 301, 318, 322, 324; 3-part 220–22; 4-part 222–5; 5-part 225–30; 6-part 230–32; adapted for use in sacred music 318–21; dedications 42, 49, 59, 102–3, 109, 110–11, 322–3; quality and variety 218–20; sacred 111–12; *see also Songs of 3, 4, 5 and 6 Parts; and individual songs*

Magdalen College, Oxford 61, 69, 81, 81n

Magnificat 203, 204, 205, 206, 276, 277, *298*, *305*, *306*, 307, *309*; Byrd's 304–5, *306*, 307, *308*

Mainwaring, Roger, dean of Worcester 154, 155, 169

Mann, Arthur 81

Manningham, John 84–5

Marenzio, Luca 78

Marlowe, Christopher 79

Marston, John 60, 151

Martin Hussingtree, Worcestershire 186–7, 236, 255, 300; church 186, *188*, 189, 190

Marwood, Richard 47, 51

Mary I 13, 14, 18, 20, 46

Mary Stuart, queen of Scotland 62, 73

366 Index

masques 268, 269
Massinger, Philip 107
Mell, Davis 139
Mell, Leonard 139
Melyonek, John 42
Merro, John 48, 49–51, 89, 93, 106, 152
Meyer, Ernst 282
Meyerstein, Edward 81
Meyrick, Francis 35
Middleton, Marmaduke, bishop of St David's 19
Middleton, Thomas 60
Mildenham Mills, Worcestershire 233
Milsom, John 112, 113, 199
Milton, John (father of poet) 83
Milton, John (poet) 99, 192
Miserere, settings of 184, 246–7, 257
Molle, Henry *see* Moule, Henry
monody 212
Monson, Craig 49
Montague, Richard 124
Monteverdi, Claudio 222, 224; *Con che soavità* 110, 222
Morehen, John 67, 68–9
Morgan, Henry, bishop of St David's 18, 19
Morgans (schoolmaster) 20
Morley, George, bishop of Worcester 189
Morley, Thomas 81–3, 223, 302; included in TT's personal anthologies 121, 235; music for Shakespeare 99; services 297, 304; *see also Plaine and Easie Introduction to Practicall Musicke; Triumphs of Oriana, The*
motets 207, 247, 320
Moule, Henry 110, 119, 156, 226
Moule, Margaret *see* Withy, Margaret
Mulliner Book 244–5, 249
Music Divine (madrigal) 111, 230
Musica Britannica 260, 274, 282
Musica Deo sacra (compiled by Nathaniel Tomkins) 112–13, 192, 197–216, 274, 276–84; acquired by Worcester Cathedral 201; anthems 87, 197, 202, 207–16, 276, 277–82; dating 200; facility for inclusion of other works 292; madrigal adaptations in 318–21; Nathaniel's instructions in Bodleian Library copy 201–2; number of books 200–201; organ accompaniments 233; preces 206, 208, 299; psalms 206–7, 299; Ramsbotham's work on 282–3; sacred pieces omitted from 285–300; services 202–6, 276–7, 278, 297, 299, 318–20; verse anthems 93, 112–13, 211–16, 315; works for special occasions 207; *see also individual works*
Musica Transalpina (madrigal collection) 78, 81, 94

My beloved spake (verse anthem) 281
My dwelling is above (verse anthem) 294
'My help cometh from the Lord' *see I will lift up mine eyes*
My shepherd is the living Lord (verse anthem) 207, 213, 281, *282*
Myriell, Thomas: anthologies 93, 94, 111, 159, 219, 227, 288, 322; career 94; as dedicatee of works by TT 111, 112, 227; friendship with Tomkins brothers 93, 94; *see also Tristitiae Remedium*

Nabbes, Thomas 119–20
Nash, Thomas 233
Nicholson, Richard 314–15, *316*
No more will I thy love importune (madrigal) 220–21
North, Roger 259, 260, 261, 265, 267
Not in the merits of what I have done (verse anthem) 112, 207
Nottingham, Charles Howard, earl of 81
Novello, Vincent 217
Nunc Dimittis 203, 204, 205, 206, 277, *298*, 305, 307, *311–12*; Byrd's 304–5, 307, *309*

O God, the heathen are come into thine inheritance (verse anthem) 112, 173–4, 286, 293
O God the proud are risen (anthem) 208, 312, *314–15*, 315
O God wonderful art thou (anthem) 312, 314
O how amiable are thy dwellings (anthem) 211
O let me die for true love (madrigal) 223, 283, 322–3
O let me live for true love (madrigal) 222–3, 322
O Lord do away as the night even so my sins (anthem) 208
O Lord God of hosts (verse anthem) 127
O Lord graciously accept see *Blessed is he that considereth*
O Lord grant the King a long life (verse anthem) 87, 207
O Lord how glorious are thy works (anthem) 320
O Lord I have loved the habitation of Thine house (anthem) 210
O Lord let me know mine end (verse anthem) 94, 212, 281
O Lord let my mouth be filled with thy praise (verse anthem) 112, 293
O Lord wipe away my sins (anthem) 290
O praise the Lord all ye heathen (anthem, *a* 5) 314
O praise the Lord all ye heathen (anthem, *a* 12) 207, 277–8
O pray for the peace of Jerusalem (verse anthem) 214, 314–15, *316–17*

Index

367

O sing unto the Lord (anthem) 208, 277–8, 312, *315*

O think upon Thy servant (verse anthem) 294

Offertory (keyboard music) *117*, 247, 248, 251, 274–5

Oft did I marle (madrigal) 230–31, 323

Okeover, John 51

Old Cheque Book of the Chapel Royal 56–8, 62–3, 121, 123, 127

Oliver, John, dean of Worcester 189

Opusculum neuer Pavanen, Galliarden, Coranten und Volten (Simpson) 268

organ books 198, 292; *see also* 'Batten' Organ Book

organ music: changes in 235; importance and volume of TT's work 233–4; importance of pitch 299–300; and *Offertory* 248; omitted from three-part anthems 279; preferred accompaniment to sacred vocal music 261; role in consort music 261; role in pre-Reformation anthems 207; role in verse anthems 211; TT's knowledge and collection of 234–5; Tudor 234, 235, 247, 248

organists, reputation of 90

organs, church: by Dallam 90–93, 103, 168, 191, 219; failure of reformers to ban 90; Gloucester Cathedral 103–4, 168; St David's Cathedral 36, 37; St Mary's Church, Shrewsbury 39; sub-standard 202; Worcester Cathedral 90–93, 173, 177, 191, 219, 275–6

ostinati 274

Our hasty life away doth post (madrigal) 49, 220

Out of the deep (verse anthem) 281, 315, *317*

Out of the deep have I called (anthem) 211

Owen, George, Lord of Kemys 34, 35, 36

Oxford, University of 107, 111, 119; *Plaine and Easie Introduction* preserved in 79–81; Tomkins family and 61, 69, 81n, 147, 192, 237; *see also* Bodleian Library; Christ Church, Oxford

Oxford Music School 51, 94

Oyez! has any found a lad? (madrigal) 134–5, 223, 273

pageants 268

parliament 125, 132, 153, 154, 164, 166, 169

Parry, Henry, bishop of Worcester 83–5, 89–91, *91*, 99, 115

Parsons, Robert 57

partbooks 268, 282, 288, 290; Gloucester bass partbook 69–70, 292, 294; Peterhouse 163, 290, 299; Tenbury MS 1382 67–9, 87, 208, 290; Worcester 119, 261; *see also Musica Deo sacra*

Patrick, Alice *see* Tomkins, Alice

Patrick, Nathaniel 61, 65, 68, 76, 77

patronage 41, 107–10

Patten, Elizabeth *see* Gibbons, Elizabeth

Patten, John 123

Pavan: Earl Strafford (keyboard music) 178, 252

Pavan in A minor (keyboard music) 249, 253, 255

Pavan: Lord Canterbury (keyboard music) 178, 252

pavans: for consort 261, 262, 265, 266, 268–9; for keyboard 178, 249, 252–5, 269; *see also Sad Pavan: for these distracted times*

Pembroke, William Herbert, earl of 107–10, *108*, 131, 143, 220

Pembrokeshire 17, 28–33, 36; *see also* St David's

Pendock, Worcestershire 38–9

Penknight, Cornwall 8, 15

Pennell, Edward 185, 186

Pereyra, Mlle 238–9

Perpetual Round, The (keyboard music) 236, 256

Petition of Right 132

Phelps, William 62

Philips, Arthur 241, 251

Philips, Peter 262, 268, 269, 302

Phillips, Morgan 18

Phillips, Peter: *English Sacred Music 1549–1649* 215

Phyllis, now cease to move me (madrigal) 119, 226–7, 228

Phyllis, yet see him dying (madrigal) 120, 228–9

Piers, Thomas 62, 107

Pike, Lionel 303

pitch 279–81, 288, 299–300

plague 70, 124, 125, 157

Plaine and Easie Introduction to Practicall Musicke, A (Morley) 79–81, *80*, *82*, 87, 120, 256

plainchants 247–8

plainsongs 235, 244–5, 256–7, 265

Playford, John 118

Poe, Dr 124

poetry 79, 99

Poher (Pore), Margaret *see* Tomkins, Margaret

Poole Court *see* Pull Court

Port Mawr, Pembrokeshire 32–3

Portland, Richard Weston, earl of 150

Potter, Christopher, dean of Worcester 155, 156–8, 159

Pownall, Nathaniel 133

Praise the Lord O ye servants (verse anthem) 212

prayer book *see* Book of Common Prayer

preces 206, 208, 286, 299

predestination, doctrine of 51, 105

preludes (keyboard music) 244

Index

Preston, Thomas 234, 246
Prideaux, John, bishop of Worcester 181–2
Princely coming of her Majesty to the Holy Communion at Easter 62–3, 248
printed music licences 43, 78, 79, 218
printers: and mensuration signs 225
proportio sesquialtera 229
Prynne, William 163–4, 169
psalms; 'Geneva' 19, 20; metrical 19–20, 112, 286, 299; penitential 211, 279, 293; settings 206–7, 276, 293; as texts for anthems 207, 211; TT's tunes 112, 286, 299
Pull Court, Worcestershire 74–7, *75*, 120, 184, 186, 189, 256
Purcell, Henry 190, 193, 283–4
Puritans 71, 73, 105, 125, 151, 161, 164
Put me not to rebuke (anthem) 211
Pym, John 166

Quarterly Music Review 259
Queen Henrietta's Company 118, 164

Rainsborough, Thomas 178
Ralegh, Walter 76–7
Ramsbotham, A. 282–3
Ramsey, Robert 293n
Ramsey Island 31–2, 41
Rathgeb, Jacob 55
Ravenscroft, Thomas 102, 112, 113, 159, 255
recusancy 55, 70–71, 73–4, 88, 118
Redford, John 234, 235
Reformation 8–9, 12–14, 268; in Wales 18
Rejoice, rejoice (verse anthem) 292, 294–5
Remelius, Henry 54
Restoration 189–92, 315
Revenge (ship) 25
Revue de Musicologie 238–9
Rhys, Philip ap 234
Ridley, Thomas 12, 13
Rimbault, Edward 56, 110, 259
Robin Hood (keyboard music) 242, 244, 255–6
Rosseter, Philip 255
Rous, John 76
Rudd, Anthony, dean of Gloucester/bishop of St David's 44
Russell, William 184

sacred music: effect of Reformation 12–14; TT and 111–13, 197; omitted from *Musica Deo sacra* 285–300; *see also* anthems; *Musica Deo sacra*; Services; verse anthems
Sad Pavan: for these distracted times (keyboard music) 179, 216, 252–3, 275, 276, 321

Sadock the Priest see *Zadok the priest*
St Catherine's Church, Gloucester 44
St David's, Pembrokeshire 7, 17, 29–33; ancient stones 32–3, 34; bishops 18–19, 27, 121, 126; bishop's palace 19, 29–30; chapels 30–32; grammar school 22, 23, 24; harbours 31; known as *Menevia* 30; Laud and 121, 126; Port Mawr 32–3; wells 33
St David's Cathedral 14, 17, 18, *21*; and Civil War 176–7; condition of cathedral music 19, 36–7; condition of organ 36, 37; deterioration of records 22, 23; discipline of vicars choral and choristers 19, 20–21; introduction of metrical psalms 19–20; loss of Tomkins family 41; lost manuscript on history of 27–36; paid stalls 24; recruitment of choristers and vicars choral 36, 37
St David's Head 32
St George's Chapel, Windsor 54, 59, 77, 179
St George's Day 207, 215
St George's guild, Lostwithiel 9, 11
St James's Palace 97
St John the Baptist church, Tredington 44
St Mary de Lode church, Gloucester 44, 45
St Mary's Church, Shrewsbury 39
St Nicholas Church, Worcester 65
St Paul's Cathedral 47, 94, 102, 134, 159, 233
St Paul's Church, Covent Garden 190
St Stephen's Day 207, 214–15
St Stephen's Walbrook 94
St Thomas's Day 287, 292
Salesbury, William 18–19
Salisbury: and Civil War 176
Salisbury Cathedral 47, 90, 116, 134, 190; dispute over appointment of Giles Tomkins 135–8
Sandie, Richard 133
Sanudo, Leonardo 81
Sarum rite 247, 248
Savoy Parish, Middlesex 190
Sayer, John 199
Scheidt, Samuel 255, 257
Schmitz, Oscar 54
Schütz, Heinrich 227
Scotland 106, 140–41, 164–6, 169, 184
Scott, Gilbert 93
secular music, increase in 77
See, see the shepherd's queen (madrigal) 226, 318
self-borrowings 318–21, 324
Senhouse, Richard, bishop of Carlisle 126
Services: 1st 202–3, 305; 2nd 203–4, 305; 3rd 204–5, 305, 307, *309*, 318, *319*; 4th 205, 276–7, 297, 304, 305, *310–11*; 5th 205, 206,

276–7, 297, 299, 305, *306*, 307, *311–12*; '6th' 286, 295–7; '7th' 286, 297; Byrd's influence on 303–12; madrigals adapted for 318–20; in *Musica Deo sacra* 202–6, 276–7, 278, 297, 299, 318–20; in other sources 286, 295–9; solo material 299; verse services 297–9, 300; Weelkes and 276, 295, 299, 305

Severn, river 74, 77

Seymour, Edward *see* Hertford, Edward Seymour, earl of

Shakespeare, William 79, 99, 107, 109, 115

Shaking Stone, Pembrokeshire 32–3, 34

Shellsley Beauchamp, Worcestershire 179–80

Shellsley Walsh, Worcestershire 179–80

Shepherd's Joy, The (keyboard music) 255

Sherfield, Henry 161–2

Shirley, James 132

Short Parliament 166

Short Pavan, A (keyboard music) 253, *254*

Shrewsbury 39

Shuter, Thomas 135

Sidney, Philip 79, 107

Simpson, Christopher 259

Simpson, Thomas 261, 268

Sing unto God (verse anthem) 281

Siri, Vittorio 84

Skinner, Robert, bishop of Worcester 191, 199–200

Smith, Miles, bishop of Gloucester 104

Smyth, William 158

Snodham, Thomas 218

Solley, Edward 173

songs: variations for keyboard 255–7; *see also* madrigals

Songs of 3, 4, 5 and 6 Parts (1622) 217–32, 235, 273–4, 287, 318, 322, 324; two editions 217–18; *see also* madrigals

'Songs to the Organ' *see* verse anthems

Southwell Minster partbook *see* Tenbury MS 1382

Spain 89, 97, 125; Armada 25, 35, 62, 70, 77

Spenser, Edmund 79, 99

sports 151

Spottiswood, John, archbishop of St Andrew's 140

Squire, Barclay 217

Star Chamber, Court of 161, 162–4

Stephens, William 172

Sternhold and Hopkins: *The Whole book of Psalms Collected into English Metre* 19–20, 295, 299

Stettin-Pomerania, duke of 60

Stevens, Denis 61, 87, 287, 295, 302

Stevens, John 87, 110, 121, 122, 125, 127, 226

Strafford, Thomas Wentworth, earl of 164, 169–70; TT's tribute to 178, 252

strings, music for 251, 282; *see also* consort music; viols

Strogers, Nicholas 68

Strowger, E. 234

Suckling, John 148

Sure there is no god of love (madrigal) 116, 221

Surrey, Henry Howard, earl of 79

Survey of Worcestershire 90

Sweelinck, Jan 187, 255

Sweet Saviour (verse anthem) 295

Swinburne, Algernon Charles 120

Tallis, Thomas: Byrd and 42–3; Catholicism 55, 301; and Chapel Royal 57; death 58, 283; *Felix namque* settings 247; music praised by TT 188; plainsong settings 235, 244–5; TT influenced by 203, 277, 296

Taverner, John 235, 260; *Missa O Michael* 207

Tayler, Richard 167, 168

Taylor, Marjorie 186, 187

Taylor, Stainton de B. 231

Taylor, Thomas 120

Te Deum 202, 203, 204, 205, 305, 307, *309–10*

Tenbury MS 1382 67–9, 87, 208, 290

Tewkesbury, Gloucestershire 74, 76, 77, 189

theatre *see* drama

Then David mourned (anthem) 209

Thirty Years War 125

Thornborough, Edward, archdeacon of Worcester 116, *117*, 251, 257

Thornborough, Giles 116, 136, 138

Thornborough, John, bishop of Worcester 115–16, 150–51, 156–8

Thorne, John 234

'Thorough', policy of 106, 116

Thorpe, Thomas 238

Thou art my King, O God (verse anthem) 212, 282

Thou healest the broken in heart (anthem) 278, 279

Three Choirs Festival 69

Tinker, John 167, 168

To the shady woods (madrigal) 225

tombeau 252

Tomkins, Alice (*née* Patrick; first wife) 76, 77, 145–6, 151, 170–72, 211

Tomkins, Anne (*née* Hargest; step-mother) 37, 39, 47, 48–9, 131, 140

Tomkins, Bridget (sister) 21, 48

Tomkins, Edward (great-uncle) 15, 37, 38

Tomkins, Edward (son of John of Worcester) 38

Tomkins, Elizabeth (half-sister) 47, 48

Tomkins, Giles (half-brother): birth 47; musical career 47, 134; as court musician 47, 134,

Index

Tomkins, Giles (half-brother) (contd) 138, 139; mother's will 48; as dedicatee of works by TT 110; disputed appointment at Salisbury Cathedral 134, 135–8, 233; finances 138; marriages and children 138–9, 190; TT's communication with 140, 152; travels to Scotland 140–41; and Civil War 176, 190; death 190, 324

Tomkins, Giles (nephew) 139, 189, 190

Tomkins, Isabella (*née* Folliott; daughter-in-law) 186–7, 255

Tomkins, Jane (*née* Hastings; sister-in-law) 140

Tomkins, John (half-brother): birth 37, 39; career as organist 47, 94, 100, 102, 128, 233; and mother's will 48; education 94, 99–100; and Myriell 94; and Phineas Fletcher 99–102, 229; as singer 102; dedicatory poem to TT 102–3; as dedicatee of works by TT 103, 231–2, 290; and Chapel Royal 128, 134, 140; marriage and children 140, 159, 167; travels to Scotland 140–41; death 159–60, 324; extant works 159; *John, come kiss me now* (keyboard variations) 235; *O thrice-blessed earthbed* (consort song) 102

Tomkins, John (nephew) 140, 159, 167, 175, 181; marriage and descendants 192; and TT's will 191–2, 234, 237

Tomkins, John, of Shrewsbury 39

Tomkins, John, of Worcester 37–8, 61, 76, 186; descendants 38–9

Tomkins, John (son of John of Worcester) 38

Tomkins, Margaret (*née* Poher; mother) 14, 21, 22

Tomkins, Margaret (half-sister) 47, 48

Tomkins, Margaret (*née* Griffiths; sister-in-law) 140, 159, 167

Tomkins, Martha (*née* Browne; second wife) 175–6, 181, 186

Tomkins, Nathaniel (son): Anthony à Wood meets 61; birth 77; as dedicatee of works by TT 110, 220, 232, 290, 318; as compiler of *Musica Deo sacra* 112, 113, 192, 197, 198–202, 278, 320; childhood 147; education 147; career at Worcester Cathedral 147; first marriage 147; becomes 'spy' for Laud 147, 149–50; house in Worcester 150; TT's communications with 152; involvement in King's School controversy 156–7, 169; and lectureship controversy 158, 159; and orphaned cousins 167, 175, 192; apologises to Worcester corporation 169; finances after Civil War 181–2; wife's death 182; second marriage 186–7, 255; moves to Martin Hussingtree with TT 186–7; TT's respect for 188; and restoration of Worcester

Cathedral 190–91; continues to be controversial 191; musical and singing ability 199–200; apparently not TT's executor 237; and list of TT's books 239, 241, 242; chamber organ performances 261; and score of Byrd anthem 287; and works omitted from *Musica Deo sacra* 292, 293, 300

Tomkins, Nicholas (half-brother) 47, 48, 110, 132, 140, 190, 221

Tomkins, Peregrine (half-brother) 47, 48, 110, 123–4, 190, 223, 274; marriage and finances 140, 183–4

Tomkins, (Reverend) Richard (great-grandson of nephew John) 237

Tomkins, Robert (half-brother) 47, 48, 110, 190, 223, 274; musical career 47, 139–40, 261, 324

Tomkins, Sylvanus (nephew) 140, 159, 167, 175, 181, 241

Tomkins, Theodosia (*née* Broad; daughter-in-law) 147, 168, 182

Tomkins, Thomas (1572–1656)

LIFE: birth and childhood 7, 22, 36, 41, 42; as possible chorister at Chapel Royal 41, 42, 43–4, 58; as pupil of Byrd 42, 43–4, 58, 60, 61, 87, 207, 217, 235; dedicatees of 42, 49, 59, 102–3, 109, 110–11, 220, 225–6, 231–2, 290, 318, 322–3; deaths of father and step-mother 48–9, 131, 140; attends Oxford University 61, 69; as gentleman extraordinary of the Chapel Royal 62, 83, 106–7; as gentleman of the Chapel Royal 58, 62, 293; appointed master of the choristers at Worcester Cathedral 61–2, 65, 69, 73; finances 65, 129, 143, 154, 168, 179, 181–2, 185; dislike of Puritans 73; meets and marries Alice 76, 77; moves into Song School 77; birth of Nathaniel 77; and Henry Parry 83, 90; and new Worcester organ 90–93; friendships 93, 94, 116–21, 123, 134; and Prince Henry's death 98; sources of lyrics 99, 112; relationship with John Tomkins 102–3; dealings with Laud 103, 106; consulted on organ for Gloucester 103–4, 168; as organist at the Chapel Royal 107, 121, 233; dedication to Pembroke 109–10; dual responsibilities and regular journeys to London 121, 154, 165; music for the funeral of James I 121–2; music for the coronation of Charles I 121, 125–8; appointment as 'Composer-in-Ordinary' subsequently revoked 129–31, 135; builds College Green house 143, 146–7; charitable donations 143–6, 211; annotations and

Index

criticisms by 152–3, 234–5, 242, 323; records 'The English Lords' answer to Scottish proposition 165; verse on political situation 166–7; provision for orphaned nephews 167; duties at Worcester 168; admiration for Strafford and Laud 170, 301; death of Alice 170; effect of Civil War on 173–4, 179–80, 181, 185–6, 301; marriage to Martha 175–6, 179, 181; compositions in later life 178–9, 184, 187, 251, 268, 275–6; tribute to Charles I 179; returns to College Green home after war 179–80; dispute with neighbour 180–81; Royalist sympathies 181, 301; respected by City of Worcester 182, *183*; death of Martha 186; moves to Martin Hussingtree with Nathaniel 186–7; sets out his 'Lessons of Worth' 187–8, 241–2; respect for son 188; illness and death 188–9; as compiler of his own music 198, 219–20; not known what instrument he owned 234; books and manuscripts owned by 234–5, 323; knowledge of contemporary music 323–4
MUSIC: *see* anthems; keyboard music; madrigals; *Musica Deo sacra*; organ music; psalms; Services; *Songs of 3, 4, 5, and 6 Parts*; verse anthems; *and individual works*
Tomkins, Thomas (elder brother) 21, 23–5
Tomkins, Thomas, the elder (father): Cornish background 7, 11, 14–15; education 22; as vicar choral at St David's 14, 17, 19, 23; first marriage 14; children 21, 22, 37, 47; accused of extramarital affair 21–2; appointed master of the choristers and organist 22, 23–4, 36; as master of grammar school 22, 23, 36; finances 23–4, 36, 43, 44, 45; as widower 24–5; manuscript on history of St David's attributed to 27–36; takes holy orders 36; second marriage 37; moves to Gloucester as minor canon 36, 39, 41–2, 43, 44–5; additional livings 44, 45; appointed precentor 47; compiles 'Account of the Bishops of Gloucester' 48; as dedicatee of works by TT 110, 220; encourages TT's musical career 303; death 48, 131, 140
Tomkins, Thomas (nephew) 140, 159, 167, 192, 199
Tomkins, Thomas, of Shoreditch 46–7
Tomkins, Ursula (daughter) 48–9
Tomkins (Tomkyn) family 7, 8, 9, 11, 15, 37–9; descendants 237; in Worcester 38–9
Too much I once lamented (madrigal) 42, 225, 302, 320–21
Townshend, Henry 179, 186, 187, 188, 189

Toy, John 120, 170–72
Toy: wrongly attributed to TT 257
Toy made at Poole Court, A (keyboard music) 74, 236, *240*, 256–7
Treaty of London 89
Treaty of Westphalia 125
Tredington, Gloucestershire 44
Tregian, Francis 268
Trevelyan, John 20
Trionfi di Dori, Il (madrigal collection) 81
triple cursus 247
Tristitiae Remedium (Myriell) 93–4, 111, 159, 227, 230, 288
Triumphs of Oriana, The (Morley) 81, 83, 217, 219, 322
Tudor Church Music 199, 201, 202n, 204, 277, 278
Tudway, Thomas 163, 215
Turbet, Richard 303, 304, 312
Turn thou us (anthem) 211
Turn unto the Lord (sacred madrigal) 112, 232, 290, 318, *319*
Tuttle, Stephen 239, 274–5, 282; *Thomas Tomkins: Keyboard Music* 244, 258

Ut re mi fa sol la variations: for consort 265; fragment written in old age 187, 251; for keyboard 251, 265, 274–5

Van den Borren, Charles 238
Van Wilder, Philip 42
Vaughan Williams, Ralph: 'London' Symphony 53–4
Velasco, Juan Fernandez de, duke of Frias 97
verse anthems ('Songs to the Organ') 93, 207, 211–16, 276, 281–2, 283, 324; choruses 212–14; difficulty of singing 211–12; for feast days 212, 214–15; high quality 215–16; influenced by other composers 312, 315–18; instrumental accompaniments 261; omitted from *Musica Deo sacra* 121–2, 285, 286, 287, 290, 292–5; role of organ 211; in Tenbury MS 1382 68; *see also individual works*
verses (keyboard music) 116, 248–9, 250–51
vicars choral 14, 19, 20–21, 24, 30, 33, 34, 35, 36, 37
Villiers, George *see* Buckingham, George Villiers, duke of
viols 245, 260, 261; as accompaniment to verse anthems 212; lost *Fancy* for 249; *see also* consort music
virginals 234
voluntaries (keyboard music) 248–50

372 *Index*

Wales 17–18; and the Reformation 18, 19; *see also* St David's
Walker, William 111
Waller, William 173, 174
Walton, William 99
Ward, John 98, 110, 220, 230, 260, 262, 305, 322, 323
Warlock, Peter 322
Warmestry, Thomas, dean of Worcester 189, 191
Warwick, Thomas 110–11, 123, 127–8, 133, 139, 230
Was ever wretch tormented (madrigal) 224–5, 274
Watson, Thomas 79
Weelkes, Thomas 53, 301; *Alleluia, I heard a voice* 274; anthems 312–14, *315*; consort music 262, 269; madrigals 79, 83, 218, 220, 227, 322; *O care, thou wilt dispatch me* 320; *O how amiable* 211; Services 276, 295, 299, 305; verse anthems 214, 215
Weep no more thou sorry boy (madrigal) 223–4, 274, 302
Weldon, Anthony 94–5
Wentworth, Thomas *see* Strafford, Thomas Wentworth, earl of
West, John E. 23
Westminster Abbey 110, 111
Weston, Richard *see* Portland, Richard Weston, earl of
Westphaling, Mr 180
Wharton, Nehemiah 143
What if a day (keyboard music) 244, 256
When David heard (anthem) 93–4, 98, 112, 209, 216, 225, 227–8, 231, 274, 276, 279, 312, 321
When I observe (madrigal) 110, 230, 274, 320
White, William, of Durham 111, 229, 262
Whitehall, Palace of 44, 55
Whitgift, John, archbishop of Canterbury 83, 85
Who is this that cometh out of the wilderness (verse anthem) 215
Who shall ascend the hill of God (anthem) 208–9, 320
Why art thou so full of heaviness (anthem) 209, 320
Wiborowe, Francis 128
Wilbye, John 79, 83, 218, 220, 322
Wild, John 145
Wiles, Thomas 110
Willaert, Adrian 78
Willcocks, David 215–16
Willetts, Pamela 49–51, 94
Williams, John, bishop of Lincoln 126, 147–50, 163, 169
Willis, Browne 28; *A Survey of the Cathedral Church of St David's…* (1717) 28–35; *Survey of the Cathedrals* 48

Willis, Francis, dean of Worcester 39, 44–5
Wilton House, Wiltshire 135
Windebank, Francis 129–31
Withdraw not Thou Thy mercy (anthem) 210, 295
Withy, Francis 118, 119
Withy, Humphrey 110, 116–18, 119, 178, 221, 251, 261, 268
Withy, John 116, 118, 119, 164, 261, 268
Withy, Margaret (*née* Moule) 119
Withy, Richard 119
Woe is me (sacred madrigal) 103, 112, 231–2, 274, 287, 290–91
Wogan, John 31, 35
Wogan, Thomas 176
Wogan family 33
Wolsey, Thomas 12
Wood, Anthony à 61, 118, 120, 259
Woodson, Thomas 57
Worcester: churches 65, 70; and Civil War 172–5, 177–8, 179, 184–5, 187, 252, 275; gates 70; King's School 119, 120, 147, 155–7, 167, 169, 176; map *73*; as market town 151; opposition to Arminianism 157; plague 70, 157; river 74; size and population 70; St Oswald's Hospital 118; Song School 77, 147; Talbot Inn 185–6; Tomkins family in 38–9; TT's charitable donations 143–6; TT's College Green house 143, 146–7, 179–81; TT's good relationship with 182, *183*; Withy family and 116, 118, 119
Worcester (psalm tune) 112, 299
Worcester, Battle of (1651) 184–5
Worcester, sieges of: 1643 173–5; 1646 177–8, 252, 275
Worcester Brawls (keyboard music) 151, 256
Worcester Cathedral *66, 71*; acquires Barnard's *Selected Church Music* 198; acquisition of books and copying of parts 201; architecture 70; belfry 120; conflict with city corporation 157–9, 168–9; dispute over Carnary Chapel 155–7, 169; effect of Civil War 172, 173, 177; efforts to improve choral standards 154–5; finances 73; improvements to exterior 155; John Fido and 65; lectureship controversy 157–9; links with other establishments 69, 106; list of choristers (1643–44) 167–8; Nathaniel Giles as organist 59; nave services 299; organs 90–93, 173, 177, 191, 219, 275–6; Parry and 90, 115; problem with treble voices 276; and Restoration 189, 190; restoration of 190–92; Tomkins family and 38, 39; TT as master of the choristers 61–2, 65, 69, 73; TT's organ music 233–4

Index

Worcestershire 143; and Catholicism 71, 73–4, 88; and Civil War 172
Wotton, William 28, 34–6; *Memoirs relating to the Cathedral-Church of St David's* 28–36
Wyatt, Thomas 79
Wynn, John, of Gwydir 19
Wynslade, Richard 234
Wyntour family 88

Xenophanes 161

Yardley, Worcestershire 38
Ye people all (verse anthem) 295
Yet again, as soon revived (madrigal) 224, 229, 274
Yonge, Nicholas 78, 94
Young, Thomas, bishop of St David's 18

Zadok the priest (anthem) 126, 127, 291

Lightning Source UK Ltd.
Milton Keynes UK
UKHW021219211218
334365UK00010B/240/P